The Queer Renaissance

Robert McRuer

The Queer Renaissance

Contemporary American Literature
and the Reinvention of
Lesbian and Gay Identities

New York University Press

New York and London

NEW YORK UNIVERSITY PRESS
New York and London

© 1997 by New York University

Library of Congress Cataloging-in-Publication Data

McRuer, Robert, 1966-
The queer renaissance : contemporary American literature and the
reinvention of lesbian and gay identities / Robert McRuer
p.   cm.
Includes bibliographical references and index.
ISBN 0-8147-5554-2 (clothbound : alk. paper). — ISBN
0-8147-5555-0 (paperbound : alk. paper)
1. Gays' writings, American—History and criticism.
2. Homosexuality and literature—United States—History—20th
century.   3. Literature and society—United States—20th century-
History and criticism.   4. American literature—20th century-
History and criticism.   5. United States—Civilization—1970-6. Gender identity
in literature.   7. Lesbians in literature.
8. Gay men in literature.   I. Title.
PS153.G38M38-1997
810.9'920664—dc21   96-51220
CIP

New York University Press books are printed on
acid-free paper, and their binding materials are chosen
for strength and durability.

Manufactured in the United States of America

10   9   8   7   6   5   4   3   2   1

Contents

Preface   vii

Acknowledgments   xi

Introduction
Reading the Queer Renaissance   1

Chapter One
Boys' Own Stories and New Spellings
of My Name: Coming Out and Other
Myths of Queer Positionality   32

Chapter Two
Queer Locations/Queer Transformations   69

Chapter Three
Unlimited Access?
Queer Theory in the Borderlands   116

Chapter Four
Queer Identities in a Crisis   155

Epilogue
Post-Queer?   205

Notes   215

Works Cited   237

Index   249

Preface

Every year, countless Americans from the forty-eight contiguous states flock to Hawaii, making tourism that state's number one industry. Travel agents, hotels, and airlines entice tourists by shaping the Aloha State into the land of beauty, romance, and imagination. A recent *Vacations by Sheraton* brochure, for instance, announces, "Hawaii is as much a place of mind as it is a place on the map. A peaceful paradise where golden sunshine warms the spirit along with the body. Where worry drifts away on azure waves." MTI Vacations adds, "Hawaii is a honeymoon paradise! You'll be inspired by the breathtaking scenery and swept up in the romance of the islands." The industry supports these claims with visual evidence, scattering pictures of men and women in luxurious settings through every brochure: men and women standing beside waterfalls or pools, walking along the beach, or watching the tropical sunset.

Gay men and lesbians, however, have disrupted the fantasy of Hawaii as a romantic (heterosexual) paradise. In 1990, three same-sex couples filed a lawsuit claiming the state violated their civil rights by refusing to grant them marriage licenses. The Hawaii Supreme Court agreed and ordered a lower court to review the couples' complaints. Since states have a long history of recognizing marriages legally performed in other states, the events in Hawaii provoked a flurry of legislative activity elsewhere. By the mid-1990s, legislators across the country had introduced bills that would ensure that their states would not have to recognize same-sex marriages performed in Hawaii. Congress even introduced the Defense of Marriage Act (DOMA), and members of both major political parties lined up behind it to show their support for the idea that marriage should be defined only as the union between one man and one woman. DOMA was passed and signed into law by President Bill Clinton in September 1996.

In this context, the already suspect metaphor of the mainland collapses under the weight of the crisis. Hawaii indeed becomes "the mainland" here, given its ability to drive the legislative agenda of the U.S. Congress and of many other states in the Union. The legislators' panic, and that of their constituents, endows Hawaii with a threatening subjectivity that belies characteristic understandings of it as an island paradise passively awaiting heterosexual travelers. No longer simply a beautiful and distant place to escape *to*, Hawaii—because it broaches the taboo subject of same-sex marriage—becomes a subject to escape *from*.

Nonetheless, to many gay men and lesbians (and indeed, to the litigating couples themselves), gay and lesbian marriage hardly constitutes a threat to civilization as we know it. On the contrary: proponents of lesbian and gay marriage openly admit that they don't want to threaten heterosexual marriage; instead, they want to *uphold* marriage by extending it to lesbians and gay men. Other gay men and lesbians see the issue somewhat differently. While not denying that lesbians and gay men should have equal access to the political and economic benefits marriage bestows on couples in American culture, they argue that the gay and lesbian marriage movement seeks admittance to an institution that gay liberationists have sharply and consistently critiqued.

The debate over marriage rights in Hawaii might actually extend those critiques, since it again makes visible the crises that circulate around marriage and "the family." The legislative panic in particular exposes the ways in which the idea of the family is grounded in a fear of *contiguous states:* that is, a fear of queer states and eroticisms that are supposed to be safely distant, marginal, and exotic but are, in actuality, always internal to the family, the community, the nation. The debate about marriage rights in Hawaii reveals that those queer states (indeed, like Hawaii) are not "naturally" distant, marginal, and exotic; rather, they are distan*ced*, mar-ginal*ized*, and exotic*ized* through the heteronormative processes that construct "the family," "the mainland," and "civilization as we know it." It is crucial that queer activists and theorists continue to draw attention to those heteronormative processes, especially since the lesbian and gay marriage movement in fact repeats them; many advocates for same-sex marriage distance queer identities and communities that don't fit their "new and improved" model of family.

The Queer Renaissance: Contemporary American Literature and the Reinvention of Lesbian and Gay Identities examines how queer writers of the past fifteen years have shaped alternative relationships, communities, and identities. The 1980s and 1990s have seen an unprecedented wave of cultural activity by openly queer poets, playwrights, and novelists. *The Queer Renaissance* not only highlights that phenomenon but also considers how it works in tandem with a "renaissance" of radical queer political analysis that reinvents lesbian and gay identities and alliances in order to challenge dominant constructions of sex, sexuality, gender, class, and race.

The queer alliances and interconnections writers and activists have shaped cannot be contained by the model of a well-behaved same-sex dyad, and *The Queer Renaissance* thus brings together both women *and* men from a variety of overlapping communities and locations: women working together as friends and lovers, female and male activists protesting homelessness and inadequate health care, lesbians of color *hacienda alianzas* (forging alliances), queers in the streets chanting, "We *are* fabulous—get used to it!" or "Safe sex—do it!" Although putting men and women together in one study will undoubtedly strike some readers as monstrously unnatural, such a queer gathering is actually more representative of the ways men and women have indeed worked together in many locations over the past fifteen years. The field of contemporary gay and lesbian literary studies, which generally focuses on writing by *either* men *or* women, in this sense lags behind gay and lesbian communities more generally.

The Queer Renaissance brings together Audre Lorde, Edmund White, Randall Kenan, Gloria Anzaldúa, Tony Kushner, and Sarah Schulman and considers how or whether these writers breed fluid and disruptive identities and communities. The conversation *The Queer Renaissance* stages among these writers intends to extend that disruption and fluidity. However, I unavoidably erect other barriers or establish new boundaries that can, and I hope will, be disrupted in turn. Most obviously, I focus here on "American" writers. Without question, the cultural phenomenon I examine crosses many different geographical and metaphorical borders, making my American focus in many ways arbitrary. My (partial) rationale for this focus is twofold. First, the field of literary studies continues to be segregated along national lines, and American literary studies provides one venue in which *The Queer Renaissance* might speak. At the same time, although this study thereby perpetuates the segregation of literary studies, it also (like lesbian and gay studies generally) questions from within many of the academic boundaries we establish. Second, disparate as the writers in this study might be, they are all subject, although in different ways, to various American institutions: religious life, the medical establishment, the U.S. Congress, the border patrol, the marketplace, and so forth. Therefore, many of the disruptions envisioned and detailed by writers in *The Queer Renaissance* are disruptions of specific American institutions or forces.

Still, the "unity" I achieve through this focus is temporary and at many points contested, and the margins of my study threaten to take it elsewhere. Latin America, China, Italy, Australia; Edmonton, Berlin, London, Tel Aviv—these are a few of the places that I tuck away in endnotes or that the writers I examine mention in passing. Other locations—Carriacou, Mexico, West Africa—already resist marginalization in my study, since they have shaped the consciousness of the writers at its center. These locations begin to reconfigure *The Queer Renaissance* and to position the writers and texts here in alliance with other people, places, or contiguous states. Such an ongoing reconfiguration, however, is desirable and necessary: although most of the writers I analyze expose the ways normative identities are structured to distance, marginalize, and exoticize others, they do not do so from some imaginary "uncontaminated" location; although they refuse to be kept in their place, they simultaneously refuse to establish a pure "paradise" elsewhere. The writers at the center of *The Queer Renaissance* perversely insist that we can and should sustain the messy processes of interrogating the exclusions our identities and communities effect and of imagining our communities and identities otherwise.

Acknowledgments

I am grateful to Eric Gardner, Robert Nowatzki, and Michael Thurston for their careful reading of each draft of this book. Our many hours of conversation about this project have been invaluable. I especially thank Michael Bérubé for his ongoing assistance, encouragement, and inspiration, and for his thoughtful criticism of my work at various stages. I am also very grateful to Lisa Duggan, Robert Dale Parker, and Paula Treichler for their insights and encouragement.

Elizabeth Davies read and commented on much of the manuscript, and many other colleagues and friends read drafts of individual chapters: Stacy Alaimo, Amanda Anderson, Steve Amarnick, Beth Coleman, Jon D'Errico, Sagri Dhairyam, Amy Farmer, Will Harris, Randall Kenan, Kenneth Kidd, Barb Sebek, Siobhan Senier, Tamise Van Pelt, and Liesl Ward. Linde Brocato and Evan Engwall advised me on the Spanish translations in chapter 3.

I want to thank Jennifer Hammer at New York University Press for soliciting this project, and for her patience and assistance along the way. This book was made possible through fellowships granted to me by the Graduate College and the Department of English at the University of Illinois at Urbana-Champaign. I am grateful to the Department of English and the Unit for Criticism and Interpretive Theory for their support of both my work and the work of lesbian and gay studies more broadly.

Finally, and most important, this project would not have been completed without the love and support of Tom Murray, who saw me through from beginning to end.

An earlier, shorter version of chapter 1 was published *Genders* 20 (1994): 260–84. Copyright 1994 by New York University Press. Reprinted with permission.

Introduction

Reading the Queer Renaissance

In one of the most fabulous moments in the introduction to her *Epistemology of the Closet*, Eve Sedgwick considers the analysis and recovery work being done in gay and lesbian literary studies on the Harlem Renaissance, the New England Renaissance, and the Renaissance in Italy and England. As Sedgwick sees it, an antihomophobic inquiry into each of these renaissances promises to reconfigure completely the ways in which we conceive of the period in question. Although we "can't possibly know in advance . . . where and how the power in [these renaissances] of gay desires, people, discourses, prohibitions, and energies were manifest," Sedgwick asserts that the questions currently being asked by scholars about these movements reveal that such desires and discourses were nonetheless undoubtedly central (58–59). She then concludes the section, characteristically, by "flaunting it": "No doubt that's how we will learn to recognize a renaissance when we see one" (59).

If the centrality of lesbian and gay desires to a moment of distinctive cultural production is indeed one marker of a renaissance, then we should recognize the past fifteen years as just such a renaissance. Before the 1969 Stonewall Riots ushered in the contemporary gay liberation movement, material representations of same-sex desire in American literature and the arts were few and far between. Even in the 1970s, although openly gay and lesbian literature had begun to appear more regularly, such work was still quite rare. In the 1980s and 1990s, however, all that changed. Literally thousands of novelists, poets, and playwrights published or performed works about lesbian and gay people. Writers' groups and workshops, such as the Violet Quill Club, Other Countries, and Flight of the Mind, helped create and nurture this literary movement; literary magazines and book reviews devoted entirely to gay and lesbian writing propelled the movement forward. Annual Lambda Literary Awards—or "Lammies"—even provided institutional recognition of outstanding achievement in lesbian and gay literature. Straight America began to take notice. As journalist David Gates observed, "At least since Edmund White's best-selling 'A Boy's Own Story' in 1982, major American houses have published more and more of such writing; even the staid Book-of-the-Month Club has announced a gay and lesbian reprint series" (Gates and Malone, 58). Gates's incredulity about the supposedly staid Book-of-the-Month Club could have been as easily directed inward: his comments about the "explosion" of gay writing appeared in a magazine no less mainstream than *Newsweek*. Not surprising, by 1993, when this *Newsweek* article was published, gay and lesbian writers and publications had been taking note of the cultural phenomenon for quite some time.[1]

The Queer Renaissance: Contemporary American Literature and the Reinvention of Lesbian and Gay Identities puts a name to this unprecedented outpouring of lesbian and gay creative work.[2] By naming and discussing this efflorescence of creative activity as a queer "event," I work in this study both to secure a context for analysis of the period and to promote critical representation of the texts and authors involved. Many gay and lesbian writers have noted this cultural renaissance; my project is among the first to analyze the movement critically.

Through this analysis, I hope to complicate and illuminate the position of lesbian and gay writers in contemporary literary studies generally. When contemporary gay or lesbian writers are studied or taught individually, they are easily exoticized; in other words, they are inserted into a general academic market for difference that is able to consider and contain queer desire temporarily, before going on with business as usual. "Business as usual" in this case entails the reproduction of multicultural narratives of American literary history that celebrate and consume difference, including sexual difference, while simultaneously positing, without acknowledgment, an unmarked (and therefore heterosexual) consumer for whom this "difference" is an addendum to the straight narrative. If contemporary queer work is articulated to the idea of a collective movement or renaissance, however, it might be seen as disrupting or transforming the straight narrative and business as usual.

This disruption or transformation will definitely not be easy or automatic. Certainly, in literary studies there are many institutional pressures and expectations (such as the expectation that a given course will "survey" a culture or time period) that are not easily overcome. At the very least, I hope my analysis complicates the tendency to have days or weeks devoted to the study of "difference." By reading contemporary gay and lesbian writers as part of a larger contemporary renaissance, I mean to move them from the margins to the center of the stories we tell ourselves about contemporary literary history.

At the same time, there is more than a little irony involved in considering a "rebirth" of any sort during a period when thousands have died of complications related to acquired immune deficiency syndrome (AIDS). For that reason, my study tries to resist—or *queer*—certain characteristic tendencies of renaissance thinking. This "renaissance" is "queer" not only because it is by and for lesbians and gay men but also because it is *different* from other renaissances. Indeed, this is not a renaissance at all, if renaissances are understood—as they traditionally are—as securing a "great nation's" cultural position through "transcendence" of that nation's historical location. Instead, this is a queer renaissance rooted in particular communities, histories, and struggles. Moreover, this is not simply a cultural renaissance but a rebirth of radical gay and lesbian political analysis, which recalls the formation of the Mattachine Society in the 1950s or the Gay Liberation Front in the 1970s—two other twentieth-century moments when lesbian and gay people came together to reimagine and reshape culture and identity.

Such a reshaping of *identity*, like the unprecedented outpouring of gay and lesbian literature that many critics have noted, has not been overlooked by contemporary commentators, who have positioned "queerness" in particular as a supplement to understandings of sexuality that posit homosexuality and heterosexuality as fixed, immutable, and—supposedly—equal and opposite identities. Influenced by both poststructuralist theory and the flamboyant queer activism of the late 1980s, these critics have theorized queer identity as an alternative to such rigid understandings of sexuality.[3] Sedgwick, for example, begins *Tendencies,* the book she wrote concurrently with *Epistemology of the Closet,* with an extended meditation on the identities being deployed around her:

At the 1992 gay pride parade in New York City, there was a handsome, intensely muscular man in full leather regalia, sporting on his distended chest a T-shirt that read, KEEP YOUR LAWS OFF OF MY UTERUS.

The two popular READ MY LIPS T-shirts marketed by ACT UP were also in evidence, and by the thousands. But for the first time it was largely gay men who were wearing the version of the shirt that features two turn-of-the-century-looking women in a passionate clinch. Most of the people wearing the version with the osculating male sailors, on the other hand, were lesbians. FAGGOT and BIG FAG were the T-shirt legends self-applied by many, many women; DYKE and the more topical LICK BUSH by many, many men. . . .

And everywhere at the march, on women and on men, there were T-shirts that said simply: QUEER.

It was a QUEER time. (*Tendencies*, xi)

Queer, indeed. Sedgwick's overview of the 1992 parade makes it clear that these new identities were, above all, not fixed in discrete gendered locations; instead, identities were reborn in the interstices between various genders and sexualities. Moreover, this queer identification across difference often sharply (and with a camp flair) critiqued powerful American institutions—most obviously here through the "Keep Your Laws Off of My Uterus" and "Lick Bush" T-shirts but also through ACT UP's graphics and T-shirts generally, since the AIDS Coalition to Unleash Power (ACT UP) was, after all, formed to address directly and explicitly the government's neglect of people living with AIDS. Indeed, the very slogan "Read My Lips" was intended both to ridicule George Bush's vacuous uses of the phrase and to draw attention to the government's overwhelming silence on issues of concern to lesbians and gay men, and to the many different people living with AIDS.

In this project, I argue that the renaissance of gay and lesbian creative work has not emerged alongside or above the renaissance of queer identities and political analyses; instead, the efflorescence of creative work is contingent on and, in turn, represents and fuels the proliferation of queer identities and political analyses. Both dimensions of the Queer Renaissance provide readers with fluid identities that are shaped and reshaped across differences and that interrogate and disrupt dominant hierarchical understandings of not only sex, gender, and sexuality but also race and class. In the chapters that follow, these identities take different names (Zami, trickster, new mestiza, AIDS activist) but share this queer commitment to fluidity and disruption. Indeed, to paraphrase Sedgwick, it is, no doubt, in such fluidity and disruption that we will learn to recognize a queer renaissance when we see one.

The remainder of this introduction locates the Queer Renaissance in and around contemporary debates about the uses and abuses of renaissance thinking. In the first section, through a brief survey of critical work on renaissances in literary studies, I consider how the critiques leveled by scholars in various literary fields might be used to read renaissance dis-course in American culture more generally (including recent discussions of the supposed cultural renaissance brought on by the AIDS crisis). I then foreground a different kind of renaissance altogether: looking to lesbian and gay history, particularly the history of the 1950s and the 1970s, I argue that the contemporary emergence of radical gay and lesbian political analysis and activism is actually a *re*emergence, with antecedents in earlier lesbian and gay communities. The cultural production of the past decade and a half can and should be read through this political and historical rebirth, rather than through more traditional, transcendent notions of a renaissance.

Reading the Queer Renaissance alongside and against other American renaissances of the twentieth century, particularly the Harlem and Chicano Renaissances, the next section of the introduction considers whether these renaissances might also be understood as antecedents to the Queer Renais-sance. The Chicano and Harlem Renaissances at times critique powerful American institutions and construct new, more fluid subjectivities, but despite these similarities, the identities shaped in both are generally less fluid than the identities shaped in the Queer Renaissance. Moreover, in the Harlem Renaissance in particular, the relationship between art and politics is much more tenuous than it is in the Queer Renaissance. Therefore, I argue that contemporary authors reconceive the identities shaped in earlier literary movements such as these.

Finally, I position my project, and the writers who are central to it, within current contested understandings of queerness. Although only a few of the writers in *The Queer Renaissance* have been associated with the movement overtly labeled New Queer Writing by Dennis Cooper and others, they share (and in many ways extend) the New Queer Writers' emphasis on a critical perversion that continuously forges unexpected alliances and gives voice to identities our heteronormative culture would like to, but cannot, silence.[4]

On Renaissances and Revolutions

Renaissances have long been staples of literary periodization, but in recent decades, scholars influenced by cultural studies and new historicism have tended to scrutinize the concept more closely. In his introduction to *The American Renaissance Reconsidered*, for example, Donald E. Pease writes:

The term *American Renaissance* designates a moment in the nation's history when the "classics," works "original" enough to lay claim to an "authentic" beginning for America's literary history, appeared. Once designated as the *locus classicus* for America's literary history, however, the American Renaissance does not remain located within the nation's secular history so much as it marks the occasion of a rebirth from it. Independent of the time kept by secular history, the American Renaissance keeps what we could call global renaissance time—the sacred time a nation claims to renew when it claims its cultural place as a great nation existing within a world of great nations. Providing each nation with the terms for cultural greatness denied to secular history, the "renaissance" is an occasion occurring not so much within any specific historical time or place as a moment of cultural achievement that repeatedly provokes rebirth. (vii)

Despite the imperative to be "reborn" outside secular history, however, the contributors to the project Pease introduces, as he goes on to explain, met specifically to *resist* such demands, supposedly characteristic of "global renaissance" thinking generally. The ensuing volume consequently purports to reconsider the American Renaissance: "the demand for rebirth was met, but this time the American Renaissance was reborn not *without* but within America's secular history" (vii). The essays that follow Pease's introduction—"Slavery, Revolution, and the American Renaissance," "The Other American Renaissance," and five others—thus consider how American works from this distinctive moment of cultural production neither transcended the contingencies of history and politics nor escaped nineteenth-century controversies about and around race, gender, and class. The volume's contributors, in short, counter the dislocating tendencies of renaissance discourse with an insistence on location and specificity.

Such an insistence is crucial, given that the dislocating tendencies of renaissance discourse in American culture are in evidence far beyond the literary sphere. Growing up outside of Detroit in the 1970s, for instance, I watched how that urban area was transformed into the "Renaissance City" (an epithet I later learned it shared with Pittsburgh). The sign of this supposed transformation was and is the colossal Renaissance Center: a circular, seventy-four-story glass and steel tower flanked by four similar, though somewhat shorter, towers. At first, this literal "center" of Detroit's renaissance might be understood as locating that movement, both geographically in the heart of the city and historically in a moment of urban renewal. Yet such an understanding of the Renaissance Center as the located sign and signature of the Renaissance City simultaneously covers over the inevitable dislocations of "urban renewal."[5] *Center* is, of course, a verb as well as a noun, and we might do well to examine the process of cente*ring* that occurred in the construction of, and that continues to occur around, this particular center. Atop the Renaissance Center, what can be seen is decidedly not the poverty, violence, and despair that continue to affect the majority of the city's inhabitants. On the contrary, one is literally above all of that: the centering of vision that takes place at such a height assists in the construction of yet another Great American City filled with glass and steel skyscrapers. Indeed, especially at night with the glittering lights reaching as far as the eye can see, one could as easily be in, say, the Sun Belt as in the Rust Belt; that is, in the region that gained jobs even as the restructuring of labor and industry in the Midwest (a restructuring that the renaming of the Motor City as the Renaissance City covers over) cost jobs.

Hence, renaissance discourse in Detroit—centered in a monument that "transcends" the material conditions of the city—*dis*locates and *de*specifies. This particular (dis)location ostensibly provides visitors with a plethora of perspectives on the city, but the revolving lounge-and-observation deck at the top of the Renaissance Center, while shifting constantly, actually goes nowhere. Furthermore, the supposed "heart of the city" is ironically empty of any long-term life; the "tallest hotel in the world" obviously does not house those who actually live in Detroit. Instead, many Detroiters, whose labor has been made marginal or superfluous by corporate and industrial restructuring, have been displaced to ghettos on the city's margins. These margins are precisely what become invisible by the centering of vision that renaissance discourse effects in Detroit.[6]

In literary studies, the dislocations of renaissance rhetoric are never, perhaps, quite as menacing as those enacted by the idea of a renaissance in Detroit's fantasy of urban renewal. However, there are similarities, and as *The American Renaissance Reconsidered* confirms, many literary scholars have begun to look carefully at how the concept is deployed. Indeed, in the past few decades an influential critical movement has worked methodically to rename another entire era in literary and historical studies, precisely to shed the negative baggage carried by "the Renaissance." As Leah S. Marcus explains, "*Early modern* carries a distinct agenda for historians, who have adopted the name quite consciously as a sign of disaffiliation from what they perceive as the elitism and cultural myopia of an older 'Renaissance' history" (41–42). Like the rhetoric of renewal in Detroit, much traditional

Renaissance scholarship, according to Marcus, centers our vision of that era at the cost of the supposed cultural margins:

> The term *Renaissance* is optimistic, upbeat—rebirth and renewal are marvelous ideas. One of the reasons many historians have become suspicious of the term is that it buys its optimism at too great a price—the neglect of other cultural currents and forms of cultural production, of a vast sea of human activity and misery that *Renaissance* either failed to include or included only marginally. The term *Renaissance* implicitly calls for a perception of historical rupture (in order to be reborn, a culture must previously have died) and, along with that, a subtle hierarchical valuation of disparate cultures. (43)

The use of the term *early modern*, in contrast, explicitly resists such hierarchical valuation and refocuses our vision, bringing critics down from the revolving lounge that "Renaissance" scholarship is always in danger of becoming.

The elitism and cultural myopia to which scholars of the early modern period object appear in characterizations of other renaissances, not least in characterizations of the renaissance of contemporary lesbian and gay culture under consideration here. Especially when the topic in question is AIDS, elitist and idealist pronouncements abound. Consciously or unconsciously, commentators often position art as the force that can "purify" the supposed stigma of AIDS. For this reason, Douglas Crimp in particular, in his introduction to the influential collection *AIDS: Cultural Analysis/Cultural Activism*, sharply chastises those who would deploy the rhetoric of renaissance when discussing the literature and art of AIDS. Writing to counter such "idealistic platitudes" as Elizabeth Taylor's assertion that "art lives on forever" (*AIDS*, 5), Crimp asserts that these clichés communicate the message "that art, because it is timeless and universal, transcends individual lives, which are time-bound and contingent" (*AIDS*, 4). Crimp is critical of any artistic ideology that positions art as outside or above the contingencies of material human existence or—even more perniciously—as that which "redeems" human suffering:

> Redemption—of course—necessitates a prior sin—the sin of homosexuality, of promiscuity, of drug use—and thus a program such as "AIDS in the Arts" [a PBS report against which Crimp is arguing] contributes to the media's distribution of innocence and guilt according to who you are and how you acquired AIDS. Promiscuous gay men and IV drug users are

unquestionably guilty in this construction, but so are all people from poor minority populations. (*AIDS*, 4n. 4)

In such an ideological context, in which the guilty offer up art as penance for their misdeeds, Michael Denneny's belief that "we're on the verge of getting a literature out of this that will be a renaissance" is insensitive and escapist (qtd. in Crimp, *AIDS*, 4), and Richard Goldstein's that "AIDS is good for art" and "will produce great works that will outlast and transcend the epidemic" is politically reactionary (qtd. in Crimp, *AIDS*, 5). These comments, and others like them, fetishize the artistic work and ignore how certain understandings of art require—and indeed, produce— the abject artist, the sinner whose transfiguration into the saint comes only through her art. Therefore, as Crimp convincingly establishes in his dismissal of such sentiments, "we don't need a cultural renaissance; we need cultural practices actively participating in the struggle against AIDS. We don't need to transcend the epidemic; we need to end it" (*AIDS*, 7).[7]

As I have already insisted, however, the term *renaissance* might be made to signify differently—might, in short, be queered. Crimp himself implicitly opens the door to such a query of the concept, I think, when he faults media reports for failing to make "any mention of *activist* responses to AIDS by cultural producers" (*AIDS*, 4). Crimp's point is not that activists are the alternative to artists, as if the two groups were always and everywhere distinct, but rather that activists resignify the "artistic," providing an alternative to the idea of art as somehow redemptive or transcendent.[8] Crimp's own subsequent analysis of *Let the Record Show* . . . , an installation produced by ACT UP in the Broadway window of New York's New Museum of Contemporary Art, presents readers with precisely such an activist/artistic project: *Let the Record Show* . . . , in contrast to exhibitions sequestered within museums, highlighted to those outside on the street the negligence and bigotry exhibited during the AIDS crisis by the Reagan administration, the medical establishment, and organized religion (*AIDS*, 7–12). Extending Crimp's linkage of art and politics, I suggest that activism similarly does not preclude us from reading the contemporary queer moment as a renaissance, as if queer politics and renaissances were always and everywhere distinct. On the contrary: we might say that the contemporary moment presents us with a "queer renaissance"—not in the sense of a cultural moment for gay men and lesbians that *dis*locates and *de*specifies, "transcending" history and politics, but in the sense of a cultural moment that engages history and politics and that recalls or cites other such moments. This is not simply a cultural renaissance, "timeless and universal," but rather a specific time of enormous cultural productivity, integrally connected to another kind of renaissance: a renaissance of radical lesbian and gay political analysis. Shaped and reshaped precisely to resist the cultural myopia of those who celebrate art and discount ongoing structural inequities, and of all who maintain such inequities, this renaissance once again focuses our vision on the queer margins that are effaced (or "redeemed") by more elitist or escapist notions of cultural production.

Two moments in twentieth-century lesbian and gay history that might be recalled in a consideration of the contemporary queer period, among the many moments that this period explicitly or implicitly cites, are the early 1950s, when the Mattachine Society was founded by Harry Hay and four other leftists, and the early 1970s, when, after the Stonewall Riots, groups of young people came together to form the Gay Liberation Front (GLF). In his groundbreaking *Sexual Politics, Sexual Communities: The Making of a Homosexual Minority in the United States, 1940–1970* and his subsequent *Making Trouble: Essays on Gay History, Politics, and the University,* John D'Emilio presents the most comprehensive analysis of these time periods. Throughout his work, D'Emilio makes clear that there has been an ongoing tension in twentieth-century gay and lesbian history between radical liberationist and liberal reformist politics.[9]

In the 1950s, D'Emilio explains, "Hay and his partners . . . brought to their discussions an interest in uncovering a systemic analysis for social problems. As Marxists they believed that injustice and oppression came not from simple prejudice or misinformation but from relationships deeply embedded in the structure of society" (*SP,* 64). For this reason, the early Mattachine Society set out to formulate a theoretical explanation for the homosexual's inferior status. The Mattachine Society began to argue that this status was not a function of individual deviance but instead resulted from the structure of American society, particularly from the structure of the dominant nuclear, heterosexual family, which "equates male, masculine, man ONLY with husband and Father . . . and which equates female, feminine, woman ONLY with wife and Mother" (qtd. in *SP,* 65). One of the main goals of the early Mattachine Society, then (which was linked to the Marxist goal of distinguishing between a class "in itself" and a class "for itself"), was to make homosexuals aware of their position as "a social minority imprisoned within a dominant culture" (qtd. in *SP,* 65).

Although D'Emilio describes the Mattachine Society's first action outside their discussion group as a "modest, undramatic one" (*MT,* 30), it is nonetheless significant if we are to read the contemporary Queer Renaissance, which repeatedly stresses coalition across differences, through this earlier period. Police in Los Angeles had a long history of harassing the Chicano community in that city.[10] Not long after the Mattachine Society began to meet in the early 1950s, incidents of harassment of Chicanos received increasing attention in the newspapers. The city government finally held public hearings on the incidents, and the founders of the Mattachine Society attended these hearings to voice their support for disciplinary action against the Los Angeles police officers involved. "The rationale for their participation," D'Emilio explains, "was their conviction that all socially oppressed minorities had something in common" (MT, 30). Hence the early Mattachine Society's radical critique of American society extended beyond an isolated analysis of the homosexual's position within that society to a promotion of intersubjective relations and alliances outside of their own group.

As the 1950s progressed and the Mattachine Society grew, however, those favoring such a systemic and far-reaching critique of American society came into conflict with those preferring a liberal reformist approach. By mid-1953, leadership had transferred to a group of men intent on redefining the mission of the Mattachine Society. These men sought to replace the structural analysis of Hay and the other founders, with its emphasis on homosexuals as a social minority within a dominant heterosexual order, with a position that argued that, except for their sexual object choice, homosexuals were "no different from anyone else." Assimilation to American society was the goal, and this goal could be met if only "false ideas" about homosexuality were corrected. Therefore, the new leadership of the Mattachine Society advocated "aiding established and recognized scientists, clinics, research organizations and institutions . . . studying sex variation problems" (qtd. in SP, 81). D'Emilio concludes:

> Accommodation to social norms replaced the affirmation of a distinctive gay identity, collective effort gave way to individual action, and confidence in the ability of gay men and lesbians to interpret their own experience yielded to the wisdom of experts. Under its new officers, the Mattachine Society shifted its focus from mobilizing a gay constituency to assisting the work of professionals. (SP, 81)

As in American culture generally in the 1950s, so too in the later Mattachine Society: the new atmosphere was no longer congenial to the Marxist insights Hay and his cohorts initially brought to the movement.

A similar "retreat to respectability" occurred not long after this within the autonomous lesbian organization the Daughters of Bilitis (*SP*, 75). Respectability, indeed, was the very basis for the formation of the Daughters of Bilitis (DOB). When the group first met in 1955, they explicitly emphasized that their organization was to be an alternative to the lesbian bars, which they considered "vulgar and limited" (Kennedy and Davis, 68). These lesbian bars, however, although not as numerous as gay male bars, were one of the few arenas where women had the opportunity and space to shape a collective lesbian identity. Elizabeth Lapovsky Kennedy and Madeline D. Davis explain:

> Tough bar lesbians . . . expanded the presence of lesbians in the world of the 1950s. As they affirmed their right to live as lesbians, they made it easier for other lesbians to find them, and more difficult for the heterosexual community to ignore them. . . . In addition, by spending as much time as possible in the bars under difficult conditions, tough bar lesbians created a strong sense of community solidarity and belonging that included women of diverse ethnic and racial groups. (111)[11]

Kennedy and Davis's language, especially its emphasis on "community solidarity," diversity, and difference from the heterosexual community, links the incipient analysis occurring in the lesbian bars to the analysis developed by Hay and the early Mattachine Society. The DOB's alternative to such group consciousness can also be linked to the "alternatives" emphasized by the leaders of the later Mattachine Society: the founders of the DOB "saw education—the dispelling of myths, misinformation, and prejudice—as the primary means of improving the status of lesbians and homosexuals" (*SP*, 102). As D'Emilio points out, the lesbian retreat to respectability, with its disavowal of bar culture, was particularly class-bound (*SP*, 106). However, the shifts in the Mattachine Society—a demonizing of Marxism, an appeal to middle-class professionals, and a refusal to acknowledge that a group's status is a function of larger societal structures—were also clearly class-bound.

Thus the radical beginnings of the lesbian and gay movement were overshadowed by a shift to liberal reformism. Although gay and lesbian organizations continued their activity throughout the 1950s and 1960s, they did so as part of a movement that "could accurately be described as a reform movement solidly implanted in the American liberal tradition" (*MT*, 239). It was not until the formation of the Gay Liberation Front in

1969 that the radical analysis of the early Mattachine Society was decisively "reborn." The time was ripe for such a rebirth. Young lesbians and gay men were already involved in the antiwar movement, the Civil Rights movement, and radical feminism—movements that had spoken and were speaking to American young people generally (*MT,* 241). When the police raided the Stonewall Inn Bar on the night of June 27, 1969, the rage and energy generated by the ensuing riots could be easily articulated to communities of young people who were already radicalized by these other movements. In such a context, the GLF was born, and many of the ideas expressed by their early Mattachine forebears were reborn:

> GLFers began to construct a rudimentary analysis of gay *oppression.* It was not a matter of simple prejudice, misinformation, or outmoded beliefs. Rather, the oppression of homosexuals was woven into the fabric of sexism. Institutionalized heterosexuality reinforced a patriarchal nuclear family that socialized men and women into narrow roles and placed homosexuality beyond the pale. These gender dichotomies also reinforced other divisions based on race and class, and thus allowed an imperial American capitalism to exploit the population and make war around the globe. (*MT,* 242)

As with the early Mattachine Society, the two main characteristics of the GLF's political vision were a commitment to an ongoing interrogation of the very structures of heterosexual, patriarchal, and capitalist society and a simultaneous recognition that resistant identities needed to be reshaped across differences. For this reason, as Terence Kissack explains, the GLF "not only acted in defense of gay and lesbian rights, but also participated in antiwar demonstrations, Black Panther rallies, and actions undertaken by radical feminists" (108). Over the next few years, GLF "kindred groups" spread to cities and college campuses all over the country (*MT,* 243).

Not long after the formation of the GLF, however, a tension between the radical vision it espoused and more traditional liberal reformist impulses, similar to the tension that shifted the Mattachine Society's goals, emerged. The Gay Activists Alliance (GAA) was formed virtually on the heels of the GLF and was, not surprising, much narrower in its focus: "Rather than try to destroy the old in order to build something new, they saw themselves as unjustly excluded from full participation in American society and wanted recognition and a place inside" (*MT,* 247). The GAA was able to achieve several victories—most notable, the removal of homosexuality from the American Psychiatric Association's list of mental disorders (*MT*, 249)—but their shift to a single-issue politics eventually trumped the GLF's broader vision.[12] A commercial subculture of restaurants, bars, and bathhouses flourished by the end of the 1970s and can be seen as an indirect consequence of activists' efforts, but this subculture was social and sexual rather than explicitly political (*MT*, 250–51). Understandably, just as women in many political movements were becoming dissatisfied with the overwhelming focus on male concerns and with ongoing sexist attitudes generally, many lesbians were dissatisfied with these new developments within the gay movement and with groups that focused on sexuality while virtually ignoring gender. This dissatisfaction led to the formation of autonomous lesbian-feminist groups. As the 1970s progressed, these autonomous groups themselves increasingly shifted from a structural critique of society to a more utopian and separatist outlook (*MT*, 252).

D'Emilio's summation of where all these shifts ended up is particularly astute. In stark contrast to the structural change envisioned by the GLF (and the early Mattachine Society), D'Emilio presents what may be the "quintessential products" of each wing of what he calls the "gendered seventies": "the elaborate, glitzy, high-tech gay male discos found in many cities, and the self-sufficient, rural communes of lesbian separatists. Here were men, in a public space, spending money, focused on themselves, and searching for sex. And here were women, in a private retreat, financially marginal, focused on group process, and nurturing loving relationships" (*MT*, 258). So much for structural critique and for identities reshaped across differences. Although D'Emilio acknowledges that "some scrambling of gender characteristics did occur," his critical insight is that traditional understandings of sex and gender were, ironically, very much intact in gay and lesbian communities as the 1970s concluded (*MT*, 258).

Despite what D'Emilio sees as a retrenchment at the end of the 1970s, he is not the only theorist to note that the AIDS crisis and other factors in the 1980s and 1990s have incited another period of political rebirth. Dennis Altman writes, "It has struck me that AIDS is leading gay men and our organizations towards some of the practices associated with the gay liberation movements of fifteen years ago" (41). Sarah Schulman broadens this observation, suggesting that feminist *critiques* of "practices associated with the gay liberation movements" have actually reconfigured "our" organizations, taking them further than they went in the early 1970s:

The coming together of feminist political perspectives and organizing experience with gay men's high sense of entitlement and huge resources proved to be a historically transforming event. Necessity was the best motivator for efficiency, and for the most part ACT UP was able to function with a wide coalition and broad divergence of opinion. . . . ACT UP produced the largest grass-roots, democratic, and most effective organizing in the history of both the gay and feminist movements. (*My American History*, 11–12)

Schulman's account of the early days of ACT UP implies that, if gay men's inability to function with "a wide coalition and broad divergence of opinion" led to the fracturing of many gay and lesbian organizations in the early 1970s, a revitalization of lesbian and gay politics occurred in part because some gay men, however tentatively, began to learn the lessons of feminism and to work more effectively with lesbian and straight feminists.

Beyond this, D'Emilio factors in three additional catalysts that provoked a widespread rebirth of radical lesbian and gay political analysis: the rise of the New Right, the "sex wars" of the early 1980s, and independent organizing by lesbians and gay men of color (*MT*, 258–62). As early as 1977, the New Right was specifically targeting gay men and lesbians through Anita Bryant's campaign to encourage voters to repeal gay rights legislation in Dade County, Florida. Bryant's campaign and others brought home to activists both the dangers of complacency and the need for an ongoing analysis of the ways in which gay and lesbian oppression is built into the very structure of society. More positively, the "collapse of the lesbian-separatist utopia" (*MT*, 259) and the ensuing sex wars of the early 1980s brought to the forefront the voices of s/m lesbians and other "sex radicals." These diverse voices called for a more consistent attention to differences within feminist and lesbian communities. The sex wars were fought over issues such as pornography, sadomasochism, sex work, and alliances with men, and they made possible an understanding of sexuality as more fluid and discontinuous than 1970s utopianism had admitted. At the same time, through a series of moves that similarly brought to the forefront voices that had been previously ignored or suppressed, independent organizing by lesbians and gay men of color finally provoked (some) white gay men and lesbians to attend to racial privilege and to the tendency to disavow racial divisions within lesbian and gay communities.[13]

To all theorists of this period, however, AIDS is the central issue that elicited a sense of political urgency among gay men and lesbians generally.

Introduction: Reading the Queer Renaissance

15

The rebirth of radical politics that AIDS sparked eventually led to the formation, in the late 1980s and early 1990s, of other groups not specifically focused on AIDS, such as Queer Nation and the Lesbian Avengers. These later groups, in turn, tended to revitalize ACT UP and AIDS activism.[14]

The consequences of this political renaissance have been profound. D'Emilio insists that the AIDS epidemic "has once again given plausibility to understandings of gay and lesbian oppression as systemic; it has exposed the complex ways in which it is tied to a host of other injustices" (*MT*, 268). In short, responses to the AIDS epidemic have brought us back to analytical practices associated with the early Mattachine Society and the GLF. A consideration of the specifically queer identities that emerge from this return, moreover, brings us back to the impudent identities with which I began this introduction: identities refusing fixation in any one sexual or gendered location, reshaped across difference and in opposition to systemic injustice. In response to the challenges of the 1980s and 1990s, queers have collectively *reinvented* gay and lesbian identities; in unexpected ways and in ever-multiplying locations, they have flaunted new, transgressive identities. And as I have indicated, contemporary queer commentators have been quick to spotlight, and have in turn fueled, this identificatory irreverence. Cherry Smyth writes, "Queer promises a refusal to apologise or assimilate into invisibility. It provides a way of asserting desires that shatter gender identities and sexualities, in the manner some early Gay Power and lesbian feminist activists once envisaged" (60). Michael Warner likewise emphasizes:

Every person who comes to a queer self-understanding knows in one way or another that her stigmatization is intricated with gender, with the family, with notions of individual freedom, the state, public speech, consumption and desire, nature and culture, maturation, reproductive politics, racial and national fantasy, class identity, truth and trust, censorship, intimate life and social display, terror and violence, health care, and deep cultural norms about the bearing of the body. Being queer means fighting about these issues all the time, locally and piecemeal but always with consequences. It means being able, more or less articulately, to challenge the common understanding of what gender difference means, or what the state is for, or what "health" entails, or what would define fairness, or what a good relation to the planet's environment would be. Queers do a kind of practical social reflection just in finding ways of being queer. (6)

Obviously, I cannot claim to address all the interrelations Warner cites here, though in the pages that follow I do engage many of them. My project is more modest. My study joins this queer parade of commentaries, and—through its reinflection of the insights of Smyth, Warner, Sedgwick, D'Emilio, and many others—aims to couple the renaissance of queer identities and political analyses with the other renaissance with which I began: the unprecedented efflorescence of queer cultural production. Of course, "couple" is not exactly the right word, if the concept assumes a prior separation of the parties involved. As I have already implied, neither renaissance was discrete in the first place.

Queer America

The renaissance under consideration here is "queer" not simply because it is by and for lesbians and gay men but because it is different from many other renaissances. As I insisted at the beginning of the last section, the Queer Renaissance resists the discourse of transcendence and historical dislocation that generally accompanies cultural renaissances. In this section of my introduction, I consider more carefully how the Queer Renaissance differs from a few specific twentieth-century renaissances. At the same time, I complicate the sense I gave of the Queer Renaissance's distinction from other renaissance moments. The Queer Renaissance is indeed fabulously distinct from renaissances that strive for transcendence of secular history, but absolute distinction from all other renaissance moments would be impossible, given the permeability of boundaries the Queer Renaissance celebrates. Moreover, many of the central figures of the Queer Renaissance would credit not only gay and lesbian history with shaping their political consciousness but also—or primarily—Chicana/o, African American, feminist, and working-class history, and hence these earlier literary and political movements are often explicitly or implicitly cited in the Queer Renaissance. The Chicano and Harlem Renaissances, in particular, share some characteristics with the contemporary Queer Renaissance. Nonetheless, vocal factions in both the Chicano and Harlem Renaissances attempted to contain fluidity, and thus writers in the Queer Renaissance who avail themselves of these movements reinvent the identities they proffer.

The Chicano Renaissance of the late 1960s and early 1970s, for instance, like the Queer Renaissance of the 1980s and 1990s, initially produced a revitalized and politicized identity. "Chicano" identity was rooted in *El Movimiento* and opposed to a hyphenated "Mexican-American" identity, which was perceived as more complacent and assimilationist. Systemic critique and an identity reshaped across differences—the two central components I identify with the Queer Renaissance—were also very much components of the Chicano Renaissance, as Rodolfo "Corky" Gonzales's epic poem *I Am Joaquín/Yo Soy Joaquín* makes clear.

I want to consider a few aspects of *I Am Joaquín* carefully, since the poem so thoroughly intertwined, in its message and its reception, the political and literary aspects of the Chicano movement. Gonzales's poem is printed in both English and Spanish. The first stanza opens by sharply criticizing *la sociedad gringa* that is destroying "Joaquín":

> I am Joaquín,
> lost in a world of confusion,
> caught up in the whirl of a
>   gringo society,
> confused by the rules,
> scorned by attitudes,
> suppressed by manipulation,
> and destroyed by modern society.

> Yo soy Joaquín,
> perdido en un mundo de confusión
> enganchado en el remolino de una
>   sociedad gringa,
> confundido por las reglas,
> despreciado por las actitudes,
> sofocado por manipulaciones,
> y destrozado por la sociedad moderna. (6–7)

Even as the poem places Joaquín within a desperate situation, however, it begins to shape a Chicano identity that will remake this "world of confusion." The English version of this first stanza appears beneath the picture of a young boy of eight or nine, who holds a sack and is seated atop boxes of El Rancho grapes. The credits identify this boy as a California grape worker (Gonzales, 118). The Spanish version of the first stanza appears on the opposing page, beneath the picture of a young *girl* of eight or nine, who leans against a wooden shack, also in California (118). The "I/Yo" that is Joaquín, then, is not individual but collective: both Spanish-

and English-speaking, female and male, child and adult. More than fifty photographs throughout *I Am Joaquín*—of farmworkers, demonstrators, veterans, children, and so forth—make Chicano identity even more expansive, as does the poem's distribution: thousands of copies were reproduced by Chicano newspapers; *teatro* groups performed the poem from California to Mexico (Teatro Campesino in particular, transforming it into a film); and—as Gonzales asserts—excerpts from the poem were "used by almost every Chicano organization in the country" (2).

The poem itself represented and refueled the Chicano movement. As Gonzales explains, "*I Am Joaquín* was the first work of poetry to be published by Chicanos for Chicanos and is the forerunner of the Chicano cultural renaissance. The poem was written first and foremost for the Chicano Movement" (3). Hence, far from transcending history or providing an alternative to *El Movimiento*, the Chicano Renaissance was understood as integrally connected to the political and the historical: "There is no inspiration without identifiable images, there is no conscience without the sharp knife of truthful exposure, and ultimately, there are no revolutions without poets" (1). Carlos Muñoz, Jr., explains that "*I Am Joaquín* did not offer its readers a well-defined radical ideology, but it did provide a critical framework for the developing student movement through its portrayal of the quest for identity and its critique of racism" (Muñoz, 60–61). In short, the poem nourished the nascent analysis taking shape within the movement. The sharpened political analysis within the movement, in turn, encouraged the formation of other literary works—such as the plays of Luis Valdez—that sustained a more well-defined critical ideology.

The poem provided the movement with a historical framework: "*I Am Joaquín* filled a vacuum, for most student activists had never read a book about Mexican American history—especially one that linked that history with Mexican history" (Muñoz, 61). To strengthen contemporary Chicano identity, Gonzales drew on a collective Chicano history. The name in the title, for instance, recalls the legend of Joaquín Murrieta, a miner who worked in California from 1849 to 1851. Gonzales explains that Anglo miners raped and killed Murrieta's wife and then drove Murrieta himself away from the claim he had staked. He was later falsely accused of horse stealing and whipped in public for this fictitious crime. Vowing revenge, Murrieta formed a band of outlaws, who commenced a series of "daring robberies and narrow escapes": "He became a legendary figure, *el bandido terrible*, the 'Robin Hood of El Dorado.' The California government offered a reward of $5,000 for him, dead or alive, and—because his last name was not well known—California became unsafe for anyone whose name happened to be Joaquín" (Gonzales, 115).

Through its citation of this legend, Gonzales's poem both valorizes a history of Chicano resistance to Anglo oppression and enacts a reversal in the service of contemporary Chicano identity. In the nineteenth-century context recalled by the legend, the statement "I am Joaquín" would have been fraught with danger; if one's name was Joaquín, silence would be the surest way to avoid certain death. Gonzales, in contrast, animates the Chicano movement by championing and disseminating the assertion "I am Joaquín." The dangerous statement is transformed into a byword for all those who join the Chicano movement and thereby becomes a sign that "Joaquín" cannot and will not be eliminated. The statement "I am Joaquín," then, is similar to ACT UP's appropriation and resignification of the pink triangle in the 1980s and 1990s. In Nazi Germany, silence about one's homosexuality was the only way to avoid being forced to wear the pink triangle and sent to extermination camps. ACT UP inverted the triangle (in Nazi Germany, it was worn with the point facing down) and appended to it the motto "Silence = Death." Wearing the triangle thus signified both one's membership in a vital, collective movement that refused to be silenced and one's belief that the government's silence on AIDS, in particular, had been murderous.

The renaissance of African American cultural production in the 1920s, especially if that movement is understood as the "New Negro Renaissance," similarly displayed a dynamic new identity. Although the New Negro Renaissance was certainly much more committed to abstract ideas of beauty than either the Queer or the Chicano Renaissance, all three nonetheless attempt to construct an identity that will speak to the presumed inadequacies of older identities: we are not simply lesbian and gay, but queer; not Mexican American, but Chicano; not Old Negroes, but New Negroes. An "Old Negro" identity might be considered politically apathetic and acquiescent in its subordination to whites, but "New Negro" identity offered an active, proud, resistant alternative. Hence the New Negro Renaissance, like the Chicano Renaissance forty years later, offered some African Americans of the 1920s a heightened and collective "race consciousness" that specifically countered from within the negative representations from without that dominated discussions of Negro life. Many in the New Negro Renaissance also saw art as the force that could bring about change. James Weldon Johnson, for instance, insisted that "artistic efforts" would enable the New Negro to overcome racism "faster than he has ever done through any other method" (qtd. in Lewis, 193).

However, there are important differences between the Queer Renaissance and both the New Negro and the Chicano Renaissance. In the New Negro Renaissance, for example, even though writers such as Johnson and W. E. B. DuBois saw politics and art as compatible and even positioned art as the highest form of social protest, the identity some of these writers favored was much less fluid than the identities favored by writers in the Queer Renaissance. DuBois and others championed the artist's ability to produce "positive images" of black people. Representations of the erotic, therefore, were often proscribed. Carla Kaplan notes that "black publication guidelines warned that nothing liable to add fuel to racist stereotypes of wanton licentiousness and primitivism would be printed" (122). Kaplan concludes that such proscriptions "were much more rigorously applied to the work of black women" (122). Male gatekeepers in the Harlem Renaissance thus scapegoated black women writers as more likely to reflect "wanton licentiousness" but simultaneously required them to embody the "highest moral values." Black women such as Bessie Smith did shape more fluid (and sexual) identities, but artists like Smith "were not often invited to New Negro salons" (Gates, "Trope of a New Negro," 148).

Furthermore, for some the question of how or whether the "political" and "aesthetic" functions of art were related remained open. The debate was ongoing and often vigorous. Alain Locke and others resisted DuBois's insistence that literature portray black people in a positive light and advocated, in contrast, unfettered individual self-expression. Locke and his cohorts understood DuBois's desire for "positive images" as propagandistic. The debate about art paralleled a more general controversy over New Negro identity. As Henry Louis Gates, Jr., argues, "At least since its usages after 1895, the name [New Negro] has implied a tension between strictly political concerns and strictly artistic concerns" ("Trope of a New Negro," 135). Locke's usage of the term to describe a literary movement, according to Gates, celebrated a mythological racial self and diluted the connotations of political activism that New Negro identity carried. Other writers took this separation of the artistic from the political to the extreme: in 1924, Charles Johnson characterized Jean Toomer as "triumphantly the negro artist, detached from propaganda, sensitive only to beauty" (qtd. in Lewis, 90). Thus, in spite of its articulation of a collective new identity for some, and in spite of some writers' linkage of the political and the aesthetic, the New Negro Renaissance as often positioned the two realms at odds, and this sharply contrasts to the Queer Renaissance, where they have consistently been mutually constitutive.[15]

Finally, if the New Negro Renaissance is understood, more traditionally, as the Harlem Renaissance, then its limited geographic location and availability contrast with the ubiquity of the Queer Renaissance. The "here" of the queer pronouncement "We're here, we're queer, get used to it" is as valid, and perhaps more threatening, in Peoria as in New York or San Francisco. I do not mean by this assertion to contradict my argument in favor of location and specificity but rather to affirm that queers in specific locations everywhere have reinvented gay and lesbian identity. We are everywhere, but the terms of our existence shift according to distinct histories and locations. Thus my first chapter is critical of how Edmund White's Ohio in *A Boy's Own Story* becomes a blank "Everyplace," whereas my second and third chapters examine specific and very different queerings of rural North Carolina and the U.S.-Mexican border region, respectively.

As with the Harlem Renaissance, there are differences between the Chicano and the Queer Renaissance—in this case, precisely to the extent that the former is, relentlessly, the Chicano Renaissance. As Lorna Dee Cervantes writes, "You cramp my style, baby / when you roll on top of me / shouting, 'Viva La Raza' / at the top of your prick" (qtd. in Gutiérrez, 48). In other words, the Chicano Renaissance, despite its expansiveness and despite the gender inclusivity suggested by the first few pages of *I Am Joaquín,* often depended for its meaning on the containment of Chicanas. "Queer," too, can and does generate its own exclusions (some of which are considered more fully in my third chapter), but I think that, at its best, the concept is unruly and undermines attempts at fixation or containment. "To queer," in my mind, is precisely "to bring out the difference that is compelled to pass under the sign of the same." As Sedgwick notes, "The most exciting recent work around 'queer' spins the term outward along dimensions that can't be subsumed under gender and sexuality at all: the ways that race, ethnicity, postcolonial nationality criss-cross with these *and other* identity-constituting, identity-fracturing discourses, for example" (*Tendencies,* 8–9). Isaac Julien, Gloria Anzaldúa, and Richard Fung are exemplars of this type of queer theory, according to Sedgwick: "[These] intellectuals and artists of color . . . are using the leverage of 'queer' to do a new kind of justice to the fractal intricacies of language, skin, migration, state. Thereby, the gravity (I mean *gravitas,* the meaning, but also the *center* of gravity) of the term 'queer' itself deepens and shifts" (*Tendencies,*

9). Such constant shifting is a central focus of all four of the chapters that follow. Only through this constant shifting can the Queer Renaissance guard against the exclusionary practices that already endanger it and that have plagued—and ultimately grounded—earlier movements.

Hence, when practitioners of the contemporary Queer Renaissance avail themselves of movements such as the New Negro or the Chicano Renaissance, they resist the tendency to contain fluidity. At the same time, they reinvoke those earlier moments' sharp critique of American culture. Cherríe Moraga, for instance, writes, "For me, 'El Movimiento' has never been a thing of the past, it has retreated into subterranean uncontaminated soils awaiting resurrection in a 'queerer,' more feminist generation" (*Last Generation*, 148). For Moraga, then, the contemporary moment signals a revitalization or rebirth of Chicano/a political/artistic practices *through the lens* of queer and feminist thought. This revitalization sustains and extends the Chicano Renaissance's and *El Movimiento's* indictment of America: *"An art that subscribes to integration into mainstream Amerika is not Chicano art"* (Moraga, *Last Generation*, 61).

Since Moraga writes openly as Chicana, feminist, and queer, understanding those identities as inextricably imbricated, and since queer art similarly indicts "mainstream Amerika," Moraga's assertion could as easily describe the Queer Renaissance of which she is a part as it does the Chicano art that is her immediate topic. In fact, the title of the collection of prose and poetry from which these quotations are taken seems to license such an ongoing linkage of "queer" and "Chicano." Calling her collection *The Last Generation*, Moraga insists that the reproduction stops here: both literally, since she is a lesbian who chooses not to have children, and figuratively, in that she is a Chicana resisting the reproduction of assimilationist "Hispanic" narratives. In short, Moraga reinvents Chicano/a identity in and through queerness and vice versa. She describes her writing as "a queer mixture of glyphs" that "shape[s] the world I know at the turn of this century. . . . Like the ancient codices, *The Last Generation* begins at the end and moves forward" (4). Judging by the writing that follows this description of her project, the "end" Moraga invokes here is the end of assimilation to Anglo-American, heterosexual, and patriarchal norms. Like all the "queer glyphs" that constitute the Queer Renaissance, Moraga's prose and poetry are dedicated to a dismantling of such norms, wherever they are encountered: "I hold a vision requiring a radical transformation of consciousness in this country, that as the people-of-color population increases . . . we will emerge as a mass movement of people to redefine what an 'American' is" (61); "We can work to teach one another that our freedom as a people is mutually dependent and cannot be parceled out—class before race before sex before sexuality" (174).

Other American renaissances of this century (I think here especially of the Native American Renaissance and the Hawaiian Renaissance), despite important differences, share with the Queer Renaissance the commitment to a systemic critique of American culture.[16] I would never argue, then, as David Bergman does in the introduction to his *Gaiety Transfigured: Gay Self-Representation in American Literature,* that "to be American is to be queer" (10). Bergman jotted this observation down on a scrap of paper during a visit to Harper's Ferry with his lover, and he insists that "in so doing I united the currents of the national spirit with my literary ancestry and my erotic desires" (10). Of course, Bergman's national epiphany here has to be read in the context of Harper's Ferry: that is, in the context of John Brown's famous attempt to *change* the America of his day. In this sense, "America" for Bergman, as for many people at various locations on the political spectrum, stands for "liberation" and "freedom." The abstractness of Bergman's formulation and his celebratory lyricism, however, prevent him from moving beyond this oversimplified nationalism. Bergman's lyricism also prevents him from questioning the potential ramifications of his thesis about "the national spirit." If "to be American is to be queer," in what sense is it or is it not the case that "to be queer is to be American"? Could "American" simply replace "Queer" on the T-shirts that so delighted Sedgwick at the gay pride parade, since the two terms are interchangeable? Of course not: "American" carries too many other contradictory and reactionary meanings that are not easily dismissed (or, to use Bergman's language, "transfigured"). Rather than teasing out these contradictions and insisting—as Moraga does—that we continuously "re-define what an 'American' is," however, Bergman uses this scrap of paper to pull together a sort of high-modernist unity from the disparate fragments of his life. Moraga, in contrast, advocates not unification but dissolution: "*If the Soviet Union could dissolve, why can't the United States?*" (*The Last Generation,* 168).[17]

If Bergman had more fully explored these contradictions, then perhaps he would have asserted that to be queer is to *contest* America. In this formulation, "Queer America" is less a description than an ongoing imperative. It is this imperative, I think, that the Queer Renaissance performs and extends, and it at times shares this imperative with, and inherits it from, the New Negro and Chicano Renaissances.

New Queer Writers

"Queerness" is not merely contestatory, however; over the past several years, activists, journalists, scholars, and many others have sharply contested the meanings of queerness itself. In many locations, and in gay and lesbian journalism in particular, *queer* is still used as a simple synonym for embodied lesbians and gay men. And indeed, such an association should remain primary; as Sedgwick notes, "Given the historical and contemporary force of the prohibitions against *every* same-sex sexual expression, for anyone to disavow those meanings, or to displace them from the term's definitional center, would be to dematerialize any possibility of queerness itself" (*Tendencies*, 8). Still, *queer* as I am using it in this project (and certainly, as Sedgwick deploys it in hers) should be seen as more expansive and not simplistically coextensive with fixed homosexual bodies.

My use of the term should be seen, for instance, as a deliberate contrast to Michelangelo Signorile's use of it in his national bestseller *Queer in America: Sex, the Media, and the Closets of Power*. Although Signorile explores a plethora of locations in his book, in each "queers" look exactly the same. Like many ethnographers before him, everywhere Signorile goes, he sees people just like himself. In sections such as "Queer in New York," "Queer in Washington," "Queer in Hollywood," and "Queer in America," Signorile positions those who engage in heterosexual activity as always automatically on the outside of "queer" ("Because they've never experienced the closet, because they have no idea what it's like to be queer, sympathetic straights often see coming out or being outed as the most excruciating, most horrible thing imaginable" [xx]), while those who engage in homosexual activity are automatically on the inside—as if, were Jesse Helms and Robert Dornan to be caught in a tabloid love nest, it would indicate that all along they have been unacknowledged members of the queer club.

To me, Signorile's use of expressions such as "all the president's queers" (165), "Pete Williams['s] . . . queerness" (104), or "closeted queer" (71) verge on the oxymoronic. In fact, I would go so far as to say that, given the current structure of the American political system "inside the Beltway" and in contrast to what Signorile implies throughout *Queer in America*, there are no "queers in power," only queer moments: Maryland senator Barbara Mikulski's characterization of the Senate Judiciary Committee as an "inquisition" and Republican senators as "grand inquisitors," an accusation she made before delivering the resounding "No!" vote that registered her opposition to the confirmation of Clarence Thomas to the Supreme Court; Surgeon General Joycelyn Elders's assertion that we should understand masturbation as part of human sexuality and even that we—gasp!—should communicate that to our children. The cross-identifications and commitments that led to these moments and many others like them indicate, certainly, that queer *processes* are alive and well on the inside, disrupting the system; but embodied "queers in power," whatever such creatures might look like, are not—Representatives Barney Frank, Gerry Studds, and, especially, Steve Gunderson notwithstanding. Indeed, I would argue that Elders, complete with sparkling heterosexual and Christian credentials, is the closest we have come to a highly visible queer in power, and that her rapid dismissal (Elders: "[The conversation] was more than one minute and less than two") attests to the difficulty of articulating queerness to the current political system, given that queerness is so intent on *changing* that system.[18]

My use of *queer* in this project has more in common with David Wojnarowicz's uses of the term than with Signorile's. For Wojnarowicz, queerness is fluid and disruptive. Wojnarowicz's use of *queer* shifts constantly throughout his *Close to the Knives: A Memoir of Disintegration,* so that at various points in the text it describes fags, dykes, junkies, hustlers, the homeless, people living with AIDS, people of color, women, and the occasional straight man—all of those who stand in opposition to what Wojnarowicz calls throughout "this pre-invented existence" (174), "the illusion of the ONE-TRIBE NATION . . . this illusion called AMERICA" (153), or more globally, this "shit planet" (168). To Wojnarowicz, "Being Queer in America" (the title of one of his essays) means constantly living "close to the knives." Living close to the knives, in turn, means dealing with danger and rage as basic components of everyday life: Will you suddenly face the knives, literally or metaphorically pinned to the wall by queer bashers, or will you instead suddenly grab the knives yourself, to use against the bashers? In short, one lives close to the knives because this is a dangerous and infuriating world in which queer lives of all sorts are expendable:

> I thought of the neo-nazis posing as politicians and religious leaders and I thought of my genuine fantasies of murder and wondered why I never crossed the line. It's not that I'm a *good* person or even that I am afraid of containment in jail; it may be more that I can't escape the ropes of my own body, my own flesh, and bottom line in the pyramids of power and confine-

Introduction: Reading the Queer Renaissance

ment one demon gets replaced by another in a moment's notice and no one gesture can erase it *all* that easily. (Wojnarowicz, 33)

On a journey through the American West, Wojnarowicz is not surprised to read in the newspaper of one city—a city he describes as "a government war town filled with a half million workers employed in the various research centers attempting to perfect a president's dream of laser warfare from the floating veil of outerspace" (30)—about a Native American teenage boy who is terrorizing civilians by driving his car onto the sidewalk. Instead, given "this pre-invented existence" and "the illusion of the ONE-TRIBE NATION," Wojnarowicz is surprised by others' surprise: "I thought of the face of our current president floating disembodied and ten stories tall over the midnight buildings. I wondered why any of these things, like the kid in his camaro, are a surprise. Why weren't more of us doing this?" (32).

Wojnarowicz carries his outrage to his art and, in photographs and paintings such as *Fuck You Faggot Fucker* (1984), translates that outrage into a queer challenge to those in "the pyramids of power." *Fuck You Faggot Fucker* displays a collage of images, including a crude drawing of anal sex flanked by the words "Fuck You Faggot Fucker." The drawing appears to be graffiti, perhaps pulled from the walls of a public restroom. Wojnarowicz places a much larger drawing of two men kissing, waist-deep in water, in the center of the collage and overlays the men's bodies with a color map of North America. The graffiti beneath these men suggests that they are embattled, surrounded by—indeed, almost drowning in—hostility, yet their kiss remains the most prominent feature of the collage. Moreover, Wojnarowicz defiantly maps queer acts and eroticisms onto countless locations everywhere, since all of North America is incorporated into the kiss between these two men. A far cry from Signorile's desire to "out" Malcolm Forbes or Jodie Foster, Wojnarowicz's desire is to represent queer identity otherwise: not as an identity one might discover tucked away in the "closets of power" but rather as a fluid and disruptive identity openly constructed and reconstructed in innumerable *pockets* of power by the many who share Wojnarowicz's opposition to a society "pre-invented" to sanction "the legalized murder of those who are diverse in their natures" (154).

In the pages that follow, I consider the various ways other poets, playwrights, essayists, and novelists have represented such queer identities. I have specifically started here with Signorile and Wojnarowicz, two white and male writers, in order to tease out differences within that group over and around queerness. Another difference worth pointing out is that some white men (in opposition to both Signorile and Wojnarowicz) have often been among the concept's greatest detractors: Bruce Bawer and Rich Tafel, for instance, are among the many white gay men who think the movement would gain more respect if we *queers* would only behave.[19]

I highlight this disjunction because there are some who would turn the most recent history of the term into the story of a split between white gay men (a group that is assumed to be monolithic) and everyone else. Consider, for instance, Ruth Novazcek's concerns: "I worry about the word queer. I still have this image of the gay clone in a black leather jacket and shaved 'blonde' head and I worry that it will perpetuate that aesthetic" (qtd. in Smyth, 34). Or take Robyn Wiegman's too-easy dismissal of queer theory: "The turn toward the word *queer* is intended to displace [the] displacement of difference, to mark a mutual eccentricity . . . as central. While I certainly agree with the political imperative of such a project, it seems to me that the deployment of *queer* so far . . . actually neutralizes difference" ("Introduction," 17n. 1). Yet rejection of *queer* might also neutralize difference; in fact, Bawer's repeated rejections of the concept suggest as much. Bawer is the editor of *Beyond Queer: Challenging Gay Left Orthodoxy,* a collection that he hopes will convey the message that it's time "for the gay rights movement to grow up" (xiv). For Bawer and his cohorts, however, growing up "beyond queer" apparently means moving *away* from difference and diversity: the contributors to *Beyond Queer* are overwhelmingly white and male; it is, indeed, difficult for me to think of a recent gay and/or lesbian collection that is less inclusive than Bawer's.

Pace Wiegman, I certainly agree that *queer* has the *potential* to neutralize difference. My point here is simply that resistance to or dismissal of the concept also has the potential to neutralize difference, and one goal of our inquiries might be to negotiate these tensions.[20] Rather than simply assuming that *queer* perpetuates a white male aesthetic, we might consider more critically how and why the concept has *failed* to speak to some white men and how it has already been deployed by many different gay and lesbian writers of color. Many white men do not want to be queer, and many women and men of color were queer before queer was hip.[21]

It is this belief that makes *The Queer Renaissance* a project that is more about writers such as Audre Lorde, Randall Kenan, and Gloria Anzaldúa than about the group that has recently been labeled explicitly the "New

Queer Writers." The New Queer Writers (Wojnarowicz, Dennis Cooper, Eric Latzky, Kevin Killian, Dodie Bellamy, and several others) are a loosely associated group of writers who nonetheless share a commitment to interrogating sexual and social identities that are made marginal by contemporary society, even (and in some cases, especially) by contemporary lesbian and gay culture. I think this group of writers is very much part of the Queer Renaissance (much more so than, say, a mainstream gay writer such as David Leavitt), which is why I have focused on Wojnarowicz here. In this project, however, I am interested in bringing together "related but disparate views [that] inform and corrupt each other," if I may appropriate one recent description of the New Queer Writing (qtd. in Latzky, 14). I want, in short, to corrupt queer writing by examining an even wider variety of "margins": not simply the high-literary "bad boys" who look back to Jean Genet and William S. Burroughs as their forebears (important as that group may be) but also those writers who look back to the various liberation movements I have surveyed in this introduction and who draw their commitment to the representation of boundary-crossing and systemic critique from them. To my mind, Wojnarowicz, Cooper, Latzky, and the rest have produced some of the most provocative and exciting contemporary queer writing to date, and I do not mean to suggest that they do not recall or cite in their writing the movements I have considered. New Queer Writers, however, come in a wide variety of forms, and the bad boys and girls I have nodded to here are only a small part of a "vast, diverse, and growing anti-assimilationist queer movement" (Cooper, xi). Hence, in the chapters that follow, I consider novelists, poets, and playwrights whose work might not, at first, be thought to represent the New Queer Writing. The theories they advance and the unruly identities they depict, however, ensure that their work is very much in concert with the work of this school.

Chapter 1 thus reads Audre Lorde's *Zami: A New Spelling of My Name* alongside Edmund White's *A Boy's Own Story* and considers how, at the outset of the Queer Renaissance, *Zami* redefines the parameters of the coming-out story. Although the Gay Liberation Front intended "coming out" to provide a starting point for radical political action, by the late 1970s the coming-out story had evolved into a predictable narrative, detailing a protagonist's teleological journey toward an essential wholeness. Examining coming out alongside feminist theories of positionality, I suggest that *Zami* resists this individual and essentialist understanding of gay identity and constructs instead an/other myth of queer positionality—not because

Lorde attempts, as White does in *A Boy's Own Story,* to construct her protagonist as an alienated, marked "other" but because *Zami* argues for collective identity, for a "self" defined in and through others.

Chapter 2 carries queer theory to another region, where "community" is not always the sustaining force it is in *Zami.* I analyze Randall Kenan's *A Visitation of Spirits*—which focuses on a black gay youth growing up in the rural African American town of Tims Creek, North Carolina—in order to consider what happens when queer desire turns up in apparently unlikely and inhospitable places. This chapter engages African American theories of signification and suggests that *A Visitation of Spirits* effects a queer trickster identity, able to reverse hierarchies of power and transform even the supposed "margins" of the queer world.

Chapter 3 focuses on Gloria Anzaldúa's *Borderlands/La Frontera* and the current academic penchant for transgressing disciplined/disciplinary boundaries. I argue that there's more than one way to cross a border: border crossings may challenge the mechanisms of power that produce borders, divided identities, and histories of exploitation, but they may also uncritically posit cosmopolitan consumers/theorists, able to move anywhere and everywhere with ease. Anzaldúa's "new mestiza" crosses the U.S.-Mexican and other borders not to escape identity and history but rather to challenge the unchecked mobility of oppressive systems of power. The new mestiza turns the searchlight away from those border residents deemed "illegal" and onto those who delimit and police the border in order to secure unlimited mobility for themselves.

Chapter 4 examines lesbian and gay work generated by the AIDS crisis. I begin by considering how Tony Kushner, in his critically acclaimed play *Angels in America,* queers the concept of perestroika in order to promote the performance of a disruptive, coalition-based identity. I then provide a genealogy of Kushner's aesthetic: using Sarah Schulman's fictionalization of ACT UP in her novel *People in Trouble,* I put Kushner's play into conversation with the queer AIDS activist identities that were being performed in the streets during the writing and production of *Angels in America.* This final chapter considers more directly how the critical aesthetic that is at play in the works that constitute the Queer Renaissance shapes, and has been shaped by, liminal sexual and activist "identities in a crisis."

Finally, in the epilogue, I conclude that the Queer Renaissance is ongoing, despite—and in the face of—the recent rise of gay neoconservatism and of studies that seek to ground homosexuality in biology. Queer inquiry

Introduction: Reading the Queer Renaissance

commences by challenging the boundaries established by others and thus thrives despite attempts by some to fix us with a well-behaved neoconservatism or an underdeveloped hypothalamus. Activists and writers in the Queer Renaissance continue to refuse such constricting identities. The queer trickster, the AIDS activist, the new mestiza, Zami—these are the identities I analyze here. Born of a wide variety of twentieth-century liberation movements, such identities have been reborn in the contemporary Queer Renaissance.

Chapter One

Boys' Own Stories and New Spellings of My Name: Coming Out and Other Myths of Queer Positionality

———→➤●◄←———

Myths of Queer Positionality

In *The Beautiful Room Is Empty*, Edmund White's nameless narrator envisions a day when gay people will claim the right to define themselves: "Then I caught myself foolishly imagining that gays might someday constitute a community rather than a diagnosis" (226). This exhilarating thought comes to White's protagonist as he finds himself in the middle of an uprising at the Stonewall Inn Bar in Greenwich Village on the night of June 27, 1969. Drawing on Civil Rights rhetoric, the protagonist and his friends reclaim and reposition their own experiences with chants such as "Gay is good" and "We're the Pink Panthers" (226).[1]

Although White's account is fictional, the riots outside the Stonewall Inn are generally considered the beginning of the contemporary gay liberation movement. They did indeed usher in a decade of redefinition by lesbian and gay communities. Within weeks, the Gay Liberation Front (GLF) had formed, employing the slogan "Out of the Closets and into the Streets!" Within a year, the Radicalesbians, influenced by both gay liberation and the women's movement, had presented feminists with the "woman-identified woman," a position that they hoped would facilitate the formation of challenging, politicized coalitions among women. By 1974, activists had successfully removed homosexuality from the American Psychiatric Association's (APA's) list of mental disorders. In short, the new names and identities embraced by White's protagonist and his friends were high on the agenda for early gay liberationists.[2]

These newly available gay and lesbian identities were claimed and proclaimed through the act of "coming out." This act provided lesbians and gay men with positions that could serve as starting points for the radical political action the early gay liberationists believed was necessary to reconfigure the systems of capitalism and patriarchy responsible for gay and lesbian oppression. Indeed, the very slogan of the gay liberationists (and the title of a 1972 essay by Allen Young), "Out of the Closets, into the Streets," suggests not simply that one claims a position ("out of the closet") but that one moves from that position to effect radical social change. Young writes, "Of course, we want to 'come out.' . . . But the movement for a new definition of sexuality does not, and cannot, end there. . . . The revolutionary goals of gay liberation, including the elimination of capitalism, imperialism and racism, are premised on the termination of the system of male supremacy" (10). Similarly, "woman-identification," according to the Radicalesbians, could be "develop[ed] with reference to ourselves, and not in relation to men. This consciousness is the revolutionary force from which all else will follow" (Radicalesbians, 176). Like the identity positions (pro)claimed by all the so-called new social movements, the identities into which gay and lesbian activists "came out" were collective identities meant to generate radical social change based on new and different ways of understanding the world.[3]

Coming out generally does not have the same radical edge for the new generation of queer activists, or for the writers of the Queer Renaissance, that it had for their gay liberationist forebears. On the contrary: coming out, along with its product—one's "coming-out story"—has been thoroughly critiqued by many contemporary lesbian and gay writers. In particular, theorists have critiqued coming-out stories for their emphasis on the "discovery" of an individual and essential gay identity, unmarked by other categories of difference, such as race or class. This chapter briefly surveys these and other criticisms but simultaneously attempts to lay the theoretical groundwork for a reclamation of coming out's radical potential. Specifically, through readings of Edmund White's *A Boy's Own Story* and Audre Lorde's *Zami: A New Spelling of My Name*, I consider whether a feminist-informed and antiracist analysis might redefine the parameters of the coming-out story, shaping it into a myth of what I call "queer (op)positionality."

Through the term *(op)positionality*, I intend to invoke the "opposition" to established and oppressive systems of power that was voiced by the GLF, the Radicalesbians, and members of all the new social movements, and that has been rearticulated in the contemporary Queer Renaissance. I also intend to invoke "positionality" theory (or "standpoint epistemology") as it has evolved in recent feminist writing. Standpoint theorists, often explicitly citing both the strengths and the weaknesses of the social movements of the 1960s and early 1970s, argue for a nonessentialized "position" from which to forge coalition-based political action.[4] Linda Alcoff, for example, argues, "If we combine the concept of identity politics with a conception of the subject as positionality, we can conceive of the subject as nonessentialized and emergent from a historical experience and yet retain our political ability to take gender as an important point of departure" (433). As Alcoff sees it, this new position is both fluid and relational: "being a 'woman' is to take up a position within a moving historical context and to be able to choose what we make of this position and how we alter this context," so that "women can themselves articulate a set of interests and ground a feminist politics" (435).

Similarly, Donna Haraway's feminist redefinition of "objectivity" argues for an openly acknowledged, although partial, position or perspective. Haraway writes, "Feminist objectivity is about limited location and situated knowledge, not about transcendence and splitting of subject and object" (190). This *partial* perspective is necessitated since, not unlike Edmund White's narrator in *The Beautiful Room Is Empty*, with his concern about psychiatric diagnoses, Haraway confesses that she has occasional paranoid fantasies about so-called *impartial*, "objective" discourses that appropriate "embodied others" as "objects" of knowledge:

> Academic and activist feminist enquiry has repeatedly tried to come to terms with the question of what *we* might mean by the curious and inescapable term "objectivity." We have used a lot of toxic ink and trees processed into paper decrying what *they* have meant and how it hurts *us*. The imagined "they" constitute a kind of invisible conspiracy of masculinist scientists and philosophers replete with grants and laboratories; and the imagined "we" are the embodied others, who are not allowed *not* to have a body. (183)

Because of these fears, Haraway's redefinition of "objectivity," like the rhetoric of gay liberation, gives preference to other ways of seeing, particularly those ways of seeing that emerge from what she calls the "standpoints of the subjugated." She writes, " 'Subjugated' standpoints are preferred because they seem to promise more adequate, sustained, objective, transforming accounts of the world" (191). Such standpoints are actually *more* "objective" because they do not claim to see, simultaneously, "everything from nowhere" (189) or "to be," as Richard Dyer puts it in his analysis of the social construction of whiteness, "everything and nothing" (Dyer, 45). Such standpoints are more "transforming" because a coalition politics that emphasizes working together across difference is fundamental to what theorists of positionality envision. Indeed, this model would not have been shaped in the first place if feminists of color had not called for a more rigorous analysis of the differences within feminism and for an ongoing interrogation of the ways in which feminist concerns overlap with the concerns of other groups. Both Haraway and Alcoff, consequently, place race as well as gender at the center of their analyses: to Haraway, the category "women of color" "marks out a self-consciously constructed space that cannot affirm the capacity to act on the basis of natural identification, but only on the basis of conscious coalition, of affinity, of political kinship" (Haraway, 156); to Alcoff, positionality theory "can be readily intuited by people of mixed races and cultures who have had to choose in some sense their identity" (Alcoff, 432).

Other theorists, recognizing the value of such coalition-based and self-reflexive positionality, have attempted to link gay male and feminist standpoint theory. Earl Jackson, Jr., for one, begins his study of Robert Glück by acknowledging, "One of the most important things gay men can learn from feminist and lesbian-feminist discursive practices is how to read and write from responsibly identified positions" (112). Nevertheless, there are drawbacks to any attempt to link, specifically, *coming out* to feminist theories of positionality; these drawbacks become evident from the critiques of coming out I alluded to earlier. The position "out of the closet," much more than the "standpoint" of recent feminist theory, has become in the past two decades a mandated and delimited position, for both men and women. In the process of forging the imperative to come out, unfortunately, some lesbian and gay communities lost the sense that coming out was, as feminist theorists now argue about the feminist standpoint, only a beginning point from which to launch political action. The collective rallying cry "Out of the Closets, into the Streets" quickly became the demand that individuals simply "Come out of the closet." Assimilation, rather than transformation, became the goal; increased visibility, it was thought, would lead to gay civil rights and acceptance into mainstream society. Martin Duberman explains that the Gay Activists Alliance emerged

Boys' Own Stories and New Spellings of My Name

as a breakaway alternative to the Gay Liberation Front, and would shortly supercede it. . . . Whereas GLF had argued that sexual liberation had to be fought for in conjunction with a variety of other social reforms and in alliance with other oppressed minorities, GAA believed in a single-minded concentration on gay civil rights and eschewed "romantic" excursions into revolutionary ideology. (*Cures*, 213–14)[5]

Maintaining the GLF's insistence that gay men and lesbians speak up but abandoning their politics of alliance, the GAA redirected the movement and circumscribed the meaning of coming out.

In addition to the dangers of quietism, coming out as a focus for gay and lesbian theory could also underwrite an apolitical essentialism. The narrowing of vision Duberman recounts could, and often does, narrow even further, so that coming out comes to signify solely the assertion of one's (supposedly long-repressed) identity. This model of coming out, by itself, exhibits little concern for how lesbian or gay identities are socially constituted, for how they are intersected by other arenas of difference, or for what sort of collective political action might develop from an assertion of one's gay or lesbian identity. Coming out here becomes a suspiciously white and middle-class move toward "self-respect," not revolutionary social change, and many contemporary coming-out narratives might be seen as products of this shift toward individualism and essentialism. To be fair, however, John D'Emilio writes, in reference to the early gay liberationists:

For a gay man or lesbian of that time, I don't think that it was possible to experience anything of comparable intensity. In a psychological sense it was an act of "revolutionary" import. No manner of political analysis could convince someone who had come out that he or she wasn't turning the world inside out and upside down. (*Making Trouble*, 249)

Still, D'Emilio's comment is less a trumpeting of the benefits of coming out than it is a note of caution. He is attempting to contextualize, but also look critically at, the psychological empowerment that coming out could bring: "Only later, as the movement matured, would it become clear that coming out was a first step only. An openly gay banker is still a banker" (*Making Trouble*, 249). By the end of the 1970s and throughout the 1980s, many lesbians and gay men no longer had the sense that coming out was a first step only. Coming out came to have one meaning, across all social locations: announcing one's homosexuality. The act no longer necessarily carried the sense that lesbians and gays should collectively move to *new* locations; one could come out, and stay out, anywhere. Although "coming out conservative" would have been a logical impossibility to members of the GLF, by 1992, because of the ways in which the act had been redefined as the assertion of one's essential, no longer repressed identity, it was the title of a popular book about Marvin Liebman, a formerly closeted anticommunist and conservative activist.

In a slightly different vein, Haraway, too, stresses that essentialism in its many guises is a pitfall for feminist theories of positionality, especially those, like hers, that foreground the "standpoints of the subjugated": "But here lies a serious danger of romanticizing and/or appropriating the vision of the less powerful while claiming to see from their positions. . . . A commitment to mobile positioning and to passionate detachment is dependent on the impossibility of innocent 'identity' politics" (191–92). Haraway's disclaimers suggest that these essentializing tendencies might not engulf feminist theories of positionality, as long as "situating knowledge" entails continually and collectively *re*positioning identity: "The knowing self is partial in all its guises, never finished, whole, simply there and original; it is always constructed and stitched together imperfectly, and *therefore* able to join with another, to see together without claiming to be another" (193).

An "innocent identity politics," however, has already engulfed the coming-out narrative, according to many lesbian and gay critics. Diana Fuss sees even in the Radicalesbians a "tension between the notions of 'developing' an identity and 'finding' an identity" that "points to a more general confusion over the very definition of 'identity' and the precise signification of 'lesbian' " (*Essentially Speaking,* 100). Biddy Martin discusses how, by the end of the 1970s, the imperative to come out is evolving into a predictable (and white) narrative, and how many coming-out stories "are tautological insofar as they describe a process of coming to know something that has always been true, a truth to which the author has returned" (89). Jeffrey Minson takes this accusation of tautology a step further, suggesting that "far from constituting a break from a repressive, closetted past, coming out might be situated as the latest in a long line of organised rituals of confession. . . . Sexual avowal therefore is a mode of social regimentation" (37). In Minson's ominous scenario, coming out simply reproduces and undergirds the homophobic notion that homosexuality wholly explains a lesbian or gay person's identity.

Finally, although Fuss's, Martin's, and Minson's criticisms might also be leveled at some feminist theories of positionality, coming out may be problematic for a unique, more mundane reason: the imperative "Come out!" is by now, for many, a worn-out refrain. "National Coming Out Day" is at this point televised yearly on *The Oprah Winfrey Show*, and encouragement, such as the exhortation in my own campus newspaper to "come out, wherever you are, and friends won't turn away" (Behrens, 19), often sounds like pandering for heterosexual "compassion." Since coming out, according to this mainstream model, is virtually synonymous with a call to "respect yourself," many gay and lesbian people are understandably bored or irritated with this focus on coming out and its product, the coming-out narrative.[6] For example, David Van Leer insists that for White, coming out is "the quintessential gay experience"; but in a review of *The Faber Book of Gay Short Stories*, which White edited, Van Leer suggests that, in its "preoccupation with the opinion of others," coming out "sometimes looks like a bid for heterosexual sympathy, even for absolution" (50). Sarah Schulman states more forcefully, "The coming out story should be permanently laid to rest. . . . It was a defining stage we had to go through, but it doesn't help us develop a literature true to our experience" (qtd. in Fries, 8).

Although I have no doubt that "we" will never construct a literature "true to our experience," since that "experience" is multiple and that "truth" is always socially constituted and continually shifting, I am nonetheless sympathetic with Schulman's frustration over the primacy given the coming-out narrative, especially when this focus comes at the expense of attention to other queer stories. Richard Hall, in a review of White's *The Beautiful Room Is Empty*, is more tentative than Schulman, suggesting, "Not that the coming-out novel in its pristine liberationist form is dead. Maybe it's just weary. . . . Here is another coming-up-and-out story, taking the narrator into adolescence and young manhood . . ." (27). Although Hall feels White's novel is told with "wit, humor and aphoristic elegance" (27), his reservations about the coming-out novel are standard fare these days in reviews of contemporary lesbian and gay literature.[7]

Thus, despite a possible affinity with recent feminist theory, as a myth of "queer positionality," coming out can be read as a worn-out concept. In the remainder of this chapter I explore more thoroughly why this is the case, but I also use the insights offered by feminist positionality theory to present an analysis that considers ways to revise or reclaim the coming-out story. Myths of queer positionality/identity need not be hopelessly lost on teleological journeys toward essential wholeness; "noninnocent" myths of queer positionality can be shaped in a queer world that is about "lived social and bodily realities [and] in which people are not afraid . . . of permanently partial identities and contradictory standpoints," as in the cyborg world Haraway envisions and argues for (154). *A Boy's Own Story* and *Zami: A New Spelling of My Name* were both published in 1982, when the cultural phenomenon I call "the Queer Renaissance" had only just begun. Through an examination of these two very different coming-out stories, I want to flaunt the ways coming out has been reinvented in the Queer Renaissance as a myth of queer (op)positionality.[8]

Queer Oppositionality/Queer Apositionality

Edmund White's *A Boy's Own Story* is the first novel in a planned three-novel series. In each text, White traces the development of his nameless, faceless narrator. *A Boy's Own Story* focuses on this development during the 1950s; *The Beautiful Room Is Empty*, on this development during the 1960s. The novel as yet unfinished (*The Farewell Symphony*) will carry the protagonist through the 1970s and 1980s.

The "invisibility" used as a mechanism in these texts works as a metaphor for the pain the protagonist goes through as a gay youth in heterosexist America. Ed Cohen writes that

> the structuring stories we commonly use in order to make sense of our daily lives provide us with very few plots that do not emplot us in normative versions of gender and sexuality. . . . [These normative narratives] have special consequences for those of us whose movements appear to transgress the possibilities of such acceptable representations, effectively rendering us "unrepresentable." ("Constructing Gender," 545)

Thus, like many other gay men and lesbians, White's protagonist feels that none of the people around him knows who he "really" is, and that he must consequently wear a (heterosexual) mask. The young narrator of *A Boy's Own Story* muses, "What if I could write about my life exactly as it was? What if I could show it in all its density and tedium and its concealed passion . . . ?" (41). The point is, however, that he cannot, given the normative versions of gender and sexuality available to him, and hence invisibility works to underscore that the narrator is forced to "live a lie" at the same time as it works to stress more generally the pain and isolation of being marginalized in and by American society. Like the narrator of Ralph Ellison's *Invisible Man,* White's protagonist might say, "I am invisible . . . because people refuse to see me" (Ellison, 3).

I mention Ellison at this point because White's use of the trope of invisibility in *A Boy's Own Story* and elsewhere is not unlike Ellison's use of the same trope in his 1952 novel: both writers use invisibility to comment on the exclusionary logic at the heart of American culture. Perhaps not surprisingly, then, White's narrators often see parallels between their experiences and the experiences of African Americans in the United States. In *A Boy's Own Story,* for example, the narrator finds himself pressured by his friends to accompany them to a whorehouse staffed by two black women and one white woman. As the protagonist sits in the waiting room, one of the black prostitutes engages him in conversation. The narrator admits, "I felt sorry for her. I thought she might really need my ten dollars. After all this was Saturday night, and yet she didn't have any customers. Somehow I equated her fatness, her blackness, her unpopularity with my own outcast status" (183). White's narrator goes on to imagine a marriage between the two, "she a Negro whore and I her little protector. . . . If this fantasy kept me a pariah by exchanging homosexuality for miscegenation, it also gave me a sacrifice to make and a companion to cherish. I would educate and protect her" (183). Since both characters are invisible "outcasts," White's narrator imagines that they might more effectively face the world together.

The identifications here and elsewhere in White with African American (and with "fat" and "unpopular") identity, however, are suspect for several reasons, and my main argument in this section is that the construction of sexuality in *A Boy's Own Story* is in tension with the construction of race in ways that forestall the possibility that the story might serve as a myth of queer (op)positionality. Although the novel is in some ways "oppositional," I argue that any "oppositionality" is ultimately undercut by the "apositionality," or invisibility, of whiteness in the text. It is not White's own story, necessarily, that produces this tension: by 1982, the standard coming-out story, with its single-minded focus on the discovery of one's essential identity, required such apositionality. The remainder of this section shows how white apositionality fixes *A Boy's Own Story* as a representative—or *the* representative—coming-out story and considers what ramifications the effacement of whiteness has for contemporary gay male writing generally. In the next section, however, I turn to an analysis of the ways in which Audre Lorde reconceives the coming-out story as a fluid and relational myth of queer (op)positionality.

Initially, White's novel may be read as "oppositional" for its disruption of linear models of sexual development in which heterosexuality is both the ultimate goal and the mark of maturity. This disruption of heterosexual telos is underscored by the very form of the text, which represents the protagonist's story in a nonlinear fashion (he is fifteen in the first chapter, seven at the beginning of the third, fifteen again by the end of the sixth, and so on).[9] Yet, despite this "opposition" to heterosexual telos, White's novel nonetheless teleologically represents his protagonist's coming to a racially unmarked gay consciousness. Although overt acts of coming out into this new gay consciousness are deemphasized in the text (the narrator confesses to a friend that he is gay only once, offhandedly [88]), it is still clear throughout *A Boy's Own Story* that homosexuality is precisely and primarily what White's nameless narrator must confront. Indeed, he uses a homosexual encounter with and betrayal of a "straight" teacher at the very end of the novel to confront this identity, which, he says, is "at once my essence and also an attribute I was totally unfamiliar with . . . this sexual allure so foreign to my understanding yet so central to my being" (198). In the end, the betrayal of his teacher finally allows White's narrator to work through the contradiction inherent in his "impossible desire to love a man but not to be a homosexual" (218). Thus, although *A Boy's Own Story* certainly disrupts the cultural mandate to develop heterosexually, it also institutes a coming-out narrative as necessary for understanding one's (essential) gay identity. In fact, White later asserted that the novel "succeeded partly because it seemed to fill an empty niche in the contemporary publishing ecology, the slot of the coming-out novel" (*Burning Library*, 372).

White's discussion of niches and slots implies that *A Boy's Own Story* was an easy fit; the publishing world was ready for a novel with a unitary focus on coming out. I would argue, however, that at the time the "contemporary publishing ecology" could provide a home for White's novel only on two, unspoken conditions. First, gay identity had to be understood, as it is in *A Boy's Own Story*, as an "essence . . . central to [one's] being." Such an understanding is what enabled the empty niche to be filled so exactly. Second, gay identity could not be explicitly intersected by other facets of identity, such as gender or race: in other words, this "gay" slot was white and male, although not *openly* white and male. Lisa Duggan's comments

Boys' Own Stories and New Spellings of My Name

suggest that these two points are, in fact, interrelated: "*Any* gay politics based on the primacy of sexual identity defined as unitary and 'essential' . . . ultimately represents the view from the subject position '20th-century Western white gay male' " ("Making It Perfectly Queer," 18). Duggan outs the subject position as white and male, however; generally, such representations are advanced without being explicitly marked as such. And indeed, in *A Boy's Own Story*, a unitary, essential gay subject position is achieved through the mechanism of invisibility.

The mechanism of invisibility in White's novel is not intentionally deployed to cover the main character's gender and race; White's narrator is "invisible" throughout the novel precisely because homosexuality is an identity that he cannot openly embrace. Yet the construction of sexuality here inadvertently colludes with hegemonic constructions of whiteness, which maintains its power precisely to the extent that it is able to remain hidden from view. As Richard Dyer argues, "White power secures its dominance by seeming not to be anything in particular" (44). What this effects in *A Boy's Own Story* is contradictory: on the one hand, the story is one of marginalization and oppression; on the other hand, the story is *representative*. White himself recently gave voice to this contradiction, insisting, "When I was growing up, I felt I was a totally freaky person . . . and then later I came to realize that my life, which I had thought was the most *exceptional* imaginable, was actually the most *representative*. All I needed to do was to say what I went through in order to say what gay people went through in their evolution toward freedom" (in Avena, 224). In the end, even White's title conveys this dual sense of the exceptional and the representative, suggesting that this "boy's own story" is as much about any (gay) boy as about White's specific protagonist. Indeed, I was struck, when I attempted to teach one of White's texts, by a student's response to my very first question, "Why do you think White chooses not to give his narrator a name or face?" A Filipino American student of mine responded, "So we can put ourselves into the story?"

My student was not "wrong" to identify with White's protagonist; he is, in fact, like White's narrator, a gay man living in a homophobic society. Yet the interrogative inflection my student gave to his response suggests that he suspected his resolution to my question might be a bit problematic. For White's character is not simply a representative "Everyboy": his mother and he play games with the classical radio station, guessing whether the composer is Haydn, Mozart, or early Beethoven (80); a (black female) maid, a (white male) therapist, and a private school are all part of his childhood; and he admits, however ironically, "Even as I made much of my present miseries I was cautiously planning my bourgeois future" (178). In short, aspects of the protagonist's identity can be read as race- and class-coded, despite his "invisible" gay identity. Indeed, his gay identity is rendered representative precisely because the "naturalness" of his racial identity is maintained through White's "god-trick" of "invisibility."[10]

The term *god-trick* is Haraway's, and she uses it to refer to seemingly innocent perspectives that claim to see the world more comprehensively while actually "being nowhere" (191). This may seem to be an unfair charge to level at White's story of gay development, but it is harder to dismiss in the context of Dyer's analysis of whiteness. Dyer suggests that

> white people . . . are difficult, if not impossible, to analyse *qua* white. The subject seems to fall apart in your hands as soon as you begin. Any instance of white representation is always immediately something more specific— *Brief Encounter* is not about white people, it is about English middle-class people; *The Godfather* is not about white people, it is about Italian-American people; but *The Color Purple* is about black people, before it is about poor, southern US people. (46)

Similarly, *A Boy's Own Story* is not about white people, it is about gay people; but *Zami* is the autobiography of a black lesbian, not of the gay community more generally. *A Boy's Own Story* posits a seemingly innocent perspective that implicitly claims to see gay identity more comprehensively, but it is able to do so because white identity is nowhere to be seen.

The very landscape of *A Boy's Own Story* underwrites white apositionality. The story takes place, alternately, in Illinois, Michigan, and Ohio. This is not Toni Morrison's Ohio, however, in which racial divisions are graphically (and in *Sula*, geographically) represented. Like the protagonist, the various settings for the novel are unmarked: a "boy's own story" presumably takes place in Anywhere, U.S.A. David Bergman argues that "the importance of Cincinnati . . . cannot be underestimated in White's fiction," but it is Bergman, not White, who actually names the "Queen City" that plays such a "prominent role in [White's] autobiographical novel *A Boy's Own Story*" ("Edmund White," 387). Of course, the Midwest has long had a reputation for being the blank "nonregion" of the United States, the land—as in Don DeLillo's *White Noise*—of supermarkets, station wagons, and "an expressway beyond the backyard" (DeLillo, 4). This unmarked regional identity, however, does not preclude White in his novel from marking *other* parts of the country regionally: the protagonist and his sister make fun of "hillbillies" from Kentucky (73), and the protagonist himself dreams of escaping to the "charm" and sophistication of New York City (52–57).

As in DeLillo, certainly, the blankness of White's Midwest might be read as simply a metaphor for the region's supposed cultural sterility. This interpretation would elide, however, the ways in which regional blankness underwrites racial invisibility in *A Boy's Own Story*. Like Kentuckians and New Yorkers, African Americans in White's Cincinnati are embodied as such, and throughout this text, it is the location of regional and racial identity in embodied "others" that enables the protagonist *not* to have a regional and racial identity of his own. This disembodiment, in turn, ensures that the protagonist's coming-out story can be read as representative. The "other," marked identities allow White's narrator to negotiate a problematic sleight of hand: while he effaces differences of race and region, he simultaneously appropriates representative "outcast" status for himself.

In *Playing in the Dark: Whiteness and the American Literary Imagination*, Toni Morrison argues that white American writers have often used their African American characters to perform such sleights of hand. Morrison's study emerges from her interest "in the way black people ignite critical moments of discovery or change or emphasis in literature not written by them" (viii). Insisting that an understanding of American literature is incomplete without an understanding of the central role an African American presence has played in the American literary imagination, she concludes, "What became transparent were the self-evident ways that [white] Americans choose to talk about themselves through and within a sometimes allegorical, sometimes metaphorical, but always choked representation of an Africanist presence" (17). In *A Boy's Own Story*, this metaphorical process begins in the second chapter. At first, the chapter might be read as starkly exposing the mechanisms of power that enable and ensure white privilege: the unmarked and privileged white identity is depicted here as depending for its very existence on the labor of a marked and African American identity. The protagonist admits:

> As a little boy, I'd thought of our house . . . as the place God had meant us to own, but now I knew in a vague way that its seclusion and ease had been artificial and that it had strenuously excluded the city at the same time we depended on the city for food, money, comfort, help, even pleasure. The black maids were the representatives of the city I'd grown up among. I'd

never wanted anything from them—nothing except their love. To win it, or at least to ward off their silent, sighing resentment, I'd learned how to make my own bed and cook my own breakfast. But nothing I could do seemed to make up to them for the terrible loss they'd endured. (36)

Although he realizes his knowledge is "vague," White's protagonist is able to recognize here that race and geography shape subjectivity, including his own.

Events later in the chapter corroborate the possibility that, at least initially, the narrator is gaining insight into the unequal distribution of power and wealth. When their maid's daughter survives a bloody fight and needs help, the protagonist's father takes him along on a journey to her home in the "dangerous" section of town. This journey forces the protagonist to confront the poverty of the African American section of their town:

That had been another city—Blanche's two rooms, scrupulously clean in contrast to the squalor of the halls, her parrot squawking under the tea towel draped over the cage, the chromo of a sad Jesus pointing to his exposed, juicy heart as though he were a free-clinic patient with a troubling symptom, the filched wedding photo of my father and stepmother in a nest of crepe-paper flowers, the bloody sheet torn into strips that had been wildly clawed off and hurled onto the flowered congoleum floor. (50)

Nonetheless, the wedding photo "filched" by Blanche from her white employer is the first sign, I think, of what Morrison might label the "choked representation" in this scene. White specifically chokes, or checks, the "silent, sighing [and potentially threatening] resentment" of "the black maids" through the representation of Blanche's shrine, which certainly suggests anything but resentment. Moreover, the identification of an/other city is already appropriated by the end of the chapter to facilitate the protagonist's *own* developing sense of self. The very use of the name Blanche foreshadows the possibility that this scene could be as much about "White" as it is about the maid herself.[11] And indeed, when he is considering running away to New York City, the protagonist appropriates—without reference to Blanche herself—the rhetoric he had earlier used to identify her: "I'd go hungry! The boardinghouse room with the toilet down the hall, blood on the linoleum, Christ in a chromo, crepe-paper flowers . . ." (56). In this entire section, difference is not so much "exposed" and challenged as it is safely contained—in White's Cincinnati, in this section of his novel, and, ultimately, in his own "outcast" protagonist.

Boys' Own Stories and New Spellings of My Name

This is White's second chapter, and racial difference becomes a crucial factor only once more in the novel: when White's protagonist and his friends, in the final chapter, visit the whorehouse. Despite the reemergence of race, though, the relations of power that determine and maintain white dominance remain safely behind in chapter 2. What was earlier an identification *of* racial difference and discrimination becomes, at the whorehouse, an identification *with* racial difference (White's protagonist, as I mentioned earlier, equates the woman's situation with his own). It is precisely the "invisibility" of the protagonist's racial identity (as well as the "blankness" of the regional scene upon which all of this is played out) that allows for this slippage and appropriation to go unnoticed. Since the narrator's regional and racialized body is invisible, he can safely appropriate "other" identities for his own limited—I would not necessarily call them "queer"—uses. Thus the blankness of the Midwestern landscape and the invisibility of whiteness in *A Boy's Own Story* are more than simply metaphors for cultural sterility. Unmarked and dislocated racial and regional identities are exactly what enable this to be a "representative" story about *gay* people, rather than about white Midwesterners.

Hence queer (op)positionality in *A Boy's Own Story* is choked by white apositionality. As I suggested, this is as much a function of how the coming-out story had evolved as it is of White's particular novel. However, in some other contexts, the ways in which the identity "Edmund White" is constructed replicates this pattern. For example, after White edited an anthology of gay fiction *(The Faber Book of Gay Short Fiction)* that included only one black writer (James Baldwin) and no women, the controversy was reported in a publication no less mainstream than *USA Today*. In the article, Kent Fordyce explicitly spells out the tension between sexuality and race: "I think Faber flubbed the title. . . . I think it should be 'Edmund White's Anthology of White Short Story Writers' " (qtd. in C. Wilson, 8D). *The book isn't about white people,* White himself seems to be saying when he explains, "[I] read dozens of stories by dozens of gay black writers and I didn't find anything too suitable. And I thought it was wrong to include them just because they were black" (qtd. in C. Wilson, 8D).

His dismissal of race notwithstanding, in the foreword to *The Faber Book,* White continues to appropriate racial identity for its comparative value: "Do gays really constitute something like an ethnic minority? Does an author's sexuality represent a more crucial part of his identity than his social class, generation, race or regional origins?" (xvii). White's persistent blindness to race (and to other arenas of difference) except when he is appropriating it to talk about his own oppression is surely what led Essex Hemphill to signify on White in his own introduction to *Brother to Brother: New Writings by Black Gay Men:* "When black gay men approached the gay community to participate in the struggle for acceptance and to forge bonds of brotherhood . . . we discovered that the beautiful rhetoric was empty" (xix).

In *Essentially Speaking: Feminism, Nature and Difference,* Diana Fuss admits to implying throughout that "the adherence to essentialism is a measure of the degree to which a particular political group has been culturally oppressed" (98). And yet, in her chapter on lesbian and gay identity politics, Fuss spends only a page early on "exposing" the "essentialism" of the Combahee River Collective, Cherríe Moraga, and Barbara Smith (99). Although Audre Lorde is mentioned in passing in an earlier chapter (44), no other openly gay or lesbian writers of color are engaged in the chapter on identity politics, or in the entire book, for that matter. To me, this hardly provides enough material to justify a sweeping statement the logical conclusion of which would be that lesbians of color are the *most* essentialist of all. In fact, in contrast to Fuss, I would propose that those who are oppressed in only one facet of their identity often stand the most to gain from essentialism.[12] As White writes in introducing his anthology of (white) gay short story writers, "Most gay men believe they did not choose to be homosexual, that this orientation was imposed on them, although whether by nature or nurture they have no way of knowing" (ix). White does not and need not necessarily speak for all white gay men here, but as in *A Boy's Own Story,* coming out into an essential and essentially oppressed gay identity is exactly what allows White to mask white and male power and to assume a voice that purports to speak for "most gay men."

The subordination of racial identity to an unmarked (white) gay identity has ramifications far beyond White's texts. It is evident in some recent criticism of gay male fiction that likewise tends not to notice the apositionality of White and whiteness. David Bergman, in his study of gay self-representation in American literature, *Gaiety Transfigured,* examines Baldwin in one chapter on "The Agony of Gay Black Literature," while White and other whites provide the material for the next chapter on "Alternative Service: Families in Recent American Gay Fiction." Yet under what discursive regime can Baldwin be understood as *not* about "family"? Indeed, I have a hard time thinking of many twentieth-century American writers

Boys' Own Stories and New Spellings of My Name

more interested in exploring the family than James Baldwin. Nonetheless, Bergman positions White under the sign *family*, while Baldwin is positioned and contained under the sign *race*.

Bergman explains, in the introduction to *Gaiety Transfigured*, that he added a chapter on "race and homosexuality" only after the "excellent suggestions" of Robert K. Martin (24), and he also concedes, "I felt some . . . reluctance when I began to explore black gay literature, namely, that as a white man I would fail to grasp the subtle—and not so subtle—differences between the black and gay experiences" (13). Although he admits that it was a challenge, he reports that he now feels "a greater sympathy with the gayness of black men than many heterosexual blacks have expressed" (13). In short, Bergman may not feel competent to write much about black gays, but he is certainly competent to make sweeping dismissals of "many" black heterosexuals. Bergman's naive oversensitivity to the positionality of blacks and his reinscription of White/white apositionality result in a chapter on "family" in which he examines without critical comment such questionable scenes from contemporary gay fiction as Andrew Holleran's description of two white men in Union Square observing a "cocoa-colored youth" whom they feel they have a right to "have" (*Gaiety Transfigured*, 188) and White's narrator's own fantasy of an expatriate white gay friend living as a "garden god" among a tribe in Mexico (*Gaiety Transfigured*, 199).

Baldwin's ghettoization under the sign *race* here connects, moreover, to the ways in which "race" is contained in the larger narrative that some critics, including Bergman, are beginning to tell us about post-Stonewall gay male literature. Around 1978 (or so the story goes), gay literature began to come of age. Since 1978, Bergman explains, "when Edmund White's *Nocturnes for the King of Naples*, Larry Kramer's *Faggots*, and Andrew Holleran's *Dancer from the Dance* gained critical and commercial success—gay books have become a regular and increasingly large portion of trade publishers' lists" (*Gaiety Transfigured*, 9–10). This version of the story is underwritten by White: "It wasn't until 1978 that three gay novels came out: Larry Kramer's *Faggots; Dancer from the Dance*, by Andrew Holleran; and my *Nocturnes for the King of Naples*. Those three books gave the impression of a new wave, of a new movement coming along" (in Bonetti, 95). White modestly appends a disclaimer—"Mine was probably the least important of those three, as a publishing event" (in Bonetti, 95)—but just as for Bergman, 1978 is the banner year for White, the turning point for post-Stonewall gay male literature. As White asserts elsewhere, "Gay male fiction was suddenly on the map" ("On the Line," xii).

Boys' Own Stories and New Spellings of My Name

Yet where was Baldwin during all of this critical and commercial success? Although Baldwin was never wholly comfortable with the term *gay*, his most comprehensive study of *black* gay desire is nonetheless a product of exactly this period. *Just Above My Head* was published in 1979, but portions of the novel had begun to appear in that "banner year," 1978. My objection here could certainly be qualified (Baldwin was nearing the end of his career, whereas the three white authors were at the beginning of theirs; and *Just Above My Head* first began to appear in *Penthouse*, hardly the premier gay venue), but this has not kept some critics from telling the White/Bergman "banner year" story otherwise. Joseph Beam, for example, in his introduction to *In the Life: A Black Gay Anthology*, positions Baldwin's novel as one of the few landmarks: "More and more each day, as I looked around the well-stocked shelves of Giovanni's Room, Philadelphia's gay, lesbian, and feminist bookstore where I worked, I wondered where was the work of Black gay men. . . . How many times could I reread Baldwin's *Just Above My Head* and Yulisa Amadu Maddy's *No Past, No Present, No Future?*" (14). The year 1978 may have been commercially successful for some gay writers, but the narrative that Bergman, White, and others tell depends on a unitary notion of what "gay" literature is. In contrast, for Beam gay literature was not necessarily "on the map," since so much territory still remained uncharted. Baldwin and Maddy, however, not White, Holleran, and Kramer, provide Beam with a place to begin the journey.

Like Beam, Emmanuel Nelson, in his preface to *Contemporary Gay American Novelists: A Bio-Bibliographical Critical Sourcebook*, makes Baldwin (and John Rechy) central to his own coming-of-age as well as to the story we might tell ourselves about contemporary gay literature. In contrast to the deracinated narratives Bergman and White provide, Nelson's narrative begins with the overbearing presence of "whiteness":

> Barely twenty years old, I had just arrived in the United States from India to work toward a doctorate in twentieth-century American literature. Before long I grew uncomfortable and impatient with a good deal of American literature that was the staple of my graduate courses: the works of white, straight authors. . . . The exclusive focus on white writers . . . was tiresome and frustrating. (xi)

Gay literature provided Nelson with alternatives. "Gay literature," however, signifies much differently for Nelson than it does for Bergman and White:

Boys' Own Stories and New Spellings of My Name

It was then that I started to discover, on my own, those literary territories whose existence was either unacknowledged or derisively dismissed in the classrooms. . . . I began to seek reflections of my own realities within the ethnic and gay spaces of American literature. In particular, I was drawn to the works of James Baldwin and John Rechy. I was drawn to Baldwin because of his elegant prose, his expansive humanity, his sharp challenges to the logic of racism, and his uncompromising deconstructions of conventional sexual assumptions. I was drawn to Rechy because of his authentic style and his rebellious stance; moreover, I imagined an affinity with his dark, Latino protagonists and their familiar and frantic journeys through the anarchic sexual underworlds. That Baldwin and Rechy were, like me, ethnic as well as sexual outsiders in American culture made their perspectives recognizable; their voices and visions became reassuring, even liberating. Their widely different styles of managing their competing ethnocultural and homosexual subjectivities offered me potential models to reconcile the conflicting claims of my own multiple identities. Above all, Baldwin and Rechy enabled me to rediscover American literature. (xi–xii)

Of course, there is more than a little irony in this alternative narrative, in which a scholar from India "rediscovers" America and its literature. In contrast to the "discoverer" of America who came to this continent and saw "Indians," Nelson comes to America, looks around at its literature, and sees nothing but white folks. By putting a face to the unmarked (white) "American" identity of his graduate studies ("I grew uncomfortable and impatient with . . . the works of white, straight authors. . . . The exclusive focus on white writers . . . was tiresome and frustrating"), Nelson is able to resist and move beyond the hegemonic narrative being told not only about contemporary gay literature but about American literature more generally.

"One of the signs of the times is that we really don't know what 'white' is," Kobena Mercer writes ("Skin Head Sex Thing," 204). Whiteness, after all, maintains its hegemony by passing itself off as no-thing. As *A Boy's Own Story* and some recent gay male criticism indicate, whiteness is apositionality; it denies "the stakes in location, embodiment, and partial perspective [and makes] it impossible to see well" (Haraway, 191). "Every gay man has polished his story through repetition," White writes in the foreword to *The Faber Book*, "and much gay fiction is a version of this first tale" (ix). Perhaps. Yet White's celebration of the coming-out story as the original gay tale obscures the ways in which the coming-out story positions some gay people as more "polished" or representative than others. In *A Boy's Own Story* and *The Faber Book,* White disavows the appropriations and erasures that enable him to transform *his* story into "a boy's own." Denying its own racial situatedness, White's coming-out novel fails as a "noninnocent" myth of queer (op)positionality. Like the texts Biddy Martin examines, White's understanding of the "story" "reproduces the demand that women [and men] of color . . . abandon their histories, the histories of their communities, their complex locations and selves, in the name of a [gay] unity that barely masks its white, middle class cultural reference/referent" (Martin, 93). The Queer Renaissance requires another myth of queer positionality, one that *renames* "gay unity" by continually reimagining and relocating the complexity of queer histories, communities, and selves.

An/other Myth of Queer Positionality

Audre Lorde's *Zami: A New Spelling of My Name* is set in roughly the same time as Edmund White's *A Boy's Own Story.* At about the same time that White's protagonist is learning the difference between Mozart and Haydn, Audre, the persona at the center of what Lorde calls her "biomythography," goes to Washington, D.C., to celebrate her graduation from the eighth grade. Stopping at a Breyer's ice-cream and soda fountain, Audre and her family are told they can get their dessert to "take out," but they cannot eat the ice cream on the premises. The bitter episode ends with Audre thinking, "The waitress was white, and the counter was white, and the ice cream I never ate in Washington, D.C. that summer I left my childhood was white, and the white heat and the white pavement and the white stone monuments . . . made me sick to my stomach for the whole rest of that trip and it wasn't much of a graduation present after all" (71). In stark contrast to *A Boy's Own Story,* the mechanisms of white power are all too visible in *Zami.*

Clearly, despite nominal similarities (the 1950s setting, the 1982 publication date, the autobiographical elements, homosexuality), *A Boy's Own Story* and *Zami* are extremely different texts. Their publication history reflects their difference as well: whereas White's novel was published in hardcover by E. P. Dutton and in paperback by Plume, both divisions of New American Library, *Zami* was rejected by a dozen or more mainstream publishing houses, including, as Barbara Smith reports, a house known for publishing gay titles ("Truth That Never Hurts," 123). Smith explains,

"The white male editor at that supposedly sympathetic house returned the manuscript saying, 'If only you were just one,' Black or lesbian" (123). So much for the "empty niche in the contemporary publishing ecology" in 1982, the "slot" waiting to be filled by the coming-out novel! To my knowledge, Lorde was never interviewed by *USA Today*.

Zami was eventually published by Persephone Press and the Crossing Press Feminist Series, and Donna Haraway, Katie King, and others have already noted *Zami's* importance for feminist theory. Haraway includes *Zami* in her discussion of "feminist cyborg stories," which "have the task of recoding communication and intelligence to subvert command and control" (175). King is more specific, suggesting:

> It is in this currently contested time/place [the lesbian bar of the 1950s] where "the passing dreams of choice" are mobilized that Lorde looks for the secrets of the making of her personal identity; the passing dreams of choice, where sexual identity is neither an existential decision nor biochemically/ psychoanalytically programmed, but instead produced in the fields of differ- ence individually *and* collectively. (332)

In this section, taking Haraway's and King's observations as a starting point, I suggest further that, in these "fields of difference" where sexual identity is "produced . . . individually *and* collectively," *Zami* also allows for a "recoding" of the coming-out story, a recoding along the lines of what I call "queer (op)positionality." In *Zami*, coming out can be seen as an/other myth of queer positionality—not because Lorde makes, as White does in *A Boy's Own Story*, an attempt to construct her protagonist into an alienated, marked "other" but rather because *Zami* is concerned, as King notes, with collective identity. A humanist, unified self is not Lorde's objective, but rather a definition of "self" as defined in and through others, particularly those "who work together as friends and lovers" (Lorde, *Zami*, 255).

Already this goes against White's objectives in *A Boy's Own Story*, which ends, after all, with a betrayal that enables the protagonist to self- define *as against* a lover. Moreover, Lorde's biomythography improves on Linda Alcoff's theory of positionality, which fears that "post-structural- ism's negation of the authority of the subject coincides nicely with classical liberal views that human particularities are irrelevant" (Alcoff, 420). In- deed, the fiction of identity Lorde constructs in *Zami* goes beyond the poststructuralism Alcoff fears, since a negation of the authority of the subject underscores here the *relevance* of human particularities. Taking its protagonist through approximately two decades of development, *Zami* is framed by a prologue and an epilogue that are meditations on the *particular* women Audre has loved. In the prologue, Lorde poses the question *"To whom do I owe the woman I have become?"* (4) and proceeds to answer it by naming and describing those who have shaped her identity. Lorde concludes the prologue by apostrophizing:

> To the battalion of arms where I often retreated for shelter and sometimes found it. To the others who helped, pushing me into the merciless sun—I, coming out blackened and whole.

> *To the journeywoman pieces of myself.*
> *Becoming.*
> *Afrekete.* (5)

Of course, the penultimate stanza of the prologue might read like another teleological myth of essential wholeness, but Lorde immediately undercuts this with fragmentation and open-endedness ("pieces of myself," "becoming"). Moreover, even the "wholeness" into which Lorde "comes out" here is unlike the myth of identity represented in White. Particular "others" have helped forge this identity, and the metonymic reference to baking underscores Lorde's emphasis on the construction, not the preexistence, of identity.

Zami constructed a collective "new spelling of my name" that was subsequently taken up and reshaped by other readers and writers in the Queer Renaissance. Lorde promoted a similar identity in her *Chosen Poems—Old and New*, which were also published in 1982. The rest of this section first overviews exactly how identity is reinvented in these two texts. Then, after examining the ways in which both Lorde and White have responded to being cast, in various contexts, as "representative," I conclude by reconnecting *Zami* to Stonewall and the myths of queer (op)positionality with which I began.

In the body of the text of *Zami*, Audre has a number of "friends and lovers," black and white, beginning with Genevieve, a friend who commits suicide while the two are still in high school. Both in her biomythography and elsewhere, Lorde stresses how important this event was for her. *"Yes, I see Gennie often,"* she acknowledged in an interview twenty-five years after the suicide. "I'll never forget what it is to see young waste and how painful it is. And I never got over wanting to help so that it would not happen again" (in Cornwell, 43). In *Zami*, the placement of the suicide in the text makes it appear that the event inaugurates Audre into an identity separate from others; after the chapter detailing Gennie's suicide concludes, the next chapter opens, "Two weeks after I graduated from high school, I moved out of my parents' home" (103).

The separation from home and parents, however, does not mark the end of Audre's development; on the contrary, this emergence into a separate identity initiates a cycle of desire that takes Audre through a series of lovers over the course of the text. Although after Gennie's suicide, the protagonist *"decided that I would never love anybody else again for the rest of my life"* (141), she admits the loss of the wholeness she felt with Gennie was actually the commencement, not the end, of desire: "It is the last dream of children, to be forever untouched" (141). That this loss was a commencement is underscored by the fact that, in the text, Lorde positions the admission that after Gennie she "would never love anybody else again" *after* she details Audre's first sexual affair with *another* woman, Ginger. Ginger helps Audre recognize that her earlier resolve to separate from others was both misguided and untrue to what she had learned from and with Gennie. After this affair, Genevieve is not often invoked in *Zami*; in fact, Audre is caught off guard at one point when she mentions the girl to a lover: "I surprised myself; usually I never talked about Gennie" (185). In general, the formation of Audre's identity and her explorations of desire proceed without explicit reference to Genevieve.

Near the end of the text, however, Audre meets Afrekete ("Kitty") at a party for black women. When the two women arrive at Afrekete's apartment, Audre notes they are "in Gennie's old neighborhood" (247). Indeed, the two are in Gennie's old neighborhood in more than one sense: Afrekete is Audre's final lover in *Zami*, and she provides a fitting conclusion/nonconclusion to the problematics of identity and desire that commenced with the loss of Gennie. On one level, the nickname Kitty recalls Audre herself, since—as AnnLouise Keating points out—Ginger had repeatedly labeled Audre the "slick kitty from the city" (Keating, 29). This is only the first link in a chain of associations, however; the identity of this final lover is highly unstable and merges freely with others. Not only does the epilogue explain what the prologue did not—that Afrekete is the name of a goddess and of a *"mischievous linguist, trickster, best-beloved, whom we must all become"* (255)—but even as Audre and Kitty make love, the scene shifts seamlessly from the present to memories of Genevieve, so that the identity of the first lover reemerges in the identity of the last. Afrekete thus completes a circle for Audre/Lorde, bringing her to the point where she can write that her "life had become increasingly a bridge and field of women" (255). In other words, whether she understands her life linearly or circularly, as a bridge over which she crosses or as a field that surrounds her on all sides, connections between women are what give that life its shape. Furthermore, in the epilogue, although "human particularities" (women's roles and names, both "real" and mythical) are present, "Audre," in her specificity as a named, individual subject, is not. In fact, the "new spelling of my name" envisioned in the title is finally explained in the epilogue, and it turns out not to be about individuality at all: "*Zami. A Carriacou name for women who work together as friends and lovers*" (255).

Alcoff wants to reclaim an "identity," fictional though it may be, from which women can construct a feminist politics (435). The queer position *Zami* establishes, however, disclaims Lorde's individual identity. Earlier in the text, Audre realizes that, for her, the passage "beyond childhood" entails recognizing herself as "a woman connecting with other women in an intricate, complex, and ever-widening network of exchanging strengths" (175). Others have thus authored "Zami," this new identity, with her. Sagri Dhairyam argues, "*Zami* . . . calls itself 'biomythography,' a description which explicitly . . . recognizes the tactical uses of fictional identity, but refuses to grant the author primacy over the textuality of her life" (231). In the end, this refusal to grant primacy to any concept of the supposedly individual author ensures that, in *Zami*, fictional identity and *nonidentity* alike construct "the very house of difference rather than the security of any one particular difference" (*Zami*, 226).

At the same time, this is not some White/white "god-trick" that disavows its own situatedness. It may be impossible to read "Audre" as a self-identical, unified individual, but the identities "black," "lesbian," and "woman" are all present in the identity "Zami."[13] In a sense, Lorde's persona comes out into a fiction of nonidentity not unlike what Trinh T. Minh-ha envisions:

A critical difference from myself means that I am not i, am within and without i. I/i can be I or i, you and me both involved. . . . "I" is, therefore, not a unified subject, a fixed identity, or that solid mass covered with layers of superficialities one has gradually to peel off before one can see its true face. "I" is, itself, *infinite layers*. Its complexity can hardly be conveyed through such typographic conventions as I, i, or I/i. Thus, I/i am compelled by the will to say/unsay, to resort to the entire gamut of personal pronouns to stay near this fleeing *and* static essence of Not-I. (90, 94)

This, it seems to me, is queer (op)positionality at its best: an effacement of, and in-your-face-ment to, the liberal humanist God/man/subject, with its notions of separation, individualism, and fixity.

As much as *Zami* works as a realization of Trinh's unstable i/I/Not-I, it also, *pace* Alcoff, maintains in its very self-definition a commitment to feminist political action; these are, after all, women actively *working* and *loving* together. *Zami* constructs a nonessentialized identity position from which to forge a coalition-based, and oppositional, politics. In fact, King and Haraway both position *Zami* as an example of Chela Sandoval's "oppositional consciousness" (K. King, 338; Haraway, 174). Sandoval herself explains that the notion of oppositional consciousness provides feminists with a new, more fluid definition of "unity": "These constantly speaking differences stand at the crux of another, mutant unity . . . mobilized in a location heretofore unrecognized. . . . This connection is a mobile unity, constantly weaving and reweaving an interaction of differences into coalition" (18). The act of reading *Zami* stands as a figure for the "weaving and reweaving . . . of differences into coalition": since the "new spelling of my name" in Lorde's biomythography is not defined until the epilogue, one must read the entire text, with all of its "constantly speaking differences" and "location[s] heretofore unrecognized," before one can begin to understand that new spelling.

Zami does not end with the epilogue, however. Indeed, there is a sense in which Lorde's biomythography cannot end, even with her death. By remembering the identities envisioned in *Zami*, readers have attested to its ongoing vitality and success at achieving an/other, mutant, mobile unity. The editors of *Afrekete: An Anthology of Black Lesbian Writing*, for instance—Catherine E. McKinley and L. Joyce Delaney—frame their collection with selections from Audre Lorde. The first selection, "Tar Beach," is the excerpt from *Zami* wherein Audre is transformed through her encounter with Afrekete. The final selection, "Today Is Not the Day," is a poem in which Lorde calls on Afrekete and resolves to continue working and loving in the face of mounting challenges (particularly cancer). Afrekete and *Zami*, then, both set the stage for the explorations of identity furthered by this anthology and sustain the writer(s) through the process.

In her introduction to *Afrekete,* McKinley explains, "This is a story at once familiar and new. You may find yourself in it" (xii). McKinley goes on to detail her own experience of first reading *Zami* and explains how and why Lorde's text provides the writers included with a useful myth of positionality:

> Afrekete, in *Zami,* is Audre's last embrace. Afrekete is a child of the South, a migrant to Harlem. She is someone you may know. She is both wonderfully common and of the substance from which myths are spun: 'round the way girl, early banjee, roots daughter, blues singer. . . . AFREKETE is many women. With contradictory selves. And while AFREKETE troubles identity politics— her vision stretches much wider. (xiii–xv)

Afrekete, then, is both ancient and new; she is mythological, historical, and visionary. With this contradictory and impetuous figure as their muse, the contributors to *Afrekete,* according to McKinley, are committed to shaping new visions, selves, and communities:

> The contributors and these editors identify as lesbian, gay, zamis, dykes, queers, Black, African, African-American, biracial—and often may use these terms and others interchangeably. And while sexuality, or race for that matter, is and is not always at the center of their work, both deeply inform the writer's vision. The work featured is written in a range of styles, a breadth of aesthetics reflecting the birthing and meshing of seemingly disparate artistic sensibilities and traditions: Black and queer, as well as others. (xvi)

Many other readers have similarly reinvented themselves and their communities because of the queer identities posited in and by Lorde and *Zami.*[14]

Lorde's *Chosen Poems—Old and New* were published in the same year as her biomythography, and the narrative she constructs about her life in this collection of poetry is similar to the narrative she constructs in *Zami,* in the sense that both texts posit a shifting positionality and a self ultimately defined in and through others. The volume opens with four poems depicting the poet's attempt to come to terms with Genevieve's death. In "Memorial II," the poet approaches her mirror and sees not her own face but Gennie's. Despite this merging of the two girls' identities, however, "Memorial II" also represents the poet's attempt to recognize that she does indeed have an identity that is separate from Genevieve's. By the last

Boys' Own Stories and New Spellings of My Name

stanza, the speaker acknowledges that any vision of Genevieve in the poet's mirror can only be a fantasy. In this early poem, the poet must recognize herself, as she gazes into her mirror, as a subject separate from Gennie; for if Genevieve were to see her again, she would not recognize the young woman the poet has become: "Are you seeking the shape of a girl / I have grown less and less / to resemble" (5). Although the separation from Gennie is painful and difficult—at the end the poet laments that "your eyes / are blinding me / Genevieve" (5)—it is, at this point, nonetheless inevitable.

"Memorial II," then, with its emphasis on the formation of an individual identity, might allow for a reading of identity that is opposed to the collective identity represented in the epilogue to *Zami*. Yet, as in *Zami*, this assumption of a separate identity in *Chosen Poems* is only the beginning of the story. The poet's new, autonomous identity never quite seems to fit. In "Change of Season," for example, she complains, "Am I to be cursed forever with becoming / somebody else on the way to myself?" (40). Beyond this, the figure of Gennie and that original loss continue to haunt "Change of Season" and many other poems: "I was so terribly sure I would come to april / with my first love who died on a sunday morning / poisoned and wondering / was summer ever coming" (41). "Memorial III: From a Phone Booth on Broadway" shows how easily the poet's supposedly stable world is thrown into disarray by the memory of that loss:

> you will blossom back into sound
> you will answer
> must answer
> answer me answer me
> answer goddammit
> answer
> please . . . (89)

In short, the death of Gennie in *Chosen Poems* provokes the poet's assumption of a separate identity, but with all the insecurities and instabilities specific to a poststructuralist account of the subject incompletely sutured into an identity. In *Chosen Poems* and *Zami* alike, however, inauguration into identity for the poet is much more than this: inauguration into identity is simultaneously inauguration into a social system dependent on racism, sexism, and homophobia, and hence into a system intent on defining and controlling all that is black, female, and queer. "Good Mirrors Are

Not Cheap" captures the lack of control the poet feels because the cultural context in which she finds herself allows only for deceitful, masked representations of her identity:

> down the street
> a glassmaker is grinning
> turning out new mirrors that lie
> selling us
> new clowns
> at cut rate. (44)

Lorde is thus caught, in *Chosen Poems*, in the paradox of recognizing the instability of any subject position and yet desperately needing to articulate an identity that has been systematically distorted. Gennie's suicide itself, in both *Chosen Poems* and *Zami*, illustrates this central paradox. In *Zami*, before detailing in prose the events surrounding Gennie's death, Lorde includes a poem that foregrounds the ways in which the event is simultaneously an effacement and an assumption of identity:

> But we wept at the sight of two men standing alone
> flat on the sky, alone,
> shoveling earth as a blanket
> to keep the young blood down.
> For we saw ourselves in the dark warm mother-blanket
> saw ourselves deep in the earth's breast-swelling—
> no longer young—
> and knew ourselves for the first time
> dead and alone. (97)

We "knew ourselves for the first time / dead and alone": obliteration of identity and assumption of identity come together in the same moment. All of this, at the same time, occurs in an oppressive system intent on "keep[ing] the young blood down."

In "Need: A Choral of Black Women's Voices," the final entry in *Chosen Poems* and one newly written for Lorde's collection, the poet further probes this paradox, reproducing on a more urgent level the exploration of identity/nonidentity found in the epilogue to *Zami*. Coming together with others is never easy (in fact, another selection in *Chosen Poems* poses the insistent question "Who Said It Was Simple" [49]), but from the title of "Need" on, Lorde implies that a collective voice is necessary for survival.

Boys' Own Stories and New Spellings of My Name

"Need" opens by giving voice to that which has been silenced and by making visible that which would otherwise be effaced:

> This woman is Black
> so her blood is shed into silence
> this woman is Black
> so her death falls to the earth
> like the dripping of birds
> to be washed away with silence and rain. (111)

The poem has three speakers, "I," "P.C.," and "B.J.G.," the latter two representing the voices of Patricia Cowan and Bobbie Jean Graham, two women murdered in Detroit and Boston in 1978 and 1979, respectively. As in *Zami*, naming is a central preoccupation in "Need." After P.C. and B.J.G. describe their violent deaths, the "I" of the poem rages, "I do not even know all their names. / My sisters deaths are not noteworthy / nor threatening enough to decorate the evening news . . . blood blood of my sisters fallen in this bloody war / with no names no medals no exchange of prisoners" (112). The three voices weave in and out in this prolonged meditation on violence and oppression, until the final stanza of the poem, when the "I" transforms into an "All": " '*We cannot live without our lives.*' / '*We cannot live without our lives*' " (115). A note explains that the italicized quotation is from a poem by Barbara Deming. The words are therefore Lorde's and not Lorde's, and the individual identities of Lorde/I/ Patricia Cowan/Bobbie Jean Graham/Barbara Deming, along with all the women named and not named in *Chosen Poems*, coalesce, as they do in the epilogue to *Zami*, into a collective and threatening identity that depends for its existence on the foregrounded yet constantly shifting positionality of the identity "black"/"lesbian"/"woman." The poem, once again, belies any notion of an essentialized self existing apart from others, and indeed, in the face of such violence and destruction, such separation seems not only unproductive but absurd.

"Need" itself is a particularly useful example of the ways in which Lorde comes out into a myth of collective identity. Lorde's *Chosen Poems—Old and New* was originally published by W. W. Norton and Company. "Need," however, was reissued as a pamphlet in 1990 by Kitchen Table: Women of Color Press as part of their Freedom Organizing Series. In the preface to this new, revised version of *Need*, Lorde traces the poem's genealogy. As 1978 was for white gay men, 1979 is a "banner year" for black and Latina lesbians. The latter banner year, however, looks significantly different from the former:

> "Need" was first written in 1979 after 12 Black women were killed in the Boston area within four months. In a grassroots movement spearheaded by Black and Latina Lesbians, Women of Color in the area rallied.... My lasting image of that spring, beyond the sick sadness and anger and worry, was of women whom I knew, loved, and trembled for: Barbara Smith, Demita Frazier, Margo Okazawa-Rey, and women whose names were unknown to me, leading a march through the streets of Boston behind a broad banner stitched with a line from Barbara Deming: "WE CANNOT LIVE WITHOUT OUR LIVES." (3)

Lorde again attributes the words to Barbara Deming, but the identity/nonidentity articulated in *Need* and in Lorde's genealogy of "Need" belies any unified authorial consciousness. Instead, the identity is an example of Haraway's "contradictory" standpoint, which gains its strength precisely because authorial consciousness is "permanently partial." Deming does not, therefore, become so much the "source" here as another element in the collective and shifting identity into which the women behind the banner come out. This collective identity is a powerful and threatening one, made more so by its lack of fixity. Indeed, the (re)issuance of *Need* reaffirms and deploys that lack of fixity: each pamphlet includes a button with the line "We Cannot Live without Our Lives" printed on top of the pan-African colors and beside the symbol for female. Neither Lorde nor Kitchen Table makes any attempt here to suture, within the reissued text, the identity being articulated; on the contrary, the button and a "Resources for Organizing" section that follows the poem encourage women (and apparently, men) reading the text to join and hence continually reshape this collective identity. Lorde herself, in fact, traces the 1990 revisions of the poem to the ways in which others had used and reshaped it since its publication: "Alterations in the text since the poem was originally published are a result of hearing the poem read aloud several times by groups of women" (*Need*, 3).[15]

The Kitchen Table version of *Need* seems at least to allow for male inclusion: the "Resources for Organizing" section that follows the poem includes the addresses for organizations such as NCBLG: The National Coalition of Black Lesbians and Gays, the National Black Men's Health Network, Men Stopping Rape, and the Oakland Men's Project (*Need*, 16–

17). Identity, as Lorde constructs it in *Zami, Need,* and elsewhere, however, while not exclusionary, does not always simplistically include men or white people; connection is not necessarily easy or automatic. Hence "Zami" is *an* "other myth of queer positionality," not *the* necessary corrective to versions of coming out such as White's. As Elizabeth Alexander notes, " 'A' new spelling (as opposed to 'the') means there is probably more to come" (704). In the Queer Renaissance, there have indeed been many more "new spellings," as subsequent chapters of this book will demonstrate.

However, Lorde often does connect with men—particularly men of color/gay men—throughout her work. In fact, one of Lorde's earliest uses of the phrase that would become the subtitle to *Zami* occurs in a poem from the late 1970s to "Brother Alvin," a boy from Lorde's second-grade class who suddenly died of tuberculosis:

> I search through the index
> of each new book
> on magic
> hoping to find some new spelling
> of your name. (*The Black Unicorn,* 54)

A more recent and particularly poignant example of connection with a man comes in her poem to the late Joe Beam. In "Dear Joe," Lorde uses as an epigraph words from "Sister, Morning Is a Time for Miracles" (*Chosen Poems,* 109–10). The words that had signified Lorde's attempt to connect with another woman, her sister, are here re-signified in her memorial to Beam: "if you have ever tried to reach me / and I could not hear you / these words are in place of the dead air / still between us" ("Dear Joe," 47). "Zami," then, may signify "women working together as friends and lovers," but the new ways of spelling identity that Lorde envisions do not preclude working with and loving others.[16]

As *Need,* "Brother Alvin," and "Dear Joe" illustrate, and as with White in and out of *A Boy's Own Story,* the construction of identity in *Zami* connects to the construction of "Audre Lorde" in other contexts. I should note before continuing, however, that my earlier account of White as the one of these two authors more likely to be published by houses such as New American Library, while Lorde is consigned to lesser-known houses such as Persephone or Crossing Press, was somewhat unfair. White's publication history, like Lorde's, has at times been rocky, and Lorde has indeed been published by both small feminist presses and mainstream houses such as Norton.[17] Both authors are therefore made available for representation in a variety of contexts. I do not want to institute an argument in this chapter that implies too much about either White's or Lorde's canonical or precanonical status: for example, that White is "more canonical" than Lorde because he is oppressed in only one facet of his identity and is hence closer to what Lorde called the "mythical norm" of American society (*Sister Outsider*, 116). The "canonicity" of either author is actually quite difficult to assess, and not only because both are contemporary authors. It would appear that both White and Lorde are fairly canonical, but in two different contexts. Although *Time* magazine declared White "America's most influential gay writer" (L. Schulman, 58), it is Lorde who is more likely to be taught in college classrooms or to be the subject of scholarly articles. The MLA (Modern Language Association) Bibliography, for instance, lists forty entries for Lorde between 1981 and 1994 and twelve for White. Ten of White's entries, however, are articles he himself has written, compared to only four such articles for Lorde. Of Lorde's forty entries, moreover, seven are dissertations, underscoring her importance to the generation of scholars who will be shaping the academy over the next few decades.

Lorde's burgeoning academic reputation is highly contestable, of course; other contemporary writers, such as Toni Morrison and Thomas Pynchon, have garnered much more attention during the same time period (Morrison, 329 MLA Bibliography entries; Pynchon, 514 entries). Nonetheless, Lorde is better known than White in academe (in part because of women's studies departments and academic feminism), while White, in contrast, is becoming ensconced as the gay author mainstream readers need to know. The Quality Paperback Book Club (QPB), for example, "proud to announce the launch of Triangle Classics, a series of landmark books illuminating the gay and lesbian experience," initially included one writer from the 1980s in their new series: Edmund White. The flyer for the series declares that QPB's edition "brings together Edmund White's landmark novels of coming-of-age and coming out," that is, *A Boy's Own Story* and *The Beautiful Room Is Empty*. The series included one black author, James Baldwin; but significantly, the Baldwin novel included, *Giovanni's Room*, is about white Europeans.[18]

If, as Richard Ohmann suggests, contemporary canon formation is the result of "both large sales . . . and the right kind of critical attention" (384), then it would seem that White is cornering the market on one necessary qualification and Lorde on the other. Michael Bérubé complicates Ohmann's thesis, suggesting that "we are no longer confronting Ohmann's mid-1970s landscape" and that academic critics "now represent contemporary writers to different audiences from those of the nonspecialist press" (31). To Bérubé, then, the Toni Morrison of academic criticism is not the same as the Toni Morrison of nonacademic journals and reviews; indeed, there is a competition between members of these two groups for what "Toni Morrison" will signify. In contemporary lesbian and gay writing, this competition, I would argue, is conducted not so much over individual authors as over the very sign *gay/lesbian literature*, and moreover, this competition tends to be split along gender lines. Hence, and very generally, the contemporary "gay(/lesbian) literature" represented in nonacademic journals and reviews is not the same contemporary "lesbian(/gay) literature" of academic criticism.

Consider, for instance, the very different observations of Ed Cohen, a professor of English at Rutgers University, and Victoria Brownworth, a lesbian journalist and fiction writer. Cohen justifies his focus on gay men in his essay on "Constructing Gender," in *The Columbia History of the American Novel*, in this way:

> If I focus now on the former [gay male writing] rather than the latter [writings by women of color/lesbians, which he acknowledges have also been important to his intellectual development] it is because I know that in a volume like this one it is likely that the works of women of many races and ethnicities will have been addressed heretofore, while the works of men who are exploring the possibilities for sexual and emotional intimacies with other men will most probably remain eccentric. (557)

In contrast, Brownworth insists:

> Unlike gay men . . . lesbians have not been part of the big queer book boom of the last few years. We haven't received the same advances as our gay male counterparts. So while there may be more lesbian writers than ever before, few of us are making a living by writing alone—most of us supplement our income with teaching or lecturing. For lesbians there's no money in being a writer. (49)

Lesbian writers and readers have witnessed a few major "publishing events" over the past few years (most notably Dorothy Allison's *Bastard out of Carolina*, which was a finalist for the National Book Award), but some have claimed that these events were made possible because the lesbian content was not always explicit in such books.

This is not to argue, by any means, that academic criticism is somehow inherently more progressive because lesbians are on top; on the contrary, in both arenas, the uses to which the winner of the gendered competition might be put are more important than who, specifically, wins. Publishers take advantage of White's purchase *outside* the academy, for example, to market his texts. The cover of White's 1978 novel *Nocturnes for the King of Naples* includes *Newsweek*'s assessment of the author, which is identical to that of *Time* magazine: "White is unquestionably the foremost American gay novelist." *Inside* the academy, in contrast, Lorde is able to cash in on a desire for "difference" that can be, nonetheless, safely contained. Anna Wilson, discussing Lorde's increasing canonization in the academy, argues:

> For feminist academia Lorde is particularly effective as a token: since she is Black, lesbian and a mother, her work compactly represents that generally repressed matter towards which white feminists wish to make a gesture of inclusion — but since Lorde conveniently represents so much at once, she can be included without her presence threatening the overall balance of the white majority vision. (77)

Certainly, the majority vision in literary studies, if not in feminist academia, is also heterosexual, or at least heterosexualized. Thus, in literary studies, Lorde can "conveniently represent," along with other "differences," a homosexuality that nonetheless does not threaten to disrupt the straight narrative.

Of course, according to Ohmann's thesis, openly lesbian and gay literature will never be canonized, since the two necessary ingredients of canon formation are not really coalescing for any individual author. I have already mentioned Bérubé's complication of Ohmann, but I include here a third, mediating context that emerged during, and even before, the Queer Renaissance and that particularly complicates the canonicity question for queers: the gay and lesbian marketplace. Lorde and White may not be "canonical" in quite the same way as other contemporary writers are, but because of the existence of a community-based marketplace, as White himself points out, "even quite celebrated heterosexual authors — watching their books go out of print or out of stock — might well envy the longevity of books written by lesbians and gay men" ("Twenty Years On," 4).

Boys' Own Stories and New Spellings of My Name

Lesbian and gay bookstores, literary reviews, award ceremonies, and the like ensure that canonization is an extremely complex affair for openly gay and lesbian writers. In this third context, the community context, White and Lorde are both among the most canonical of contemporary writers.

Thus both Edmund White and Audre Lorde are positioned by others, in various ways, as "representative," and as representative of overlapping and competing constituencies with varying degrees of access to the "center." Each author, however, responds differently to the ways in which he or she has been represented by others, and in general, White's and Lorde's responses parallel the ways in which each constructs identity within the texts I have been examining. In 1990, when Lorde was presented with the second annual Bill Whitehead Memorial Award, in recognition of outstanding contributions to lesbian and gay literature, she informed the audience, "One award will not counterbalance a continuing invisibility of Lesbian and Gay writers of color" ("What Is at Stake," 66). Using her individual location to emphasize how her identity had been shaped in and through others, Lorde went on to explain that the best way to honor her was to honor those she had loved and worked with: "If this group wishes to truly honor my work, built upon the creative use of differences for all our survivals, then I charge you, as a group, to include and further expose the work of new Lesbian and Gay writers of color within the coming year, and to report on what has been done at next year's award ceremony" ("What Is at Stake," 66).[19] In contrast, Edmund White, the recipient of the first annual Bill Whitehead Memorial Award in 1989, concluded his speech with the reflection, "Oddly enough, what literature has always taught us is that only in tracing our individuality can we become universal" ("Twenty Years On," 5). "We," "our," and "us," of course, signify quite differently in White's speech from how "our" signifies in Lorde's "creative use of differences for all our survivals." Despite his stress on "the recording of our differences" in gay and lesbian literature, when White himself acknowledges that "it has struck me as no coincidence that many of the most original writers of this century have been gay" (5), the list he produces in support of this claim includes no people of color.[20]

Then I caught myself foolishly imagining that gays might someday constitute a community rather than a diagnosis. White's protagonist's thoughts during the Stonewall Riots, with which I began this chapter, apparently contradict the points I have been making about White/white apositionality and appear to participate in a more productive myth of identity, akin to those articulated in *Zami* and "Need." This moment of potentiality in *The Beautiful Room Is Empty*, however, is trumped by the novel's notorious ending:

> I stayed over at Lou's [one of the nameless narrator's friends]. We hugged each other in bed like brothers, but we were too excited to sleep. We rushed down to buy the morning papers to see how the Stonewall Uprising had been described. "It's really our Bastille Day," Lou said. But we couldn't find a single mention in the press of the turning point of our lives." (227–28)

At the end of *The Beautiful Room Is Empty*, bittersweet isolation and invisibility triumph over the possibility of community.[21]

Yet the story of Stonewall has been told otherwise. Martin Duberman's historical overview, *Stonewall*, interweaves the stories of six people who were active in lesbian and gay communities during the time of the Stonewall Riots. Craig Rodwell was one of the men actually present when the riots broke out, and Duberman details his reaction: "Craig dashed to a nearby phone booth. Ever conscious of the need for publicity—for *visibility*—and realizing that a critical moment had arrived, he called all three daily papers, the *Times*, the *Post*, and the *News*, and alerted them that 'a major story was breaking.' Then he ran to his apartment a few blocks away to get his camera" (*Stonewall*, 198; emphasis mine). Rodwell's photographs never came out, but Duberman's "day after" is nonetheless not characterized by the existential alienation White's protagonist and his friend feel:

> Word of the confrontation spread through the gay grapevine all day Saturday. Moreover, all three of the dailies wrote about the riot (the *News* put the story on page one), and local television and radio reported it as well. The extensive coverage brought out the crowds, just as Craig had predicted (and had worked to achieve). All day Saturday, curious knots of people gathered outside the bar to gape at the damage and warily celebrate the fact that, for once, cops, not gays, had been routed. (*Stonewall*, 202)

At Stonewall and in *Stonewall*, gay men and lesbians "come out" into a myth of collective identity, and the ramifications of that collective act are still being felt today.

During high school, the protagonist of *A Boy's Own Story* and Tommy, his current obsession, go slumming: "He and I had trekked more than once downtown . . . to listen, frightened and transported, to a big black Lesbian with a crew cut moan her way through the blues" (120–21). Of course, this exoticization of the "big black Lesbian" is only a minor incident for the narrator, unconnected to the larger project of coming out into his own, individual, gay consciousness. And yet the black lesbian singing the blues in *A Boy's Own Story* is not as out of place as she might at first appear. Teleological and essential (white) "boys' own stories" at this point offer feminism and queer politics little in the way of queer (op)positionality. Like the protagonist of Lorde's *Zami*, whose "heart ached and ached for something [she] could not name" (85), the blues singer in White's novel needs an/other myth of queer positionality. Coming out into an essential wholeness may be the myth that lesbians and gay men are told they must embrace, but as Audre's teacher declares early on, when the young protagonist of *Zami* refuses to take dictation in the same manner as the rest of the class, Audre is "a young lady who does not want to do as she is told" (26). Lorde responds instead with a nonessentialized, non-self-identical "new spelling of my name" in *Zami*, and only through this new construction is she able to envision a queer and powerful community of women, whose new identities are permanently partial and whose coalitions are conscious.

Chapter Two
Queer Locations/Queer Transformations

"Vito Russo pointed out in cinema . . . that historically, the gay character always had to end up with his head in the oven or in some similar state," Henry Louis Gates, Jr., explained in a 1991 interview. "It was like a Hays rule that you had to come to a bad end. *Giovanni's Room* isn't really an exception to this; and in Randall Kenan's book you get a brilliant tormented homosexual, Horace, who commits suicide" (in Rowell, 454).[1] Gates praised Kenan's novel *A Visitation of Spirits* but was nonetheless wary of the suicidal ending: "There's another way of reading this [suicide]: which is just as a way of registering some pretty tragic facts of history. . . . But I want Randall Kenan to, as it were, take Horace to the big city in his next novel" (in Rowell, 454).

Gates's prescription for Kenan is in many ways predictable; the "migration to the big city" is a widely available trope in contemporary lesbian and gay literature, with a long and illustrious history.[2] And yet I find the need to transport characters like Horace off to "the big city" symptomatic of a regional elision in queer theory generally. What Gates elides in his suggestion to Kenan is the fact that taking Horace *to* anywhere also entails taking him *from* somewhere. In this case, the unmentioned "somewhere" is the fictional Fundamentalist Christian, rural, African American community of Tims Creek, North Carolina. Not the most conducive atmosphere for the expression of queer desire, certainly; but as liberal lesbian and gay thought likes to remind us, "we are everywhere," and rather than concede that "everywhere" actually means New York and San Francisco, I am interested in the (perhaps more radical) implications of recognizing that "everywhere" includes such an apparently marginal and inhospitable place.

Gates's vision of Horace in the big city is understandable given the tragic suicide that ends the novel, yet the desire to fix Horace's situation is not exactly true to Gates's own theories of signification. In *The Signifying Monkey* (and elsewhere), Gates examines the rhetorical process of "Signifyin(g)" as it has evolved in diverse African Caribbean and African American communities.[3] "The Afro-American concept of Signifyin(g)," Gates writes, involves "formal revision that is at all points double-voiced" (22). Gates sees this double-voiced rhetorical principle at play in the Signifying Monkey tales, which have been passed on and revised by African American speakers in "barrooms, pool halls, and [on] street corners" (54). The Signifying Monkey tales present listeners with a master of trickery: the Signifying Monkey bests his opponent, the Lion, by skillfully opening up a play of meaning. Through a series of insults directed at the Lion and attributed to the Elephant, the Signifying Monkey tricks the Lion into sparring with the Elephant, who—in turn—always physically defeats this supposed "king of the jungle." The Signifying Monkey succeeds because the Lion, who always equates the figurative with the literal, is unable to see through the Monkey's linguistic games. "Another way of reading" *A Visitation of Spirits* could position the text within the tradition of Signifyin(g), considering how the novel shapes a queer trickster identity that rewrites both the "pretty tragic facts of history" that Gates acknowledges and the "corrective" he offers: the migration to the big city.

Contemporary gay fiction that deals with "family" or "community" often exposes the ways those concepts cover over difference: the group achieves a cohesive identity through disavowal of "aberrant" individual identities. Thus, as Gates suggests, "One thing that a good deal of contemporary fiction that deals realistically with gay themes achieves, which I think is very important, is to desentimentalize the notion of 'community' as an unadulterated good" (in Rowell, 454). In my mind, this is precisely what Kenan does with the story of Horace in *A Visitation of Spirits*; yet Gates is uncomfortable enough with Horace's suicide to envision *another* community for Horace in "the big city." Certainly, the narrative in which Gates places Horace allows for the possibility of an *alternative* community, perhaps one more akin to the sustaining community envisioned in *Zami: A New Spelling of My Name*. Difference, however, is again suppressed by transporting Horace off to a community of others "like him," and away from the community he threatens. Locating Horace in an urban area where, presumably, a "black gay identity" is more developed and secure[4] effaces the possibility of transforming the community in which Horace is already located and—more important—undermines Kenan's critique of the "regime of sameness" embodied by the people of Tims Creek.

The term *regime of sameness* is Marcos Becquer's, and before I proceed with my reading of Horace and "transformation" in Tims Creek, North

Carolina, I want to use Becquer's analysis to center my own. Becquer analyzes "snapping" and "vogueing," two of the black gay discursive practices celebrated in and by Marlon Riggs's critically acclaimed film *Tongues Untied*.[5] Since the discursive practices in Riggs's film "emerge both from within and against the cultural and historical discourses operating around them" (8), Becquer argues that "*Tongues Untied* can confront and condemn the regime of sameness which alienates black gays from the black community, the white gay community, and discourse/representation in general" (14). In other words, black gays, confronted by black heterosexual or white gay communities with the compulsion to be "the same," can, in turn, use the discourses made available by those very communities to contest such a compulsion.[6] Becquer's analysis thus foregrounds "difference" while nonetheless arguing for the connective, political importance of a subverted and subversive "sameness":

> It is, then, however ironically or heroically, just that differentiated voice within sameness which *Tongues Untied* attempts to distill, so as to ensure not only that black gays speak up, but that they remain audible in discourse. It proceeds, then, not by nullifying the value of sameness within difference . . . but by acknowledging its political importance and admitting, within the logic of "constructed identity," that sameness is always already a part of difference, as well as vice versa. (15)

Becquer's theory, with its focus on snapping and vogueing, is particularly relevant when discussing the tremendous outpouring of urban and secular black gay cultural production represented in films such as Riggs's *Tongues Untied* and Jennie Livingston's *Paris Is Burning*. Indeed, Becquer explicitly elaborates on "black gays' *secular* use of snapping as a means by which to metaphorically awaken one out of the codes of (discursive) domination" and on vogueing's "reconstitut[ion of] the literal *urban* battlefield of bloody violence . . . into a figurative arena upon which these confrontations between images are played out" (9, 12; my emphasis). In this urban and secular context, snapping and vogueing address the exclusionary practices of black heterosexual and white gay communities: Becquer concludes, for instance, that the segment on snapping in *Tongues Untied* "depicts the snap precisely in its ability to overcome the discursive mechanisms which position black gays beneath both black heterosexuals and white gays" (9). Through the snap, black gays reposition themselves as apart from and yet a part of, on the one hand, white gays, and on the

Queer Locations/Queer Transformations

other hand, black heterosexuals, and "the very binarism of sameness/difference" (15) is thereby deconstructed. In other words, snapping (and elsewhere in Becquer's article, vogueing) works as an empowering and signifying difference for black gays, but this signifying difference nonetheless forges connections with the groups it critiques. With this revised idea of sameness in mind, Becquer concludes, "*Tongues Untied* is not a separatist film" (15).

Becquer's analysis is fueled by "recent revisions of identity politics," which understand identity as a construction and thus allow for "the hope of deconstructing the binarism of otherness which marks discursive alienation and domination by acknowledging that the other is always already a part of ourselves and vice-versa" (7). Yet, although putting sameness back into difference forges connections and hence undermines, as Becquer argues, black homophobia and white gay racism, this queer theoretical move should not overshadow the ongoing need for a queer theory that challenges the "regime of sameness," even when that regime is reproduced *inside* the cultural category "black gay." Despite Becquer's best efforts, indeed, his article concludes with the inscription of a fairly monolithic, snapping and vogueing "black gay identity" singular (16). Although he begins the article decrying "the essentialism inherent in notions of *the* black subject or *the* gay sensibility" (7), Becquer himself subtly moves from plurality to singularity in his discussion of black gay identities: *Tongues Untied* is, at the beginning, "a condensed version of black gay (collective) experiences" (8) but has become, by the end, a celebration of "the emergence of a black gay difference that is unique" (15).

This slippage does not invalidate Becquer's argument; it simply demonstrates, as Ed Cohen suggests, that "no matter how sensitively we go about it, 'identity politics' has great difficulty in affirming difference(s)" ("Who Are 'We'?" 76). Becquer's article, with its critique of white gay and black heterosexual hegemony, recognizes the difficulty of affirming difference but simultaneously affirms the "sameness" that is always already present within "difference." Cohen argues, however, with a nod to Diana Fuss, that "identity politics is predicated on denying the difference that is already there in 'the same'" ("Who Are 'We'?" 76). This predication ensures that difference can be denied or repressed even when identity politics is grounded in sophisticated poststructuralist attempts, such as Becquer's, to move beyond the sameness/difference binarism.

While black gays are undeniably marginalized by black heterosexuals and by both heterosexual and gay whites, and hence are strategically positioned to disrupt and decenter heterosexual and white hegemony, a focus on *urban* black gays will always, in turn, produce other margins. Still, I want to extend rather than disarm Becquer's analysis. By pushing his ideas further, I hope to create a space in which to consider black gay cultural production (and perhaps queer cultural production generally) *outside* an urban, secular arena.[7] It was no accident that I used Becquer's analysis to "center" my own. Until quite recently, queer theory has predominantly "centered" on urban areas. Such a focus is in some ways inevitable: after all, as John D'Emilio and Estelle B. Freedman explain, it was initially in American cities that a gay subculture flourished in the middle of the twentieth century (288). The urban "center" that D'Emilio, Freedman, and other queer theorists and historians have analyzed, though, might be productively understood as part of a complex array of "centers" and "margins," since both concepts emerge relationally. Moreover, in the Queer Renaissance, critical interrogation of the processes of marginalization might proceed hand in hand with the establishment of unexpected, even unlikely, new centers. Thus we would do well to consider—before placing Kenan's Horace "safely" (or more "appropriately"?) in an urban "center"—just what black queer desire is doing in, or does to, rural North Carolina. Essex Hemphill's words, with their subtle promise/threat that black gays will transform *whatever* community they are in, seem appropriate to me here: "I ask you brother: Does your mama *really* know about you? Does she *really* know what I am? . . . I hope so, because *I am* coming home" (*Ceremonies*, 42).[8]

Transformations (I): Horace Thomas Cross

A Visitation of Spirits concerns itself with several members of the Cross-Greene clan, an African American family living in Tims Creek, North Carolina, in the mid-1980s.[9] The novel focuses particularly on Horace, the youngest member of the Cross family, and on Jimmy Greene, Horace's cousin, the young minister at the First Baptist Church of Tims Creek and the first black principal of Tims Creek Elementary School. *A Visitation of Spirits* is organized around two days in the life of the Cross-Greene family: December 8, 1985, and April 29–30, 1984. The text moves back and forth between these two days, and each section heading further specifies the exact placement of events in time: for instance, "December 8, 1985 / 8:45 A.M. . . . April 30, 1984 / 1:15 A.M." (3, 66). This temporal precision gives each section of the novel the appearance of measurable, scientific "fact";

the events of *A Visitation of Spirits*, however, belie any easy distinction between "fact" and "fiction." Unable to live up to the (heterosexual) expectations of the community and consequently dissatisfied with his life, Horace Cross attempts to use a magic spell to transform himself into a bird. When the transformation fails, "spirits" and "demons" reveal themselves to Horace in order to lead him on a whirlwind journey through his own life. Past, present, and future blur together as freely as fact and fantasy as Horace's journey progresses. Even Horace himself is confused as to whether what he is seeing is "real" or not. One of the demons attempts to explain: "Ghosts? Yeah, you might call them ghosts. Ghosts of the past. The presence of the present. The very stuff of which the future is made. This is the effluvium of souls that surround men daily" (73).

The echoes here are of the humanistic, transformative experience of Ebenezer Scrooge, and in fact, Kenan begins his novel with an epigraph from *A Christmas Carol*. In *A Visitation of Spirits*, however, Horace is not in a position to experience the same sort of happy ending as Scrooge does in *A Christmas Carol*. In contrast to the miserly gentleman of Charles Dickens's tale, Horace, after observing the constraint and confusion he has endured throughout his young life, does not undergo some humanistic "redemption"; instead, he commits suicide. In the end, it is not Horace the individual but the position and the place in which he finds himself that are in need of transformation.

After spending weeks preparing the spell, Horace decides that his transformation into a bird will occur at midnight on April 29, 1984. Horace performs the necessary incantation, and a few minutes after midnight, someone or something begins to call: "The voice said: Come" (27). The remainder of Horace's story, like Ebenezer Scrooge's, is told in three episodes, roughly corresponding to Horace's past, present, and future. In the first episode, the voice/demon shows Horace the "ghosts" of his own past. Horace finds himself in front of the First Baptist Church of Tims Creek, where a service is in progress. His entire family (including a five-year-old version of Horace himself) is present in the congregation. This community, to Horace, is the embodiment of what he is attempting to escape:

> They were fat and thin, light and dark, tall and short, farmers, salesmen, mechanics, barbers, nurses, mothers, fathers, aunts, uncles, cousins, lovers, friends. Here was community, not a word but a being. Horace felt it as though for the first time. Here, amid these singing, fanning, breathing

beings were his folk, his kin. Did he know them? Had they known him? It was from them he was running. Why? (73)

Clearly, "community" in this episode signifies much differently than it did in Audre Lorde's *Zami: A New Spelling of My Name.* In my previous chapter, I used *Zami* to argue for "other" identities; that is, for identities defined in and through others. The community re-presented to Horace by the demon, however, is a far cry from Lorde's sustaining vision of women working together as friends and lovers. The enumeration of various identities here suggests that this is another "house of difference," but—*pace Zami*—Horace at this point wants to define himself only *against,* not *through,* this group.

In this chapter, consequently, I look more critically at the idea of community. I explore the ways in which this community incites the "transformation" of Horace the *individual,* but I also consider, conversely, how the location of Horace and his queer story in rural North Carolina puts into play a critique that has the potential to transform this *community,* and others like it, on the supposed margins of the queer world. After examining the importance of North Carolina to Horace's story, I look specifically at the institution in Tims Creek most in need of transformation: the church. I then expand my argument, looking to the community more generally, to consider some strategies (à la Becquer and Gates) that Horace might use to begin the queer work of transforming this community and its institutions. Although this section concludes with some of the ways in which Horace apparently fails to effect change, the next section insists that failure is always *only* apparent or temporary. Through a reading of Horace's cousin Jimmy Greene, I argue that *A Visitation of Spirits* ultimately succeeds in establishing a queer trickster identity intent on exposing the queerness at the center of identification and desire, disrupting the exclusionary logic on which "community" is often founded, and sustaining a transformative critique of this community.

Horace himself underscores the urgency of transformation occurring in rural North Carolina: "Cats had a physical freedom he loved to watch, the svelte, smooth, sliding motion of the great cats of Africa, but he could not see transforming himself into anything that would not fit the swampy woodlands of Southeastern North Carolina. He had to stay here" (11). Horace is imagining his own transformation, not the community's, but his thoughts here nonetheless provide a point of departure for an interrogation of this queer location. For some reason, Horace feels compelled to stay in Tims Creek; something about the location proscribes the possibility that his story take place elsewhere.

Horace never solves the riddle of why he feels this compulsion to stay, but near the end of the story there is an allusion to a text that could provide some clues. Horace

> wrote his autobiography, without stopping, one long suspended effort, words upon words flowing out of him, expressing his grief. But he never read what he had written, hoping rather to exorcise his confusion. So strong was his belief in words—perhaps they would lead him out of this strange world in which he had suddenly found himself. In the end, after reams and reams of paper and thousands of lines of scribble, he had found no answers. In frustration he burned it. (239)

In frustration he burned it; the text that could facilitate an understanding of Horace's position in "this strange world" is apparently lost. Nothing in this magical realist novel mandates that this "autobiography" *remain* destroyed, however, and near the end, readers are presented with a short section narrated in Horace's own voice. This section, "Horace Thomas Cross: Confessions" (245–51), is the only part of the novel in which Horace speaks in the first person. Although it is not "reams and reams of paper," it does read like the autobiography described above. Almost every sentence of this section in which Horace meditates on his life in Tims Creek begins with the phrase "I remember": "I remember the first time I saw Granddaddy kill a chicken. I remember it, dirty-white and squawking, and Granddaddy putting it down on a stump" (245). Similar vignettes fill out this representation of life in rural North Carolina as Horace's "confessions" continue.

Horace himself "never read what he had written," but it quickly becomes clear to those who do that, despite the hardships Horace endured, this rural setting is not simply the site of "backwardness" or "repression." Like other communities in which black gay men find themselves, Tims Creek, North Carolina, is a site of struggle and possible transformation. And like the snapping and vogueing black gay men of Becquer's analysis, Horace's own queer sense of self emerges both from within and against the community around him:

> I remember my Aunt Ruthester's chocolate-chip cookies and how she would make an extra batch for me. . . . I remember the way it made my mouth happy, dissolving almost as soon as I ate it, buttery and hot.

I remember finally touching a man, finally kissing him. I remember the surprise and shock of someone else's tongue in my mouth. I remember the taste of someone else's saliva. I remember actually feeling someone else's flesh, warm, smooth. . . . I remember being happy that I was taking a chance with my immortal soul, thinking that I would somehow win in the end and live still, feeling immortal in a mortal's arms. I remember then regretting that it was such a sin. I remember the feeling I got after we climaxed, feeling hollow and undone, wishing I were some kind of animal, a wolf or a bird or a dolphin, so I would not have to worry about wanting to do it again; I remember worrying how the other person felt.

I remember church and praying. I remember revival meetings and the testifying of women who began to cry before the congregation and ended their plea of hardships and sorrow and faithfulness to the Lord with the request for those who knew the word of prayer to pray much for me. I remember taking Communion and wondering how the bread was the body and the grape juice was the blood and thinking how that made us all cannibals. . . . Then I remember the day I realized that I was probably not going to go home to heaven, cause the rules were too hard for me to keep. That I was too weak.

I remember me. (250–51)

I quote at length from this passage because, as I suggested, this autobiography might provide clues as to what queer desire is doing in, and does to, this community. Clearly, Horace's desire arises in opposition to the mores of this community; as far as they are concerned, queer desire is simply "sinful." Because of their stringent moral codes, Horace feels like an outcast and wants to escape by transforming himself into an animal. At the same time, however, Horace's desire emerges from *within* this community. The very language of the fire-and-brimstone sermons he has endured ("I remember being happy that I was taking a chance with my immortal soul") heightens the eroticism of his encounters and helps solidify his developing queer identity. Moreover, despite the fact that Horace ultimately feels weak in the face of such a powerful religious institution, his confessions highlight his attempts to appropriate and re-signify the language of that institution (e.g., "feeling immortal in a mortal's arms"). In short, this may be a sin, but it is also, nonetheless, a contestation—however temporary—of the community's ideas about "sin" and "mortality." As Lisa Duggan writes, the "project of constructing identities" is "a historical process in which contrasting 'stories' of the self and others—stories of difference—are told, appropriated, and retold as stories of loca-

Queer Locations/Queer Transformations

tion in the social world of structured inequalities" ("Trials," 793). In the fictional social world that is the First Baptist Church of Tims Creek, North Carolina (a "social world of structured inequalities," certainly), Horace must learn, somehow, to make sense of his identity, and he does so by appropriating the language of this institution for his own queer uses.

Other elements of this autobiography underscore the extent to which Horace uses this particular location to construct and make sense of his own identity. A description of the sumptuous tastes and smells of a country home, for example (the batch of cookies "made my mouth happy . . . buttery and hot"), immediately precedes and influences Horace's attempt to find a language for making sense of his erotic encounters with men ("I remember the surprise and shock of someone else's tongue in my mouth. I remember the taste of someone else's saliva"). And if this sharp juxtaposition were not enough to demonstrate how intertwined the various elements of Horace's life are, food and flesh come together yet once more in the Communion, as Horace muses on the "cannibalism" of that familiar ritual.

Immediately before the final sentence of these confessions, Horace asserts, "I was too weak." And yet his "I remember me," with its placement in a paragraph of its own at the very end of his "Confessions," overrides such an assertion of weakness and implies that he will not relinquish any part of his identity. The sentence "I remember me" solidifies the confessions that have preceded it as indelible parts of who Horace is. Despite his difference(s), Horace's identity has been shaped not simply against but also within the community of Tims Creek, North Carolina. Duggan writes that "identity" can be understood "as a narrative of a subject's location within social structure. . . . Never created out of whole cloth, never uniquely individual, each narrative is a retelling, an act of social interaction, a positioned intervention in the shared, contested narratives of a given culture" ("Trials," 793–94). Horace concludes that he has lost this "contest"; he feels he must transform himself, since he is "too weak" to live up to the community's expectations. Yet Horace's "positioned intervention" might be read differently, in a way that is less "uniquely individual." Since Horace's story is an act of social interaction, we might ask ourselves what significance that story and its violent conclusion have for this particular North Carolina community. I contend that Kenan makes the "margins" central to his vision of a transformed community: through and against the tragic trajectory of *A Visitation of Spirits*, a queer trickster identity materializes. Although such an identity is seemingly deferred during Horace's brief life, it nonetheless survives after Horace's death to begin the work of transforming the social structure in which his story is located.

The foundation of the social structure of Tims Creek is the church, and not surprising, the church is the institution sending Horace the loudest message that he, as an individual, is in need of transformation. I have already mentioned Horace's discomfort at the vision of the congregation of the First Baptist Church of Tims Creek. His discomfort is compounded by the sermon he hears during that vision. The Reverend Hezekiah Barden, minister of the church in the days before Horace's cousin Jimmy, informs the congregation that he is "gone step on some toes this morning" (77) and proceeds to read from the first chapter of Romans:

> They are without excuse: Because that, when they knew God, they glorified him not as God, neither were thankful . . . for even their women did change the natural use into that which is against nature:
>
> And likewise also the men, leaving the natural use of the woman, burned in their lust one toward another; men with men working that which is unseemly, and receiving in themselves that recompense of their error which was meet. (77)

As the sermon continues, the opposition between Horace and this religious community is spelled out in stark terms: "Now you can say, 'Well, Brother Barden, you ain't *liberated*. You ain't up with the *times*.'. . . *Liberated? Behind the times?* Brothers and sisters, there is no time but now, and now I am telling you: It's unclean. You heard what Paul wrote to the Romans: Unclean" (78–79). The voice of the congregation serves as a chorus behind Barden's sermon, giving its approval to everything he says: "Unclean. . . . Go head, Reverend, and preach, now. . . . Go on ahead. Tell it. . . ." (79–80). The community/chorus positions the Reverend Barden as its voice or representative, and as far as he is concerned, homosexuality and Christianity are mutually exclusive; being "clean" means *not* being gay.[10] Hence, when the queer individual confronts this religious institution, something clearly has to give.

That religion, and not Horace, should be what gives is corroborated by Kenan's signification on other texts. I have already mentioned how *A Visitation of Spirits* reverses the individualistic equation of Dickens's *A Christmas Carol*. Beyond this, however, Kenan's novel is a complex signification on James Baldwin's 1953 *Go Tell It on the Mountain*.[11] The story of a young boy torn between sin and the church, after all, has been told before. Through *A Visitation of Spirits*, Kenan rewrites Baldwin's story of John Grimes, bringing it—if you will—out of the closet. Even the epigraphs to the various sections of Kenan's novel occasionally repeat, with a difference, the epigraphs in Baldwin's; for example, both authors employ, in some way, Revelation 22:17: "And the Spirit and the bride say, Come. And let him that heareth say, Come. And let him that is athirst come. And whosoever will, let him take the water of life freely." As an epigraph to the first section of his novel, Baldwin simply repeats verbatim the King James Version of this text. As an epigraph to the second section of *his* novel, Kenan reworks and shortens the passage: "Whosoever will, let him come . . ." (29). This epigraph not only echoes Baldwin; it also echoes the voice Horace hears after his attempt to turn himself into a bird fails. In this context, Kenan's epigraph repeats with a difference: "let him come" takes on a queer new meaning. In *A Visitation of Spirits*, which openly details one young boy's confrontation with his homosexuality and in which a deep voice repeatedly tells him to "come," the homoerotic pun on the word is difficult to miss. Kenan's signification, in turn, makes it well-nigh impossible to read Baldwin's epigraph "straight." Beginning with the epigraphs, then, the two texts come together, and Baldwin's "closeted" text is, in effect, "outed" by Kenan's.

Kenan's signification on Baldwin is much more complex than a simple reworking of epigraphs, however. *A Visitation of Spirits* in general reads like an openly gay version of *Go Tell It on the Mountain*, and it is Kenan's more general signification on Baldwin that suggests the church and community in *A Visitation of Spirits*, not Horace, are in need of transformation. In *Go Tell It on the Mountain*, John—like Horace—struggles against sin: "all the pressures of church and home [were] uniting to drive him to the altar" (13). Moreover, just as it does for Horace and the community of Tims Creek, North Carolina, "sin" for John and the others in *Go Tell It on the Mountain* particularly connotes "sins of the flesh." John watches the pastor's nephew Elisha and his girlfriend, Ella Mae, for instance, when they are brought before the church for a "public warning" designed to keep them from having sex, which would be the "ultimate" transgression: "Sin was not in their minds—not yet; yet sin was in the flesh; and should they continue with their walking out alone together, their secrets and laughter, and touching of hands, they would surely sin a sin beyond all forgiveness" (17). In his own life, likewise, John's fear of sin and damnation is always connected to the "flesh":

He had sinned. In spite of the saints, his mother and his father, the warnings he had heard from his earliest beginnings, he had sinned with his hands a sin that was hard to forgive. In the school lavatory, alone, thinking of the boys, older, bigger, braver, who made bets with each other as to whose urine could arch higher, he had watched in himself a transformation of which he would never dare to speak. (18–19)

As this passage makes clear, however, even though both young men struggle against the "flesh," there is a significant difference between the "temptations" Elisha faces and those facing John. Although it is not as explicitly gay as Horace's story in *A Visitation of Spirits,* John's struggle against "sin" has an implicit homoerotic dimension. In fact, the "un-speakability" of John's desires here only confirms this particular dimension of his struggle. As Eve Sedgwick makes clear, there is a "centuries-long historical chain of substantive uses of space-clearing negatives to void and at the same time to underline the possibility of male same-sex genitality" (*Epistemology,* 202). According to Sedgwick, "the speakable nonmedical terms, in Christian tradition, for the homosexual possibility for men" were (and are), paradoxically, such terms as *unspeakable, unmentionable, things fearful to name,* and *the love that dare not speak its name* (202–3). Hence John's attempt to shield himself here is ironically his undoing; he speaks (queer) volumes in his very efforts to remain silent.[12]

In addition to the masturbatory fantasies growing out of his observation of the genital play of the "older, bigger, braver" boys, John is virtually obsessed with Elisha, and that obsession is almost always detailed in *physical* terms: "John stared at Elisha all during the [Sunday school] lesson, admiring the timbre of Elisha's voice, much deeper and manlier than his own, admiring the leanness, and grace, and strength, and darkness of Elisha in his Sunday suit, wondering if he would ever be holy as Elisha was holy" (13). Baldwin goes no further with John's obsession than this, but in his signification on *Go Tell It on the Mountain,* Kenan does. Horace in *A Visitation of Spirits* is much more specific about the ways in which such homoerotic preoccupations bring discomfort to a young boy in the church: "He would be lying to himself if he said he had not been attracted to Gideon. . . . Why couldn't the Lord take this bit of torture, this careful trap away? Give him larceny to fight instead. Let his piety be questioned. Try to force him to lie, to worship false gods, to dishonor his mother and father, to covet his neighbor's home . . . but why Gideon?" (146).

The differences between the two texts are not reducible to their relative openness or secrecy about homoerotic desire, however. Horace's story diverges from John's at key points, and it is ultimately in the two texts' divergence, more than in their convergence, that Kenan's sharp indictment of the church comes out. Like Horace throughout *A Visitation of Spirits*, John goes through a harrowing, "supernatural" experience in the last section of *Go Tell It on the Mountain*. John falls to the floor of the church in some sort of ecstatic, spiritual trance, and like Horace, begins to hear voices calling to him. Eventually, one voice in particular pulls John out of this trance: " 'Rise up, Johnny,' said Elisha. . . . 'Are you saved, boy?' 'Yes,' said John, 'oh, yes!' " (206). Like Horace, John is "transformed" by his supernatural experience; unlike Horace, John is "saved." Of course, there is a fair amount of irony in Baldwin's novel; Baldwin is by no means uncritical of the church, and consequently, exactly how or whether John's life will be different remains unclear in the last line of the novel: " 'I'm ready,' John said, 'I'm coming. I'm on my way' " (221). Still, John himself claims to be positively transformed by his experience. He ultimately submits to the church's authority, even though that submission is channeled through his homoerotic obsession for Elisha: "Elisha . . . no matter what happens to me, where I go, what folks say about me, no matter what *any*body says, you remember—please remember—I was saved. I was *there*" (220).

In Kenan's re-vision of the confrontation between a young boy and the church, however, accommodation to this religious institution, as it is, is no longer possible. Through Horace's suicide, *A Visitation of Spirits* suggests, in contrast to *Go Tell It on the Mountain*, that the gay individual cannot and does not survive such attempts at accommodation with the church. In the end, the religious institution, and not John/Horace, needs to be "saved." Salvation, certainly, is a seemingly difficult concept to queer, but *A Visitation of Spirits* nonetheless sets just such a queering into motion. If the straight definition of the term fixes the meaning of actions (as, for instance, "sin") or individuals (as "redeemed" or "damned"), then the queer concept opens up a play of meaning that disrupts these fixations and establishes another sort of church altogether.[13]

Religion is just one facet—the most prominent and oppressive facet—of community life in Tims Creek. The church is not the only place, however, where Horace feels he does not belong, and the church is hence not the only part of the community in need of transformation. Indeed, Horace confronts the "regime of sameness" almost everywhere he goes in Tims

Creek. None of the subcommunities of which Horace is a part is comfortable with "difference" within its ranks; thus, in none of the locations in which Horace finds himself is he able to be comfortable with "sameness." The compulsion to be "the same," even as it is reproduced within the cultural category "black gay," invalidates any of Horace's attempts to come to terms with his own identity. "You black, ain't you?" Horace's aunt asks him (186). One of Horace's lovers from the community theater where he works taunts him, "Faggot. . . . What's the matter? Don't like to be called what you are?" (225). Even Gideon, another black gay character who is Horace's first affair, says to Horace in the heat of an argument, "But remember, black boy, you heard it here first: You're a faggot, Horace. . . . At least I know what I am" (164).

In each confrontation, it is not that the labels are wholly inappropriate for Horace; it is just that every question of identity in *A Visitation of Spirits* needs to be followed by a "yes, but . . ." Judith Butler's comments are particularly relevant to Horace's situation here: "The prospect of *being* anything . . . seems to be more than a simple injunction to become who or what I already am" ("Imitation," 13). Throughout *A Visitation of Spirits*, the discordant and demanding chorus of voices surrounding Horace immobilizes him, apparently preventing any strategic resistance of the compulsion to be the same.

As a black gay teenager in Tims Creek, Horace always finds himself embodying what are—at least, to the other members of the groups of which he is a part—contradictory identities: in his own family, as in the church, he is "black," but not "gay"; at the community theater where he works, he (along with many of the other actors) is openly "gay," but his "blackness" is rendered invisible (particularly by the production itself, which is about the history of the Cross family—the *white* Cross family— in North Carolina); with his "alternative" and white high school friends, he is "smart and black" (237), but he is not "gay," and he feels his "blackness" is tokenized. Only with Gideon does Horace find a "niche," where he should "fit" exactly. But, although their relationship is consummated, Horace and Gideon do not embrace a "black gay identity" together, an identity with which they subvert and expose the contradictions of the various communities of which they are constituents. Instead, the pressure from each of these communities precludes the possibility of Gideon and Horace coming together. Horace, caught up in the belief that he is in need of transformation, is ultimately unable to imagine that he and Gideon might work together to transform others. Gideon comes to signify, for

Horace, everything about himself that must be obliterated. In his final scene with Gideon, Horace literalizes this belief by attacking Gideon: "Horace hit Gideon. Full square in the mouth, so quickly he himself did not realize what he had done, so hard he could not doubt he meant to do it. But had he wanted to hit Gideon, or himself for not wanting to hit him?" (163).

The reflection of himself that Horace sees in Gideon is, in an earlier scene, even more explicit: "Gideon turned around and looked at Horace. He paid no attention to the snickering boys who stood about Horace; he just fixed Horace with a gaze whose intensity frightened him. Now, looking at the phantoms, Horace realized how it had seemed to be more than an angry glare. It was more of a curse. A prophecy" (100). This defiant gaze links Gideon, and the potential for a black gay identity that Gideon embodies, to Horace. Horace (mis)recognizes himself in Gideon, and this event—in a world where every community appears to legislate against the very possibility of such an identity—propels Horace forward onto a path fraught with anxiety. Throughout *A Visitation of Spirits*, Horace is caught in a cycle of recognition and disavowal, which his confrontation with Gideon instigates. Horace does not see his identification with Gideon as a locus of possibility; he cannot comprehend "black gay identity" as a multivalent sign that has the potential to open up or disrupt the meanings of "community" that debilitate him. Instead, believing he has seen the final "truth" about himself in Gideon, Horace feels compelled to repudiate such a truth, due to the prohibitions he feels from various communities against embracing such an identity.

In a pivotal scene near the end of the novel (in a section where, à la Dickens, the voice of the ghost has disappeared, even though a presence remains behind to show Horace visions of things yet to come), although Gideon is no longer present, there is a final repetition of what has become for Horace the terrifying cycle of recognition and disavowal. On entering a room at the theater, Horace sees a black man, dressed as a clown, applying white makeup. As Horace comes closer to the figure, he realizes that it is himself: "The double stood up. He was exactly the same height as Horace, the same build. In his sparkling color, he turned to look at both their reflections in the mirror: Horace in his brown nakedness, covered with dirt and ash and grass in his hair, a gun in his hand, and the other Horace, white-faced, dressed as a clown" (220). Horace (mis)recognizes himself and himself and himself, but like his encounters with Gideon, this recognition is not ultimately reassuring but rather the sign of some terrible inadequacy: "Of all the things he had seen this night, all the memories he had confronted, all the ghouls and ghosts and specters, this shook him the most. Stunned, confused, bewildered, he could only stare at his reflection, seeing him and him and him" (219).

Horace's reaction here is, not surprisingly, a far cry from the strategic, subversive use to which some (urban) black gay men put mirrors. Becquer writes that

> the voguer creates a scenario in which s/he first carefully arranges him/ herself before a mirror. . . . Once satisfied with his/her own constructed image, the voguer then turns the mirror onto his/her opponent. This is done in the hopes of making evident how badly the opponent is in need of a dramatic make-up job, that is, of a drastic reconstruction and reconceptualization of his/her own identity. . . . While the Lacanian subject *mis*recognizes him/herself as a whole before the mirror, the voguer recognizes him/herself as a construction. In this sense the voguer can be seen to make use of the very simulacrum by which the Lacanian subject is duped. (13)

In *A Visitation of Spirits,* exactly the opposite happens to Horace. Turning to the mirror, he can see only how badly he himself is in need of reconstruction/reconceptualization. The terror for Horace in all of this doubling and redoubling lies in the recognition of what he believes is the "truth" about himself, which he can no longer escape: he is a clown, he wears a mask, he only plays a role, he betrays the communities of which he is a part.

In *The Signifying Monkey,* Gates suggests, "Thinking about the black concept of Signifyin(g) is a bit like stumbling unaware into a hall of mirrors: the sign itself appears to be doubled, at the very least, and (re)doubled upon ever closer examination" (44). But although Becquer's voguers—like, indeed, the Signifying Monkey himself, who might be understood as their analogue—would be able to "work" the indeterminacy of the signifier that such a stumbling into a hall of mirrors would entail (Becquer writes, "The voguer 'reads' the simulacrum" [13]), Horace, even as he literally stumbles into just such a hall, is not. Despite the literal proliferation of meanings and identities in this scene, Horace believes he is stuck with one wholly inadequate identity, which is always and only "disgusting," "unclean," an "abomination" (100). Equating the figurative with the literal (or the reflection/representation with the essence) and reading the literal as inescapable, Horace is unable to recognize and deploy the constructedness of identity against the multiple communities that surround him.

The Signifying Monkey of Gates's analysis succeeds precisely because of his ability to luxuriate in the indeterminacy of meaning. Horace, however, explicitly rejects such a potentially liberating strategy. In the end, like the lion who is always signified on in the Signifying Monkey tales, Horace is undone by the indeterminacy of meaning:

> Then . . . he saw what he had led himself to see, the reason, the logic, the point. It was round and square. It was hard and soft, black and white, cold and hot, smooth and rough, young and old. It had depth and was shallow, was bright and dull, took light and gave light, was generous and greedy. Holy and profane. Ignorant and wise. Horace saw it and it saw Horace, like the moon, like the sea, like the mountain—so large he could not miss it, so small he could barely see it. The most simple, the most complex, the most wrong, the most right. . . . Horace saw clearly through a glass darkly and understood where he fit. Understood what was asked of him.
>
> Horace shook his head. No. He turned away. No. He turned his heart away. No.
>
> This had been Horace's redemption, and Horace said no. (232, 234)

Exactly what "it" is that might have been Horace's redemption is unclear in this list of oxymorons, although Horace's rejection of this redemption is clear. The "meaning," or signified, of this vision, however, may be beside the point. What Horace refuses by turning away from this list of oxymorons is not the signified but—as Gates might put it—the "sheer materiality, and the willful play, of the signifier itself" (*Signifying Monkey*, 59). Horace is apparently unable to deploy the instability of the signifier to his advantage, in contrast to secular and urban black gays who "read" the inadequacies of the communities in which they are positioned by snapping and vogueing, and in contrast to that exemplary trickster figure, the Signifying Monkey. Instead, Horace turns away from such strategies and maintains until the end that he himself, and not his location, needs transformation.

A Visitation of Spirits is, after all, a tragedy, and from this point in the text Horace's story moves with apocalyptic rapidity toward its suicidal conclusion. In my placement of voguers and the Signifying Monkey alongside Horace's final vision, however, I mean to suggest that the text points to another possibility: a queer trickster identity might make evident to the communities of Tims Creek how badly they are in need of a "dramatic make-up job." In the Signifying Monkey tales, the Monkey repeatedly trounces his opponents by luxuriating in the indeterminacy of meaning. Gates writes, "Motivated Signifyin(g) is the sort in which the Monkey delights; it functions to redress an imbalance of power, to clear a space, rhetorically. To achieve occupancy in this desired space, the Monkey re-writes the received order by exploiting the Lion's hubris and his inability to read the figurative other than as the literal" (*Signifying Monkey*, 124). Horace's vision likewise affords him the opportunity to rewrite the re-ceived order; the string of oxymorons directs attention away from the signified and toward the sheer materiality of the signifier, providing Hor-ace with a glimpse of a world where what is profane is holy, and what is most wrong is most right. Gates explains, "The Signifying Monkey tales . . . can be thought of as versions of daydreams, the Daydream of the Black Other, chiastic fantasies of reversal of power relationships" (*Signifying Monkey*, 85). Horace's final vision is a textbook example of such a day-dream in which power relationships are reversed, and although he refuses to embrace and deploy what had been his "redemption," his vision at the very least suggests that these fantasies are always already in circulation, even within a community as apparently "marginal" and "stable" as Tims Creek, North Carolina.

The Signifying Monkey's strategy depends on repetition, with a differ-ence, of the signifier; in other words, the Monkey understands and exploits the impossibility of attaching the signifier to one fixed signified. This "repetition with a difference" might be productively linked to Judith But-ler's idea of "subversive repetition" (in fact, Butler's subversive repetition can be said to depend on repetition with a difference). Particularly in light of Horace's "inevitable" tragedy, Butler's comments seem appropriate:

> Heterosexuality offers normative sexual positions that are intrinsically im-possible to embody, and the persistent failure to identify fully and without incoherence with these positions reveals heterosexuality itself not only as a compulsory law, but as an inevitable comedy. Indeed, I would offer this insight into heterosexuality as both a compulsory system and an intrinsic comedy, a constant parody of itself, as an alternative gay/lesbian perspective. (*Gender Trouble*, 122)

To Butler, identity is constituted through a series of attempts to embody normative gender and sexual identities. She argues that the compulsive repetition these normative positions engender exposes the "truth" of identity as a fiction: "The injunction *to be* a given gender produces necessary failures, a variety of incoherent configurations that in their multiplicity exceed and defy the injunction by which they are generated" (*Gender Trouble*, 145). Butch/femme and drag performances are among the "subversive bodily acts" that particularly foreground this defiance. Such practices parody the idea of an original gender identity and in the process "*reveal . . . the imitative structure of gender itself—as well as its contingency*" (*Gender Trouble*, 137). The attention to style over substance suggests an affinity between the cultural practice of drag or butch/femme and the practice of Signifyin(g), which similarly turns on an awareness of the distinction between manner and matter (Gates, *Signifying Monkey*, 70). Horace refuses to admit such a distinction and is thus unable to claim an "alternative gay/lesbian perspective," such as the perspective Butler envisions. Instead, the compulsion to be the same has engendered in Horace the belief that his identity must be fixed, once and for all. Neither a single individual nor the regime of sameness with which he contends, however, can entirely contain the gender trouble Horace's story spotlights. As the next section argues, gender trouble keeps in play not only the meaning of Horace's identity but even the meaning, or the supposed certainty, of his inevitable "tragedy" and "death."

At this point in the novel, however, it would *seem* that Horace's journey—in contrast to Ebenezer Scrooge's—does indeed end in death.[14] The neo-Dickensian specter finally leads Horace to a cemetery: "Convincing himself he knew the outcome of this story, he fully expected to see his own grave. Though he did not understand the point of this transparent charade, he was convinced that would be the best end" (231). Prior to his suicide, and standing before the grave, Horace confronts his double one last time. Following Gates and Butler, I propose that this double, because of the "redemptive" vision he provokes, embodies the "sheer materiality" and "willful play" of the signifier. Face-to-face with the slipperiness of signification, however, Horace determines to end it once and for all:

> His reflection stood there, his hand extended. I'm your way, he said. . . . You can follow the demon if you want. It's your choice.
>
> Horace looked at his hand. His hand. Never had he felt such self-loathing, and by and by, his depression became anger as he glared at the spirit. . . .
>
> In such a rage he could barely see, Horace raised his gun and fired. The report was not as loud as he had expected. But there on the ground he lay,

himself, a gory red gash through his chest. His face caught in a grimace, moaning and speaking incoherently. Please. No. No. He looked at his hand, covered in blood, and Horace looked up at Horace, his eyes full of horror, but in recognition too, as if to say: You meant it, didn't you? You actually hate me? (234–35)

Gates writes that "the Signifying Monkey is often called the Signifier, he who wreaks havoc upon the Signified" (*Signifying Monkey*, 52). In stark contrast, Horace in the end wreaks havoc on the Signifier, his "redemption," and consequently, it is he himself who is undone.

Even as it questions it ("Why? Why. You didn't have to"), the text itself thus graphically stages Horace's rejection of the Signifyin(g) alternative. In some ways, then, neither Gates's nor my vision of and for Horace is realized: Horace is not transported "safely" off to the big city, and neither is he able to begin a much-needed transformation of the place where he is already located. Indeed, as early as the scene in which he hits Gideon, Horace—confirmed in the belief that he, and not his surroundings, must change—dismisses the idea of "another world, another place": "He imagined another world, another place, in which he could gladly have complied with Gideon's wish and fallen into lusty, steamy, lascivious abandon—but no" (164).

His inability to imagine such a place, along with his subsequent suicide, demonstrates what the compulsion to be the same has done to Horace. In the context of all the demands put on him by various communities, Horace's suicide can be seen as an apt re-presentation of the violence involved in the attempt to "alienate conclusively, *definitionally*, from anyone on any theoretical ground the authority to describe and name their own sexual desire" (Sedgwick, *Epistemology*, 26), or indeed, any component of their own identity. That *A Visitation of Spirits* appeared in the same year (1989) that right-wing religious and political leaders attempted to suppress the findings of the Department of Health and Human Services' Report of the Secretary's Task Force on Youth Suicide, which claimed that gay teenagers account for 30 percent of all teenage suicides (Ruta, 12), only underscores the validity of representing the compulsion toward sameness as violence.[15] Horace's suicide is detailed in stark, scientific (and hence "real") prose and is juxtaposed to the "fantastic" events in this postmodern, magical realist text. The realness of the suicide moves the theoretical opposition "Is It Real?"/"Is It Fantasy?" to a more urgent level and, in the process, starkly confronts and condemns the community where Horace is located: What if it is real? How is the community implicated in such violence?

In spite of Horace's violent rejection of the Signifyin(g) possibilities embodied in his double, then, the text itself provokes a critique of the community. Immediately after the suicide, the question of what queer desire (and its violent extermination) is doing in and to rural North Carolina is foregrounded. As the novel concludes, the narration shifts to the second person in a nostalgic section called "Requiem for Tobacco":

> You remember, though perhaps you don't, that once upon a time men harvested tobacco by hand. There was a time when folk were bound together in a community, as one, and helped one person this day and that day another, and another the next, to see that everyone got his tobacco crop in the barn each week, and that it was fired and cured and taken to a packhouse to be graded and eventually sent to market. But this was once upon a time. (254)

The section continues, lamenting the tragic loss of this idyllic way of life. But this section is already and inescapably in dialogue with the suicide that immediately precedes it. Because of this dialogue, the "time when folk were bound together in a community, as one," is exposed even as it is being constructed. The mythical, pastoral wholeness of this "community" is ripped apart as surely as "the bullet did break the skin of his forehead, pierce the cranium, slice through the cortex and cerebellum, irreparably bruising the cerebrum and medulla oblongata, and emerge from the back of the skull, all with a wet and lightning crack. This did happen" (253). Mikhail Bakhtin argues that "sexuality is almost always incorporated into the idyll only in sublimated form," since the idyllic form in literature demands a unity of time and place that smooths over differences and avoids the "naked realistic aspect" of life (226). Kenan's juxtaposition here of idyll and suicide foregrounds the murderous consequences of such a sublimation. Kenan himself insists, in a recent interview, "It seemed, and it seems . . . that for that community to change they have to understand the devastation that they're wreaking on certain people" (in Hunt, 416). In the end, Horace's story highlights the need for transformation of this community on the margins of the queer world. Kenan's shift to second-person narration in the conclusion further emphasizes this need: although "you remember" what this community was like, you should not, after *A Visitation of Spirits*, be able to consider this or any community without a queer sense that something is amiss.

The "Requiem for Tobacco" section that concludes *A Visitation of Spirits* is not the first time in the text that the narrator addresses the reader directly. The very first section of the novel—"December 8, 1985 / 8:45 A.M." (3)—concludes with a similar account of a "time when folk were bound together in a community, as one." This section, "ADVENT (or The Beginning of the End)" (6), describes a community coming together for a hog killing and, like "Requiem for Tobacco," includes direct appeals to the reader:

> You've been to a hog killing before, haven't you? They don't happen as often as they once did. People simply don't raise hogs like they used to.
>
> Once, in this very North Carolina town, practically everyone with a piece of land kept a hog or two, at least. And come the cold months of December and January folk would begin to butcher and salt and smoke and pickle. In those days a hog was a mighty good thing to have, to see you through the winter. But you know all this, don't you? (6)

Nostalgia for "those days" permeates the section, yet the jeering tone of the second-person appeals undercuts any sense of security that the nostalgia might have brought. As in "Requiem for Tobacco," the second-person narration taunts "you," instilling a queer sense of uneasiness, suggesting that something is wrong with this idyllic communal picture and that "you" are somehow complicit in the problem.

Everyone in the community has an expected role to play in the hog killing, as they do at the end of the text, in "Requiem for Tobacco." Women and men alike know their place, and each group entrusts to the other the socialization of girls and boys, respectively. "Advent" is associated with the beginning of a new cycle, and this Advent is no exception. Through shared and recurrent rituals such as this hog killing, the socialization of the community's youth into fixed gender roles commences:

> Beneath the shed, the women would be busy, with knives, with grinders, with spoons and forks; the greasy tables littered with salts and peppers and spices, hunks of meat, bloody and in pans to be made into sausages, pans of cooked liver to be made into liver pudding. Remember the odor of cooking meats and spices, so thick, so heady? . . . Some older man will give a young boy a gun, perhaps, and instruct him not to be afraid, to take his time, to aim straight. The men will all look at one another and the boy with a sense of mutual pride, as the man goes over to the gate and with some effort moves the three slats that close off the hogpen. (8)

The boy *cum* man then takes his gun and slaughters the hog, whose sacrifice will guarantee the continued vitality of this community and its rituals.

"But," as the narrator says, "I'm sure you've witnessed all this, of course" (8). And in a sense, this community has indeed witnessed such a "sacrifice" before: even though Horace has not yet been introduced into the text, chronologically this hog killing (December 8, 1985) *follows* Horace's suicide (April 30, 1984). Kenan's manipulation of time makes each of these scenes echo the other; "you" should hear echoes of the hog killing in the suicide/idyll at the end of the novel, but since the suicide actually predates the hog killing, the latter already contains echoes of the former. The hog killing is, after all, not the first time this community has "instructed" a young boy to "aim straight" and has given him a gun.

Once the suicide/idyll is put into conversation with the hog killing, it is impossible not to suspect that Horace's death, like the hog's, is a sacrifice carried out for the "good of the community."[16] That is, this community can exist only in the sort of (heterosexual) pastoral wholeness represented in "ADVENT" and "Requiem for Tobacco," through disavowal or outright elimination of some of its members. The hog and Horace both play a sacrificial role for this community, and the passages detailing their individual moments of death underscore this similarity of purpose:

> The hog rears up on its hind legs like a horse, bucking, tossing its head, but only once, twice. It seems to land miraculously on its front legs, but only for a split second. It topples, hitting the ground with a thud, and lets out a sound that you might call a death rattle—all in a matter of seconds. Its eyes fix intently on nothing. (9)

> His entire body convulsed several times; it excreted urine. Defecated. The tongue hung out of the mouth and during the convulsions was clamped down upon, releasing blood to be mixed with the ropes of saliva stringing down. His heartbeat slowly decreased in pressure and intensity, soon coming to a halt; the arteries, veins, and capillaries slowly collapsed. The pupils of his eyes, now tainted in a film of pink, stopped dilating, resting like huge drops of ink surrounded by brown liquid in a pool of milk. Finally the eyes themselves rolled back, staring up, as though examining the sun through the canopy of tree limbs. (253–54)

After both deaths, the community is once again free to celebrate a mythical wholeness.

Kenan's placement of the events on December 8 and on April 29–30, respectively, corroborates this reading of each as a sacrifice intended for the good of the community. In Christian mythology, Advent is the beginning, in early December, of the church year. Like the hog killing, it is supposedly a happy time, when Christians celebrate the arrival of the one who is born to die so that the community can live. The "salvation" of the Christian community is contingent on the death of Christ, and in *A Visitation of Spirits*, Kenan uses this sacrificial idea to sharply indict the Christian community of Tims Creek, North Carolina. Nonetheless, as with Kenan's use of *Go Tell It on the Mountain* and *A Christmas Carol*, this is no simple appropriation of someone else's story. Horace's very name—Horace "Cross"—links him to the "sacrificial lamb" of Christianity, but Kenan repeats even the Christian story with a difference: although April 30, 1984, did indeed fall during the Easter season ("This," as the narrator of *A Visitation of Spirits* might say, "is a fact"), this Easter is characterized not by a resurrection but rather by a graphic and apparently irreversible suicide. Horace Cross might die for this community's sins, but—it would seem—he does not rise again.

Transformations (II): James Malachai Greene

Through both the hog killing and the tobacco harvest, it is presumably the reader who recognizes the disavowal of difference on which this community is founded; the community itself simply proceeds with its celebration of mythical wholeness, oblivious to the violence its rituals demand and effect. In fact, the reader's transformation is virtually contingent on the community's nontransformation: because the community is unable to adapt and is consequently responsible for Horace's death, readers learn to view such communities askance, to perceive something queer in their very disavowal of queerness. Yet analyzing Horace as simply dead fails to account for death's ironic lack of finality in the Kenan corpus, and understanding the community as simply untransformed disregards how Horace, even in death, ultimately does become the sort of trickster figure Gates finds in the Signifying Monkey tales in particular and in the African American literary tradition in general. At the end of the novel, Horace—apparently "possessed" by a visitation of spirits—emerges from the woods and shoots himself in front of his cousin Jimmy Greene. Jimmy, who at the time of Horace's suicide is both the minister at the First Baptist Church of Tims Creek and the first black principal of Tims Creek Elementary

School, had earlier attempted to transform Horace, explaining to him that being gay is "wrong" (113). In the end, however, it is Jimmy who is transformed by Horace, and since he is the head of two community institutions, the ramifications of this transformation are far-reaching. The transformations Horace initiates are always incomplete (or, in the language of the previous chapter, "permanently partial"), but they are simultaneously inevitable and ongoing: the closet that the regime of sameness requires and constructs can never fully contain the "visitation of (queer) spirits" its exclusionary logic unleashes.

The very title of Kenan's second work suggests that we look carefully at "death" in his works. *Let the Dead Bury Their Dead* is a collection of twelve stories, most of them once again set in Tims Creek, North Carolina. The collection takes its title from Christ's injunction, in Matthew 8:22, to a would-be disciple: "But Jesus said unto him, Follow me; and let the dead bury their dead" (KJV). Christ's words in this passage are simply a poetic way of saying "drop everything and look to the future with me" or "put what's dead and gone behind you." In Kenan's rewriting of the Christian injunction, however, such an interpretation is no longer possible; the "dead" in Kenan's work tend not to *stay* dead. In both *A Visitation of Spirits* and *Let the Dead Bury Their Dead*, the dead are constantly coming back, in various and perturbing ways, to haunt and disrupt the present. In fact, the very first story of Kenan's collection underscores the futility of attempts to "let the dead bury their dead."

"Clarence *and* the Dead (*And* What Do They Tell You, Clarence? *And* the Dead Speak to Clarence)," the first selection in *Let the Dead Bury Their Dead*, is the story of a young boy who conveys cryptic, unsettling messages to the friends and neighbors who come to visit his grandparents' home. What is especially peculiar about these particular messages is that they come from people in the community who have long since died. For example, Clarence tells Emma Chaney, whose mother died long before Clarence was born, "Your mama says Joe Hattan is stepping out on you with that strumpet Viola Stokes" (5). Clarence and his "queer knowledge" (12) wreak havoc on the comfortable security of the present-day Tims Creek community, reversing people's assumptions about their pasts, their families, their marriages. Anyone who wanted to abide by the biblical dictum is effectively precluded from doing so: "Clarence told people things a four-year-old boy ain't had no business knowing the language for, let alone the circumstances around them. All from people dead five, six, ten, twenty, and more years" (8).

Hence, even though I have just argued that there is no resurrection in *A Visitation of Spirits*, we would do well to view the apparent "irreversibility" of Horace's suicide with suspicion. Granted, Horace doesn't return to Tims Creek in exactly the same way as the dead in Clarence's story, but I contend that he nonetheless wreaks havoc on the (heterosexual) stability of the community. Ultimately, Horace does become the sort of trickster figure Gates locates throughout the African American literary tradition, "surfacing when we least expect him, at a crossroads of destiny" (*Signifying Monkey*, 64). Like the dead in Clarence's story, Horace (re)surfaces in order to disrupt the complacent security of Tims Creek, to render unstable the binary oppositions (center/margin, clean/unclean, etc.) that ground the life of this community. And because Kenan relates *A Visitation of Spirits* in a nonlinear fashion, with the events of April 29–30, 1984 (the day of Horace's suicide), interwoven with the events of December 8, 1985, Horace's (comedic) postsuicide trickster role wreaks havoc even as the (tragic) events leading to his death are teleologically represented.

The first and apparently unlikely power relation that Horace reverses is the "opposition" between the "ghosts" and "Ebenezer Scrooge." As I have suggested throughout this chapter, Kenan's novel is a complex signification on Dickens's famous story, with Horace cast in the role of Scrooge. As early as the epigraph from *A Christmas Carol*, however, there is evidence that Horace has been miscast:

> "Are spirits' lives so short?" asked Scrooge.
> "My life upon this globe is very brief," replied the Ghost. "It ends to-night."
> "To-night!" cried Scrooge.
> "To-night at midnight. Hark! The time is drawing near." (*A Visitation of Spirits*, epigraph page)

The epigraph introduces Kenan's text and thereby suggests that *A Visitation of Spirits* will be some sort of retelling of *A Christmas Carol*. At the same time, this epigraph complicates any easy equivalency between Dickens's characters and Kenan's. Although Horace's whirlwind journey through past, present, and future apparently links him to Scrooge, the epigraph belies such a reading, linking him instead to the spirit. After all, it is Horace, in *A Visitation of Spirits*, whose "life upon this globe is very brief," and at the stroke of midnight on April 30, 1984, it is Horace's life that rapidly heads toward its conclusion.[17]

Queer Locations/Queer Transformations

As the text continues, Horace's metaphorical link to Scrooge is obvious; nonetheless, his metonymic link to the ghosts (which, since it is introduced in the epigraph, actually precedes the metaphorical link to Scrooge) continues to surface when we least expect it. For instance, the hog killing of the first section ends with the assertion "But the ghosts of those times are stubborn; and though the hog stalls are empty, a herd can be heard, trampling the grasses and flowers and fancy bushes, trampling the foreign trees of the new families, living in their new homes. A ghostly herd waiting to be butchered" (10). As I have said, Horace is linked to the hog in that both serve as sacrifices for the good of the community. This passage replays that connection, underscoring as well how both disrupt the idyllic stability of the community, "trampling the grasses and flowers and fancy bushes . . . living in their new homes." Beyond that, however, the linkage here of hogs and ghosts extends the metonymic chain: the ghosts call to mind the hogs who call to mind Horace who calls to mind the ghosts. And if this were not enough, the next section graphically links both the hogs and the ghosts to Horace. This section, the first in which Horace appears, opens with an ellipsis: ". . . What to become?" (11). The ellipsis serves a dual function here. On the surface, it stands in for the process of thought Horace is going through as he decides to turn himself into a bird. On another level, however, the ellipsis serves as a visual link to what has immediately preceded, and Horace is once again connected to both the hogs and the ghosts.

The identification of Horace with the ghosts, as opposed to identification with Scrooge, is crucial for understanding Horace's reemergence as a trickster in *A Visitation of Spirits*, since this identification means that, in the end, he may not be so much the *object* as the *agent* of transformation. (Scrooge's ghosts, after all, are responsible for his own radical transformation.) Perhaps, then, we are wrong to read Horace as simply "dead" after his suicide, despite the fact that his death is detailed with such graphic and scientific exactness. Perhaps—to repeat (with a difference) the Gates quotation with which I began this chapter—*A Visitation of Spirits* is *not* so much about "a brilliant tormented homosexual, Horace, who commits suicide" (in Rowell, 454). Perhaps such a description particularly overlooks the cryptic pronouncement by the narrator that concludes the suicide scene: "Ifs and maybes and weres and perhapses are of no use in this case. The facts are enough, unless they too are subject to doubt" (*A Visitation of Spirits*, 254). Indeed, the "fact" of Horace's complete annihilation should very well be subject to doubt, given how Horace—even after his suicide—

continues to "live" as the Signifying Monkey *cum* queer agent of transformation, "haunting" the community in general and Jimmy in particular.

Jimmy's story unfolds in two ways over the course of *A Visitation of Spirits*. First, he is one of the main characters in the December 8, 1985, sections of the novel. These sections ostensibly focus on Jimmy's journey, with his Aunt Ruth and Uncle Zeke (two elderly members of the Cross clan), to visit a cousin who is in the hospital in Fayetteville, North Carolina. More precisely, however, these sections focus on the internal monologues of various characters as they sort out their conflicts with and connections to other members of the family (this is Kenan's answer to *Go Tell It on the Mountain*'s "Prayers of the Saints" section).

Second, and more important, Jimmy's character comes out in all his complexity in three personal "Confessions" sections. These confessions are not dated, but since Horace's suicide haunts each of them, they must be considered as written after Horace's death and are probably roughly contemporaneous with the events of late 1985. Overall, the novel is divided into five sections, each of which is then divided into even smaller sections ("December 8, 1985"; "April 29, 1984"; etc.). Three of the five main sections open with these "Confessions" from Jimmy; the final section opens with Horace's own "Confessions" (which I analyzed in the previous section). As is often the case with events in *A Visitation of Spirits*, Horace's confessions actually *predate* Jimmy's, despite the fact that they are not included until the novel's final section. Of course, there is no way Jimmy could have seen Horace's "Confessions"; as we know, Horace burned his autobiography in frustration. Nonetheless, Jimmy's own writings betray an ironic anxiety about Horace's influence. The very heading of Jimmy's text is, stylistically, a direct echo of Horace's own: "Horace Thomas Cross: Confessions" (245); "James Malachai Greene: Confessions" (31, 107, 171). Hence, even though Jimmy could not possibly have read Horace's text, Horace's story appears to have profoundly influenced the way Jimmy documents his own private thoughts.

There is at least one major difference between Horace's confessions and Jimmy's. Although Horace's "Confessions" section is an extended prose meditation on his own life, Jimmy's three "Confessions" sections are not—so to speak—straight prose. Each of Jimmy's "Confessions" sections is interrupted by a short script, complete with stage directions. Significantly, each of these dramatic episodes is a re-presentation of a critical moment in *Horace's* life: the first sketches out the strange conversation between

Jimmy and Horace a few minutes before the suicide; the second relates an earlier scene, in June 1983, when Horace first "comes out" to Jimmy, looking to his cousin for pastoral guidance; the third, later in 1983, replays a Thanksgiving dinner where Horace offends the entire family by showing up with a pierced ear. Although "confessions" tend to signify uncensored, "unmediated" prose meditations for some reason, Jimmy cannot face his most intense, gay-identified memories of Horace so directly. These memories demand another form; Jimmy desires or needs to distance himself from them. Perhaps Jimmy indulges a fantasy that these dramatic passages somehow position him on the outside, passively observing events onstage from a comfortable seat in the audience. Nonetheless, these passages are contained within his "autobiographical" sections and are thus framed by highly personal revelations of Jimmy's weaknesses and fears. No matter how much Jimmy would like to distance himself from these memories, they are implicated in his most private and personal attempts to define himself.

These dramatic interruptions are early indications of how Jimmy has been and continues to be transformed by Horace, who, in the role of trickster, delights in reversing the received order of things. In particular, these dramatic passages, and Jimmy's "Confessions" in general, illustrate how decidedly unstable the heterosexual/homosexual binary has become for Jimmy. Kenan's revision of Baldwin helps illustrate this point: if Horace can be compared to John Grimes, then Jimmy can be compared to Elisha, the young religious figure whom John admires and counts on for spiritual guidance. Yet to the degree that identity in *A Visitation of Spirits*, as opposed to *Go Tell It on the Mountain*, is more explicitly homosexual for Horace, so too is identity less convincingly heterosexual for Jimmy. Of course, Elisha's performance of heterosexuality is a tough act to follow: Elisha is, after all, a spectacular heterosexual, in the sense that the church makes a spectacle of him and Ella Mae, so convinced are they of the couple's (hetero)sexual designs. But whereas in *Go Tell It on the Mountain* the community is convinced in advance of Elisha's heterosexual prowess (Elisha is, in a way, *too* heterosexual), in *A Visitation of Spirits* Jimmy has trouble convincing anyone, including himself, that he is unequivocally heterosexual; instead, in each of Jimmy's "Confessions," Horace's haunting of Jimmy foregrounds the irresolvable instability of the heterosexual/ homosexual binary which Jimmy thought he was on top of. Sedgwick's analysis of the ironies of *Billy Budd* is apropos here: "The death of the text's homosexual marks . . . not a terminus but an initiation . . . into the narrative circulation of male desire" (*Epistemology*, 99–100). For Jimmy, this "initiation" transforms his life on two levels, private and public, and since Jimmy is representative of the larger community, the transformation of his public role ensures that, in the end, Horace's story does indeed set into play a transformation of this community on the supposed "margins" of the queer world.

The ending of Jimmy's first "Confessions" section serves as a good introduction to the ways in which Horace, after his suicide, haunts Jimmy's private life. The dramatic interruption of this particular section replays the conversation between the two on the morning of Horace's death. After observing this drama, Jimmy returns again to his private thoughts. These thoughts are decidedly restless, however, and are made more so by their placement beneath Jimmy's recollection of his earlier conversation with Horace:

(Jimmy's eyes grow wide with horror. He swallows.)
JIMMY: I'm supposed to believe my cousin has been possessed? By a demon?
HORACE: Yeah. Something like that.

> I don't prepare elaborate meals for myself. Many is the night that I have eaten from a can. On the nights that I have no church business, no deacon board meetings, no prayer meetings, no auxiliary meetings or trustee board meetings, I try to read. I still enjoy Augustine and Erasmus. Maybe Freud, or Jung, or Foucault. Black history: Franklin, Quarles, Fanon. Occasionally fiction. But invariably I wind up asleep after about ninety minutes, only to awaken without fail around eleven o'clock to watch the late news. Then it's back to bed, which in many ways seems the object of leaving bed in the first place. (43–44)

Call me queer, but the question "Why is Jimmy reading Foucault?" is too tempting to pass up here. After Horace's death, Jimmy clearly has trouble focusing his attention; consequently, he drifts from activity to activity. His scurrying from text to text, in particular, comes across as a restless search for "meaning." Horace's undead intrusion into Jimmy's private life, however, has destabilized the secure meanings around which Jimmy's life was organized. The inclusion of Foucault on Jimmy's reading list especially highlights the process of transformation that is at work in Jimmy.[18] And particularly in the context of a list beginning with Freud, it is difficult not to imagine that Jimmy is turning to *The History of Sexuality* for answers. The imagination runs first, perhaps, to some of Foucault's more famous formulations:

> The nineteenth-century homosexual became a personage, a past, a case history, and a childhood, in addition to being a type of life, a life form, and a morphology, with an indiscreet anatomy and possibly a mysterious physiology. Nothing that went into his total composition was unaffected by his sexuality. . . . It was a secret that always gave itself away. . . . The sodomite had been a temporary aberration; the homosexual was now a species. (Foucault, 43)

But why limit Jimmy? Perhaps he has long since mastered the basic texts of Foucault and is now reading, in the French original, some of the more obscure interviews. The possibilities are titillating:

> I should like to say "it is necessary to work increasingly at being gay," to place oneself in a dimension where the sexual choices that one makes are present and have their effects on the ensemble of our life. I should like to say also that sexual choices must be at the same time creators of ways of life. To be gay signifies that these choices diffuse themselves across the entire life; it is also a certain manner of refusing the modes of life offered; it is to make a sexual choice the impetus for a change of existence. (Foucault, qtd. in Cohen, "Foucauldian Necrologies," 91) [19]

Of course, the Foucauldian fantasies I have conjured up for Jimmy here are not intended to name, definitively, the specific text or texts Jimmy may be reading.[20] Quite the contrary: my intent is not to have the final say about what Jimmy's experiences mean but rather to foreground the ways in which Horace, as trickster, has set into motion an inescapable play of meaning, so that the very *impossibility* of fixing the specific text effectively produces *possibilities* in Jimmy that he has, until now, consistently (and homophobically) disavowed. Hence neither of the Foucault selections above should be taken as my vote for what Jimmy is reading, as if I could somehow fix Kenan's intention. Likewise, I do not intend here to label Jimmy—in a minoritized sense—as "gay."[21] Instead, I propose that Jimmy's own attempt to fix meaning has redounded on him, destabilizing particularly the heterosexual securities around which his life (and the life of the community) is organized. Before the suicide, gay identity/desire was "safely" embodied by Horace, who was—à la Foucault—a personage, a past, a case history, and the like. After the suicide, Jimmy wants to maintain some sort of security by "containing" gay identity/desire in the dramatic supplements to his "Confessions." Yet, immediately after coming out of one of these dramatic interruptions, it is clear that Jimmy is unable to leave queerness behind; as Sedgwick suggests, "In the wake of the homosexual, the wake incessantly produced since first there *were* homosexuals, every human relation is pulled into its shining representational furrow" (*Epistemology*, 128). In this case, Jimmy attempts to leave Horace behind in the dramatic supplement, only to stumble into Foucault.

Furthermore, even *within* the Foucault passages I have included above, a movement from a minoritized and contained gay identity to a more pervasive, inescapable queerness is reproduced: what is, in the first passage, a discrete and embodied identity, located in others, has become, in the second, more free-floating, "diffus[ing] across the entire life." One of the *Oxford English Dictionary*'s definitions of "spirit" is "a particular character, disposition, or temper existing in, *pervading*, or animating a person or set of persons" (emphasis mine). In this sense, then, perhaps "a visitation of spirits" refers less to the ghostly crew that leads Horace on his whirlwind journey than to the queer spirit pervading Jimmy's life after Horace's death. Ironically, it is Jimmy, not Horace, who seems to have "a secret that always gives itself away." In the end, Jimmy's attempts to "contain" a homosexual are undone by the juxtaposition (or is it the coming together?) of Horace and Foucault. The queerness Jimmy is trying to "fix" may very well be within himself.

An episode from one of the other dramatic supplements to Jimmy's "Confessions" illustrates even more clearly how freely queer meanings circulate beyond Jimmy's control, despite his best efforts to contain them. It is Horace's last Thanksgiving, November 1983. Horace arrives onstage late, as the Reverend Barden, the family's guest, is praying over the food. Jonnie Mae (Jimmy's grandmother and Horace's great-aunt) scolds the boy lightly for being late, but when she realizes he has pierced his ear, her scolding becomes severe. She drops a spoon loudly into a dish of corn, and everyone at the table looks up in horror at Horace. The stage directions explain that "JIMMY *seems bewildered by the reaction of the women*" (183). Nonetheless, Jimmy has trouble finding the appropriate language to counter his aunts' and grandmother's reactions:

JONNIE MAE: (to ZEKE): Uh-huh. You see, Zeke? You see? What did I tell you? Now it starts this way, but how will it end? *(Stands.)* No better sense

Queer Locations/Queer Transformations

than to go on and follow whatever them white fools do. You'd follow them
to hell, wouldn't you? I—

RUTHESTER *(moving to comfort her):* Mamma, it ain't that bad. He just—

JONNIE MAE: He *just* pierced his ear. Like some little girl. Like one of them
perverts.

JIMMY: Mamma, it's really not that big a deal. Boys pierce their ears nowadays all the time. It's not thought of as—(184)

Can you say "gay"? For some reason, Jimmy can not; but then again, he
can't entirely *not* say it, either. Certainly, everyone in this scene is having
trouble finding the right words, but it is to Jimmy, more than anyone else,
that a trace of queer meaning attaches. Indeed, the very unspeakability of
the word (and Jimmy's is the only fragmented sentence here that could
possibly be completed by a single word) speaks queerness.

Moreover, although at the time Jimmy argues that "it's really not that
big a deal," Horace and his earring come back here to haunt Jimmy's
private confessions. In *The Signifying Monkey,* Gates traces a "signifying
chain" from the slave narrative of Ukawsaw Gronniosaw to Ralph Ellison's
Invisible Man. In Gronniosaw's narrative, this signifying chain is a literal
gold chain that serves as a marker for the African heritage Gronniosaw
seeks to discard; in Ellison, the literal chain from Brother Tarp's days
on the prison gang "signifies a heap more" and helps Ellison's narrator
"remember what we're really fighting against" (*Signifying Monkey,* 135–
36). In Kenan's novel, Gates's signifying chain becomes a signifying earring, a marker of both a particular "cultural heritage" and—in an ironic
inversion of Ellison—the disruptive force that Jimmy and the others are
"really fighting against."

The dash that signifies the presence-absence of gayness in Jimmy's
speech is a graphic representation of the queer meanings that, once again,
Jimmy is unable to contain "safely" in the dramatic supplements to his
"Confessions." The play of meaning that Horace initiates again spills
over into the prose sections of these "Confessions," wresting authoritative
control away from Jimmy. Ironically, Horace's conspirator in this disruptive project is Jimmy's wife, Anne, whose death comes a year or two before
Horace's. Jimmy often invokes the two characters at the same point in his
narrative ("I sit on the porch and wait for the sun. All the while pondering
dreams of Anne. And Horace" [36]), and his memories of Anne are often
as disruptive as his memories of Horace. Indeed, although one might
expect that his wife would help stabilize Jimmy's heterosexual identity, it

is with Anne that the inevitable failure of that identity is often most pronounced.

The possibility of failure is evident in Jimmy's recollections of the couple's first years together:

> I met Anne during the second semester of my sophomore year. I didn't sleep with her for almost two years; bedding her had not been my original goal. She fascinated me. . . .
>
> One autumn day, one of the few days in which there were no meetings for her to rush to, she turned to me as we stood beneath a huge cottonwood tree on campus and asked, "Why haven't you tried to screw me?"
>
> I didn't know whether to laugh, cry, or just stare. She had light brown eyes and sometimes she focused them with such unbridled sincerity that they belied her canniness. I kissed her long and hard.
>
> "So you aren't a faggot?"
>
> I chuckled.
>
> "Good."
>
> The first time she took me into her bed I was impotent. "Are you sure you're not a faggot?" she asked. We laughed at the entire situation and went out for Chinese food. I never had that problem again. (174, 175–76)

Jimmy never had "that problem" with Anne again, but as this passage makes clear, he can not seem to shake that *other* problem: even when he does not speak them, gay meanings attach themselves to Jimmy. Indeed, as with the dash in the Thanksgiving scene, the chuckle and the laugh speak most explicitly in their very refusal to speak. Once again Jimmy cannot say (he is) "gay," but then again, he can't entirely *not* say it, either. Or, more precisely, Jimmy relies on a (sexual) performance to solidify what he cannot convincingly put into words: his gendered heterosexual identity. As Butler might put it, "The abiding gendered self [is] . . . structured by repeated acts that seek to approximate the ideal of a substantial ground of identity, but which, in their occasional *dis*continuity, reveal the temporal and contingent groundlessness of this 'ground' " (*Gender Trouble*, 141). In this sense, the chuckle and the laugh might be seen as only part of a more general laugh *track* for this inevitable heterosexual sitcom, and Jimmy and Anne's affair here may be just one more episode in which heterosexuality attempts to cover its all-too-obvious discontinuities.

Anne has joined with Horace, then, in a monstrous, unnatural coupling that re-members the stable heterosexual meanings of Jimmy's life for

Queer Locations/Queer Transformations

him and flaunts the impossibility of embodying normative heterosexual identities. The opening of Jimmy's third and final "Confessions" confirms Anne in this role. Jimmy's narration (at this point, a rhapsody about Anne's physical beauty and about her hold on Jimmy's life) is interrupted by a series of direct challenges from Anne: "Look at me. . . . What do you see? . . . Do you really see me? . . . Me? . . . Do you? . . . Do you even want to, really? . . . Are you even capable?" (171–72). Like Anne's suggestion that he is a "faggot," these challenges push Jimmy toward (hetero)sexual assertion, and he concludes: "The metaphysics called it a little death. I think they were right" (172). Yet heterosex for Jimmy is never quite as much fun as it is for John Donne, and Jimmy's reiteration of the metaphysical poets' metaphor for sex is not without irony; in what way, exactly, does Jimmy "die a little death" every time he is with Anne? The next paragraph opens with Jimmy's confession "I have lied. To myself" (172), and although Jimmy has ostensibly moved on to a new topic, it is difficult not to see this admission as a commentary on what has immediately preceded: Anne's "Are you even capable?" and Jimmy's defensive answer in the form of a sexual performance.

All of Jimmy's sexual memories, then, suggest that he is "in the closet"—not the gay closet, exactly, but a closet of crisis, what Sedgwick might label "the closet of, simply, the homosexual secret—the closet of imagining a homosexual secret" (*Epistemology*, 205). This queer possibility—never substantiated—lurks behind all of Jimmy's recollections. For example, he writes of the wild adventures he had in college before meeting Anne:

> I slept with anything that was willing. I got drunk almost every weekend of my freshman year, many times during the week as well . . . my only regret being that my aunts and my grandmother never seemed to suspect that I was a hypocrite, a liar. For when I came home I still read the Scriptures in church and taught Bible school, only to return to school and recruit the first co-ed who gave me a willing glance. I realize that this was the true sin. (174)

As usual, Jimmy's "double life" here is not *necessarily* gay; his "co-eds," after all, effectively gender that which is so ambiguous in "anything that was willing." Yet the "secret" that is produced by Jimmy's closet is never definitely *not* a homosexual secret, "so permeative has the suffusing stain of homo/heterosexual crisis" been to crises of masculine definition more generally (Sedgwick, *Epistemology*, 72–73). Indeed, like the dash or the chuckle or the laugh, Jimmy's "closet" in this memory takes on queer meanings not because it specifically articulates such possibilities but rather because the metaphor of the closet that he implicitly invokes can never entirely *dis*articulate them.

Moreover, Jimmy's prose memories are always read in the context of those "other" memories, the memories of Horace, which he can never completely contain. Horace, as trickster, ensures that queerness can never be entirely cleaned out of any of Jimmy's closets, and the one dramatic supplement to Jimmy's "Confessions" that I have not yet discussed demonstrates this most clearly. In this scene, Jimmy is confronted by Horace's explicitly "gay" closet and, in his ministerial role, confidently admonishes the boy, "You know as well as I what the Bible says" (113). Despite his pastoral assurance that homosexuality is "wrong," however, Jimmy is again unable to keep traces of gay meaning from attaching to himself. Furthermore, this scene, in turn, transforms how straight we read Jimmy's other private memories; in particular, "anything that was willing" is thrown, decidedly, into gay relief. This time, the semantic marker for the presence-absence of gayness is not the dash, the chuckle, the laugh, or the "double life," but, well, ". . . you know":

HORACE *(quickly):* I think I'm a homosexual.

JIMMY *(smiling, puts his hand on Horace's shoulder):* Horace, we've all done a little . . . you know . . . experimenting. It's a part of growing up. It's . . . well, it's kind of important to—
HORACE: But it's not experimenting. I like men. I don't like women. There's something wrong with me.
JIMMY: Horace, really. I have reason to believe it's just a phase. I went through a period where I . . . you know, experimented.
HORACE: Did you enjoy it?
JIMMY *(slightly stunned):* En . . . Enjoy it? Well . . . I . . . you know. Well, the physical pleasure was . . . I guess pleasant. I really don't remember.
HORACE: Did you ever fall in love with a man?
JIMMY: Fall in love? No. *(Laughs.)* Oh, Horace. Don't be so somber. Really. I think this is something that will pass. I've known you all your life. You're perfectly normal. (112–13)

"Like me" is the implicit subtext here—"You're perfectly normal, *like me*." Horace, however, reverses this compulsion toward sameness, substituting instead what Kobena Mercer has called the "challenge of sameness"

Queer Locations/Queer Transformations

("1968," 427).[22] Maybe, just maybe, Jimmy, *you* are like *me:* Did you enjoy it (as I have enjoyed it)? Did you ever fall in love with a man (as I have fallen in love with a man)? In spite of Jimmy's best efforts, Horace transforms Jimmy's understanding of himself, and after Horace's suicide, that transformation grows even more pronounced. "I have never lost my fear of the dead," Jimmy admits in one of his "Confessions" sections. "No matter how many funerals I attend, perhaps no matter how old I get, I will fear the dead. In my dreams the dead rise" (189).

The challenge of sameness embodied by Horace transforms Jimmy's private life; Horace destabilizes the heteronormative laws around which Jimmy's life is organized. This transformation, however, has far-reaching ramifications: Jimmy, as minister, is representative of and for this community. And although Jimmy feels that this community could never accept Horace's "deviation," he nonetheless writes that Horace's "reason for existing, it would seem, was for the salvation of his people" (188). Consequently, the transformation Horace brings about is not merely the private transformation of Jimmy. If Horace exists "for the salvation of his people," then Jimmy is the minister entrusted to bring Horace's message to the rest of the community.

One of Jimmy's professors at seminary inadvertently prepares him for this public role by facilitating the connection between Horace and Jimmy. The professor's name is Philip Schnider: "We called him Rabbi. He got a kick out of it too, he being one of the rarest of birds, a Christian Jew" (31). This unorthodox character—the very first person introduced into Jimmy's "Confessions"—tells Jimmy, "You, Greene, will make a great theologian" (33). Rabbi's opinion does not come from his belief that Jimmy has the ability to adhere to a strict code of conduct or to expound how others ought to live their lives. Instead, Rabbi's opinion comes from his observation of Jimmy's "Curiosity": "Curiosity with a capital C. Understand what I'm saying? This is a gift, now. Don't get me wrong. There are plenty of guys here who've got curiosity. But they don't have it with a capital C. Understand? They're bright, sure. Some maybe brighter than you. . . . [But] they don't have desire. A *real* desire. Few people nowadays do" (33). Jimmy can not understand what Rabbi means by this cryptic observation, and Rabbi's subsequent attempts to elaborate do little to clear up confusion. Yet, later in the same "Confessions" section, Jimmy returns to Rabbi's words. Thinking, as usual, about Anne and Horace, Jimmy concludes, "Anne was not a romantic; I am. So was Horace. But he had something more, that damned curiosity . . . with a capital C" (36). Suddenly, what was so enigmatic to Jimmy earlier exactly describes his connection to Horace. Apparently, after Horace's suicide, the transformation Jimmy undergoes enables him to understand what had only baffled him before.

"Curiosity" and "desire" are not ingredients that normally go into the making of a Tims Creek minister; desire, in fact, because of the unlikely, unsanctioned, and queer connections it affirms, is usually equated with sin in this community. Still, although Rabbi never clearly explains what he means by these concepts, something that might be called "Curiosity" or "*real* desire" indeed appears to fuel Jimmy's ministry, particularly after Horace's death. After the dramatic episode detailing Horace's conflict with the family over the earring, for instance, Jimmy returns to his prose "Confessions" with more questions than answers:

> [Horace] didn't quite know who he was. That, I don't fully understand, for they had told him, taught him from the cradle on. I guess they didn't reckon the world they were sending him into was different from the world they had conquered, a world peopled with new and hateful monsters that exacted a different price.
>
> What has happened to us? Can I cry out like the prophet Jonah and ask God to guide my hand and direct me toward the proper remedy? Once, oh once, this beautiful, strong, defiant, glorious group could wrestle the world down, unshackle themselves, part seas, walk on water, rise on the winds. What happened? Why are we now sick and dying? . . . How, Lord? How? How can we defend ourselves and grow strong again? How can we regain the power to lift up our heads and sing? When will the Host of Hosts visit us with favor and strength? (188–89)

Behind this string of questions is a desperate curiosity about why the world is as it is, and an urgent desire for it to be better, freer, more loving. The group had assumed that the "proper remedy" was expulsion of the "abomination." This expulsion was to guarantee a return to mythical wholeness. Jimmy realizes at this point that such attempts at "purification" actually guarantee not health and wholeness but sickness and death. "Salvation" will not entail securing the distinction between "clean" and "unclean" and expelling the latter. Instead, Jimmy realizes, these fixed and exclusionary understandings of salvation are precisely the problem. "He was a son of this community," Jimmy writes of Horace, "more than most" (188). With this simple recognition, Jimmy questions and reverses the community's easy assumptions that queerness belongs elsewhere.

Questions such as these were far from the mind of the Reverend Barden, the minister who preceded Jimmy. Rev. Barden had only answers, no questions. I have already mentioned, for example, his unequivocal use of Paul's letter to the Romans to condemn homosexuality. In the same sermon, Barden turns Jimmy's questions about weakness into a quick and easy answer:

> "I can't look at evil and turn my back. It saddens me. . . . And you know what it is, don't you? You know what causes it? . . . Why a weak spirit. Ain't nothing more. Can't say the folks don't know, cause they do. But it's like the writer said another time: The spirit is willing—O my Jesus, help me this morning—but the flesh is weak. Ain't nothing else but weak-willed people. What else is gone cause this mess, children?" . . . Go head, Reverend, and preach now. (79)

To Barden—and the congregation, which is more than willing to jump on the bandwagon of moral superiority—the answer to the world's ills lies in overcoming "weakness." Success in such an effort will be measured by the extent to which one can stand apart from and condemn those who fail to live up to a legalistic, heteronormative code of conduct. To a transformed Jimmy, in contrast, this moral code is the very *mark* of weakness, and his searching questions signal a queer desire to move away from such an impoverished worldview.

After Horace's death, this shift is most apparent in a scene that ostensibly has nothing to do with Horace. Despite Horace's absence, however, Jimmy's interpretation of this scene (and of the ways in which he is complicit in the community's repeated failures) has everything to do with how his life has been transformed by Horace. The summer after Horace's suicide, Jonnie Mae dies, and Jimmy's mother, Rose, returns to Tims Creek for the funeral. The family sees Rose as an ungrateful "tramp," a woman who loved pleasure more than she loved her mother, Jonnie Mae. Rose's three sisters had been the "good" girls; Rose, in contrast, was the pariah. After returning home three times, pregnant and alone, she finally left Tims Creek for good, unable to bear the community's disdain. Jonnie Mae's funeral is the first time in his adult life that Jimmy has seen the woman. During the service, she stands apart from the family: "Rose stood at the graveside ceremony as Reverend Raines eulogized my grandmother, reading Paul's letters to the Corinthians ('Though I speak with the tongues of men and of angels, and have not charity, I am become as sounding brass, or a tinkling cymbal')" (120). When Rose is overcome with grief, all but one in the community refuse to comfort her. The haunting refrain from First Corinthians measures this community against a more inclusive vision of society, and the community is found wanting:

> When she began to cry, a calm and low sob, she looked suddenly forlorn and forsaken, a child lost and alone. And even now I cannot believe that no one, not Aunt Rebecca, not Aunt Ruthester, not Aunt Rachel [Rose's sisters], not Isador, not Franklin, not I [Rose's children], especially not I, turned to comfort her. ("Charity suffereth long, and is kind; charity envieth not; charity vaunteth not itself, is not puffed up.") Until finally, in a moment of such black tension, huddled over the lowering casket, a thin, invisible line separating the prodigal from the faithful, my Uncle Lester stepped over that line and put his hand on her shoulder. ("For we know in part, and we prophesy in part. But when that which is perfect is come, then that which is part shall be done away.") It was a crude and clumsy gesture, but in all its lack of grace it was full of grace. ("For now we see through a glass, darkly; but then face to face: now I know in part; but then shall I know even as also I am known.") Seeing that, I knew my sin, but was unrepentant. (120–21)

The passage from First Corinthians that serves as a refrain here is an ironic commentary on the other Pauline passage that so sharply condemned Horace. At Jonnie Mae's funeral, the individual "pariahs" (Horace, Rose) are no longer the ones who need transforming, as Rev. Barden's interpretation of that passage from Romans implied. Without love ("charity" in the King James Version), all the community's pompous words are no better than "sounding brass, or a tinkling cymbal," and suddenly, Jimmy sees this clearly, despite his inability to act. When Horace was first introduced into the text, the narrator explained, "More than anything else, he wanted to have grace" (11). Rose's brother Lester, in contrast to Jimmy and the rest of the community, acts with grace in this scene and, in so doing, allies himself with Horace. Ironically, Lester is only a peripheral character in *A Visitation of Spirits*; he is repeatedly depicted as inept, hardly worthy of notice. Rose, Lester, and Horace reverse such characterizations, however, making the periphery central to a transformed/transforming vision of a new community.

The "Confessions" section in which the story of Rose appears is also the section in which Horace "comes out" during the dramatic interruption to Jimmy's prose. The two episodes are related in that both represent the failure of Jimmy's ministry. They are "confessions" in the limited sense; Jimmy's inclusion of them is an admission that he has done something wrong. The episode that opens this "Confessions" section, however, suggests that Jimmy has learned his lesson and that Horace and Rose both have disrupted and transformed not only his private life but his public role as the community's minister, the community's "representative." In the opening scene, Jimmy goes to visit a woman in his congregation: Margurette Honeyblue, a seventy-three-year-old woman who is presumably on her deathbed. This scene opens the section, but it actually follows the other two episodes chronologically. More important, however, it follows the other two episodes *developmentally*: gone is the Jimmy who feels it his duty to explain the "rules" to Horace or who—along with the rest of the family—ostracizes Rose, the "sinner."

Jimmy arrives at "Miss Margurette's" a few minutes before she is scheduled to take her medicine. Looking directly at Jimmy, Miss Margurette instructs her daughter to bring her a beer so she can wash down her pills. It is a minor incident, but Jimmy recognizes it as a test, and the thoughts this scene elicits confirm not only that Jimmy is a changed man, individually, but also that he has a different vision of how members of the community might relate to one another:

> How could I communicate that I was not, did not want to be the holy and pious dictator of a pastor they had been used to for all their lives, that my very presence had nothing to do with my condemnation of their way of life, that I couldn't give a flying fuck about the still [Miss Margurette's son-in-law] Lucius had out in the woods behind the house, or how [the family] sold all sorts of regulated beverages illegally from their kitchen, or that the last time they had been to church was to funeralize Margurette's husband twenty years ago. There was no way to say: I have not come here to judge you. To say: I want to introduce a new way of approaching Christian faith, a way of caring for people. I don't want to be a watchdog of sin, an inquisitor who binds his people with rules and regulations and thou shalts and thou shalt nots. (110)

Humbled by the incident, Jimmy feels inadequate to bring this new way of living into being: "But looking past those eyes so full of past hurt and past

Queer Locations/Queer Transformations

rejection and past accusation, I could only smile and let be what was" (110). "Letting be," however, in this instance is precisely the place to begin, and Miss Margurette's reaction to Jimmy's nonchalance indicates that the process of healing has already begun: "She lay there quiet and as still as the bed. A warm breeze troubled the curtains and she gave me a wink, took a deep long breath, and sighed" (110). Outside the window, Jimmy notes, "a small bird flapped its wings against the wind" (110). Horace, of course, had earlier hoped to escape the regime of sameness in Tims Creek by transforming himself into a bird, and this bird recalls that attempt at transformation. The literal success or failure of that particular transformation, however ("Is it real?," "Is it fantasy?"), is at this point irrelevant next to other, more far-reaching transformations. After his suicide, Horace survives to haunt Jimmy and open up the meanings that have hitherto grounded the life of this community.

Thus, Horace begins the work of transforming this community by first transforming Jimmy's public role as the community's minister. Although the transformation—of this community, of the meanings of "community"—is (always) incomplete, Jimmy's "new way of approaching Christian faith," which resists founding a community on exclusion but which no longer resists queer identifications and desires, assures that transformation will be ongoing. The re-vision of Christianity that Horace incites in Jimmy is the flip side of Kenan's signification on Baldwin. Jimmy Greene, after all, is not the first "Jimmy" in the African American tradition to envision a spirituality more dedicated to justice and love. Baldwin himself writes:

> It is not too much to say that whoever wishes to become a truly moral human being (and let us not ask whether or not this is possible; I think we must *believe* that it is possible) must first divorce himself from all the prohibitions, crimes, and hypocrisies of the Christian church. If the concept of God has any validity or any use, it can only be to make us larger, freer, more loving. If God cannot do this, then it is time we got rid of Him. (*Fire Next Time*, 67)

Jimmy Greene's Christianity, which rejects the God of "thou shalt nots" and seeks to transform the community into a freer, more caring place, is at least one possible resolution of Baldwin's injunction here. Through Jimmy, Kenan introduces a crucial distinction between "religiosity" and "faith."

Queer Locations/Queer Transformations

Rejecting the pomposity and homophobia of religiosity, Kenan nonetheless validates faith as a genuine force, capable of bringing about connections between human beings (McRuer, "Randall Kenan," 234).[23]

Baldwin's desire is to forge connections between people who do not necessarily share identificatory locations, or who share some locations and not others. Hence, like Kenan's Jimmy, Baldwin does not need to count on "Christians" to be the group that of necessity institutes this freer, more loving society. In fact, Kenan's Rabbi is prefigured in Baldwin's essay by another Jewish character: the young James Baldwin's best friend, who inadvertently teaches him a lesson about the amount of hate in the "Christian" world. Baldwin writes:

> My best friend in high school was a Jew. He came to our house once, and afterward my father asked, as he asked about everyone, "Is he a Christian?"—by which he meant "Is he saved?" I really do not know whether my answer came out of innocence or venom, but I said coldly, "No. He's Jewish." My father slammed me across the face with his great palm, and in that moment everything flooded back—all the hatred and all the fear. . . . I wondered if I was expected to be glad that a friend of mine, or anyone, was to be tormented forever in Hell, and I also thought, suddenly, of the Jews in another Christian nation, Germany. They were not so far from the fiery furnace after all, and my best friend might have been one of them. I told my father, "He's a better Christian than you are," and walked out of the house. (Fire Next Time, 54–55)

In *A Visitation of Spirits*, Baldwin's best friend grows up and goes to—of all places—a Christian seminary, where he continues teaching "Christians" about "*real* desire": the desire for justice, the desire for love—subjects about which they appear to know so very little.[24]

Kenan's tribute to Baldwin complicates the theories of signification Gates develops in *The Signifying Monkey*. In a review of Mary Helen Washington's anthology *Invented Lives*, Gates writes, "[Black] female authors claim other black women as their ancestors (such as Zora Neale Hurston and Ann Petry) whereas most older black male writers denied any black influence at all—or worse, eagerly claimed a white paternity" (qtd. in V. Smith, 66). In other words, women writers' desire to bond lovingly with female ancestors—a characteristic of what Gates calls "unmotivated" signification—stands in stark contrast to what most male writers tend to feel: an anxiety of influence that leads them to critique other (male) writers who have preceded them, repeating and revising those writers' tropes and narrative strategies. Kenan, however, tends to fit neither of Gates's gendered categories; he rewrites/reverses Baldwin's story of a young boy in conflict with the church, but he also repeats, *without* negative critique, Baldwin's vision of a more just society. Contrary to Gates's implication, then, some men "lovingly bond" with other men as readily as women bond with women.[25] Thus, although I agree with Gates's reading in *The Signifying Monkey* of the profundity of Alice Walker's bond with Hurston, I propose that the Kenan-Baldwin relation disrupts the gendered dichotomy at work in Gates's theories. Kenan's embrace of Baldwin, like Walker's of Hurston, is one of "the most loving revision[s] . . . we have seen in the tradition" (*Signifying Monkey*, 255).[26]

"It rit quar. Aint spose ta be lak dat": Outing the Signifying Monkey

In the title story to Kenan's collection *Let the Dead Bury Their Dead*, a young slave girl named Phoebe—one of many slaves living on the antebellum North Carolina plantation (Canaan) of U.S. Senator Owen Alexander Cross—complains to her mistress about a mysterious slave named Menes: "*Misress . . . He Big an Black an Hateful and der aint no cause fuh such ta be ober usens in de Big House. It rit quar. Aint spose ta be lak dat*" (308). Despite Phoebe's concerns, the crisis that commences with this big, dark slave's control over the "Big House" escalates as the story continues: Menes (also known as Pharaoh) burns down the house and leads a band of slaves into the North Carolina bogs, where they found a "maroon society" dedicated to the perpetual disruption of "business as usual" on the Cross plantation. Although Phoebe initially has misgivings about Menes, eventually she too joins the ranks of those who escape from Canaan.

This story is discovered among the Greene papers after Jimmy's death in 1998. In the introduction to "Let the Dead Bury Their Dead," dated August 5, 2000, Reginald Kain—or "RK"—of Brooklyn, New York, informs readers: "On March 12, 1998, the Reverend James Malachai Greene died in a car accident on the way home from a conference of ministers in Atlanta; he had just entered the town limits of Tims Creek, North Carolina" (277). According to RK, the story of Menes and the maroon society is part of an "oral annotated history" of Tims Creek and is one of the more interesting documents to be discovered among the Greene papers after the accident.[27]

Jimmy's death suggests that Kenan has a habit of killing off characters not long after they come to an awareness of the ways in which their community needs transforming. One might expect, after *A Visitation of Spirits*, that Jimmy would begin to promote radical change in Tims Creek and elsewhere, but instead, Kenan kills him in a car accident. As in *A Visitation of Spirits*, however, the "facts" may be "subject to doubt," and I argue in conclusion that the existence of Menes/Pharaoh marks yet another resurrection of the queer trickster embodied first by Horace and later—because of his desire to reverse the received meanings of Christianity—by Jimmy.[28] Menes/Pharaoh, in fact, "literally" rises from the dead: after his death, Menes/Pharaoh's grave is discovered to be empty, and later in the story, he once again returns to transform the community, which has fallen into complacency. In Menes/Pharaoh, Kenan draws on characteristics from both Jimmy and Horace. For example, Menes/Pharaoh actually carries out the work Jimmy envisions: the maroon society would

> come to Pharaoh and he'd . . . tell em to keep themselves ready, to look out for one another, not to be like the white man, reaching and grabbing and trying to own everything, even people. Told em to remember that they come from a great land and a great people and such-like. Wont preaching he done, more like learning, learning em to love themselves and the world round em. (305)

Moreover, Menes/Pharaoh's very appearance carries on the work of "queering" the Signifying Monkey begun by Horace in *A Visitation of Spirits*. As the notice Senator Cross circulates for Menes/Pharaoh's apprehension describes him: "MENES, African-born, about 35 to 40 Years of Age, about Six-Feet-One Inches High, Square made, Left Ear pierced with Silver Metal Ring, Queer Markings about Face" (302).

Of course, you might argue, the fact that Menes wears an earring and is "marked" as "queer" means nothing, particularly in this nineteenth-century context. Lots of African slaves wore earrings. It's not such a big deal. It's not thought of as—. Yet I submit that Kenan's work as a whole repeatedly inscribes the presence-absence of queerness into the Signifying Monkey as decidedly as the evasions in *A Visitation of Spirits* attached gay meanings to Jimmy. Certainly, the signifying earring that reappears here need not be, in Jimmy's words, "thought of as—"; yet even when Kenan's tricksters are not *exactly* "gay," they are not exactly "straight" either. Menes/Pharaoh may not embody a twentieth-century category such as "gay," but the signifying earring ensures that we nonetheless read him (and his commitment to disrupting, from the "margins," the hegemonic "center") *through* Horace. The heterosexual/homosexual binary is always included among the hierarchies of power that Kenan's characters have the ability to upset, and in this sense, Kenan's work "outs" the Signifying Monkey.

Since he is already the African American "figure of indeterminacy" (Gates, *Signifying Monkey,* 11), it is more than a little redundant to "out" as "queer" the Signifying Monkey. Still, I think Kenan actualizes, in both *A Visitation of Spirits* and *Let the Dead Bury Their Dead,* what is only potentially queer in Gates's analysis of the Signifying Monkey tales. "Outing" the Signifying Monkey entails explicitly adding the heterosexual/homosexual binary to the repertoire of reversals the Signifying Monkey effects; it entails envisioning the sort of "necessarily and desirably queer world" that Michael Warner suggests will overcome the totalizing tendencies of heteronormativity (8). In the Queer Renaissance, the "queer world" has not been "contained" in New York and San Francisco; indeed, the term *queer* suggests that resistance to heteronormativity will continue to turn up and transform even the most apparently "inappropriate" places. Kenan does not hustle Horace off to the big city in his collection of stories, but despite his initial misgivings about *A Visitation of Spirits,* Gates does not complain. Instead, on the back cover of *Let the Dead Bury Their Dead,* Gates calls Kenan, with his "generous moral imagination," a "fabulist for our times." Queer transformations can begin in the queerest of locations; as "fabulist for our times," Kenan transforms a place on the so-called margins into a center of the queer world.

Queer Locations/Queer Transformations

Chapter Three

Unlimited Access?
Queer Theory in the Borderlands

———◦———

I want to begin in a queer place. My central text in this chapter is Gloria Anzaldúa's eclectic mix of theory, poetry, and nonfiction prose in her 1987 collection *Borderlands/La Frontera: The New Mestiza*, and my central subjects are those Anzaldúa calls *los atravesados*: "the squint-eyed, the perverse, the queer, the troublesome, the mongrel, the mulato, the half-breed, the half dead: in short, those who cross over, pass over, or go through the confines of the 'normal' " (3). *Los atravesados* are those who live in the "borderlands" of Anzaldúa's title; caught between two colliding cultures, this queer group of "outcasts" emerges from attempts to separate, definitively, "us" from "them." Before discussing *los atravesados de Anzaldúa*, however, I examine briefly another group of fictional "outcasts" who "crossed over" earlier in the century in Jack Kerouac's *On the Road.*

Although Kerouac might likely play a leading role in a study of homo-*sociality* in the American canon, he is certainly an unlikely candidate for inclusion in a study of the contemporary Queer Renaissance.[1] Yet I want to begin this chapter elsewhere, temporarily outside of the Queer Renaissance and the queer communities that are my subject. The two chapters that have preceded this one have examined variations on the idea of queer "community," focusing on, respectively, what queers do in and to the communities of which they are a part. This chapter initially approaches the issue from a different direction, considering what *other* "communities" might do with and to queerness.

Kerouac's appropriation of the trope of "the border" sets the stage for my analysis of contemporary deployments of borders and of queerness. Using Kerouac, I make the somewhat unremarkable assertion that there is more than one way to cross a border. Using Anzaldúa, who stands at the crossroads where "border theory" and queer theory intersect, I expand on this assertion in order to consider how there are different ways to cross the theoretical border. Queer theory is definitely part of what might be called the "theoretical border-transgressing boom," but instead of deploying queer theory as some sort of theoretical NAFTA that provides cultural critics with "unlimited access" to new markets, Anzaldúa's particular brand of queer/Chicana theory challenges the unchecked mobility of oppressive systems of power. Some overly celebratory understandings of queerness, not unlike Kerouac's "outcasts" in *On the Road,* tend to efface the ways in which identities and histories are structured in domination, so that some identities are immobilized while white, male, and heterosexual power is able to travel anywhere and everywhere with ease. Anzaldúa's work undermines this structural domination by insistently foregrounding a "mestiza queer" identity.[2]

For Anzaldúa, "the border" and "queerness" stand as figures for the failure of easy separation. Rather than establishing two discrete entities, each attempt at separation actually produces (mestiza/queer) identities that do not wholly fit in either location. Such identities are consequently marked as "other" (undocumented, illegal, perverse) by those with the power to police the border. The marking and fixing of "other" identities directs attention away from the border guards themselves, who in turn pass unmarked and unrestrained. The opposition of "unmarked" and "marked" is, at times, far from metaphorical. In a recent article in the *Arizona Daily Star,* physicist Bill Wattenburg suggests that a "florescent glowing dust" be used on the border to police "illegals"; those who cross over *(los atravesados)* would pass through the dust, and authorities could then use "ultraviolet lights and lasers [to] track down the marked people" (qtd. in Dayan, 812). The mestiza queer identity theorized by Anzaldúa, however, counters the border guards' absolute mobility with another, critical mobility.

The Kerouacian hipsters with whom I begin my analysis are hardly a pure coextension of these border guards or of ominous, all-pervasive "systems of power." I begin with *On the Road,* however, in an attempt to situate the history of borders and border crossings as multifaceted, involving more than two sides. Relations between the multiple players are often contradictory. There is doubtless much in the Beat project as a whole that is oppositional to the restrictive white middle-class mores of the 1950s, even while that project is simultaneously implicated in the very forces it opposes. In *On the Road,* the hipsters' and border guards' locations are contiguous but are not reducible to each other; hence the hipsters' border

crossing marks an extremely complex concourse of oppositional and hegemonic forces. So, too, with border crossings in the academy: there is not,
on the one side, a group that establishes borders, and opposite it, another
that transgresses them. The particular logic of the "fad," for instance,
demonstrates how complicated border crossings may be. Fads (such as the
theoretical border-transgressing boom) may, in the first place, speak to the
desire for community, the desire for transformation, or the desire to cross
over to something new that opposes the status quo. At the same time, fads
are part of a much larger network: they are marketable, and market forces
demand and ensure that a fad will inevitably disappoint and eventually
disappear, clearing the way for the next fad.

The mestiza queer locates and manipulates these and other contradictions effected by the border and by border crossings. Not content to remain
a casualty of binaristic thinking or to be merely celebrated for her hip
transgressions, Anzaldúa's mestiza queer redraws the boundaries, mobilizing a critique that spotlights the location and history of all the players in a
given border conflict, and in the process unmasks the border guards' and
others' attempts to escape identity and history.

Escape from Identity and History: Crossing the Border in *On the Road*

In Kerouac's 1957 novel, the protagonist Sal Paradise is a young writer
who "want[s] to take off": "Somewhere along the line I knew there'd be
girls, visions, everything; somewhere along the line the pearl would be
handed to me" (11). "Beaten down" by a world that lacks "vision," Kerouac's protagonist takes to the road to find it, along with "girls" and "everything." And indeed, in one of the final sections of the text, it seems as if
this desire to have it all might actually be realized. Sal and his friends Stan
Shephard and Dean Moriarty head south toward "the magic land at the
end of the road" (276). As the trio approaches the U.S.-Mexican border
(the "magic border" [273]), a shift occurs:

> To our amazement, it looked exactly like Mexico. It was three in the morn-
> ing, and fellows in straw hats and white pants were lounging by the dozen
> against battered pocky storefronts.
>
> "Look—at—those—cats!" whispered Dean. . . . We couldn't take our
> eyes from across the street. We were longing to rush right up there and get
> lost in those mysterious Spanish streets. (274)

Kerouac's protagonists assume that "crossing the border" means one thing: the signifier "Mexico" and its signified fit together "exactly." Mexico here, like the fellows "lounging" against the storefronts, is passive and immediately accessible; one can "rush right up there and get lost in" this magical union of desire and object. What these characters elide, however, is that theirs is a particular *construction* of Mexico: it is the hip, exotic land of excess Kerouac's boys have dreamed about discovering.

The protagonists are held up by the border officials, but ultimately, even the police in this new world fit the exotic picture they are constructing:

> They weren't like officials at all. They were lazy and tender. Dean couldn't stop staring at them. He turned to me. "See how the *cops* are in this country. I can't believe it!" He rubbed his eyes. "I'm dreaming." Then it was time to change our money. We saw great stacks of pesos on a table and learned that eight of them made an American buck, or thereabouts. We changed most of our money and stuffed the big rolls in our pockets with delight. (274–75)

Crossing the border is a transcendent (or, we might say, "beatific") experience for Kerouac's characters—an experience that finally allows them to escape the banality and rigidity of (white) American middle-class life. To them, the land they have discovered on crossing the border is "magical" and "delightful." The powerful and bulging pockets with which this chapter of *On the Road* concludes, however, suggest—and perhaps not so subtly—that someone, at least, is about to get fucked. As the journey continues, this connection between American buying power and white heterosexual male sexual power is literalized. Victor, the boys' hip new Mexican friend, takes them to a whorehouse where, as Sal Paradise explains, they can "buy *señorita*" (281). The protagonists spend several hours at the establishment to which Victor takes them, patronizing women from several Central and South American countries. The narrator proclaims, "Through our deliriums we began to discern [the girls'] varying personalities" (287), but none of the women is given a name. In fact, the "wildest," who was "half Indian, half white, and came from Venezuela" (287), becomes, in only a few pages, coextensive with her supposed homeland: "Venezuela clung about my neck and begged for drinks. . . . With Venezuela writhing and suffering in my arms I had a longing to take her in the back and undress her" (289). Apparently, white male power in Kerouac's text buys not only individuals but entire nations. The reduction of this woman to Venezuela is particularly ironic, given that her mestiza identity and Mexican location complicate any easy notion of "origin." Despite how "wild" she is, the boys "keep her in her place" with the epithet "Venezuela."

This border crossing undoubtedly reveals more about the white male protagonists than it does about the inhabitants of Mexico; to these "hip" bohemians, "all of Mexico [is] one vast Bohemian camp" (302) that allows them to transcend their own rigid and restricting identities and cultural contexts. This "transcendence" is not entirely negative: Beat writers despised what they saw as the materialism and stultifying conformity of middle America, and, without question, they effectively shaped alternative visions that had a major impact on the next generation. Andrew Ross, examining a passage from *On the Road* where Sal Paradise walks the streets of Denver "wishing [he] were a Negro," suggests that "[white] fantasies, however romantic . . . had real and powerful social effects . . . for the white students in SNCC [the Student Nonviolent Coordinating Committee] who participated in the struggle for civil rights, and who supported the black liberation movements of the sixties" (68–69). Despite the potential positive impact of the Beat writers' racial fantasies, however, the example Ross chooses—a fleeting fantasy on the streets of Denver— pales in comparison to the extreme exploitation represented later in the novel, when the protagonists cross the border into Mexico.

In fact, Ross's observation might be inflected somewhat differently: if we admit that white fantasies such as Sal's had "real and powerful social effects," then we would have to admit simultaneously that Kerouacian *male* fantasies also had such real and powerful effects—an admission that is borne out historically by the New Left's callous disdain for, even outright hostility toward, feminism in the 1960s. This misogyny, coupled with the romanticism Ross details (which is nonetheless racist), would have particularly disastrous consequences for women of color, who "experience racism not as 'blacks' [or 'Latinos'], but as black women" and Latinas (de Lauretis, "Eccentric Subjects," 134).[3] Sal Paradise, of course, walks the streets of Denver wishing he were a Negro *man*. In Denver, Sal's desire to escape his own identity can be read as simply a romantic fantasy that (perhaps) lays the groundwork for powerful, and potentially positive, social effects; in Mexico, when this fantasy is symbolically realized, the negative material consequences for the women on the other side of the border are far more difficult to dismiss.[4]

Ironically, the constricting white American identities that Kerouac's protagonists try to escape are reproduced in the Mexican section of *On the*

Road. As John Tytell confirms, in Mexico "Dean and Sal act without grace, as 'self-important moneybag Americans'" (168). *On the Road* demonstrates that the logic of a border crossing that seeks to escape identity actually facilitates the emergence of the self-important American. Dean insists that they are "leaving everything behind us and entering a new and unknown phase of things . . . so that we can safely think of nothing else and just go on ahead with our faces stuck out like this, you see, and *understand* the world as, really and genuinely speaking, other Americans haven't done before us" (276). However, his admission that they can and will "safely think of nothing else" guarantees that the boys never fully consider how "other Americans" before them *have* understood the world, how they inadvertently replicate American perspectives, or how the path they have taken parallels the path taken earlier by others. The boys' "wonderful Mexican money that went so far" buys them anything they want and can take them "right on to South America" if they so desire (276, 277). As they get closer to Mexico City, Dean's wristwatch even buys them the authenticity they left home to discover. Encountering a three-year-old girl standing in front of a group of Indians, Dean exclaims, "She'll never, never leave here and know anything about the outside world. It's a nation. Think of the wild chief they must have! . . . How different they must be in their private concerns and evaluations and wishes!" (297–98). Not paying for this "difference" makes Dean uncomfortable, and he presents the little girl with his wristwatch: "She whimpered with glee. The others crowded around with amazement. Then Dean poked in the little girl's hand for 'the sweetest and purest and smallest crystal she has personally picked from the mountain for me'" (298). In a sense, Dean gives up his wristwatch and buys the "timelessness" and "authenticity" that countless American travelers before and after him have sought to discover.

Nothing could be more alien to Kerouac's protagonists, however, than the thought that they are participating in a history of exploitation of the region they are exploring. On the contrary, in their minds, they have left banal American identities behind them at the border and now freely merge with what they see as a hip new Mexican identity. This escape from their own identities, however, necessarily obscures that history of exploitation. Sal's thoughts as the other boys sleep illustrate just how glaring their effacement of history is:

> The boys were sleeping, and I was alone in my eternity at the wheel, and the road ran straight as an arrow. Not like driving across Carolina, or Texas,

or Arizona, or Illinois; but like driving across the world and into the places where we would finally learn ourselves among the Fellahin Indians of the world, the essential strain of the basic primitive, wailing humanity that stretches in a belt around the equatorial belly of the world from Malaya (the long fingernail of China) to India the great subcontinent to Arabia to Morocco to the selfsame deserts and jungles of Mexico and over the waves to Polynesia to mystic Siam of the Yellow Robe and on around, on around, so that you hear the same mournful wail by the rotted walls of Cadiz, Spain, that you hear 12,000 miles around in the depths of Benares the Capital of the World. These people were unmistakably Indians and were not at all like the Pedros and Panchos of silly civilized American lore—they had high cheekbones, and slanted eyes, and soft ways; they were not fools, they were not clowns; they were great, grave Indians and they were the source of mankind and the fathers of it. The waves are Chinese, but the earth is an Indian thing. As essential as rocks in the desert are they in the desert of "history." (280–81)

In this passage, specific histories and struggles are effaced as people of color the world over are blurred into one exotic, hip lump: Malaysia is China is India is Arabia is Morocco is Mexico is Polynesia is Siam. Ultimately, the narrator settles on Benares, a sacred Hindu city on the Ganges River in India, to stand in for the "Capital of the World." Of course, it is more than a little ironic that this invocation of India is followed in the text by the narrator's observation that "these people were unmistakably Indians," since the history of white exploitation of indigenous peoples on this continent begins with just such a mistake, or (mis)naming. As the passage concludes, history indeed requires the distancing quotation marks Kerouac employs, for this is not so much history as it is history's effacement. Centuries of exploitation are erased as Kerouac's neo-Columbian hipster once again "discovers" a New World full of abundant resources that are his for the taking.

Even when *On the Road* was published, however, the "border" was a contested site. In 1958, one year after the publication of *On the Road*, Américo Paredes published his important study of Chicano *corridos* (ballads, folk songs), *"With His Pistol in His Hand": A Border Ballad and Its Hero*. Paredes was the first of many Chicano scholars to respond to Walter Prescott Webb's studies of the Texas Rangers, which championed the supposed "heroics" of the Rangers and denigrated the Mexicans and Mexican

Americans who lived within the Rangers' jurisdiction and who were often victims of their attempts to maintain "law and order" (J. Saldívar, 49–53). Through an extended analysis of "El Corrido de Gregorio Cortez," Paredes contested Webb's characterization of the Texas Rangers and the U.S.-Mexican border region. In contrast to both Webb's representation of the border region as the site of Anglo-American "heroics" and romanticized Anglo understandings of the region as "Old Spain in Our Southwest," Paredes "redefined the border . . . [as] a historically determined geopolitical zone of military, linguistic, and cultural conflict" (Calderón and Saldívar, 5). "El Corrido de Gregorio Cortez" was, for Paredes, paradigmatic of early twentieth-century border *corridos* in general, which he saw as tending "toward one theme, border conflict," and "toward one concept of the hero, the man fighting for his right with his pistol in his hand" (Paredes, 149; qtd. in R. Saldívar, 28).[5]

Far from providing an escape from identity, the border thus becomes a metaphor for the complex and oppressive social and historical forces that have shaped and continue to shape Chicano identity. Teresa McKenna writes that the border between Texas and Mexico "stands as figure and metaphor for the transition between nations and the complex of connections which continue to exist for all Mexicans whether border residents or not" (qtd. in J. Saldívar, 54). The meanings borne by border *crossings*, in turn, are also very different in Chicana/o scholarship from the meanings borne by the "magical" border crossing in Kerouac's novel. In 1981, for example, Cherríe Moraga and Gloria Anzaldúa compiled a collection of prose and poetry that complicates easy, celebratory notions about the transgression of boundaries. "Literally, for years," Moraga writes in her preface to that volume, "I have dreamed of a bridge" (xviii). That dream is realized with the publication of *This Bridge Called My Back: Writings by Radical Women of Color*, but the editors' title complicates the idea of "crossing over" by introducing history and embodiment: this crossing is not simply celebratory but is rather inscribed onto the bodies of women of color; "this bridge," according to Moraga and Anzaldúa, is "called my back."

This Bridge Called My Back stands at the crossroads where border theory, feminism, and a nascent queer theory intersect. Indeed, I would argue that, because of its construction of relational and critical identities, the collection is one of the first texts of the Queer Renaissance. Moraga writes, "But the passage is *through*, not over, not by, not around, but through" (xiv); she goes on to explain her hope that *This Bridge Called*

My Back "will function for others, colored or white, in the same way" (xiv). In spite of the hope for coalition, however, Moraga's emphasis ("the passage is *through*") suggests that *This Bridge Called My Back* (and other books for which it will eventually function as an antecedent) cannot and will not advocate "crossings" that allow for an avoidance of identity and history. Anzaldúa and she have put together a collection that is about border crossings and connections between women, Moraga explains, but connection is possible only if readers are willing to ask difficult questions about the many silences surrounding race, class, and sexuality in feminism, and to admit they do not have all the answers (xiv–xv).

In the end, *On the Road* in fact demonstrates that an avoidance of the difficult questions of history and identity cannot be easily sustained; ultimately, the hipsters succumb to the history they were trying to escape. Sal Paradise and his friends come down from the emotional, transcendental high that crossing the border facilitated, only to return once again, "beaten down," to the United States. "Crossing the border" inevitably disappoints these American boys, since "the magic land at the end of the road" turned out to be little more than a passing fad.

Queer Theory in the Borderlands

Academic border crossings are all the rage. Cultural studies, promising to break down the borders between disciplines or between the academy and outside communities, trumpets the advent of "postdisciplinary knowledge"; in literary studies, the Modern Language Association (MLA) has recently published an assessment of the profession explicitly titled *Redrawing the Boundaries*. The editors of that collection, Stephen Greenblatt and Giles Gunn, write that "our profession has become increasingly concerned with the problem of boundaries. . . . These boundaries can be crossed, confused, consolidated, and collapsed; they can also be revised, reconceived, redesigned, or replaced" (4). Likewise, in the field of education, theorist Henry Giroux has developed the idea of "border pedagogy" in his book *Border Crossings: Cultural Workers and the Politics of Education*.

Queer theory, fashionably late yet central to this theoretical border-crossing party, similarly champions the crossing and recrossing of borders. As queer theorist Lisa Duggan writes:

The notion of a "queer community" . . . is often used to construct a collectivity no longer defined solely by the gender of its members' sexual partners.

This new community is unified only by a shared dissent from the dominant organization of sex and gender.... The "queer" nation is a newly defined political entity, better able to cross boundaries and construct more fluid identities. ("Making It Perfectly Queer," 20–21)

I do not intend to be disingenuous toward any of the critical schools mentioned here or to dismiss what theorists are doing as "trendy" or unreflective. On the contrary: one of my intentions in this chapter is to question the ways in which queer theory in particular gets interpellated as a "fad" and to disarticulate it from that which is, supposedly, merely trendy. In this section of my chapter, I begin that disarticulation by considering briefly two types of theoretical border crossings: first, the crossing that interrogates the construction of borders, identities, and histories; and second, the crossing that implicitly posits a cosmopolitan consumer/theorist, able to move everywhere with ease, and that is consequently more celebratory of transgression for transgression's sake. I then offer an extended reading of Gloria Anzaldúa's queer Chicana border theory and argue that Anzaldúa's work, which ironically both interrogates and celebrates critical border crossings, redefines mobility through its deployment of the mestiza queer. *Borderlands/La Frontera* does represent a mestiza queer subject able to cross borders skillfully, but her movement, even when it is celebratory, is always in the service of locating other identities and histories that seek to maintain power by escaping detection.

The theorists and critical schools mentioned above generally represent the first sort of border crossing. They constantly question what "border crossings" might mean; each seeks to examine how and where power is located in both the demarcation and transgression of boundaries. In fact, Greenblatt and Gunn's insistence that "boundaries can be crossed, confused, consolidated, and collapsed" syntactically links the consolidation — or reestablishment — of power to its confusion or collapse: as in Kerouac's work, the crossing of one boundary may entail the reinforcement of others. After their delineation of what can be done with and to boundaries, Greenblatt and Gunn go on to insist that we not take them lightly: "The one thing they cannot be in literary studies is entirely abolished" (4). Giroux likewise connects his theory of "border pedagogy" to an interrogation of configurations of power: border pedagogy allows for "forms of transgression in which existing borders forged in domination can be challenged and redefined.... Border pedagogy must take up the dual task of not only creating new objects of knowledge but also addressing how inequalities, power, and human suffering are rooted in basic institutional structures" (28–29). Finally, Duggan also attends to "basic institutional structures" when she stresses that queer border crossings are unified only by their "shared dissent from the dominant organization of sex and gender." In short, scholars in cultural studies, radical pedagogy, queer theory, and the like are aware that the crossing of borders is no simple matter. Borders and boundaries are not inviolate, but they are almost always the products of configurations of power that are not easily displaced.

At the other end of the spectrum, seemingly, are border crossings that tend to affirm the transgression of boundaries for transgression's sake. Such celebratory transgressions are perhaps more in evidence outside the academy: as Lauren Berlant and Michael Warner point out, "There are even components of the national mass media, such as *Details* and MTV, that have cultivated a language of queerness in their highly capitalized forums" (346). In these consumer contexts, queerness and the transgression of boundaries are marketable. It was such marketability that supposedly made 1993 the year of "lesbian chic" and that, oddly enough, packaged both Tony Kushner and Jack Kerouac as Gap ads ("Kerouac," the ad insists, "wore khakis"). As Phillip Brian Harper writes, "The easy appropriability of the signifiers of certain forms of social marginality makes them prime commodities in the mass-cultural drive to market the effects of disfranchisement for the social cachet that can paradoxically attach to it" (188). The marketing of queerness puts transgressive "new" (in the case of Kerouac, reissued) identities up for sale, but what get elided in the transaction are the systemic forces that construct all identities, marking some as exotic and marketable while others are allowed to pass unmarked.[6] At first, the consumption of a fashionable queerness in videos, in magazines, and on talk shows might seem far removed from a critical academic queerness. Yet the academy, certainly, is also a consumer context, and in the 1990s, queer theory inside the academy (like lesbian chic or *Details* on the outside) is—for many—decidedly "hip"; it is often casually characterized as the "latest thing" or the "next wave." One of the problems with such "hipness" is that—as with Sal Paradise's border crossing or any "passing fad"—inevitable disappointment and failure become structural components of queer theory.[7]

We can look carefully at the contradictions inherent in queer theory's academic location and marketability without forgoing its critical promise, however. Academic and consumer border crossings overlap but are not absolutely reducible to each other, and we need not be, like Kerouac's hipsters, blind to contiguities and contradictions. Because of the existence of more celebratory variants of queer theory, however, some critics have been quick to deny queer theory's transformative potential. Such critics would see the critical type of theoretical border crossing as simply and totally reducible to the celebratory. Donald Morton, for instance, argues that the queer theory of Eve Sedgwick and others in the academy is "basically nothing more than the politics of shocking the sensibilities of the bourgeois reader by 'performing difference' " (134). Against what he sees as a "ludic (post)modern theory [that] demands the de-essentialization, de-naturalization, and de-centering of *signs* and *representations* in the name of personal libidinal liberation," Morton posits "resistance (post)-modernism [that] demands collective emancipation by the overthrow of existing exploitative and oppressive structures and a rebuilding of the space of the public sphere along new lines of coherence" (138). Despite the fact that many practitioners of queer theory not only commit to the "de-essentializations, de-naturalizations, and de-centerings" he denounces but understand these as the precondition for shaping precisely such "new lines of coherence," Morton—because of what he sees, and demonizes, as pure "performance"—is determined not to see queer theory as at all participating in this collective rebuilding. Instead, he homogenizes queer theorists into one apolitical, flaming lump. To paraphrase Emma Goldman: apparently one can't dance in Donald Morton's revolution.

In a way, Morton's denunciations of queer theory can be read as homophobic calls not to "flaunt it." Moreover, Morton reduces the players in this border conflict to two (the "redeemed" and the "damned," to borrow language from my last chapter). In contrast to Morton, we might recognize that, even though I have sketched out two types of theoretical border crossings, the boundary between these two types is not absolute. It is, indeed, impossible for any border crossing to be purely one or the other. In fact, it is the desire for a pure critical and political space (the magic land at the end of the road?) that both produces queer theory as the "latest thing" and allows for it to be dismissed as a "passing fad." Rather than acceding to either characterization, however, queer theory might expose the desire for purity (as opposed to, say, perversion?) as a fantasy and as an impediment to the critical work it seeks to advance. We might envision the best queer theory, then, as aware of the tensions caused by its contradictory location and on guard against attempts to cast its critical transgressions as (merely) hip, even as it simultaneously puts the "celebration" or "performance" back into "politics"—or rather, uses performance to spotlight and challenge, as Morton would have it, "existing exploitative and oppressive structures."

With this goal in mind, I turn to the particular convergence of queer theory and border theory in the work of Anzaldúa. Anzaldúa's work puts into play a new and transgressive identity but at the same time resists mere transgression for transgression's sake. Anzaldúa exhibits an awareness of the complexity of "existing borders forged in domination" and controverts queer theorists who do not. She even queries "queerness" if and when it seeks to escape the complexities of history and identity. There's more than one way to cross the theoretical border, and *Borderlands/La Frontera: The New Mestiza* crosses the border in ways that challenge the unchecked mobility of oppressive systems of power: Anzaldúa exposes the supposed "authorities" who mark her as "other" while attempting to pass unmarked themselves. More than just a passing fad for appropriation by disembodied theoretical hipsters, queer theory as practiced by Anzaldúa becomes a tool for the difficult work of shaping and performing what she calls *"la concien- cia de la mestiza ... a new mestiza consciousness, una conciencia de mujer"* (77). This critical mestiza, woman-centered consciousness is the "consciousness of the Borderlands" that the text celebrates (77).

The remainder of this chapter explores how Anzaldúa shapes mestiza queer identity in *Borderlands/La Frontera*. First, I analyze the poem that opens Anzaldúa's first essay, since that poem provides a blueprint, of sorts, for the text as a whole. In her opening poem, Anzaldúa transforms the abject identity into which she has been interpellated into a resistant iden- tity, intent on exposing and dismantling the history of oppression to which both her identity and the border stand as citations. Second, I examine how that transformation is reproduced on a larger scale in *Borderlands/La Frontera* more generally. Third, and finally, I consider the ways in which Anzaldúa theorizes mestiza identity in and through queerness and vice versa. Although Anzaldúa has at times been relegated to the theoretical margins,[8] this chapter redraws the boundaries in an attempt to position her (and the "positions" she advocates) as central to the theoretical agenda of queer theory. Like Zami and the theories of queer positionality I examined in my first chapter, the queer trickster identity I delineated in my second, and the bisexual artistic/activist identity I explore in my last, the mestiza queer identity Anzaldúa posits exposes and undermines the dominant, normative organizations of sexuality, gender, and race that police *los atravesados* in an attempt to "keep them in their place."

Anzaldúa divides *Borderlands/La Frontera* into two sections: *"Atravesando Fronteras/*Crossing Borders," which consists of seven autobiographical/ poetical/theoretical essays, and *"Un Agitado Viento* [An agitated wind]/ *Ehécatl,* The Wind," which is made up of six sections of Anzaldúa's poetry. Border crossings are central to the entire text, but Anzaldúa's crossings are not simply hip migrations to an exotic land of excess. Anzaldúa's first representation of a border crossing comes in a poem she includes in her first essay, "The Homeland, Aztlán/*El otro México* [The other Mexico]." In this poem, Anzaldúa reinvents the marked identity the border compels her to embody and thereby establishes a pattern of transformation that is replicated in the text as a whole. The poem commences in Border Field Park, on the U.S.-Mexican border south of San Diego:

> I walk   through the hole in the fence
> to the other side.
> Under my fingers I feel the gritty wire
> rusted by 139 years
> of the salty breath of the sea.

> Beneath the iron sky
> Mexican children kick their soccer ball across,
> run after it, entering the U.S. (2)

This is not the "end of the road" for Anzaldúa; crossing the border here marks the *beginning* of the poet's journey in *Borderlands/La Frontera,* and there is nothing very magical or transcendent about it. On the contrary: the children's soccer ball, accidentally kicked across this border, underscores the everyday triviality of this event. At the same time, the children's trivial "accident" contrasts ominously with the other historical "accident" that has occurred "beneath the iron sky": the accident that produced the artificial border in the first place.

Like the soccer ball, Anzaldúa is no respecter of borders. The very text of "The Homeland, Aztlán/*El otro México*" crosses back and forth freely between prose and poetry, between sections consisting of Anzaldúa's "original" writing and excerpts (of prose, poetry, song) from other writers whom she has found useful and pleasurable. Her lack of respect for the border, however, is accompanied by a profound respect for the people whose lives and histories have been shaped by the border, and who have resisted, in various ways, the oppression that this accident of history has

Unlimited Access? Queer Theory in the Borderlands

generated. This multifaceted understanding of the border, introduced in her opening poem, fuels Anzaldúa's entire theoretical project. Her lack of respect is evident in the ease with which the poet walks across the border. Unlike Kerouac's protagonists, her crossing is not sanctioned by hip authorities; she is not likely to gape in amazement at the "cats" who patrol the border. At the same time, even as she crosses, she reveals her awareness of how long the border has engendered both oppression and resistance: "I feel the gritty wire / rusted by 139 years / of the salty breath of the sea."

The border and its history in this text are not picturesque; Anzaldúa uses harsh adjectives ("gritty," "iron") to describe the setting, and the wavelike structure of the poem itself reproduces the insistent pounding of the sea that has gouged the hole in this fence ("silver waves marbled with spume / gashing a hole under the border fence" [1]). Yet Anzaldúa's lack of respect for the border, coupled with her simultaneous awareness of its oppressive history, leads her to yearn for something different, and she begins to identify with the harsh, insistent pounding of the ocean. She begins to look—as it were—for other holes in the fence, for ruptures in the seemingly monolithic force field that would separate her from "the other side." In this poem, and in Anzaldúa's theoretical project in general, mestiza queer identity comes out as one of those ruptures, and she repeatedly deploys this identity as a challenge to those who have created the border and who police it in order to maintain the division of "us" from "them."

"I walk   through the hole in the fence" suggests nothing remarkable or dreamlike about crossing the border. Earlier in the poem, however, prior to the poet's crossing-over, there is at least one magical moment of sorts:

> Miro el mar atacar [I watch the sea attack]
> la cerca en [the fence in] Border Field Park
> con sus buchones de agua [with its cleansing watery maw],
> an Easter Sunday resurrection
> of the brown blood in my veins. (2)

In this passage, the pounding of the sea—though violent—is far from negative, since it leads to a "resurrection of the brown blood" in the poet's veins. This resurrection, however, is different from the transcendence of identity experienced by Kerouac's protagonists; it actuates a renewed understanding of and appreciation for the poet's specific identity and history

Unlimited Access? Queer Theory in the Borderlands

that contrast sharply with the hipsters' attempts to escape both. Furthermore, the poet conceives her mestiza identity here as something that defies the history of oppression that the border signifies, just as the powerful ocean gnaws away at the gritty wire fence.

One of the institutions that literally secures that fence, and the corresponding opposition between "us" and "them," is the Immigration and Naturalization Service (INS), the branch of the U.S. Justice Department responsible for policing the border. Significantly, the INS has been exposed as one of the more discriminatory of government agencies; a group of black agents in Los Angeles filed a suit charging that the INS repeatedly denied them promotions and that people of color are extremely underrepresented in positions of power within the agency. Joyce Jones reports that of approximately four thousand border patrol employees, only thirty-eight are black (18). Hence the current organization of the INS reproduces the "us" (white power structure)/"them" ("illegal" brown or black "others") binary that Anzaldúa contests. If the department were less discriminatory, presumably this division would be harder to uphold.

However, neither in this poem nor elsewhere does Anzaldúa depict mestiza identity as that which *automatically* disrupts institutions such as the INS. Instead, Anzaldúa's work represents a process, whereby the mestiza queer comprehends her multiple identities (mestiza, queer, "outcast") as results of unsuccessful attempts to divide people and transposes the meaning of those identities, turning them against ongoing attempts to maintain hierarchical divisions.[9] Without such transpositions, mestizo/a identity might trouble such institutions, but it will certainly not disrupt them.

Anzaldúa makes this clear in her bilingual book for children, *Friends from the Other Side/Amigos del otro lado*. Prietita is a young Chicana, living in Texas, who befriends an undocumented Mexican boy and his mother. When the border authorities search Prietita's town, one of these authorities is Chicano:

> From behind the curtains, Prietita and the herb woman watched the Border Patrol van cruise slowly up the street. It stopped in front of every house. While the white patrolman stayed in the van, the Chicano *migra* got out and asked, "Does anyone know of any illegals living in this area?" Prietita and the herb woman saw a couple of people shake their heads and a few others withdraw into their houses.
>
> They heard a woman say, "Yes, I saw some over there," pointing to the

gringo side of town—the white side. Everybody laughed, even the Chicano *migra.*

Detrás de las cortinas, Prietita y la señora miraban la camioneta de la migra pasar despacito por la calle. Se paraba frente a cada casa y uno de los dos agentes de la migra se bajaba. Casi todas las veces se bajaba el agente chicano para preguntar, "¿Saben ustedes dónde se esconden los mojados?" Algunos indicaban que no con la cabeza y otros se quedaban callados. Algunos se metían en sus casas.

Siempre había una persona que contestaba, "Sí, ví a unos por allá," apuntando al lado del pueblo donde vivían los gringos. Todos se reían, hasta el agente chicano. (not paginated)

The Chicano's (uneasy?) laughter indicates that his presence complicates, but does not disrupt or disable, the power relations in this scene. The Chicano border guard still participates in the system that would mark as "illegal" and then deport Prietita's friend and his mother. Indeed, the Chicano character literally translates that system for the predominantly white, English-speaking agents, thereby securing the border patrol's ability to move freely. Another character, however, makes visible that which the Chicano border guard would mask: the "illegal" *gringo* side of town. Hence disruption comes not from an essential mestiza/o or Chicana/o identity but from an identity committed to re-vision. Anzaldúa's new mestiza refuses to be kept in her place and instead spotlights the inconsistencies and elisions the border conceals.

In contrast to the Chicano border guard, who eventually gets back into his van and drives away with the other (white) officers, the speaker in the initial poem in *Borderlands/La Frontera* moves from the recognition of a history of oppression toward the strategic deployment of mestiza identity as that which challenges the attempt to maintain divisions between people. To illustrate this trajectory, I quote at length from the final part of Anzaldúa's poem:

> 1,950 mile-long open wound
> > dividing a *pueblo,* a culture,
> > running down the length of my body,
> > > staking fence rods in my flesh,
> > > splits me   splits me
> > > > *me raja   me raja*

This is my home
this thin edge of
barbwire.

But the skin of the earth is seamless.
The sea cannot be fenced,
el mar does not stop at borders.
To show the white man what she thought of his
arrogance,
Yemaya blew that wire fence down.

This land was Mexican once,
was Indian always
and is.
And   will be again.

Yo soy un puente tendido
del mundo gabacho al del mojado,
lo pasado me estirá pa' 'trás
y lo presente pa' 'delante.
Que la Virgen de Guadalupe me cuide
Ay ay ay, soy mexicana de este lado.

[I am a bridge extending
from the world of the Spaniard/European to that of the "wetback,"
The past stretches me backward
and the present forward.
The Virgin of Guadalupe watches over me
Ay ay ay, I am a Mexican woman of this side.] (2–3)

In the first stanza of this passage, Anzaldúa foregrounds an ongoing history of oppression by reading the border as an open wound that divides a people, a culture, even individuals ("splits me   splits me / *me ra-ja   me raja*"). But this history of oppression, inscribed onto the poet's very body, simultaneously secures the possibility—indeed, the inevitability—of resistance. Here and throughout *Borderlands/La Frontera*, Anzaldúa aptly demonstrates that the attempt to divide absolutely "us" from "them" can never fully succeed, since it always produces groups of people who do not fit either category. These groups find themselves in an in-

Unlimited Access? Queer Theory in the Borderlands
———————

between position that could disrupt or destroy—just as *Yemaya* destroys the border fence—the dualistic foundation on which binary thinking rests. Binary thinking casts the poet into an abject position here, but Anzaldúa works that abject, mestiza position against the very ideology that produces it.

In this poem, Anzaldúa reproduces a disruptive, in-between position in several ways. First, Anzaldúa writes bilingually or multilingually, switching codes without always bothering to translate. Diane Freedman points out that Anzaldúa's code switching signals for some privileged readers that there are "borders they cannot cross" (53); hence, even as Anzaldúa challenges the border patrol in the name of those whom the border would mark and separate, she implicitly insists that no one should have unlimited access to others' lives and histories. Throughout *Borderlands/La Frontera,* Anzaldúa employs not only Spanish and English but Chicano/a and working-class variants of both, as well as an occasional word or phrase of Nahuatl. As she explains later in the text, "*Deslenguadas. Somos los del español deficiente* [Foul-mouthed, shameless. We speak the deficient Spanish]. We are your linguistic nightmare, your linguistic aberration, your linguistic *mestisaje* [mongrels/half-breeds], the subject of your *burla* [joke]" (58). Anzaldúa's switching of linguistic codes stands as the figure for a disruptive and vital mestiza/o existence more generally: "Chicano Spanish is a border tongue . . . *un nuevo lenguaje* [a new language]. *Un lenguaje que corresponde a un modo de vivir* [a language that corresponds to a way of life]. Chicano Spanish is not incorrect, it is a living language" (55).

Second, Anzaldúa reproduces the in-between position in this poem by describing the land as simultaneously Mexican and Indian, despite attempts by Anglos (during the 139 years that have elapsed between the Treaty of Guadalupe-Hidalgo and the writing of this text) to confine Mexican identity to *el otro lado* (the other side). The poet herself exclaims that she is a "*mexicana de* este *lado,*" in order to conclude the poem with literal evidence (again, inscribed on her body) that the divisions enacted by Anglo tyranny have not been ultimately successful.

Finally, the poet deploys a cultural mestiza identity through her use of various mythical and religious figures, such as *la Virgen de Guadalupe* ("the single most potent religious, political and cultural image of the Chicano/*mexicano*" [30]) and Yemaya, who is the Yoruban and Afro-Cuban goddess of the sea (Freixas, 27; Lorde, *Black Unicorn,* 121–22). Later in the text, Yemayá is also identified as "the wind," and Anzaldúa positions herself as the daughter of both Yemayá and Oyá, "the whirlwind" (95n. 7). Both Anzaldúa and her text, then, embody this cultural mestiza identity.

Since she begins the poem with a metonymic linkage of woman and land ("1,950 mile-long open wound ... running down the length of my body"), Anzaldúa also redeploys a masculinist and colonialist trope that would figure both (as in *On the Road*) as passively waiting to be conquered. Anzaldúa links woman and land, however, not to reenact but to indict the colonial history of which such a trope is a part. Her indictment is sustained throughout the poem and can be heard in the poet's final anguished cry. Although *Ay ay ay* can, on one level, be read as a simple lament, it is simultaneously a defiant, resistant cry. The poet's body, which had earlier been marked as divided, with an open wound running down its length, becomes in the end a bridge connecting past and present. The poem's trajectory works to transform mestiza identity from a casualty of oppression and division into a sign of resistance and connection.

Still, Anzaldúa's bridge imagery in this conclusion is not simply celebratory, just as it was not in *This Bridge Called My Back*. That the conclusion can be read as a lament reminds readers that this transformation has come at some cost. Moreover, the image of a body connecting the "Old" and the "New" World recalls La Malinche, the Aztec woman whom some, such as Octavio Paz, have denigrated as La Chingada, "the fucked one," who supposedly "betrayed" her people through her union with Hernán Cortés. Alfredo Mirandé and Evangelina Enríquez dispute Paz and the others, emphasizing instead La Malinche's passivity:

> One persistent indictment of La Malinche in folklore, concerning the fact that she was Cortés's mistress or whore, implies active volition on her part, but this need not have been the case. Paz ... suggests that Malinche's sexual transgression derives precisely from passive volition on her part, an openness or willingness to be violated. Whether active or passive, history does not ascribe volition to Malinche in becoming Cortés's mistress; she was presented to him as a slave along with nineteen other women when he arrived on the coast of Mexico. (24)

La Malinche thus passes from critic to critic and interpretation to interpretation in a bizarre parody of the transaction between Cortés and those who met him on the coast of Mexico.

Through her invocation of the La Malinche story, however, Anzaldúa intervenes in the myth on several levels, replacing captivity with freedom

Unlimited Access? Queer Theory in the Borderlands

("The sea cannot be fenced"), betrayal with steadfastness ("This land was Mexican once, / was Indian always / and is"), and passivity with agency ("To show the white man what she thought of his arrogance, / *Yemaya* blew that wire fence down"). Most important, the poem's final line replaces the historical and critical objectification of La Malinche (and the nineteen other women) with a new subjectivity: *"Ay ay ay, soy mexicana de este lado."* *Soy mexicana* is already a subjective construction, but since the poem is both multilingual and constantly shifting between various linguistic codes, readers can hear (multiple) subjectivity in *Ay ay ay* as well, since the phrase aurally recalls the English "I I I." The end of Anzaldúa's poem thereby literalizes Sidonie Smith's argument: "For Anzaldúa the topography of the borderland is simultaneously the suturing space of multiple oppressions and the potentially liberatory space through which to migrate toward a new subject position" (200).

Anzaldúa's first poem in *Borderlands/La Frontera*, with its border crossing from one understanding of the borderlands and of mestiza identity to another, serves as a blueprint for the text as a whole. The desperate and oppressive "borderlands" that dominate "The Homeland, Aztlán/*El otro México*," the first essay, have been transformed into *el camino de la mestiza* (the mestiza way) in the final essay, "*La conciencia de la mestiza/* Towards a New Consciousness." The six sections of "*Un Agitado Viento/ Ehécatl*, The Wind" that follow the final essay and that conclude *Borderlands/La Frontera* can then be read as poetic explorations/performances of this new mestiza consciousness. Despite Anzaldúa's turn to the lyrical and poetic in the second half of her text, however, *Borderlands/La Frontera* contains no transcendent escape from identity and history à la Sal Paradise; rather, Anzaldúa's liminal and disruptive identity "puts history through a sieve, winnows out the lies, looks at the forces that we as a race, as women, have been a part of" (82). Over the course of the text, Anzaldúa's mestiza queer refocuses her (and her reader's) vision on the border conflicts that more celebratory travelers disavow.

After the opening poem, which concludes with the defiant assertion that she is what Anglo-American binary thinking would like to disavow (a "Mexican woman of *this* side"), Anzaldúa moves immediately into the borderlands. In the first essay, the region that is the borderlands remains a desperate and dangerous place, inhabited by the "prohibited" and "forbidden"; that is, by those whose identities are proscribed by dualistic thinking:

The U.S.-Mexican border *es una herida abierta* [is an open wound] where the Third World grates against the first and bleeds. And before a scab forms it hemorrhages again, the lifeblood of two worlds merging to form a third country—a border culture. Borders are set up to define the places that are safe and unsafe, to distinguish *us* from *them*. A border is a dividing line, a narrow strip along a steep edge. A borderland is a vague and undetermined place created by the emotional residue of an unnatural boundary. It is in a constant state of transition. The prohibited and forbidden are its inhabitants. *Los atravesados* live here. . . . The only "legitimate" inhabitants are those in power, the whites and those who align themselves with whites. Tension grips the inhabitants of the borderlands like a virus. Ambivalence and unrest reside there and death is no stranger. (3–4)

Anzaldúa's borderlands stand in stark contrast to the tension-free land that Kerouac's protagonists enter, where everything is pleasantly "mysterious" and even the authorities are "lazy and tender" (*On the Road*, 274). In fact, the passage immediately after this description of the borderlands in Anzaldúa's text highlights instead *conflict* with the "authorities." The passage consists of an anecdote about *la migra*, who deport a character named Pedro to Guadalajara, despite the fact that Pedro is a fifth-generation American. In his terror, Pedro is unable to find the English words to explain his situation, and since he has not brought his birth certificate with him to work in the fields, the white authorities deport him (*Borderlands/La Frontera*, 4).

Anzaldúa's anecdote thus ironizes the Kerouac passage I examined earlier, in which "these people were unmistakably Indians and were not at all like the Pedros and Panchos of silly civilized American lore" (*On the Road*, 280). Although this passage criticizes Americans, Sal and his friends remain blind both to the ways in which their exoticization and primitivization of "these people" are implicated in "silly civilized American lore" and to the ways in which they themselves carry "America" with them. The effacement of an ongoing Anglo-American history of exploitation of Mexico inevitably effaces the material conditions that actual Pedros (and Panchos) face. Not surprising, this is not the last complication of celebratory border-crossing tropes that Anzaldúa effects. In *On the Road*, Kerouac's hipsters are flabbergasted by the "great stacks of pesos" they receive in exchange for American dollars (275). Anzaldúa's essay in *Borderlands/La Frontera* reveals how such North-to-South border crossings are part of a larger exploitative economy:

Unlimited Access? Queer Theory in the Borderlands

137

> Los gringos had not stopped at the border. . . . Currently, Mexico and her
> eighty million citizens are almost completely dependent on the U.S. market.
> The Mexican government and wealthy growers are in partnership with such
> American conglomerates as American Motors, IT&T and Du Pont which
> own factories called *maquiladoras*. One-fourth of all Mexicans work at
> *maquiladoras;* most are young women. . . . The devaluation of the *peso* and
> Mexico's dependency on the U.S. have brought on what the Mexicans call *la
> crisis. No hay trabajo* [There is no work]. Half of the Mexican people are
> unemployed. In the U.S. a man or woman can make eight times what they
> can in Mexico. By March, 1987, 1,088 pesos were worth one U.S. dollar. I
> remember when I was growing up in Texas how we'd cross the border at
> Reynosa or Progreso to buy sugar or medicine when the dollar was worth
> eight *pesos* and fifty *centavos*. (10)

In contrast to those moving North to South, those making the migration
from South to North do so out of material necessity, brought on by the
position of economic dependency into which the United States has cast
Mexico. When these travelers cross the border, moreover, they do not
receive great stacks of either pesos or dollars.

The bulk of "The Homeland, Aztlán/*El otro México*" combines history,
mythology, philosophy, and poetry in order to document the existence of
those who reside in the borderlands. The title refers to Aztlán, the region
of the southwestern United States that is the mythological homeland of
Chicanos/as. At the same time, Anzaldúa's theory of the borderlands is
about other, less literally geographic borderlands; those who live in Anzaldúa's borderlands, to return to the quote with which I began this chapter,
are "the squint-eyed, the perverse, the queer, the troublesome, the mongrel, the mulato, the half-breed, the half dead; in short, those who cross
over, pass over, or go through the confines of the 'normal' " (3). This large
cast of characters notwithstanding, Anzaldúa concludes "The Homeland
Aztlán/*El otro México*" by focusing on how the U.S.-Mexican border and
the borderlands provoke danger for one very specific figure:

> La mojada, la mujer indocumentada [the female "wetback," the undocu-
> mented woman], is doubly threatened in this country. Not only does she
> have to contend with sexual violence, but like all women, she is prey to a
> sense of physical helplessness. As a refugee, she leaves the familiar and safe
> homeground to venture into unknown and possibly dangerous terrain.

                    This is her home
                  this thin edge of
                  barbwire. (12–13)

The poetic echo at the end of the essay is from the poem that opens *Borderlands/La Frontera*, in which Anzaldúa asserted, "This is my home / this thin edge of / barbwire" (3). Although the experience of the borderlands extends beyond specific figures and geographic locations, Anzaldúa's pronominal shift as she returns to the language of her earlier poem ("This is *my* home . . . This is *her* home") simultaneously grounds borderlands existence materially in the endangered figure of *la mujer indocumentada*.

The end of "The Homeland, Aztlán/*El otro México*," with these images of tension and danger, places the essay firmly within the first part of the trajectory I have been sketching out: Anzaldúa demonstrates the ways in which subjects are cast into abject positions as a result of binary thinking and how identities emerge as casualties of oppression, but she does not yet indicate fully whether such locations might be transformed into sites of resistance. In the second essay, *"Movimientos de rebeldía y las culturas que traicionan"* (Movements of rebellion and cultures of betrayal), however, that possibility once again emerges: "There in front of us is the crossroads and choice: to feel a victim where someone else is in control . . . or to feel strong, and, for the most part, in control. My Chicana identity is grounded in the Indian woman's history of resistance" (21). By the final essay, *"La conciencia de la mestiza/*Towards a New Consciousness," the transformation that is initiated in the early essays (and that is presented in microcosm in Anzaldúa's first poem) is complete.

Anzaldúa returns to material conditions such as those experienced by *la mujer indocumentada* throughout *Borderlands/La Frontera*. Hence the transformation represented in the text is not one that smooths over or escapes from conflict but rather one that locates and engages conflict. Anzaldúa's border crossings do not perpetuate but instead bring to light the effacement of identity and history that patriarchal, Anglo-American power encourages. *Borderlands/La Frontera* also discourages purely celebratory appropriations (by theoretical hipsters) of borderlands existence, since such appropriations would universalize away specific experiences. Anzaldúa's pronominal shift, in fact, reverses the course of appropriation. Instead of taking what is "yours" and making it "mine," Anzaldúa moves

Unlimited Access? Queer Theory in the Borderlands

in the opposite direction: "This is my home . . . This is her home." This is not to say, by any means, that Anzaldúa discourages critical dialogue or coalition; it is simply to say that Anzaldúa's text in many ways resists what Annamarie Jagose calls "utopic undifferentiation" (152) and, indeed, insists that critical dialogue proceed by specifying all the players in any given border conflict.[10]

Jagose reads Anzaldúa's *liminal* position as a *transcendent* one and mistakes the critical mobility of the mestiza for an absolute mobility that would escape conflict. Jagose insists, "*Borderlands* installs and valorizes the *mestiza* as a figure whose traversals of the border between inside and outside ensure only a utopic undifferentiation, merging and indistinguishability" (152). Although I would not deny that *Borderlands/La Frontera* contains utopic moments, Jagose's argument necessarily discounts Anzaldúa's persistent attention to the material conditions of borderlands existence. Jagose's "only" purifies *Borderlands/La Frontera* of its perverse insistence on specificity. Jagose argues that the text "ultimately represses" its understanding of the border and the mestiza "as the paradoxical site of undifferentiation and distinction" (157); *only* "utopic undifferentiation" remains in the end. According to Jagose's "ultimate" logic, Anzaldúa's concluding essay should valorize *nothing but* "merging and indistinguishability."

In actuality, even in the final pages of the essay, the mestiza advances by differentiating and distinguishing the particular histories and conflicts the border cites:

This land has survived possession and ill-use by five countries: Spain, Mexico, the Republic of Texas, the U.S., the Confederacy, and the U.S. again. It has survived Anglo-Mexican blood feuds, lynchings, burnings, rapes, pillage.

Today I see the Valley still struggling to survive. . . . The borderlands depression that was set off by the 1982 peso devaluation in Mexico resulted in the closure of hundreds of Valley businesses. Many people lost their homes, cars, land. Prior to 1982, U.S. store owners thrived on retail sales to Mexicans who came across the border for groceries and clothes and appliances. While goods on the U.S. side have become 10, 100, 1000 times more expensive for Mexican buyers, goods on the Mexican side have become 10, 100, 1000 times cheaper for Americans. Because the Valley is heavily dependent on agriculture and Mexican retail trade, it has the highest unemployment rates along the entire border region; it is the Valley that has been hardest hit. (90)

Unlimited Access? Queer Theory in the Borderlands

"Spain, Mexico, the Republic of Texas, the U.S., the Confederacy"—these signs mark specific restructurings of the borderlands. Furthermore, each restructuring repositions, and even multiplies, the players in this border conflict—players whom Anzaldúa's account, in turn, renders *distinguishable:* the homeless, the unemployed, U.S. store owners, Mexican buyers, American shoppers. As this passage indicates, then, liminality might be understood as the opposite of transcendence: the mestiza sees more clearly not because she is "above it all" but because she is caught between colliding cultures.[11]

Thus, in "*La conciencia de la mestiza/*Towards a New Consciousness," Anzaldúa participates in the Chicano/a critical tradition in which the border marks not a site of transcendence but a geographical and metaphorical site of struggle. The "new consciousness" that the text enacts, however, encourages the mestiza to see herself as enabled, not immobilized, by the struggle. The final essay makes the transformation explicit:

> The new *mestiza* copes by developing a tolerance for contradictions, a tolerance for ambiguity. She learns to be an Indian in Mexican culture, to be Mexican from an Anglo point of view. She learns to juggle cultures. She has a plural personality, she operates in a pluralistic mode—nothing is thrust out, the good, the bad and the ugly, nothing rejected, nothing abandoned. Not only does she sustain the contradictions, she turns the ambivalence into something else. (79)

Anzaldúa's "something else" is akin to the "something else" enacted by various texts in the Queer Renaissance: like Audre Lorde's Zami, Anzaldúa's mestiza queer understands identity through collectivity; like Randall Kenan's queer trickster, she is determined to disrupt and transform both a specific locale and the dualistic, hierarchical systems of power that oppress her. In one of Anzaldúa's earlier essays, included in *This Bridge Called My Back,* the collectivity-transformation equation is made explicit:

> We are the queer groups, the people that don't belong anywhere, not in the dominant world nor completely within our own respective cultures. Combined we cover so many oppressions. But the overwhelming oppression is the collective fact that we do not fit, and because we do not fit *we are a threat.* In El Mundo Zurdo [the Left-Handed World] I with my affinities and my people with theirs can live together and transform the planet. ("La Prieta," 209)

Unlimited Access? Queer Theory in the Borderlands

Six years later, in *Borderlands/La Frontera*, this disruptive figure emerges once again, more fully developed: "Let us hope that the left hand, that of darkness, of femaleness, of 'primitiveness,' can divert the indifferent, right-handed, 'rational' suicidal drive that, unchecked, could blow us into acid rain in a fraction of a millisecond" (69). Over the course of the text, the mestiza queer moves from being a casualty of dualistic thinking to being an agent of transformation: "*Su cuerpo es una bocacalle* [Her body is an intersection]. *La mestiza* has gone from being the sacrificial goat to becoming the officiating priestess at the crossroads" (80). Earlier, "life in the borderlands" had been characterized by paralysis: "Petrified, she can't respond, her face caught between *los intersticios,* the spaces between the different worlds she inhabits" (20). In contrast, in the final essay, *la mestiza* uses the seemingly interminable condition of being "caught between" identities and cultures to actively mediate with and contest the various cultures and identities that come together at the crossroads.

The terms *mestiza* and *queer* function similarly in Anzaldúa's work. Although she never obscures the specificity of oppressions that people experience (say, "homosexuals and others who deviate from the sexual common" [18], on the one hand, and people of color, such as *la mujer indocumentada,* on the other), Anzaldúa nonetheless sees "queer" and "mestiza" identity coming together in similar liminal and disruptive ways. Both mestizas and queers, after all, are among *los atravesados,* "those who cross over." In "*La conciencia de la mestiza*/Towards a New Consciousness," Anzaldúa explicitly probes how these identities inform each other, and in her work after *Borderlands/La Frontera,* she continues, insistently, to link them.

One of the first ways in which Anzaldúa brings these two identities together is in their formation: both result from attempts to identify and police deviant "others." Judith Raiskin explains how the conflation of a marked sexual and racial "deviance" occurred historically and argues that Anzaldúa rewrites that legacy:

> Categories of sexual behavior and identity created by nineteenth-and twentieth-century sexologists were also influenced by the classification systems of race, whereby people of color, particularly "mixed race" people, and homosexuals were conflated through the ideas of evolution and degeneration in the late nineteenth century. . . . Gloria Anzaldúa allows homosexuality and mixed-race identity to reflect each other by using and reworking the language of nineteenth-century evolutionary theory. (157; 159) [12]

In the queer context, the "marking" of "degeneration" is most evident in "La Prieta" (The dark-skinned one), the essay from *This Bridge Called My Back* that ends with the defiant assertion "We are the queer groups . . . and because we do not fit *we are a threat*" (209). In that essay, Anzaldúa subjects queerness to a transformation similar to the one she will later perform on mestiza identity in *Borderlands/La Frontera*. In contrast to the defiant assertion with which the essay ends, "La Prieta" begins with an exclusionary marking. After explaining that her mother "fucked before the wedding ceremony" (199), Anzaldúa writes that her mother felt "guilt at having borne a child who was marked 'con la seña [with the sin],' thinking she had made me a victim of her sin. In her eyes and in the eyes of others I saw myself reflected as 'strange,' 'abnormal,' 'QUEER.' I saw no other reflection. Helpless to change that image, I retreated into books and solitude and kept away from others" (199). Like Horace in Kenan's *A Visitation of Spirits*, Anzaldúa has looked in various "mirrors" and seen only inadequacy. At the end of "La Prieta," however, Anzaldúa moves from a debilitating solitude to an enabling collectivity, as "we . . . the queer groups" turn the reflection/(mis)recognition against the glassmakers, whose ideology of "normalcy" requires and produces the "abnormal" and the "strange."

Hence, and more important, Anzaldúa links mestiza and queer identities in terms of their function: to unmask Anglo, patriarchal, and heterosexual systems of power, which rest on binaristic foundations and which declare that some people "fit" while others do not. Nowhere, perhaps, is this similarity of purpose more clear than in "*La conciencia de la mestiza/*Towards a New Consciousness," where mestiza identity is bolstered by queerness and vice versa. There, immediately after situating *la mestiza* as the "officiating priestess at the crossroads," Anzaldúa links mestiza identity to queerness. Furthermore, in this passage Anzaldúa reproduces even in her syntax the movement away from an understanding of mestiza and queer identity as individual and abject and toward an understanding of both as collective and transformative:

As a *mestiza* I have no country, my homeland cast me out, yet all countries are mine because I am every woman's sister or potential lover. (As a lesbian I have no race, my own people disclaim me; but I am all races because there is the queer of me in all races.) . . . *Soy un amasamiento,* I am an act of kneading, of uniting and joining that not only has produced both a creature of darkness and a creature of light, but also a creature that questions the definitions of light and dark and gives them new meanings. (80–81)

From being outcast and disclaimed to being at the center of "all countries . . . all races"—Anzaldúa's syntax "gives new meaning" to "deviant" and individual mestiza/queer identities, reinventing them as collective and ensuring thereby that echoes of *multiple* subjectivity be heard around her *(Yo) soy* construction.

As the essay continues, the mediating, transformative role Anzaldúa assigns to *la mestiza* is clearly delegated to queers as well:

> Being the supreme crossers of cultures, homosexuals have strong bonds with the queer white, Black, Asian, Native American, Latino, and with the queer in Italy, Australia and the rest of the planet. Our role is to link people with each other. . . . People, listen to what your *jotería* [queer contingent] is saying.
>
> The mestizo and the queer exist at this time and point on the evolutionary continuum for a purpose. We are a blending that proves that all blood is intricately woven together, and that we are spawned out of similar souls. (84–85)

Significantly, the section heading that immediately follows this passage declares, "*Somos una gente* [We are a people]" (85), emphasizing a connected collectivity that is then underscored by the epigraph Anzaldúa employs for the ensuing section, which she takes from Gina Valdés's *Puentes y Fronteras: Coplas Chicanas* (Bridges and borders: Chicana ballads):

> Hay tantísimas fronteras
> que dividen a la gente,
> pero por cada frontera
> existe también un puente.
>
> [There are many, many borders
> which divide people,
> but for every border
> there exists also a bridge.]
> (*Borderlands/La Frontera*, 85)

"What your *jotería* is saying," then, is that attempts to separate absolutely "us" from "them" will fail, since bridges are always already conjoined to borders. The border crossing celebrated at the end of Anzaldúa's essay section certainly engages conflict and is still only the beginning of a process, the results of which cannot be wholly predicted in advance. "Your *jotería*," however, boldly envisions a transformed, less hierarchical world: "A massive uprooting of dualistic thinking in the individual and collective consciousness is the beginning of a long struggle, but one that could, in our best hopes, bring us to the end of rape, of violence, of war" (80).

Anzaldúa's reference to rape, violence, and war suggests that her mestiza queer comprehends the dangers of nationalism. Moreover, perhaps because of those dangers, the mestiza queer does not seek a hip Queer or Chicano "Nation" that would supplant, however metaphorically, the existing nations she criticizes. In this respect, Anzaldúa's linkage of queer and mestiza identity differs from Cherríe Moraga's linkage of queer and Chicana identity in "Queer Aztlán: The Re-formation of Chicano Tribe" (*Last Generation*, 145–74). In my mind, Anzaldúa's mestiza queer has more theoretical promise than Moraga's Queer Aztlán, which Moraga describes as a "Chicano homeland that could embrace *all* its people, including its jotería" (147). Moraga's theory, like Anzaldúa's, affirms identification across difference ("Chicana lesbians and gay men ... seek a nation strong enough to embrace a full range of racial diversities, human sexualities, and expressions of gender" [164]), but it nonetheless ends up locating (or "fixing") another "nation," whereas Anzaldúa's theory, in the end, more rigorously queries both nations and nationalisms. (*Borderlands/La Frontera*, remember, moves *from* "The Homeland, Aztlán," and *to* a new and flexible mestiza consciousness.)

Although Anzaldúa understands where more nationalistic theories are coming from, she nonetheless is fairly consistent, in *Borderlands/La Frontera* and elsewhere, in her advocacy for more connections outside of oneself or one's groups:

> A bridge excludes racial separatism. So the concept has taken a beating recently because of the reactionary times we're going through and the upsurge in racism and white supremacy. But I can see that in the '90s a rainbow *serpent* bridge composed of the new mestizas/os, bi- and multiracial queer people who are mixed and politicized will rise up and become important voices in our gay, ethnic and other communities. ("To(o) Queer," 260–61)

In this passage, the new mestiza again brings to light contradiction and conflict (racial separatism, reactionary times, racism, white supremacy),

Unlimited Access? Queer Theory in the Borderlands

but she simultaneously envisions the impossible "something else": a rainbow bridge, a bridge without borders.

After mestiza queer identity emerges as a disruptive, transformative force at the end of the essay section of *Borderlands/La Frontera*, Anzaldúa celebrates/performs this critical "new consciousness" in *"Un Agitado Viento/Ehécatl*, The Wind," the poetry section that comprises the second half of that text. The poems in this section reproduce the liminal linguistic position Anzaldúa introduces in the essays: some are written entirely in English, some in Spanish, some in a combination of the two. Some of the Spanish poems are followed by English translations; some are not. Once again, the liminality of these poems is also not simply linguistic; Anzaldúa forges a cultural mestiza identity by continuing to mix various myths and traditions (Spanish, Mexican, Native American). Finally, as with the Lorde poems I examined in my first chapter, the poetic voice itself often represents a coming together of various voices. At times, it is ambiguous whether the speaker is Anzaldúa, the women she loves, or a larger group of oppositional voices.

In *"Arriba mi gente"* (Rise up, my people), for example, Anzaldúa performs the mestiza queer consciousness that she advocated in her essays:

> Chorus: *Arriba mi gente* [Rise up, my people],
> *toda gente arriba* [all people, rise up].
> In spirit as one,
> all people arising
> *Toda la gente junta* [all the people united]
> *en busca del Mundo Zurdo* [in search of the Left-
> Handed World]
> *en busca del Mundo Zurdo.* (192)

The chorus to this poem is mestiza in its mixture of Spanish and English and queer in its invocation of *el Mundo Zurdo*, which Anzaldúa previously identified as the world of "the queer groups, the people that don't belong anywhere" ("La Prieta," 209). *El Mundo Zurdo* is also the place where transformation is possible, and here again, queer mestiza identity and *el Mundo Zurdo* are linked to collectivity and transformation: the poem ends with the imperative *"Arriba, despierta mi gente* [Rise up, awake my people] / *a liberar los pueblos* [to liberate the masses] / *Arriba mi gente, despierta* [Rise up my people, awake]" (193). The dedication to the poem— "*para* Tirsa Quiñones who wrote the music and Cherríe Moraga who sang it" (192)—underscores that this is a performance; mestiza queer identity is literally "staged" here and is at once individual and collective: Anzaldúa, Quiñones, and Moraga come together as one mestiza queer voice. In this context also, "chorus" might be read as "a group of people singing together" or as what Lorde envisions in *Need* as "a chorale of women's voices" (7), rather than simply as "a refrain," so that the collective identity extends even beyond those Anzaldúa explicitly names.

Hence, in *Borderlands/La Frontera*, Anzaldúa—"trapped" by identities ("queer," "mestiza") that are not supposed to fit anywhere—works those identities against the systemic forces that produce them as "other," "deviant." In the process, mestiza queer identity moves from being a site of individual abjection to one of collective transformation. The transformation mestiza queer identity advances is a transformation of hierarchies that perpetuate domination of individuals and groups on the basis of race, class, gender, and sexuality: "mestiza" speaks to and for those subordinated because of their race, class, and gender; "queer," to those subordinated because of their sexuality, gender, and—because Anzaldúa understands it as a "working-class word"—class ("To(o) Queer," 250). Even this schematization, however, is ultimately too easy, too neat. The mestiza queer as Anzaldúa deploys her moves away from easy categorizations, seeking instead to understand, for instance, how race complicates gendered issues or how class confounds simplistic, unexamined assumptions about sexuality.[13] Anzaldúa contests the demarcation of borders intended to divide people neatly, highlighting instead the overlapping margins that belie such attempts to divide absolutely.

In her work after *Borderlands/La Frontera*, Anzaldúa continues to reinvent mestiza/queer identity. In "Bridge, Drawbridge, Sandbar or Island: *Lesbians-of-Color Hacienda Alianzas* [Forging Alliances]," she writes, "The mestiza queer is mobile, constantly on the move, a traveler, *callejera* [gadabout], a *cortacalles* [jaywalker]. Moving at the blink of an eye, from one space, one world to another, each world with its own peculiar and distinct inhabitants, not comfortable in anyone of them, none of them 'home,' yet none of them 'not home' either" (218). The mestiza queer "mobility" detailed here is quite different from various white, male, and heterosexual mobilities. In contrast to the extreme comfort Kerouac's boys feel among the "peculiar and distinct inhabitants" of Mexico (inhabitants who, despite their peculiarity, are nonetheless recognizably hip, as far as Sal and the boys are concerned), the mestiza queer feels discomfort everywhere she goes. There is no magical end of the road for this gadabout as she drifts from place to place, and her travels and crossings are, like jaywalking, usually unsanctioned by, and in opposition to, "the law." Furthermore, as Anzaldúa's essay continues, it becomes clear that this traveler's goal is to identify those who claim unlimited access to her life and experience: those who attempt to "fix" her, to mark her as "other," to name and dismiss her experience. She calls her family and Chicana/o communities generally to task for their "heterosexist bullshit" and anti-feminism (218); she critiques white lesbians for their "exclusionary or racist remarks" (218); she feels empathy with men of color, "only to be saddened that they need ... to be educated about women-only space" (219).

In short, Anzaldúa counters the unchecked mobility of others with a mobility intent on unmasking the hierarchies and exclusions they perpetuate. This critical mobility animates a politics of alliance:[14]

> In alliance we are confronted with the problem of how we share or don't share space, how we can position ourselves with individuals or groups who are different from and at odds with each other, how can we reconcile one's love for diverse groups when members of these groups do not love each other, cannot relate to each other, and don't know how to work together. (219)

As "Bridge, Drawbridge, Sandbar or Island" continues, Anzaldúa emphasizes (literally) the importance of identifying and countering oppressive relations of power: *"coalition work attempts to balance power relations and undermine and subvert the system of domination-subordination* that affects even our most unconscious thoughts" (224–25).

In "To(o) Queer the Writer—Loca, escritora y chicana [Crazy woman, writer, and Chicana]," Anzaldúa again brings together queer and mestiza identities, asserting, "The new mestiza queers have the ability, the flexibility, the malleability, the amorphous quality of being able to stretch this way and that way. We can add new labels, names and identities as we mix with others" (279). This malleability and amorphism, used in the service of unmasking the operations of domination-subordination, is not unlike the image with which Anzaldúa closes the essay section of *Borderlands/La Frontera*. Although the earlier image in *Borderlands/La Frontera* is not so much a "working" of identity as a more literal working of the land, both images emerge from the desire for a radically different world:

> The Chicano and Chicana have always taken care of growing things and the land. . . . Growth, death, decay, birth. The soil prepared again and again,

impregnated, worked on. A constant changing of forms, *renacimientos de la tierra madre* [renascences of Mother Earth].

> This land was Mexican once
> was Indian always
> and is.
> And will be again.
> (*Borderlands/La Frontera*, 91)

Significantly, Anzaldúa's *renacimientos* here intersect with the understanding of "renaissances" I am advancing as a critical context for all the writers of the Queer Renaissance. Anzaldúa does not seek an escape from history and location; instead, her *renacimientos*, with their "constant changing of forms," seek a re-vision of history, identity, and location. The reemergence of the refrain from Anzaldúa's earliest poem in *Borderlands/La Frontera* ("This land was Mexican once / was Indian always / and is") underscores her connection of these *renacimientos* to alternative histories of resistance. Moreover, because of the transformation Anzaldúa puts into play over the course of the text, the refrain at this point is even more of a defiant assertion than it was in the earlier essay. It is, literally and symbolically, the last word of Anzaldúa's essay section. Because of Chicano/a, mestizo/a, and queer flexibility and malleability, Anzaldúa is able to shape life in the borderlands, where formerly "ambivalence and unrest" resided and death was "no stranger" (4), into something vibrant and triumphant, like the plants that emerge out of the dead ground.

Mestiza Queer Agents

The note of triumph sounds most clearly in "*La conciencia de la mestiza/* Towards a New Consciousness," but it is foreshadowed as early as the preface to *Borderlands/La Frontera*, where Anzaldúa asserts, "There is an exhilaration in being a participant in the further evolution of humankind, in being 'worked' on. I have the sense that certain 'faculties'—not just in me but in every border resident, colored or non-colored—and dormant areas of consciousness are being activated, awakened. Strange, huh?" (preface, no page number). Over the course of *Borderlands/La Frontera*, Anzaldúa establishes that the evolutionary process is ongoing. The "exhilaration" she feels is not transcendence; "work" here, as the image of working the land much later in the text suggests, entails a grounding in location and history. Moreover, the mestiza queer's own work is not done once she has shed light on the border guards. Instead, the "faculties being activated" within the mestiza queer provide her with the mobility necessary to shed light on all the players and overlapping locations in this border struggle. Anzaldúa encourages those in all the geographical and theoretical communities through which she moves to consider the tensions and contradictions they embody and the ways in which their locations overlap with other locations, whether privileged or marginalized. Thus, Anzaldúa even queers "queer" if she sees the concept interpellated as a fad and appropriated by theoretical hipsters seeking escape from identity and history.

The work of Judith Butler can help both in considering how such a queering moves forward and in complicating questions of agency in *Borderlands/La Frontera*. As the invocation of evolution should confirm, the mestiza queer's movement is not simplistically voluntaristic; instead, the queer agency Anzaldúa theorizes (where certain unexpected "faculties" are "awakened") exemplifies Butler's insistence that the subject "is always the nexus, the non-space of cultural collision, in which the demand to resignify or repeat the very terms which constitute the 'we' cannot be summarily refused, but neither can they be followed in strict obedience" (Butler, *Bodies That Matter*, 124). Butler's understanding of performativity as *"working the weakness in the norm"* (237), in turn, glosses Anzaldúa's own performance of mestiza queer identity as that which is produced but never fully contained by the border or border guards.

In a parody of the ways in which some have understood her notion of "gender performativity" from *Gender Trouble*, Butler writes in *Bodies That Matter: On the Discursive Limits of "Sex,"* "If I were to argue that genders are performative, that could mean that I thought that one woke in the morning, perused the closet or some more open space for the gender of choice, donned that gender for the day, and then restored the garment to its place at night" (x). Distancing herself from such voluntarism, Butler explores in *Bodies That Matter* the possibility of a "repetition that fails to repeat loyally" the identities into which one has already been cast (220). If binaristic systems of power demand that some embody, over and over, abject identity positions (say, "mestiza," "queer"), those same abjecting systems also provide "the occasion to work the mobilizing power of injury, of an interpellation one never chose" (123). Using recent theoretical and political citations of "queer" as an example, Butler explains:

> Paradoxically, but also with great promise, the subject who is "queered" into public discourse through homophobic interpellations of various kinds *takes*

up or *cites* that very term as the discursive basis for an opposition. This kind of citation will emerge as *theatrical* to the extent that it *mimes and renders hyperbolic* the discursive convention that it also *reverses*. The hyperbolic gesture is crucial to the exposure of the homophobic "law" that can no longer control the terms of its own abjecting strategies. (232)

Likewise, Anzaldúa, in the process of "citing" the mestiza identity she did not choose and that she experiences as an open wound at the beginning of *Borderlands/La Frontera*, renders hyperbolic and reverses the conventions of an Anglo-American discursive regime that would subordinate mestizas/os, "keeping them in their place" while reserving unchecked mobility for itself. Anzaldúa's "disloyal repetition" of mestiza queer identity both figures the border as always already transgressed by those who were supposed to be immobilized by it and turns the searchlight on those who fixed the border in the first place.

Repetitions can be "disloyal," however, not only to dualistic ideologies that would compel mestizas, queers, and others to embody abjection but also to "alternative" discursive regimes that would compel them to embody "hipness." Anzaldúa writes:

> If I have to pick an identity label in the English language, I pick "dyke" or "queer," though these working-class words (formerly having "sick" connotations) have been taken over by white middle-class lesbians in the academy. Queer is used as a false unifying umbrella which all "queers" of all races, ethnicities and classes are shoved under. At times we need this umbrella to solidify our ranks against outsiders. But even when we seek shelter under it we must not forget that it homogenizes, erases our differences. ("To(o) Queer," 250)

In this passage, Anzaldúa repeats with a difference even her own previous endorsement of queerness; "queers" here are no longer simply "the supreme crossers of cultures" who have bonds with "the rest of the planet." Still, despite the shift, Anzaldúa's cautions here reiterate one of the main tenets of her theory: what is needed is not an effacement of identity and history but a grappling with specific identities and histories, particularly histories of oppression and exploitation. The mestiza queer theory Anzaldúa advocates refuses to let dominant identities travel unmarked under the banner of a unifying hipness—in this case, an overly celebratory, transcendent, and unmarked white queerness that elides its contiguity to privilege and disavows any policing role it might continue to play in and around the borderlands. Queerness may provide a useful bridge, but as always for Anzaldúa, a bridge is never *in and of itself* cause for celebration. She writes elsewhere that "being a bridge . . . may mean a partial loss of self. Being 'there' for people *all the time, mediating all the time* means risking being 'walked' on, being 'used.' I and my publishing credentials are often 'used' to 'colorize' white women's grant proposals, projects, lecture series, and conferences. If I don't cooperate I am letting the whole feminist movement down" ("Bridge, Drawbridge," 223). As with feminism, so too with queer theory: even (or perhaps particularly) beneath the sign of queerness, whiteness must be marked and white privilege challenged. When white middle-class lesbians and gay men "frame the terms of debate," Anzaldúa suggests, "they police the queer person of color with theory. . . . Their theories limit the ways we think about being queer" ("To(o) Queer," 251).[15]

Anzaldúa's cautions here, in her comments and in the title of this later essay ("To(o) Queer the Writer"), signal a certain retreat from the identity "queer." Yet this is the essay that includes the bold assertion I have already quoted: "The new mestiza queers have the ability, the flexibility, the malleability, the amorphous quality of being able to stretch this way and that way" (249). Anzaldúa's retreat, then, is not from queerness per se but from monolithic and overly celebratory understandings of it.[16] Indeed, Anzaldúa's title obviously anticipates this double move: "to queer" calls readers and writers to action at the same time that "too queer" cautions them. Anzaldúa shapes—as she has since *This Bridge Called My Back*, long before queerness was hip—what Butler might call a *"critical queerness"* (*Bodies That Matter*, 223): a queerness that is both critically necessary and critical of itself; a queerness that insists on foregrounding, and hence undermining, the ways in which identities (even, potentially, other queer identities) are structured in domination so that certain histories of exploitation or appropriation are effaced. As Butler explains:

As expansive as the term "queer" is meant to be, it is used in ways that enforce a set of overlapping divisions: in some contexts, the term appeals to a younger generation who want to resist the more institutionalized and reformist politics sometimes signified by "lesbian and gay"; in some contexts, sometimes the same, it has marked a predominantly white movement that has not fully addressed the way in which "queer" plays—or fails to play—within non-white communities; and whereas in some instances it has mobilized a lesbian activism, in others the term represents a false unity of women and men. Indeed, it may be that the critique of the term will initiate a resurgence of both feminist and anti-racist mobilization within lesbian and gay politics or open up new possibilities for coalitional alliances that do not presume that these constituencies are radically distinct from one another. (*Bodies That Matter*, 228–29)

Anzaldúa's titular use of the phrase "to(o) queer" is a critical redeployment of the term precisely in the service of the "feminist and anti-racist mobilization" Butler envisions here. Butler's call for attention to how *queer* may or may not play in nonwhite communities, in turn, is a recognition, à la Anzaldúa, that it should not be solely white middle-class lesbians and gay men (such as Butler or myself) who "frame the terms of the debate."

Anzaldúa and Butler come together at this point not only in their critical understanding of queerness but also in their emphasis on coalition. Just as mestiza queer agency is not simplistically voluntaristic, neither is it simply individual. Indeed, as with Zami in my first chapter, mestiza queer identity is not simplistically voluntaristic precisely *because* it is not individual. I have already examined some ways in which Anzaldúa performs a collective mestiza queer identity in the poetry section of *Borderlands/La Frontera*. The emphasis on "coalition and alliance building" ("Bridge, Drawbridge," 229) is evident throughout her work and is a central component of the mestiza queer identity she theorizes: "*Dime con quien andas*," she writes, quoting a Mexican saying, "*y te diré quien eres* [Tell me who your friends are and I'll tell you who you are]" (*Borderlands/La Frontera*, 62). Her commitment to identity through collectivity is undoubtedly one reason why two of Anzaldúa's most important contributions to feminist, multiethnic, and lesbian/gay studies have been anthologies: *This Bridge Called My Back*, which she coedited with Cherríe Moraga, and *Making Face, Making Soul/Haciendo Caras*. The former text has been credited by many with revolutionizing feminism, and although neither text is marketed as "lesbian/gay," I would argue that both—because of the collective and disruptive queer positions they advance—should be seen as central texts in queer studies and in the Queer Renaissance as well.[17]

Long before taking the magical journey across the border, Kerouac's Sal Paradise heads to San Francisco. He explains, "There were plenty of queers. Several times I went to San Fran with my gun and when a queer approached me in a bar john I took out the gun and said 'Eh? Eh? What's that you say?' He bolted. I've never understood why I did that; I knew

Unlimited Access? Queer Theory in the Borderlands

queers all over the country" (*On the Road,* 73). Despite Sal's incredulity at his own actions, queer readers of *On the Road* might provide an answer to his quandary: Sal acts as he does to ensure an unlimited mobility for himself (indeed, "all over the country" and beyond), while simultaneously policing "others" who, with *their* mobility, might expose and disrupt the privileged positions he occupies. Such a mobility, which ultimately reinforces relations of domination-subordination, stands in stark contrast to the mestiza queer mobility Anzaldúa champions. "Allies," Anzaldúa writes, "remember that the foreign woman, 'the alien,' is *nonacayocapo* which in Nahuatl means one who possesses body (flesh) and blood like me. *Aliadas, recuerda que la mujer ajena tambien es nonacayocapo, la que tiene cuerpos y sangre como yo*" ("Bridge, Drawbridge," 229). Queer mestizas cross borders not in order to consolidate definitions of "self" and "other" or to appropriate the "exotic" and transcend the "self" but rather to unmask the separations and disavowals the border perpetuates and to locate, in a transformed borderlands, others/allies who can similarly imagine a queer, more humane, new world.

Chapter Four

Queer Identities in a Crisis

And then came *Angels in America*. There is something predictable, per-haps, about ending with the play that has received more attention than any gay or lesbian work of the past fifteen years, and indeed, more attention than any American play of the past half century. Tony Kushner's *Angels in America: A Gay Fantasia on National Themes* is a two-part, seven-hour spectacle that has been showered with praise by gay and nongay critics alike. In 1993 the first part—*Millennium Approaches*—won the Pulitzer Prize for drama and received four Tony Awards, including the awards for best play, best director, and best actor. *Millennium Approaches* was also presented with the Lambda Literary Award for gay and lesbian drama. The second part, *Perestroika*, received three Tony Awards in 1994, including for best play and best actor. Undoubtedly, this unprece-dented success contributed to John Clum's decision to put a still from *Angels in America* on the cover of his study *Acting Gay: Male Homosexu-ality in Modern Drama* and to label his discussion of Kushner's play "The Culmination" (313).

I certainly agree that Kushner's play merits praise; nonetheless, this chapter attempts to resist such teleological thinking. I am not simply celebrating *Angels in America* here, as if mainstream success were itself sufficient for ensuring a work's inclusion in the Queer Renaissance, and as if *Angels in America* were thus somehow the crowning glory of this contemporary literary and cultural movement. As my previous chapter indicated, in fact, a purely celebratory stance is in many ways inimical to the critical work the Queer Renaissance advances. Hence this chapter begins by considering how *Angels in America* stages queer identity and theory in ways akin to the other queer works I have been examining throughout. I argue that *Angels in America* provides audiences with a demonstration of how contradiction and disruption can be deployed criti-cally and communally. Focusing mostly on *Perestroika*, I explore how

Kushner queers that particular concept to promote the performance of an openly disruptive, contradictory, mingling, and—consequently—hopeful identity. The performance of this identity secures hope by articulating the messiness and mingling that the characters ultimately champion to a collective identity that can and will be continually reshaped in the fight against AIDS.

The chapter then attempts to provide a genealogy, of sorts, for this queer aesthetic. The second half of the chapter surveys Sarah Schulman's fictionalization of the early days of the AIDS Coalition to Unleash Power (ACT UP) in her novel *People in Trouble*, in order to put Kushner's theories more explicitly into conversation with other "demonstrations." AIDS activism premiered in the streets during the writing and production of *Angels in America*, and the queer identities that activists performed during their "successful run" parallel those performed onstage in Kushner's "gay fantasia." If, as both *Webster's New World Dictionary* and the *American Heritage Dictionary* suggest, a fantasia is "a medley of familiar tunes," then Kushner's gay fantasia, like any other, draws its themes and variations from the work of many different (mostly unnamed) composers. This chapter demonstrates how such an artistic collaboration proceeds.

The liminal queer identities that have been the focus of previous chapters are again central here, but I am particularly concerned at this point with the relationship between these new sexual and political identities and the aesthetic: with how those sexual and political identities incite the reinvention of artistic identities and visions, and vice versa. That relationship is one of the main foci of Schulman's novel, which depicts the exposure of Kate, a visual artist, to both the queer activist identities shaped by Justice (Schulman's fictional answer to ACT UP) and a liminal queer sexual identity (Kate is a bisexual woman migrating between life with Peter, her husband, and with Molly, her lesbian lover). Kate's negotiation of new sexual and political identities profoundly alters her understanding of art and leads her to a critical postmodern aesthetic intent on disrupting the harmonious use of space that her corporate sponsors exact. This chapter, then, is concerned less with applauding Kushner's mainstream success story than it is with examining the ways in which liminal sexual and activist identities—the "identities in a crisis" of my title—have shaped the critical aesthetic not only of *Angels in America* but also of the many other works that constitute the contemporary Queer Renaissance.

Staging the Queer Renaissance

Angels in America is set in New York City during 1985 and 1986. This is, as the play repeatedly reminds audiences, Ronald Reagan's America—a bleak world that offers its inhabitants little in the way of hope. As Louis Ironson, one of the central characters, muses:

> Maybe we are free. To do whatever.
>
> Children of the new morning, criminal minds. Selfish and greedy and loveless and blind. Reagan's children.
>
> You're scared. So am I. Everybody is in the land of the free. God help us all. (*MA*, 74)[1]

Despite this sardonic cry for help, however, and despite the apocalyptic rumblings that pepper *Millennium Approaches*, neither God nor Reagan appears to be coming to these characters' aid. Quite the opposite, in fact: *Millennium Approaches* presents a world in disarray, moving further and further into chaos. Louis's lover, Prior Walter, is diagnosed with AIDS, and their relationship is strained to the breaking point when Prior is rushed to the hospital in the middle of the night. "Tell him goodbye, tell him I had to go," Louis instructs the nurse before walking away from the hospital and from Prior (*MA*, 52).

Meanwhile, Roy Cohn—Kushner's dramatic representation of the arch-conservative lawyer and former aide to Senator Joseph McCarthy—is also diagnosed with AIDS. He responds to this diagnosis by threatening his doctor:

> Say: "Roy Cohn, you are a homosexual."
>
> *(Pause)*
>
> And I will proceed, systematically, to destroy your reputation and your practice and your career in New York State, Henry. Which you know I can do. . . . No, Henry, no. AIDS is what homosexuals have. I have liver cancer. (*MA*, 44, 46)

Finally, the other focal relationship of *Millennium Approaches* also fractures over the course of the play, as Joe Pitt, Roy's protégé in the federal court of appeals, acknowledges his homosexuality and abandons his wife, Harper. Joe and Harper's Mormon marriage no longer serves as a protective covering, and Harper is left alone with her Valium addiction as Joe departs in search of sex in Central Park.

Queer Identities in a Crisis

Millennium Approaches concludes with the arrival of an angel, who bursts into Prior's bedroom only to literalize the devastation that has been implicit throughout the play: *"As the room reaches darkness, we hear a terrifying* CRASH *as something immense strikes earth; the whole building shudders and a part of the bedroom ceiling, lots of plaster and lathe and wiring, crashes to the floor"* (*MA*, 118). The angel declares Prior a "Prophet" and informs him that "the Great Work begins" (*MA*, 119). The second half of *Angels in America*, then, emerges out of this literal and metaphoric wreckage. *Perestroika*, which Kushner dubs "essentially a comedy" (*P*, 8), reconfigures the relationships and resolves (in part) the crises of *Millennium Approaches*: Louis, after an affair with Joe characterized by passionate sex and intense disagreements about politics, rejects Joe's conservatism and attempts reconciliation with Prior. Harper, too, self-confidently puts Joe behind her, along with the ugliness she associates with their New York life, and catches a night flight to San Francisco, which she has learned is "unspeakably beautiful" (*P*, 122). Prior assures Louis that he still loves him but insists nonetheless that Louis not move back in. Roy Cohn dies, and Prior continues to live with AIDS, developing along the way a rather eccentric friendship with Hannah, Joe's Mormon mother, who has flown in from Utah to attend to the crisis between her son and Harper.

Most important, over the course of *Perestroika*, Prior works to understand and reject the vision the angel brings him. "YOU MUST STOP MOVING!" the angel commands:

> Forsake the Open Road:
> Neither Mix Nor Intermarry: Let Deep Roots Grow:
> If you do not MINGLE you will Cease to Progress:
> Seek Not to Fathom the World and its Delicate Particle Logic:
> You cannot Understand, You can only Destroy,
> You do not Advance, You only Trample.
> Poor blind Children, abandoned on the Earth,
> Groping terrified, misguided, over
> Fields of Slaughter, over bodies of the Slain:
> HOBBLE YOURSELVES! (*P*, 52)

The angel and her celestial colleagues feel that chaotic human movement, mingling, and progress have driven God away; Prior's role as prophet, consequently, is to preach resignation and stasis. After a struggle with the angel and the vision she brings, Prior follows her to heaven, where he at last refuses the death-in-life existence she and the other angels call for, demanding instead to be blessed with "More Life" (*P*, 135–36).

In this section, I consider the ways in which Kushner stages queer identity and theory in *Angels in America*, and for this reason I focus on the Prior plot. The queer identities I have traced throughout this study have a clear analogue in the identity performed by Prior; through the Prior plot, Kushner probes perestroika in order to present audiences with a queer political theory advocating interdependence, increased openness, and ongoing democratic participation and contestation. Sexuality provides Kushner with the ground upon which to forge this theory, but sexuality also serves as a figure for his broader political vision. *Angels in America* deploys the messiness and interconnectedness of sex as a metaphor for the collective and contested identities-in-process shaped and reshaped in the ongoing struggle against AIDS. Rather than renouncing the contradictions of human existence, as the angel demands, Prior embraces them and insists that they sustain a more radical democracy—a radical democracy I call "queer perestroika."

Prior's story, based on the biblical story of Jacob's nocturnal struggle with an angel in the book of Genesis—or more properly, the *Book of J*, as interpreted by Harold Bloom[2]—is ultimately about the survival of a people who thrive not in spite of but because of their migrating and mingling. J's Jacob, alone at night in a strange land, encounters a mysterious figure who wrestles with him until daylight. At the end of this struggle, Bloom writes, "the angel acknowledges the difference between the victim he had expected . . . and the hero he has encountered throughout the night" (218). Jacob demands that the angel bless him, which he does by granting Jacob the name of Israel, "God-clutcher." Bloom explains that one possible interpretation of this exchange is that the stranger is named Israel himself, and that he loses his name to Jacob (218). *Perestroika* likewise enacts such a renaming. "Angels in America," which at the end of *Millennium Approaches* would appear to refer to supernatural beings such as the one who crashes into Prior's bedroom, seems, at the end of *Perestroika*, a more apt designation for those like Prior, who cling to desire, hope, and life even as they are told by apparently all-powerful forces to "Creep away to Death" (*P*, 135). Prior resists this celestial injunction, ensuring that in the end, as with J's Jacob/Israel, "what matters . . . is not so much the identity of the more-than-human that could not hold on, but the new identity of the human that refused to let go" (Bloom, 218).

In what follows, I trace this exchange of identities more carefully,

Queer Identities in a Crisis

focusing initially on what it is about this forbidding angel that would make an exchange desirable. I argue that the logic of the angel's identity undermines itself, since her reactionary message is in tension with her fabulous and queer sexuality. Prior clings to the latter component of the angel's identity and—in the deconstructive struggle—articulates that fabulous sexuality to a collective political vision that affirms queer perestroika rather than the isolation and individualism the angel preaches.

Initially, the identity of the angel is enigmatic. In the first part of *Angels in America*, she does not even appear onstage until the final scene, when she crashes through Prior's bedroom ceiling. Earlier in the play, however, in keeping with the apocalyptic rumblings throughout *Millennium Approaches*, the angel's voice periodically interrupts Prior's scenes:

> Look up, look up,
> prepare the way
> the infinite descent
> A breath in air
> floating down
> Glory to . . . (*MA*, 35)

Stage directions indicate that this voice is *"incredibly beautiful"* (*MA*, 34) and that its approach causes *"dramatic change[s] in lighting"* (*MA*, 35). The angel is thus simultaneously beautiful and powerful, but beyond this, Kushner gives us few clues into the nature of her identity. Her role throughout *Millennium Approaches* is apparently to announce the approach of someone or something—though not necessarily of God, since here and elsewhere the refrain "Glory to God" is truncated. Audiences learn something about the angel's identity only from the effect she has on Prior: "I want the voice," Prior tells Belize, an African American former drag queen who is Prior's best friend and Roy Cohn's nurse. "It's all that's keeping me alive. . . . You know what happens? When I hear it, I get hard" (*MA*, 60). Neither Prior nor Belize can particularly explain such a reaction at this point, but Prior extracts a promise from Belize that he will not let the doctors change Prior's drugs.

The queer connections between desire, sexuality, and the angel solidify in *Perestroika*. Kushner titles the first act of *Perestroika* "Spooj" (*P*, 13), and although audiences do not learn immediately what the term *Spooj* (printed in their program) means—or, more important, what occurs in the meeting between Prior and the angel after she bursts into his bedroom—

this act nonetheless picks up where *Millennium Approaches* left off. Again we are introduced to the angel's identity indirectly, by seeing the effect she has on Prior. Immediately after she leaves his apartment, Prior calls Belize at the hospital to report. The meaning of "Spooj" comes—so to speak—as soon as Belize picks up the phone:

> BELIZE: Ten East.
> PRIOR: I am drenched in spooj.
> BELIZE: Spooj?
> PRIOR: Cum. Jiz. Ejaculate.
> BELIZE: Spooj?
> PRIOR: Onomatapoetic, isn't it?
>   I've had a wet dream.
> BELIZE: Well about time. Miss Thing has been abstemious.
>   She has stored up beaucoup de spooj.
> PRIOR: It was a woman.
> BELIZE: You turning straight on me?
> PRIOR: Not a *conventional* woman. . . . An angel. (P, 23)

When Belize and Prior meet in the second act, Prior explains in more detail exactly what took place during his meeting with the angel. Kushner uses a flashback scene in order to stage, finally, the actual encounter. The angel appears to Prior to declare him a prophet and to supply him with "The Book" (P, 47), whose contents he is to communicate to the people. These contents are revealed, however, only after a very queer and erotic episode that bears out the connections between the angel and sex that the audience has been primed to expect. I quote from this episode at length to stress how completely it satisfies these sexual expectations:

> *(The Angel's lines are continuous through this section. Prior's lines overlap.*
>   *They both get very turned-on.)*
>
> PRIOR *(Hit by a wave of intense sexual feeling):* Hmmmm . . .
> ANGEL: The Pulse, the Pull, the Throb, the Ooze . . .
> PRIOR: Wait, please, I. . . . Excuse me for just a minute, just a minute OK
>   I . . .
> ANGEL: Priapsis, Dilation, Engorgement, Flow:
> The Universe Aflame with Angelic Ejaculate . . .
> PRIOR *(Losing control, he starts to hump the book):* Oh shit. . .

Queer Identities in a Crisis

ANGEL: The Feathery Joinings of the Higher Orders,
    Infinite, Unceasing, The Blood-Pump of Creation!
PRIOR: OH! OH! I . . . OH! Oh! Oh, oh . . .
ANGEL *(Simultaneously):* HOLY Estrus! HOLY Orifice! Ecstasis in Excelsis!
    AMEN!

(Pause. If they had cigarettes they'd smoke them now.) (P, 47–48)

The angel and Prior's interaction here is, if you will, queer as fuck; as
Prior explains to Belize, "The sexual politics of this are *very* confusing" (P,
49). The Chicago production of *Angels in America* staged this scene with
the angel (Carolyn Swift) suspended just above the head of the bed on
which Prior (Robert Sella) was lying.[3] Prior initially retreated to the foot
of the bed when the angel crashed through his ceiling, but as he was more
and more overcome by the "intense sexual feeling," he moved back onto
the bed, turned over, and raised his ass up to the angel. The angel and Prior
thus appeared to be engaging in anal sex, with the angel on top. Throughout this scene, Swift's angel maintained a thrusting motion as she delivered
her lines, until the final "AMEN," which was spoken—or rather, ecstatically
shouted—with the first syllable drawn out: "AAAAAAAA-MEN!" The impression given was that the angel, with this exclamation, had ejaculated in
Prior's ass, and this was substantiated by Prior's immediate response:

PRIOR: What *was* that?
ANGEL: Plasma Orgasmata.
PRIOR: Yeah well no doubt. (P, 48)

After this erotic encounter, Belize and the audience finally hear, for the
first time, what the angel and her cohorts want from Prior. The angel
explains to Prior that God apparently created in humankind the potential
for change, for movement forward (P, 49). However, "Bored with His
Angels, Bewitched by Humanity, / In Mortifying Imitation of You," God
Himself began to move and migrate, until one day—the day of the Great
San Francisco Earthquake of 1906—He left and never came back (P, 50–
51). Since the angels feel that the messiness of human existence and
progress drove God away, they are convinced that the only way to bring
back God is through a cessation of movement and mingling: "FOR THIS
AGE OF ANOMIE: A NEW LAW!" (P, 56). The angel even suggests, obliquely,
that AIDS is to be a figure for this new law:

Queer Identities in a Crisis

On you in you in your blood we write have written:
STASIS!
The END. (*P,* 54)

In other words: your constant motion (one might even say "promiscuity") has brought you to this point and has marked you; there is nothing left for you to do but resign yourself to this conclusion, and tell others to do the same.

Given the foreplay audiences (and Prior himself) have experienced with this angel, the demand that he commence a sort of death-in-life existence should be a bit of a surprise. Prior is stunned by the contradiction: "What are you? Did you come here to save me or destroy me?" (*P,* 53). Belize, in contrast, forgets completely the sexual ecstasy that has preceded and tries to focus Prior's attention solely on the problematic content of this "prophecy": "This is . . . worse than nuts, it's . . . well, don't migrate, don't mingle, that's . . . malevolent, some of us didn't exactly *choose* to migrate, know what I'm saying. . . . This is just you, Prior, afraid of the future, afraid of time. Longing to go backwards so bad you made this angel up, a cosmic reactionary" (*P,* 55). With its focus on malevolence, Belize's interpretation intersects with Bloom's rereading of the Jacob story. Bloom reads Jacob's angel as relatively hostile, in spite of normative Christian and Judaic interpretations that suggest otherwise. " 'Wrestling Jacob' is a powerful image, particularly in Protestantism," Bloom writes, "where the agon is essentially seen as a loving struggle between Jacob and God. But . . . there is absolutely nothing loving about this sublime night encounter" (216). Likewise, the angel's message in *Perestroika* can be read as hostile to human vitality.

Since she appears onstage only at the very end of the first play, there is not much in *Millennium Approaches* that foreshadows the angel's gloomy message in *Perestroika.* Kushner does provide a few indirect hints in the first play of what is to come, however. In both *Millennium Approaches* and *Perestroika,* all of the minor characters are played by actors who are also playing major roles. Sister Ella Chapter, for instance, is the real estate agent who agrees to sell Hannah's house in Salt Lake City when Hannah decides to head to New York to help Joe and Harper. Kushner's instructions call for the actor playing the angel to play Sister Ella Chapter (*MA,* 4)— and with good reason, as Sister Ella's philosophy is similar to what the angel will preach in *Perestroika.* Sister Ella explains to Hannah, "I always thought: People ought to stay put. That's why I got my license to sell real estate. It's a way of saying: Have a house! Stay put! It's a way of saying traveling's no good" (*MA*, 82). Prior's nurse, Emily, is played by the same actor, and Kushner likewise has this character, quite literally, speak for the angel. At one point Emily unexpectedly begins yelling at Prior in Hebrew:

> EMILY: There's really nothing to worry about. I think that shochen bam-romim hamtzeh menucho nechono al kanfey haschino. (*MA*, 98)

Prior becomes extremely agitated, but Emily denies that she has said anything out of the ordinary: "*Hebrew? (Laughs)* I'm basically Italian-American. No. I didn't speak in Hebrew" (*MA*, 98). Emily's denial confirms for audiences that they are getting not *her* personality but rather a literal foreshadowing of the angel's personality. In the Chicago production, when Swift delivered her Hebrew lines, she added to the impression that the angel's personality would be fairly hostile by having her Emily face Prior and scream.

The Hebrew words Emily screams here, and in two more outbursts in this scene, both compound and complicate the angel's hostility. The Hebrew, from the *Daily Prayer Book/Ha-Siddur Ha-Shalem*, asks the spirit of God to bring quietness and peace to Prior. These are not necessarily hostile sentiments, but since this is a prayer for the dead, and since Prior— in this scene and throughout *Angels in America*—continues to *live* with AIDS, the angel's words could be understood as betraying a death wish for Prior. Most American audiences would likely see only hostility if and when the actor playing Emily screamed these lines, since—like Prior (or myself)—they would be unlikely to have a working knowledge of Hebrew.[4]

Yet despite this hostility, and despite the fact that—given her message of resignation or death wish—the angel is indeed a "cosmic reactionary," the contradiction remains: she is repulsive because of her demand that human movement and interaction cease, but at the same time, she is eminently attractive in that she is responsible for not only the hottest sex Prior has had in months but possibly the queerest sex he has ever had. Moreover, later in the play, she has this effect on others: Hannah, who is sitting with Prior in his hospital room, "*has an enormous orgasm as the Angel flies away to the accompanying glissando of a baroque piccolo trumpet*" (*P*, 120). This scene takes place after Prior has left the room, and again, the performance of sexuality is both queer and intense. Swift's angel in the Chicago production turned to Hannah (Barbara Robertson) with a lascivious look on her face and proceeded to rub the inside of her thigh invitingly, as Hannah watched from across the room, exclaiming, "What? What? You've got no business with me, I didn't call you, you're *his* fever dream not mine, and he's gone now and you should go too, I'm waking up right ... NOW!" (*P*, 120). Instead of waking up, however, Hannah is seduced; she walks over to the angel, and the two fall into a passionate kiss. After this kiss, Robertson performed her orgasm by falling back on Prior's bed and shaking all over as the angel disappeared in a flash of light. The kiss between Swift and Robertson and Robertson's exuberant orgasm elicited vigorous applause from Chicago audiences. Audiences may not have agreed with or may have been baffled by the hostile angelic message, but their applause clearly bespoke approval of the women's sexual performance.

Earlier in *Perestroika*, as Hannah struggles to come to terms with her son Joe's homosexuality, she explains to Prior, "It just seems ... ungainly. Two men together. It isn't an appetizing notion but then, for me, men in *any* configuration ... well they're so lumpish and stupid" (*P*, 104). Hannah's statement is thrown into ironic relief when she eventually gets a taste of sex with the angel; not finding men palatable apparently does not forestall, and may even facilitate, Hannah's extreme satisfaction with this female angel. In the end, Hannah's sex scene only underscores the angel's contradictions: she brings intense pleasure to everyone, including the audience, while demanding, in effect, that all such pleasure cease.

John Clum, working with an earlier draft of *Perestroika*, glosses over this contradiction by reading the sexuality of the angels not as paradoxically similar to the acts they denounce but rather as a sort of safeguard against those very acts. For Clum, apparently, angelic sex itself is not movement and mingling but is, instead, that which keeps the angels from moving. It is this sex-as-stasis, Clum implies, that God ultimately rejects: "Having tired of the eternal sexual bliss of paradise and its ever adoring angels, he followed the example of his creation, man" (314). To support this opposition, Clum provides an earlier version of the lines Kushner has the angel say, which I quoted above:

> His lust gave way to wanderlust
> In mortifying imitation of you, his least creation. (Clum, 314)

Given these lines, with their suggestion that lust gives way to wanderlust, Clum is entirely justified in the opposition he sets up between angelic sex and human movement/migration. But Kushner removed this line from later versions, including the published version of *Perestroika;* through this removal, Kushner makes it more difficult to naturalize away the contradiction I have been drawing out. Contradiction, for Kushner, is one of the angel's central components: "She's the contradictory spirit of America. . . . She's the angel of history. She's the intermediary between the divine and the material world. She's also the angel of theatricality. And yes . . . she's a human body in God-like drag" (qtd. in Kroll, 58).[5] Hence, Kushner dispenses with a line that might position the angels' sexuality itself, and not simply the angelic message, in opposition to vitality and, through this alteration, explicitly heightens the tension between the angels' sexuality and their message.

Ultimately, this tension facilitates the exchange of identities and the queer theory that *Angels in America* stages. That exchange of identities commences, I would argue, with another tension and another exchange that is performed in *Perestroika:* an exchange of glances between Prior and the angel immediately after she demands that humankind stop moving. A lot is communicated through this exchange of glances, including, I think, Prior's acknowledgment to the angel that he sees the contradiction between the fatalistic prophecy she has just given and the hot sex that preceded it. The angel, in turn, sees this acknowledgment in Prior's glance and is, not surprisingly, uncomfortable with his recognition of her contradictions:

PRIOR: Whatever you are, I don't understand this visitation, I don't under-
     stand what you want from me, I'm not a prophet, I'm a sick, lonely man,
     I . . . Stop. Moving. That's what you want. Answer me! You want me dead.

(Pause. The Angel and Prior look at each other.)

ANGEL: YES. NO. NO.
     (Coughs)
     YES.
     This is not in the Text, We *deviate* . . . (*P,* 53)

We deviate, indeed. Prior's "deviation" here, with its complementary destabilizing gaze, is his first explicit challenge to the new order that the angels seek to fashion. In the Chicago production, Carolyn Swift sharply differentiated her "yes" and "no," highlighting how little the angel expected this sudden alteration in "the Text"; her "yes" was delivered softly, as though she and Prior were locked together in a spell (as indeed they were a few moments earlier, as Robert Sella's Prior listened, entranced, to her demand that he stop moving), but her "no" was shouted, as she abruptly came to realize that Prior would resist her demands. Through such nascent acts of deviation, Prior begins to usurp the authority of the angel's position. As the angel acknowledges, Prior's performance marks a moment of textual transgression, or what we might call a moment of queering.

In this scene, the players present audiences with a literal dramatization of the transgressions the other texts in my study have written. In fact, the angel's italicized response to Prior's gaze ("We *deviate* . . .") could be a byword for my entire project, since in each chapter I have examined the ways in which lesbian and gay writers in the Queer Renaissance shape queer identities that, in their deviation from heteronormativity, are disruptive and transformative. *Collective* deviation is again crucial here. As the play continues, Prior moves to a location where multiple actors envision a more radical democracy emerging from the contradiction and chaos the angel resists. Such movement from contradiction to community is not automatic: Roy Cohn, for instance, takes his understanding of chaos in the opposite direction. Roy says to Joe in his very first scene, "I see the universe . . . as a kind of sandstorm in outer space with winds of mega-hurricane velocity, but instead of grains of sand it's shards and splinters of glass" (*MA*, 13). Roy's understanding of chaos fuels ruthlessness and individualism, not community. In contrast, Prior's affirmation of the messiness of human existence encourages him to appropriate and disseminate not only the angel's authority but also her ironic and unintended acknowledgment that deviation is threatening when it takes place in the first-person plural. In the Queer Renaissance, multiple actors in many different locations have declared, "We deviate." Hence, despite the fact that Prior himself suggests this is one of his weakest, most isolated moments ("I'm a sick, lonely man"), it is in this scene that *Angels in America* effectively begins to stage the Queer Renaissance: not because it is clear to audiences at this point that Kushner's play is an individual artistic achievement but rather because Kushner and the actors, along with all of those involved in the "production" of queerness in *Angels in America*, implicitly connect Prior's performance here to the widespread "rebirth" of radical gay and lesbian political analysis occurring offstage. Actors onstage and offstage authorize the Queer Renaissance; Prior's identity in this scene mingles with the new queer and resistant identities performed in the streets.

The political analysis that is central to the Queer Renaissance seeks to

Queer Identities in a Crisis

expose and undermine the ways in which domination is structurally secured in and through the construction of normative identities. In the preceding chapter, for Gloria Anzaldúa this involved working sexual and racial categories against themselves, so that mestiza queer identity was no longer simply a mark of abjection but rather a force that might unsettle the system of binaristic thinking on which normative identities depend. Similarly, in this scene, Prior's recognition of the angel's contradictions begins to undermine the identificatory regime she and her cohorts seek to institute. Initially, the angel, with her demand that human movement and migration cease, appears virtually all-powerful. Prior begins to recognize, however, that the angel attempts to deny or exclude what she has already incorporated into her own identity. The struggle between them, then, is a comically deconstructive one, through which Prior is able to effect both an explicit reversal of power relations and an implicit exchange of names.

I call the struggle "comic" not only because Kushner himself dubs *Perestroika* a "comedy" but also because of the ways in which it inscribes a deconstructive relationship onto the bodies of these characters: the struggle between the angel and Prior is an ironic *performance* of deconstruction. Generally, deconstructive analyses expose how the logic of a system of meaning undermines itself. More specifically, binary oppositions that present themselves as apparently, "naturally" equal and opposite (man/woman, straight/gay) can be shown to exist actually in relationships of domination and subordination that valorize the first term and disparage the second. Despite this positioning of the second term as ancillary, however, the first term secures its identity and dominance only through the ongoing exclusion of the second term; the first term must repeatedly define itself in opposition to what it is not. Ironically, this act of exclusion ensures that the first term actually depends for its meaning on the second term, and this dependence, in turn, puts the supposed "dominance" of the first term into perpetual jeopardy. Hence the first term not only excludes but *incorporates* the second term, and this simultaneous exclusion and incorporation makes the structuring of systems of meaning in terms of binary oppositions irresolvably unstable.[6]

In *Perestroika*, Kushner's performance of deconstruction is comic in that his characters literally re-present a deconstructive scenario. The angel seeks to establish an opposition between order and stasis, which are to be valorized, and mingling and migration, which are to be subordinated. However, this opposition is ripe for deconstruction, since the angel cannot even describe the new order she desires without opposing it to the human action she claims to repudiate: the angels value stasis precisely because it is *not* movement or mingling. Yet Kushner takes this strict opposition, and the subsequent performance of deconstruction, one step further, since the angel literally incorporates, for the audience, the movement she would exclude from her identity: the angel calls for inaction but at the same time *embodies* the hottest action Prior has had in months. The reversal of power relations that takes place will thus be a true disruption from within, as the logic of the angel's identity undermines itself.

The orgasmic yell the angel emits during her initial encounter with Prior ("HOLY Estrus! HOLY Orifice! Ecstasis in Excelsis! AMEN!" [*P,* 48]), juxtaposed with the prophecy she later gives him ("STASIS!/The END" [*P,* 54]), spotlights the foundational illogic of her identity. She preaches a morbid stasis and yet both preaches and *performs* ec-stasis ("in the highest! So be it!"). This contradiction is not lost on Prior, who explains to Belize that the angels are "basically incredibly powerful bureaucrats . . . they're sort of fabulous and dull all at once" (*P,* 49). *Fabulous,* used for decades in gay male vernacular communities, is an important term in the Kushner lexicon. In "Notes Toward a Theater of the Fabulous," Kushner's foreword to a recent anthology of contemporary gay plays, he writes:

> *Fabulous* became a popular word in the queer community—well, it was never *un*popular, but for a while it became a battle cry of a new queer politics, carnival and camp, aggressively fruity, celebratory and tough like a streetwise drag queen: *"FAAAAABULOUS!"* . . . *Fabulous* is one of those words that provide a measure of the degree to which a person or event manifests a particular, usually oppressed, subculture's most distinctive, invigorating features. (vii)

It is to the most fabulous—and thus, as Kushner's notes make clear, to the "queerest"—aspects of the angel's identity that Prior eventually clutches, explaining to all the angels in the last act that although he rejects their prophecy of resignation, he nonetheless wants to be blessed, by them, with "more life." Sensing a tradition of fabulousness beneath the angel's dullness and desire for stasis, Prior seizes on the former. As Walter Benjamin insists, "In every era the attempt must be made anew to wrest tradition away from a conformism that is about to overpower it" (255). The deconstructive struggle Prior wages against the angel wrests a fabulous tradition away from straight conformism and thereby implicitly responds to Benjamin's call to "brush history against the grain" (257).

Queer Identities in a Crisis
———

Clum writes, "Prior ... wants more life and will, like Jacob, wrestle with the angel to get it" (319); Clum does not clarify, however, *why* Prior would want "more life" from this angel and her cohorts, who come across as fairly stuffy celestial prudes in his analysis. Since Clum never moves beyond the angels' calls for "stasis, death" (319), or their desire for "an end to human movement, migration, change" (314), Prior's motives remain unclear in Clum's interpretation, unless Prior wrestles a blessing from the angel simply because she is a powerful figure or—more insipidly—because Jacob did so. My argument, in contrast, is that queer sex generally and the angels' sexuality specifically are crucial to understanding not only the exchange between Prior and the angel but *Angels in America* as a whole. Prior deconstructs the angel's message of doom by clinging to the fabulous and erotic sexuality he has shared with her, and in the end, this vitality wins out. Prior returns the Book containing the prophecy and informs the angels, "We can't just stop. We're not rocks—progress, migration, motion is ... modernity. It's *animate*, it's what living things do. We desire" (*P,* 132). Prior's appropriation of the angel's "we" disregards the anxiety inherent in her "We deviate" and instead celebrates connection among "living things." Prior's "we," moreover, cannot but encompass the angel at this point, given that his only *performance* of desire in *Perestroika* is with her. And although the angel initially appears incredulous ("Oh who asks of the Orders Blessing/With Apocalypse Descending?/Who demands: More Life?" [*P,* 135]), her own internal contradictions ultimately sanction the reversal of her message. Indeed, even the casting and staging of this scene, as in many others, represent interconnectedness and mingling: just as the actor playing the angel takes on additional roles throughout *Angels in America*, the actors playing Harper, Joe, Hannah, Belize, Louis, and Roy all take on additional roles as angels here.[7]

Angels in America revels in the eros of this interconnectedness. Clum suggests, "AIDS drama may not be erotic, but it is unabashedly romantic" (74); this argument, however, is difficult to sustain given *Perestroika*, which includes several onstage sex scenes in addition to the human and angelic orgasms I have detailed.[8] Indeed, Kathleen Chalfant, who played Hannah on Broadway, actually suggested, "An unmentioned subtext ... is we'd like the whole audience to have a simultaneous orgasm" (qtd. in Friend, 160). In my mind, it is this queer insistence on sex, sexuality, and interconnectedness that both sets *Angels in America* apart from more "unabashedly romantic" and individualistic AIDS plays and makes it central to the Queer Renaissance. The outcome of *Perestroika* both celebrates queer sexuality and, more important, deploys it as a figure for Kushner's broader political vision of queer perestroika.

Some critics, however, deemphasize the physical in *Angels in America* and focus instead on the spiritual, rebinarizing the oppositions the play deconstructs. Rob Baker, for example, reads the play as alluding to the alchemical process whereby "the inner soul" is transformed from a "basic instinctual self into a higher spiritual being" (214). When the angel announces the "Great Work" at the end of *Millennium Approaches*, Baker argues, the capitalization particularly suggests that Kushner has in mind the alchemical "Great Work," the transformation of base lead into pure gold that served as a symbol for the transformation of the soul (214). Baker's account of the breadth of Kushner's allusiveness is useful, but he does not go far enough. Although he denies his reading is connected to "New Age religiosity" (220), he nonetheless grounds his argument about spirituality with a predictable New Age emphasis on self-transformation: the angel "is the force (and perhaps the only force) which can meet AIDS head-on and combat that other brutally real/unreal mysterious phantom force in a fight to the finish. Once Prior has known her, he can face that same struggle in himself" (221). The emphasis on personal struggle and transformation allows Baker, at his weakest, to endow AIDS itself with mystical qualities. It is one thing to say characters *use* AIDS to achieve transformation but quite another to mystify AIDS by suggesting it is some sort of *prerequisite* to transformation: "AIDS itself, in all its horror, ironically may be the very Philosopher's Stone that the characters . . . must 'possess' in order to achieve the necessary transformation, be it political or spiritual" (215).

Despite Baker's nod here to the political as well as the spiritual, he emphasizes only the spiritual in his analysis. He insists that Kushner's play is both political and sexual, but he never explains how; nor does he consider how the various elements (spiritual, political, sexual) might be interdependent. By contrast, in my reading of the play, the sexual is both the ground for Prior's spiritual struggle with the angel and the element that ensures he will prevail against her prophecy of resignation. The result of this spiritual struggle is, in turn, a political theory that I label *queer perestroika*: that is, a politics of sexuality emphasizing interdependence, coalition, openness, and democratic participation and contestation—or, if you prefer more physical terms, coming together, mingling, messiness, and disruption. Not surprising, as Kushner's "Notes Toward a Theater of the Fabulous" acknowledges, numerous variations on this theory were playing

Queer Identities in a Crisis

successfully in the streets during the writing and production of *Angels in America*, breeding such slogans as "We're here, we're queer, we're fabulous, get used to it" and "Safe sex—Do it!" In fact, Michael Mayer, the director of the Chicago production, explicitly acknowledged that one of the messages of the play was "We *are* fabulous—get used to it!" (qtd. in Hamilton-Little, 18).

Clum suggests that the "key words" in *Perestroika* are "blessing" and "forgiveness" (322). Without disputing this, I would add the titular term *perestroika* or the concept *queer perestroika* to Clum's list, despite the fact that "perestroika" itself is not spoken onstage until the play's epilogue, and "queer perestroika" is not spoken at all. The term *queer perestroika* is actually mine, but I think it is nonetheless a key concept and a useful and logical label for the theory Kushner advances in *Angels in America*. The Russian word means "a restructuring of all social relations" (Miracky, 12) and was used during the 1980s to refer to President Mikhail Gorbachev's comprehensive plan for reform of the Soviet Union. Gorbachev's goal was to build *glasnost*, or "openness," into the political process, increasing citizen participation and decreasing government bureaucratization. Political institutions were to be decentralized, and Soviet foreign policies were to include, overtly, recognition of international interdependence.

In the epilogue to the play, "Bethesda," the characters comment directly on this process. It is February 1990, and four years have passed since the end of the last act; as Prior explains, "I've been living with AIDS for five years. That's six whole months longer than I lived with Louis" (*P*, 146). Prior, Louis, Belize, and Hannah (who is now fully transformed into a hip New Yorker) are gathered at the Bethesda Fountain in Central Park. Louis is celebrating global change:

> LOUIS: Gorbachev is the greatest political thinker since Lenin. . . . Remember back four years ago? The whole time we were feeling everything everywhere was stuck, while in Russia! Look! Perestroika! The Thaw! It's the end of the Cold War! The whole world is changing! Overnight!
>
> HANNAH: I wonder what'll happen now in places like Czechoslovakia and Yugoslavia. (*P*, 145–46)

As Hannah's comment makes clear, there is more than a little dramatic irony in this celebration of perestroika. Audiences know what the characters do not: "places like Czechoslovakia and Yugoslavia" no longer exist, and indeed, the Soviet Union itself has fallen; nationalistic fervor and ethnic conflict in those same places have brought about untold carnage;

Gorbachev himself has been removed from power, along with his plans for reform within socialism.

The dramatic irony of Hannah's musings about Yugoslavia and Czechoslovakia, however, intersects irony of another sort: reports of perestroika's death may have been exaggerated, since the queer perestroika that has already succeeded overshadows the perestroika that has already "failed." The play juxtaposes Gorbachev's "failure" here with Prior's success. Prior's success, furthermore, is both ongoing and larger than Prior the individual:

> PRIOR: [to the audience] . . . This disease will be the end of many of us, but not nearly all, and the dead will be commemorated and will struggle on with the living, and we are not going away. We won't die secret deaths anymore. The world only spins forward. We will be citizens. The time has come.
> Bye now.
> You are fabulous creatures, each and every one.
> And I bless you: *More Life.*
> The Great Work Begins. (*P*, 148)

Perestroika thus ends with Prior's appropriation not only of the angel's "we" but also of her pronouncement from the end of *Millennium Approaches*: "The Great Work begins." Rejecting the angel's demand for death-in-life and clinging instead to queer perestroika, Prior reverses the relations of power and appropriates for himself the most fabulous aspects of the angel's identity. The "Angels in America" are, at the end of the play, not those seemingly supernatural visitors who, in this play, crash into human lives and demand resignation but rather those fabulous (and entirely human) creatures who struggle on in the fight against AIDS— moving forward, acting up, demanding that we not die secret deaths any longer. Moreover, Prior's "Great Work" here is no longer Baker's alchemical, spiritual, and individual process; instead, it is linked to the very political and public work of forging a more radically democratic citizenship.

This link explicitly puts *Angels in America* into conversation with the new and hopeful queer identities being performed offstage, in groups such as ACT UP and Queer Nation. It is thus appropriate that Prior is, at this point, literally in conversation with those seated offstage, in the audience. In this scene, Kushner both commemorates the transformative queer work that angels in America have performed in the previous four years, and— through Prior's direct address to the audience—recruits others to carry on that work, which has only just begun. Such commemoration of the past, coupled with the recognition of an ongoing struggle for more life, is represented by the Bethesda Fountain itself, which depicts the Jewish myth of a fountain in Jerusalem that could cleanse those who bathed in it of pain and disease. As Prior explains about the Bethesda angels whose statues grace the fountain in Central Park, "They commemorate death but they suggest a world without dying" (*P*, 147). Certainly, Prior's comments about these mythical figures could be seen as a return to the supernatural, opposed once more to the earthly and the political. Yet the resignification of "angels" that has already occurred in this play complicates such a reading, focusing attention instead on those figures who, during the writing and production of *Angels in America*, were indeed both commemorating death (in collective works such as the AIDS memorial quilt) and actively demanding (in demonstrations around the country) an end to the dying.

At one point in *Millennium Approaches*, Louis—wracked with guilt over his abandonment of Prior—tells Belize, "There are no angels in America" (*MA*, 92). Of course, since Louis says this while performing in a play called *Angels in America*, his observation is already a bit ironic. Yet the irony goes much further than this, given Prior's "deviation" from the celestial text of resignation—a deviation which guarantees that the trajectory of the play will advance toward his appropriation and dissemination of the queer and fabulous aspects of the angel's identity. In fact, the very staging of this scene renders Louis's thoughts ironic by causing audiences to focus on Prior. The scene is split: Louis and Belize are in a coffee shop on one side of the stage, while Prior and his nurse Emily are in an examination room on the other. The split scene ensures that even as Louis denies their existence, audiences are confronted with at least two potential angels in America: Emily, who is played by the actor who plays the angel (and this is the scene that later underscores that connection, when Emily unexpectedly shouts at Prior in Hebrew), and Prior, who will eventually claim the title after wresting "more life" from her. In the Chicago production, the irony was compounded even further by Belize (Reg Flowers), who—as he sat listening skeptically to Louis—wore a denim jacket with an angel's wings embossed on the back. Hence there are multiple angels in America, even as Louis speaks. He simply cannot see them, so intent is he, after leaving Prior, on a performance of isolated individualism.

Isolation and individualism are frequent targets of Kushner's wrath, so it is not surprising that *Angels in America* ultimately rejects both in favor of the vision of collectivity represented in the epilogue. In the afterword to *Perestroika*—called, appropriately enough, "With a Little Help from My Friends"—Kushner writes, "We pay high prices for the maintenance of the myth of the Individual: we have no system of universal health care, we don't educate our children, we can't pass sane gun control laws, we elect presidents like Reagan, we hate and fear inevitable processes like aging and death, and on and on" (*P*, 150). *Angels in America's* theory of queer perestroika, in contrast, like Audre Lorde's understanding of the identity "Zami," ensures the survival of the group. Just as the name Jacob wins from the angel in *The Book of J*—Israel—symbolizes the survival of a people, so, too, the exchange of identities performed in *Angels in America* underscores ongoing solidarity and interconnectedness.[9]

Scott Tucker is one of the only critics to address directly the issue of solidarity in *Angels in America*, and—in contrast to my reading here— he does so negatively: "Solidarity, if it means anything, must be harder to come by than this very kind of unearned inclusion" (34). What elicits such a response from Tucker is Kushner's allusion, in a *Village Voice* interview, to an earlier version of the epilogue at the Bethesda Fountain:

> Prior used to have a section in his final speech where he said these very confrontational things: "We won't die for you anymore, and fuck you if you can't accept it." I changed it because all the straight people in the cast came to me and said, "We feel hurt by this. You ask us to go on this journey with you, and we go, and at the end you turn it into us-and-them."
>
> I felt very angry at first: "Come on, grow up." . . . It felt like the whiny American thing of "We're one big family. We are the world." . . . On the other hand, these were political, deeply decent people who were feeling something I did not want people to be feeling at the end of the play. That kind of political note would only work if it could be understood in the context of an embracing gesture the play is making that I want the play to make. (qtd. in Tucker, 34)

Tucker concludes from this episode that "Kushner responded like a social worker keeping harmony in a support group" (34) and suggests that "any playwright dealing with AIDS in America must lead the audience through a *convincing* stretch of hell before revealing a bit of heaven. Or even before revealing a bit more decency on earth" (35).

Yet Kushner's "compromise" might be read otherwise, as part and parcel

Queer Identities in a Crisis

of the queer theory of perestroika Kushner advances throughout *Angels in America*, particularly in the second half. Queer perestroika admits a wide variety of transformations, in contrast to Tucker's attack on Kushner with its queerer-than-thou implication that there are acceptable and unacceptable transformations. Generally, the Queer Renaissance resists such fixed notions of queerness. As my previous chapters have demonstrated, different contexts and locations (rural North Carolina, the U.S.-Mexican border region) require and produce different understandings of queerness. Moreover, in coalitions across difference and in conversations with "political, deeply decent people" (even if they are, in one sense, "the straight people in the cast"), multiple actors continually reinvent these local queer identities.

Tucker admits that he has not yet seen *Perestroika* (35)—a significant admission, since his conclusions might differ considerably if the event he objects to were read in the context of the play as a whole. Prior's comments are staged, after all, and their meaning is contingent on that staging. In the epilogue, Prior is flanked by three characters, and three characters only: Belize, Louis, and Hannah. All three have come through Prior's struggle with him, and two of these characters (Louis and Hannah) have been substantially transformed in the process. Hannah, particularly, should be seen as someone who, over the course of the play, enters into a conversation with queerness, and whose personal and political identity is shaped in new and critical ways as a result of that conversation. If this is not—*pace* Tucker—"meaningful" solidarity, not to mention a primary goal of queer theory and activism, I'm not sure what is. Moreover, this scene obviously locates several characters *offstage*—most notably, Roy Cohn and his protégé Joe Pitt. Certainly, *Angels in America* affirms the "humanity" of both characters (no one deserves to die of AIDS, not even Roy Cohn, and the play maintains this profoundly), but neither Roy's nor Joe's philosophy admits either character to the vision of political solidarity Kushner stages in the end.[10] In fact, in one of Louis's most important developmental scenes, he literally and *physically* rejects Joe's politics. After researching and reading the opinions Joe wrote during the early 1980s for Judge Theodore Wilson, Second Circuit Court of Appeals, Louis confronts Joe, and a fight breaks out.[11] Louis receives a cut eye and mouth in the process and says to Joe, who is mortified at having hit Louis, "I could have you arrested. . . . They'd think I put you in jail for beating me up. . . . But it'd really be for those decisions" (*P*, 112).

Tucker feels Kushner is premature in his celebration of "decency on earth," and that the characters need to go through a "convincing stretch of hell." Ironically, Louis opens this confrontation with Joe by quoting Joseph Welch, who, at the Army-McCarthy Hearings, exclaimed, *"Have you no decency, at long last, sir, have you no decency at all?"* (*P*, 110). In other words, Kushner/Louis, far from celebrating decency on earth, invokes one of the most glaring and famous examples of political *indecency* and implicitly suggests that those who engage in such politics—whether in the 1950s or the 1980s—cannot be part of the progressive vision of inclusion performed in the epilogue.[12] These are not easy lessons for Louis to learn—one might even say that he goes through a convincing stretch of hell—but they are crucial for his development away from the individualism and betrayal he performs for the bulk of the play.

Given what Louis and some of the other characters *do* go through, then, it is hard not to think that Kushner's straight cast members had a point when they insisted they were with him for the journey. And Kushner's acceptance of that point, I think, might be read as part of the queer perestroika staged by *Angels in America*, if ongoing democratic contestation is indeed part of that queer theory. Significantly, although Tucker casts the actors in a relationship of dependency (Kushner as social worker, actors as support group), Kushner himself *refuses* such a relationship: dispensing with his initial impulse to interpret his actors as whiny children ("Come on, grow up"), Kushner moves instead toward understanding them as adults with political commitments, including the commitment to fight alongside him.[13] At the same time, Kushner rejects compromise when it obscures that commitment. When a Broadway producer asked him to delete the play's subtitle—*A Gay Fantasia on National Themes*—rather than risk alienating potential theatergoers, Kushner refused (Sandla, 31). With the Broadway producer, Kushner rightly saw an effort to mask *Angels in America*'s queer political perspective and to pander to those who might be made uncomfortable by that perspective; with the actors, who compose this "gay fantasia" with him, he acknowledged that gay and nongay others *share* that critical queer perspective, and that queer perestroika demands a recognition of such interdependence.

"Political identities remaking identities are . . . productive of collective political struggle," Douglas Crimp writes, "but only if they result in a broadening of alliances rather than an exacerbation of antagonisms. And the latter often seems to result when, from within development toward a politics of alliance based on relational identities, old antagonisms based on fixed identities reemerge" ("Right On," 16). In *Angels in America*, Kushner attempts to negotiate this dilemma, using a constantly shifting yet insistent queer sexuality as a figure for the progressive theory his play stages. Moving characters toward a renunciation of stasis, isolation, and fixed identities, *Angels in America* proffers as an alternative the performance of queer perestroika: messy, mingling, and ultimately hopeful. "Marx was right," Kushner insists in his afterword, "the smallest indivisible human unit is two people, not one; one is a fiction. From such nets of souls societies, the social world, human life springs. And also plays" (*P*, 158). Kushner's staging of Marx's queer theory makes *Angels in America* one of the central texts of the contemporary Queer Renaissance.

The Queer Renaissance: Taking It to the Streets

Earlier in his analysis of "political identities," Crimp cites Teresa de Lauretis's observation that "it takes two women, not one, to make a lesbian" and concludes that "we can begin to rethink identity politics as a politics of relational identities formed through political identifications that constantly remake those identities" (Crimp, "Right On," 12; de Lauretis, "Film and the Visible," 232). Crimp's invocation of de Lauretis in an article on ACT UP links desire and activism; constantly shifting queer *sexual* identities are here articulated to shifting, coalition-based *activist* identities. As the previous section demonstrated, *Angels in America* performs a similar articulation: Prior's understanding and appropriation of the angel's fabulous sexuality provides a basis for the collective queer political theory envisioned in the end.

The theater can be an important site both for the transmission of such queer theories and for the constant remaking of identities that Crimp advocates. David Román suggests as much when he writes:

> For critics who argue that gay and lesbian performance only preaches to the "choir," it is important to recognize that such a choir does not exist unless one presupposes . . . that there is only possible a singular monolithic community of activists which reflect the "ideal spectator." In any event conversion entails more than simply rhetoric; it demands conversion of ideas and belief systems into direct action, a possibility only beginning to come into fruition. (217–18)

For Román, the "community" is neither monolithic nor necessarily shaped in advance. Furthermore, the "conversion of ideas and belief systems into direct action" Román calls for implies that the theater is contiguous to other locations. Kushner himself champions that contiguity; in fact, for Kushner, conversion moves in both directions. *Angels in America* reshapes the ideas *of* gay and lesbian direct action and insists, in turn, that the ideas performed in the play be reshaped yet again *in and through* direct action. As Kushner's closing remarks in the keynote address he delivered to the Fifth Annual OutWrite Conference suggest, the conversion of belief systems and identities takes place in many different and ever-multiplying locations: "See you in Washington. See you on the Internet. See you on the streets" (*Thinking*, 79). Hence, the reifying force of a Pulitzer Prize and Tony Awards notwithstanding, Kushner's achievement is not isolated: *Angels in America* speaks directly to and with contemporaneous developments in queer theory and activism.

This is not to deny that powerful mainstreaming forces occlude such a connection. Indeed, the mainstream culture industry's mystification of social relations could be seen quite clearly when Kushner accepted his Tony Awards (particularly his second). As Kushner attempted to verbalize his debt to his "lesbian and gay brothers and sisters" who continued to struggle against AIDS and homophobia, the orchestral music swelled to indicate that his time was up and that the television broadcast was about to cut to a commercial. In this scenario (and in awards ceremonies generally), the supposed singularity of Kushner's achievement was the important thing, not the ongoing dialogue he wanted to highlight.

In this section, then, I aim to amplify, rather than drown out, the critical conversation between art and activism by turning to Sarah Schulman's novel *People in Trouble*.[14] I continue to argue here, through an examination of Schulman's character Kate, that various liminal (sexual, activist) "identities in crisis" can breed queer artistic identities and visions. Schulman places Kate in a context that specifically evokes the tax abatements granted by Ed Koch to Donald Trump for the construction of Trump Tower, his multimillion-dollar luxury shopping mall and apartment complex, but that—with its representation of privatization and of tax cuts for wealthy entrepreneurs—more generally records the mayoral strategy since Koch came to power.[15] In Schulman's novel, the mayor of New York City offers real-estate developers millions in tax rebates if they agree to fund public artwork on their properties. Kate, a visual artist, suddenly finds herself commissioned to produce a major public artwork outside a former public building that the city is converting into private office space. Significant changes in Kate's private life, however, are simultaneous to this professional development: first, her identity as a married and heterosexual woman is disrupted as she begins to juggle life with her husband, Peter, and her lesbian lover, Molly; and second, her complacent political identity is thrown into crisis by her exposure to an ACT UP-like organization called Justice. Analyzing each of Kate's identities (sexual, political, artistic) in turn, I argue here that the critical postmodern aesthetic Kate eventually brings to her commission emerges directly from these new sexual and activist identities. This portrait of the artist as an emergent queer then sets the stage for some concluding thoughts on *Angels in America* and—in the epilogue that follows this chapter—for some final reflections on the Queer Renaissance generally.

As with *Angels in America, People in Trouble* rumbles with apocalyptic anxiety; like the first half of Kushner's play, Schulman's novel could easily be subtitled "Millennium Approaches." The novel opens: "It was the beginning of the end of the world but not everyone noticed right away. Some people were dying. Some people were busy. Some people were cleaning their houses while the war movie played on television" (1). In the midst of this chaos Schulman places Kate, who is happily buying two bras for Molly: "Which one would Molly wear first? . . . There was the demure lace that opened from the front, like walking in through a garden gate. Then there was the really dirty push-up that didn't need to open. Kate could lift Molly's breasts right out over the top" (2). The immediate juxtaposition of chaos and desire serves somewhat contradictory functions. On the one hand, Kate's desire keeps her from noticing right away that the world is spinning out of control. She is not one of those who is "dying" but rather one of those who is "busy": she is buying bras for her lover and "enjoying herself thoroughly" (1). On the other hand, *People in Trouble* constructs desire as something that cannot and will not be eradicated; in the midst of the apocalypse, people are still having sex. As Prior comes to see in *Angels in America,* and as the central argument of the first section of this chapter insisted, "We can't just stop. . . . It's *animate,* it's what living things do. We desire" (P, 132).

Hence, although Kate is apparently oblivious in this scene to the chaos outside, her budding desires nonetheless connect her (along with almost everyone) to the ongoing messiness and vitality of human existence. Such contradictions are central to Schulman's characterization of Kate, and as Kate begins to face these contradictions, they propel her supposedly stable identity into crisis. In general, especially early in the novel, Kate and Peter are almost cartoons, expressing cartoon liberal views: "They talked details. All details. The contents of that day's *Times*, including which airlines had proposed merger. The plight of the American farmer. Something having to do with percentage points. Both Kate and Peter clearly believed in quoting statistics" (54). About gay men, lesbians, and AIDS, in particular, the two are virtual parodies of themselves: "*These are men with AIDS*, Peter realized. . . . *But that one doesn't look like he has it. He looks like he works out. . . . That black man*, thought Peter. *I wonder if he's gay or if he got it from drugs*" (58). Although Peter is by far the worst, Kate shares many of his naive conceptions. She worries, "With Molly so many things could go wrong. . . . She'd trap me, try to turn me into a lesbian" (21), and she insists defensively, even late in the novel, "I don't want to live in a ghetto like lesbians do. I like men. I want to be universal" (186). Both Peter and Kate repeatedly express regret that Molly "hates men," despite over-whelming evidence to the contrary. In fact, Molly has many more male friends than either Kate or Peter; they are simply gay men, men with AIDS, men of color, homeless men. These men cannot disrupt Kate and Peter's thesis, since for this couple, "man" equals "Peter" and those like Peter and is unmediated by any other arena of difference.

But Kate's introduction and persistent connection to the vicissitudes of desire complicate Schulman's construction of the couple as liberal-hetero cartoon. Because of the queer changes occurring in Kate's life, profound differences between Peter and her eventually materialize. As the novel progresses, Peter shores up the unexamined liberal belief in a secure distinction between self and other, even as that belief disintegrates for Kate. Initially, both characters are presented behind walls or windows, with the world on the other side: "It had been a hallucinatorily hot summer with AIDS wastes and other signs of the Apocalypse washing up on the beaches. Kate had spent it working in her studio, only in the evening" (12).[16] One evening, in particular, Kate witnesses the Tompkins Square Park Riots, in which four hundred police officers, in August 1988, rioted against the homeless, housing activists, punks, anarchists, and other locals, who were protesting a curfew.[17] As she watches this struggle, Kate con-sciously decides to maintain the barrier between herself and the chaos outside: "She stayed at the window watching and then made the decision not to enter into it" (12). Peter, likewise, first appears with barriers between himself and the world outside; one early chapter has him safely ensconced in a coffee shop as he watches a gay funeral across the street. But whereas Peter uses "the other side" to reinforce his (heterosexual) sense of self, Kate probes queer desire in ways that begin to reshape her identity.

I certainly do not mean to suggest, however, that Peter's heterosexuality is not (always already) an "identity in crisis," or that his identity is not reshaped by the lesbians and gay men he encounters.[18] In the coffee-shop scene, for example, as he watched the mourners file into the church, Peter noted—"with some relief" that their life was so "clearly defined"—that "his and Kate's inner circle were all heterosexual couples. It had just turned out that way" (31). Peter's remembrance of a brief gay affair from his past, though, immediately undercuts this observation. Peter, who is a lighting and set designer (or, we might say, a master at compelling others to believe in illusory identities and locations), dismisses the affair as "part of being in theater" (32), but his incessant need to situate himself *as against* the queer other ("that's not me") nonetheless manifests his anxiety about his performance as "heterosexual male." This definition as against the other resurfaces as Peter's curiosity gets the best of him and he crosses the street to the church where the funeral is taking place. Although crossing the street apparently belies the separation of self and other Peter seeks to maintain, he thinks of what he is doing as "touring," and notes to himself that he "had learned from traveling in Mexico that when you are watching another culture in church it is best to stand in back" (33). The gay mourners thus become the foreign others who provide an identity for the nervous tourist, who can supposedly leave at any time.

Peter's need to establish such a "secure" identity, repeatedly, suggests that in an important sense, Peter's identity, like Kate's, is unstable and "in crisis." The couple diverge, however, in their responses to that instability. Peter is always on the defensive and desirous of moving *away from* queerness; he anxiously demands of a woman he meets after he and Kate have begun to drift apart, "You're not gay, are you? You're not bi or unsure or in transition? You're heterosexual, right?" (170). Kate, in contrast, although not entirely free of anxious disavowals of lesbian identity ("I want to be universal"), eventually moves *toward* queerness and allows her "heterosexual" identity to be radically reshaped.

Ironically, the language describing Peter's visit to the gay church resurfaces near the beginning of Kate's affair, when Molly takes Kate on "a guided tour of all the lesbian bars below Fourteenth Street" (81). However, the effect this trip has on Kate, the "tourist," helps illustrate her difference from Peter, since by the end of the chapter, the word no longer seems quite

Queer Identities in a Crisis

appropriate. At the first bar they visit, Kate encounters a woman she knows whose husband is a sculptor. Kate turns to Molly: "Isn't that great? . . . That a straight woman like Susan can feel comfortable coming to a place like this" (81–82). Kate's cheerful exuberance is checked, however, when she learns from Molly—who goes on to imply that "straight" is as inadequate a descriptor for Kate as it is for Susan—that Susan came to this bar to meet her female lover. Kate muses, "How weird about Susan. . . . It makes me feel like I don't really know her. Like I don't have any idea of who she is" (82). Kate's sense of dislocation soon escalates when, at the next bar, Molly attempts to explain butch and femme identities:

"Everyone here is femme."

"How can you tell who's femme?"

"That's the question of the year. After a while you just know. Usually it's the one who puts her arms around the other woman's shoulders when they're dancing."

"Which one of us is femme?"

"Neither. That's a joke. It's too early to tell because you still act straight. You have to be out a little longer before these subtle nuances take shape."

"Why are you always telling me what I'm going to become and what I'm going to think? How do you know?" (82)

Although Kate's reaction again bespeaks some anxiety about new and queer identities, her curiosity gets the best of her and she pursues the butch/femme issue further, telling Molly at the next bar that she still cannot see the difference. To clarify, Molly asks Kate which women she finds attractive and then informs her, "Those are all butches" (84). Kate then begins to sort this out on her own as Molly moves onto the dance floor with someone else. The crisis intensifies as Kate watches the two women:

Kate watched them for a while, the way they picked up each other's rhythm and figured out how to move together. They figured it out rather quickly.

What do you know? she thought. *Molly dances hot with everyone. It's not just me. That's the way she dances.*

And for the first time ever, Kate felt jealous.

"Excuse me," she said, cutting in abruptly, "but I have to dance with my girlfriend." And took her to the floor, noticing immediately that Molly's arms went around her neck. (84)

Queer Identities in a Crisis

The conclusion of this passage in particular suggests that Kate is no longer a tourist in the queer world she and Molly have been exploring; moving literally from the margins to the center, Kate declares aloud her implication in that world: "Excuse me, but I have to dance with my girlfriend."[19] Moreover, Kate "notices immediately" that her incorporation into this system of desire does not secure for her a fixed identity position but rather one that is constantly shifting: although her initial identifications of the women she finds attractive position her temporarily as "femme," Molly's arms around her neck reposition Kate, a page later, as "butch."

Ultimately, Kate's re-formation around butch and femme identities marks only a beginning for the larger transformation incited by her night out with Molly. Molly begins to trouble Kate's unconscious need to return to a default, normative position: her need to "set things straight," as it were. The reshaping of this normative position, and of Kate's former identities ("heterosexual," "tourist"), continues even as the evening concludes:

> Molly announced one last stop.
> "Where could we possibly be going now?"
> . . . "It's a vintage gay porn store. You know the necessities stay open later than frivolous indulgences."
> Kate felt one second of resistance before walking through the front door.
> (84)

Once inside the porn store, pictures of "cocks . . . on beautiful young men" entrance Kate (85). At first, this experience again appears to fix Kate's identity: "This is how I know I'm not a lesbian. . . . Because I'm turned on by cock. I like cock" (86). Molly, however, once again disrupts this identification, bringing attention not only to the normative voices *speaking through* Kate but also to the voices *silenced* by the compulsion to set things straight:

> "Good for you. Does Peter have to hear you say, 'I like pussy'? Bet not. . . . Have you ever said to Peter, 'I like pussy'?"
> "No I haven't," [Kate] said. "It has never occurred to me to say that. It wouldn't be appropriate."
> Then she felt uncomfortable. (85)

Molly's challenge and Kate's discomfort spotlight the new location into which Kate has moved: "it wouldn't be appropriate," any longer, for her to

Queer Identities in a Crisis

ground her sexual identity through a definition that positions her as against queerness. Kate's discomfort here attests to her nascent understanding that she has inappropriately used disclaimers to shore up an impenetrable heterosexual identity, from which she excludes her love for women. It can certainly be true, given her desire for men and her ongoing relationship with Peter, that she is "not a lesbian," but Molly's comments implicitly remind Kate that it is true because she is bisexual or because she is queer, not because her love of "cock" insulates her heterosexual life. Just as her love for men continues to resonate in her "lesbian" world, so, too, her love for women now resonates in and reshapes her "straight" world.

The chapter ends with images that serve as analogues for the "in-between" position into which Kate has moved. Alone in her studio, Kate thinks about the evening and masturbates: "Her face showed great pleasure. She could rock down on her hips and swing into a low moan. She could dance around her studio being led by her own hand" (86). This erotic moment is stimulated by a magazine—a present Molly gave her at the end of their evening on the town. Molly purchased the magazine at the porn store because it made her think of Kate immediately, but she waited until they were alone to present it and insisted that Kate not open it until Molly was gone. "That had been a week ago," the narrator explains. "She'd opened it a dozen times since then. It was a collection of transsexuals in various poses. . . . It was packed with photos of euphorically happy men in sexy, slimy, girly getups with hard pricks and big boobs. They looked so turned on. They turned her on with their dicks and tits, how excited they were" (86). The pictures of transsexuals underscore, especially in their depiction of these men as "euphorically happy," the promise of the shifting location Kate now occupies. Appropriately enough, given the identity crisis that has commenced in this chapter, Kate masturbates in front of the mirror. At this point, both magazine and mirror reflect identities that are no longer fixed in any one gendered or sexual location.

Molly's gift again unsettles Kate and Peter's easy assumption that "Molly hates men." Quite the opposite is true, it would seem, since Molly is so comfortable giving a magazine full of "men" to her girlfriend, knowing all the while that the magazine will fuel Kate's erotic fantasies. Kate and Peter (mis)read as "hate" Molly's adeptness at making "gender trouble," in Judith Butler's sense: "subverting and displacing those naturalized and reified notions of gender that support masculine hegemony and heterosexist power . . . through the mobilization, subversive confusion, and proliferation of precisely those constitutive categories that seek to keep gender in its place by posturing as the foundational illusions of identity" (*Gender Trouble*, 33–34). Ironically, the "cock" itself is a constitutive force here, since Kate uses it, when she enters the porn store, to shore up a safe location for herself ("not a lesbian"). This safety is exposed as an illusion by Molly's gift, however, which actually proliferates cocks, thereby detaching them from a fixed location and draining them of their ability to confer on Kate a rigid heterosexual identity.

Significantly, though, and in contrast to Peter, Kate begins to take pleasure in that loss of rigidity and moves toward queerness. While masturbating in front of the mirror, for instance, Kate "could feel her orgone rushing inside her like a waterfall, like crowds of teenage girls held back from the Beatles, who suddenly in a tearful frenzy, break free of the police and lose control. She was open in every way. There were no obstacles. She was streaming" (86). Kate's erotic thoughts reveal that she has learned the lesson of the porn store: there is no sign (whether that sign be "cocks" or "teenage girls thrusting toward the Beatles") that is established, absolutely, as heterosexual. Molly has taught Kate that signs can be "queered," and Kate here demonstrates what a good student she is. Kate queers the ostensibly heterosexual image of the girls and the Beatles: her desire is directed much more toward the crowd of surging females than toward the Beatles, the pleasure in the image comes more from the idea of women collectively thwarting (presumably male) police control than from connection with the band, and the whole image is metonymically connected to the queer images of transsexuals to which Kate is masturbating. At this point, moreover, Molly no longer choreographs Kate's development alone. Instead, larger queer forces (happy men in slimy, sexy, girly getups; thrusting teenage girls), now welcomed by Kate herself, begin to move Kate's transformation forward.

When Molly and her friend Pearl unexpectedly notice Kate walking past the park, Molly's surprise at what she sees shows how far Kate has come. Pearl's comments, in fact, suggest that Molly herself has not yet recognized the pleasure Kate takes in her new identities, or—for that matter—Kate's agency in the transformation process: "You say she's not coming out, but take a look at that" (89). The two women watch as Kate, dressed as a man, walks down the street:

> Kate was a man. Anyone in the street would have thought so. But she was a better man than most because she was so strikingly handsome in her black suit. She strode powerful and erect like a well-bred charming man. A male

Queer Identities in a Crisis

model perhaps. A movie star. She didn't wear a white button-down. She was much too stylish for that. Kate, the man, wore a soft blue shirt designed for a sexy strong man's leisure. It was cut to hang from his neck and muscles. Kate was thrilling. She was the most handsome man on the street. (89–90)

When Pearl asks Molly if she knows what's going on with Kate, Molly "stop[s] one more time to take a hard last look" and responds, "I have no idea" (90). Kate's willingness to move toward queerness reshapes her identity to such an extent that it cannot be contained by those observing her; neither side of the heterosexual/homosexual binary can fully account for her emerging queer subjectivity.

These developments in Kate's "personal" life are simultaneous to, and intertwined with, new developments in her "political" life. Although Kate smugly understands herself as "progressive" or even "radical," she is fairly complacent politically at the beginning of *People in Trouble*, subscribing to little more than a vague humanism. An encounter she has in a coffee shop exemplifies her complacency. A woman in the coffee shop informs Kate that she has just bought a new raincoat. Kate's self-satisfied political identity is thrown into crisis by this encounter as decidedly as her "heterosexual" identity is by her travels with Molly:

> "When you get something new," [the woman] said conspiratorially, "you have to watch out that it doesn't get stolen. You have to avoid people who need money and people who need raincoats and keep them away from yours. But I feel bad being dry on the street when my brothers and sisters have nowhere to sleep."
>
> "And contradictions are what let us know that we are fully human," Kate said.
>
> "But?" the woman answered, waiting.
>
> "But?"
>
> "But," she said running old-looking hands over a young-looking face. "But then what?" (13)

Kate is bothered by the challenge, to which she can provide no response. She had wanted to use "contradictions" to *settle* her identity: contradictions "let us know that we are fully human." Yet, just as the contradictions in Kate's sexual identity begin to reshape that identity, so, too, do contradictions in scenes such as this one unsettle and reshape Kate's "human(ist)"

Queer Identities in a Crisis

political identity. In the text, the encounter in the coffee shop follows Kate's memory of watching the Tompkins Square Riots from her studio. Unsettling or disruptive events are thus multiplying before Kate's very eyes, and at a rate that mocks her attempts to smooth over or harmonize the contradictions through appeals to the "human" or "universal."

As unrest in the New York City of *People in Trouble* ferments, Schulman again positions Kate initially on the outside: Kate is not present in the chapter that introduces Justice, the fledgling AIDS activist organization. Nonetheless, Justice brings attention to issues of crisis and liminality similar to those I have been examining in conjunction with Kate, and as Molly infers at the end of the chapter, Kate and Justice could go well together. Initially, Molly alone attends a vigil for those lost to AIDS. The vigil underscores both the ways in which Molly's life has been altered by AIDS and—through its direct echo of Kate's appeal to the "human"—the insufficiencies of Kate's political philosophy:

> It made [Molly] feel something very human; a kind of nostalgia with public sadness and the sharing of emotions. But then what?
> This dying had been going on for a long time already. So long, in fact, that there were people alive who didn't remember life before AIDS. And for Molly it had made all her relations with men more deliberate and detailed. First, the men changed. They were more vulnerable and open and needed to talk. So she changed. Passing acquaintances became friends. And when her friends actually did get sick there was a lot of shopping to do, picking up laundry and looking into each other's eyes. She had never held so many crying men before in her life. (44–45)

The vigil commemorates these friends of Molly's, and the many others, male and female, who have died. But as Molly watches balloons with the names of the dead rise to the sky, and as groups of people break into small groups and depart, her mourning is checked: "Molly felt enormous anger. These were her friends. These were her dead friends. She saw their faces. Were their lives worth less than the lives of heterosexuals? Where was Kate? She should be here at a time like this" (46). Molly's sense that her mourning is not validated represents a common response to societal complacency about AIDS. Crimp explains that "for anyone living daily with the AIDS crisis, ruthless interference with our bereavement is as ordinary an occurrence as reading the *New York Times*. The violence we encounter is relentless, the violence of silence and omission almost as impossible to endure as the violence of unleashed hatred and outright murder" ("Mourning and Militancy," 237). In this scene, Schulman, like Crimp, connects complacency and quietism to an entire system that values only "straight" lives. In the process, she once again inverts the stereotype that lesbians hate men. As Crimp's placement of "silence and omission" on a continuum with "unleashed hatred" demonstrates, and as Molly's angry meditations confirm, it is not lesbians (who have, after all, "never held so many crying men before") but rather the heterosexual system that "hates (gay) men" and people with AIDS in general. Awareness of this systemic hatred unsettles Molly and elicits a string of questions for which she has no answers.

Like Prior, however, Molly prepares to move from an uncertain position to a contiguous, communal location. As in *Angels in America* (and many other works in the Queer Renaissance), it is not contradiction per se but contradiction articulated as a collective and ongoing challenge to oppressive systems of power (we—first-person *plural*—deviate) that provides a basis for action and change. Schulman depicts this movement from contradiction to collectivity by turning directly from Molly's questions, in one paragraph, to Justice, in the next:

> Molly saw two men handing out leaflets. . . . The first thing she saw was that they were wearing black T-shirts. On their chests were large pink triangles with the word *Justice* scrawled, graffiti style. . . .
> DO YOU THINK IT'S RIGHT?
> *That people are dying and the government does nothing? If you do not think that this is right then do something about it.*
> The flyer went on to invite people to a weekly meeting. Molly folded it four times and pushed it into her pocket. She missed Kate very much. She wished Kate were there. Molly walked home feeling open and vulnerable and then very angry with an energy that had nowhere to go. (47)

The chapter thus concludes with a return to Kate—another character who might be described as having an energy with nowhere to go. At the same time, though, the chapter belies the idea that such queer energy need go nowhere. Kate and Molly can come together with other "people in trouble" in a group like Justice, and it is there that the Butlerian implications of "trouble" come out. Schulman's title, certainly, can call to mind weak or helpless people, caught or undone by trouble: "victims" in need of rescue. As the novel progresses, however, that passive and objective sense of the title gives way to a more active and subjective sense: these people collectively *make and mobilize* trouble to disrupt governmental and societal complacency and bring an end to the dying.

Molly carries her newfound uneasiness and dislocation back to her relationship with Kate: "Here we are trying to have a run-of-the-mill illicit lesbian love affair. . . . And all around us people are dying and asking for money" (113). Kate shares Molly's dismay at the suffering all around them, but she nonetheless tries to smooth over the contradiction Molly sees by invoking her own identity as "artist":

> "I'm not protected," Kate said. "I'm a poor artist. I am not a powerful person in this society. Don't be so self-deprecating, it's unbearably righteous."
> "You're not poor. Neither am I."
> "Listen, Molly, when I was your age I was a lot more radical than you are, so don't lay that on me. That's your trip."
> "Let's go to the meeting," Molly said. "Let's go there now." (114)

This scene between the two women generates a paradox. On the one hand, Kate—up to her old tricks again—disavows elements of her identity that might disrupt the ways in which she perceives herself. Ironically, she disavows the *privileged* part of her identity here, but the effect is similar to her earlier disavowals of queerness: Kate constitutes her identity as "artist" and "radical" as fixed and insulated (in fact, with her appeal to the past, she practically *embalms* her radical identity). On the other hand, Kate reveals, however tentatively, the impossibility of absolute fixity and insulation. She contends that AIDS or homelessness "could happen to me. . . . It could happen to you" (113). Although she makes this pronouncement with a fair amount of smugness and with the intent of "winning" a debate with Molly, Kate has a valid point here, if we take seriously her earlier negotiations of self and other in the lesbian bars, the porn store, and even the coffee shop, where the woman in the raincoat spoke of her "brothers and sisters" on the street. Kate learns that the separation between self and other is not absolutely secure, and in many ways, the queer identity she brings to this conversation—an identity Schulman reinvokes by describing Kate here as "a peacock in a man's overcoat" (114)—attests to that point. Perhaps this explains why Molly ends the conversation (and the chapter) not with an insistence that Kate is simply wrong or misguided

Queer Identities in a Crisis

but with the suggestion, "Let's go to the meeting. . . . Let's go there now." Kate indeed may be somewhat misguided in her self-satisfied understanding of artists and radicals, but Molly also apparently recognizes in Kate's willingness to see herself as implicated in the struggles of the homeless and of people with AIDS an "energy" not unlike Molly's own. The repetition of *go* ("go to the meeting," "go there now") reanimates Molly's earlier "energy that had nowhere to go." Molly comprehends her uneasiness and dislocation, along with Kate's naive but promising identity-in-process, as preconditions for involvement in Justice.

In her description of the direct action by Justice that follows, Schulman draws on more than one actual ACT UP event. In June 1987, when the Third International Conference on AIDS was set to open in Washington, D.C., activists descended on the White House to protest the Reagan administration's apathy toward AIDS issues. (Ronald Reagan had spoken the word *AIDS* publicly only in the previous month.) Police officers wearing bright yellow gloves arrested sixty-four protesters at the White House. Activists, desirous of drawing attention to the officers' paranoia, which would feed public hysteria about "catching" AIDS through casual contact, chanted for the television cameras, "You're gloves don't match your shoes! You'll see it on the news!" (Crimp and Rolston, 32–33). Schulman relocates the yellow-glove incident and the chants to New York City.

More centrally, however, Schulman re-presents a November 1988 action, when ACT UP rallied to protest the fact that five thousand to ten thousand homeless New Yorkers were living with AIDS. ACT UP demonstrated at the Trump Tower in New York City on the day after Thanksgiving, "the biggest shopping day of the year" (Crimp and Rolston, 122). The flyer activists distributed during the demonstration explained the reasons for their anger:

*Donald Trump received a tax abatement of $6,208,773 to build Trump Tower. This money could have rehabilitated about 1,200 city-owned apartments. Instead Trump gets richer while homeless people get sicker.

*The city favors private developers like Trump over small community-based organizations that are committed to providing low-income housing and housing for PWAs. The AIDS Center of Queens County, for example, never even received an acknowledgment of the proposal it submitted for 20 scattered-site apartments for homeless PWAs.

*Mayor Koch and the city allow Trump to displace people from their apart-

Queer Identities in a Crisis

ments when he wants to build a building. Trump is symbolic of a system that lets the rich do whatever they want while letting the poor die. (Crimp and Rolston, 122)

The Trump Tower was the ideal location for the points activists wanted to make. Containing both a luxury shopping mall and million-dollar apartments, the Tower stands, for a few, as the symbol of a "healthy economy." For activists, however, the Tower stood and stands for the ways in which the economic system *denies* health, well-being, and housing to many.

ACT UP's flyer exemplifies Rosalyn Deutsche's reworking of Walter Benjamin's famous dictum "There is no document of civilization which is not at the same time a document of barbarism" (Benjamin, 256). With a nod to Benjamin, Deutsche insists that "New York's spatial documents of ascendancy" and redevelopment are always at the same time "documents of homelessness" and eviction ("Uneven Development," 123). In Schulman's re-presentation in *People in Trouble* of ACT UP's demonstration, this central paradox fuels the action Justice takes. At the meeting, activists discuss Ronald Horne (Schulman's fictional answer to Donald Trump), with no illusions about how his wealth requires and engenders other people's poverty:

"This week many of you received eviction notices from Ronald Horne's development company. This is the man who has warehoused thousands of empty apartments while ninety thousand people live in the subways and stairwells and public bathrooms of this city. Now we have learned that he has purposely bought buildings with more than fifty percent gay tenants in the hope that we will drop dead and leave him with empty apartments. He files these eviction notices anticipating that some of us will be too ill to contest. Now let me ask you, what are we going to do to get *justice?*"

There was a great steamy silence when [the speaker] finished, almost like *subito piano* in music; the quiet after a crescendo, like falling off a cliff. . . .

"We should go there now," [one man] said. "We're angry now, so we should go now." (118–19)

Like the bass in a jazz ensemble, Schulman's throbbing "go . . . go . . . go" keeps the beat here, reappearing once again to channel the collective energy generated by the band. The "quiet after a crescendo" is like Molly's "energy that had nowhere to go," and again Schulman implicitly suggests that such energy can produce a disruptive queer identity. Additionally, this scene lends credence to Kate's earlier points about the tenuousness of the separation between self and other: gay people can indeed be threatened with eviction and homelessness. Justice, however, takes that point much further than Kate—or rather, Justice provides Kate with a "demonstration" of what might be done with those points. Through this demonstration, Schulman represents some of the basic tenets of ACT UP. First, it is an AIDS *Coalition*: AIDS activism entails recognizing that discrete, or apparently discrete, identities ("gay," "lesbian," "homeless," "PWA [Person with AIDS]") can come together to "unleash power" and create change.[20] Second, the identity of this queer creature—the "AIDS activist"—is not located in advance but is, instead, as constantly shifting as the location of her politics: the Trump Tower, St. Patrick's Cathedral, the White House, the Food and Drug Administration, the streets.

Schulman shifts the location of Justice's initial action from the Trump Tower of ACT UP fame to the fictional Horne Castle, which the narrator describes as "the biggest, lushest, most ostentatious and expensive hotel from the Eastern Seaboard to Rodeo Drive . . . renowned, not only for its lavishness, but also for the transplanted tropical rain forest that had been re-created inside the lobby to serve as a symbolic moat with actual crocodiles" (119). Schulman's shift to Ronald Horne's Castle makes even more explicit the systemic connections between homelessness and economic "growth" that ACT UP sought to spotlight: Horne, in *People in Trouble*, is not simply "housed" while evicting others but housed in a literal and luxurious *castle*. Furthermore, Schulman's ironic inclusion of a "transplanted tropical rain forest" places the crisis in an even larger, global system, since actual rain forests in the Southern Hemisphere are being, in effect, "transplanted" North, as the South labors to support the North's consumption habits. Activists in *People in Trouble* descend on and occupy this "castle" to draw attention to these systemic inequities and to protest the city's housing policies. Fifty pairs of Playtex Living Gloves, "which turned out to be an unfortunate lemon yellow" (126), are ordered by the hotel overseers for use in removing the demonstrators, who immediately begin to chant, "Your gloves don't match your shoes," for the television cameras (126–27).

The cameras capture the activists on film, but Schulman shifts the focus, exposing the ways in which the camera's eye is itself far from innocent. In the process, Schulman reveals how her own participation in experimental queer film and video production may have influenced *People in Trouble*. Schulman has, in fact, been centrally involved in contemporary film and

Queer Identities in a Crisis

video production: in 1987, she and Jim Hubbard founded the New York Lesbian and Gay Experimental Film Festival, and she is herself a member of ACT UP, which has produced several experimental videos. From its inception, ACT UP displayed a heightened awareness of media strategies; activists, particularly activists with video cameras, both critiqued the ways in which the mainstream media has written "the story of AIDS" and documented that story otherwise, using a variety of experimental techniques.[21] Paula Treichler writes that AIDS activist video work "demonstrates the manipulation of conventional cultural narratives and representations to tell an alternate story" (79).

In her representation of Justice's action at the Castle, Schulman manipulates the "conventional cultural narrative" through the use of a jump cut. After the chapter describing the meeting that Molly and Kate attend, Schulman shifts abruptly to a chapter focusing on Peter, who is watching a newscast on TV at a bar on Second Avenue. The television thus mediates most of the action. As the anchorman tells the story, "Hundreds of AIDS victims have occupied the restaurant and lobby of Ronald Horne's Castle in midtown Manhattan. They are demanding that the superstar developer rescind eviction notices sent to homosexual men in Horne-owned buildings" (123). By splicing preparations for the demonstration together with newscast, however, Schulman complicates the televisual mediation: although the news anchor tells the same old story, that story speaks differently next to Justice's rally, which readers have just witnessed. Schulman's jump cut from the rally to the television newscast brings out *contesting* narratives. The TV reporter, whose sympathies clearly lie with the "superstar developer," calls these people "victims," but the group itself refuses to be victimized. Schulman's wide angle exposes the media: journalists do not "objectively" report preexisting stories; instead, they actively produce both the stories and the interpretations that should accompany them. In this scene, Schulman's own camera work produces a story that demonstrates how the news aligns itself with corporate interests and contains the threat of activism.

Kate's political identity, however, now resists containment. *People in Trouble* at this point positions Kate as a central player in issues of representation and contestation. Peter in fact recognizes that Kate is in the middle of it all: though he is "barely able to get out the words," he suddenly exclaims aloud to those in the bar, "That's my wife" (124). When the bartender challenges Peter with the suggestion that there are only men in the crowd on the screen, Peter insists, "No, that's her. The redhead with the crew cut in a suit and tie. That's my wife" (124). Kate appears on TV, in "earnest conversation" with another activist, her "orange hair look[ing] more mandarin on the eerie color TV" (124). Readers never learn the topic of Kate's "earnest conversation," but Kate does inform Molly later that this has been an "important night" for her and that it has given her "a lot of ideas" (127). Perhaps, given that Schulman places this visual artist at the center of a televised event seen by the people of New York City, we might imagine Kate discussing the conjunction of representation and activism. The cameras transmitting her image to viewers all over the city momentarily fix Kate in earnest conversation. Kate herself, however, has recently received funding for the production of a "public artwork" that—as her agent explains—will likewise be "seen by the people of New York City" (99). The "ideas" to which Kate refers, then, are very likely ideas about how to refocus the city's gaze through her artwork, which she undoubtedly sees in a different light after her experience with Justice.

As *People in Trouble* progresses, Justice engages in several more direct actions that shape and reshape a queer AIDS activist identity. Fury, a group focusing on the specific needs of women with AIDS, joins Justice, and both groups demonstrate, for various issues, at locations around the city. Kate is not directly involved in all of these actions, but the changes in both her "personal" and her "political" identity persist, transforming her aesthetic. Antifoundational sexual and activist communities and movements trouble the heterosexual and humanist foundations of Kate's identity. As Deutsche writes, "To localize meaning and identity—to assert that they are confined in discrete sites and determinate origins—is to deny the worldly relations that, in the absence of transcendental sources of truth, both constitute meanings and, crucially, put them at risk" ("Art and Public Space," 44). Kate cannot deny the queer relations that reconfigure her world as the text continues; these relations *de*localize her identity and consequently put at risk the meanings she has heretofore invested in her artwork.

At the beginning of the novel, Kate's aesthetic might be described as "high modernist": she strives in her artwork for purity of form; she wants her artwork to be "universal," to "let us know that we are fully human," and to somehow rise above the contingencies of history and politics. But, as the narrator explains early in the novel, "something was changing in the way she was seeing and it had started to affect her drawing" (14). People in trouble, identities in crisis—these are the referents for the elusive "something" that alters Kate's aesthetic.

Queer Identities in a Crisis

Kate's meditation on the changes in her drawing follows the troubling scene in the coffee shop where the woman with the raincoat challenges her: "But then what?" The narrator's comments after this challenge confirm that it has provoked a crisis for Kate: "There were three or four things that terrified Kate and they came to her in moments. . . . Kate feared the consequences of chaos, but was comfortable with fragments, when they were freely chosen" (14). Kate founds her comfort, and her artistic practices, on "free choice," but terror threatens to overcome her comfort and alter her artistic practices as the inadequacies of her high-modernist aesthetic ideal of "fragments freely chosen" become more and more apparent. The motto for Kate's aesthetic at the beginning of the novel—a motto that encapsulates both her fear of the consequences of chaos and her comfort with freely-chosen fragments—might be T.S. Eliot's famous line "These fragments I have shored against my ruins" (Eliot, 50). Yet this motto encapsulates all that is proving to be inadequate about Kate's high modernism as *People in Trouble* continues: Eliot's declaration implicitly invokes a fully formed and autonomous self, both in danger of ruin from without and capable of shaping art that "transcends" chaos and history by unifying or harmonizing fragments and contradictions. In Eliot's poem, the possibility of transcendence brings peace in the final line ("Shantih shantih shantih" [50]), which onomatopoeically intimates that rain finally arrives to settle the contradictions and chaos of the Waste Land. In *People in Trouble*, in contrast, Kate's "terror" suggests that this peace cannot be sustained; instead, Kate's identities in crisis unsettle the possibility of reliance on a fully formed, autonomous self.

Kate thinks "free choice" can secure order and lock out chaos. As Linda Hutcheon writes in *The Politics of Postmodernism*, however, "Postmodernism has called into question the messianic faith of modernism, the faith that technical innovation and purity of form can assure social order" (12). Hutcheon suggests that "messianic faith" in art is no longer possible precisely because postmodernism is always "complicitous" in the very systems of power (such as "economic capitalism and cultural humanism") it "chooses" to critique (13). Like the hipsters I considered in the previous chapter, Kate initially disclaims any complicity in systems of power. She argues instead for a pure artistic space outside such systems. Yet, as Hutcheon writes, "unacknowledged modernist assumptions about closure, distance, artistic autonomy, and the apolitical nature of representation are what postmodernism sets out to uncover and deconstruct" (99). In terms of *People in Trouble*, this might suggest that the postmodern "identities in crisis" Kate embraces (identities that, following Hutcheon, are *not* closed, distant, autonomous, or apolitical) will "uncover and deconstruct" the "unacknowledged modernist assumptions" Kate brings to her artwork.

Kate does not subscribe unequivocally to all of these high-modernist tenets; she does insist, for instance, that her artwork is "political": "It teaches people to see things in a new way.... Form is content. New forms are revolutionary" (113). Still, Kate grounds her "politics" on a disavowal of art's *complicity* in the systems of power her "revolution" would supposedly topple. At the same time, the queer identities Kate contends with make it more difficult for her to deny that complicity. During Justice's action at Horne's Castle, for instance, she experiences firsthand the ways in which that space has multiple meanings: the Castle is simultaneously a "document of ascendancy and homelessness." Since Kate comes away from that action with "a lot of ideas," and since the public artwork she is commissioned to produce will grace another of Horne's buildings, it is not surprising that Kate begins to question the assumption that her artwork will have a unified and critical meaning (whether "universally human" or "politically revolutionary"). Indeed, she even begins to recognize how her desire for unity and transcendence is complicitous with the economic and social philosophies of her patron Horne and those like him. Ultimately, Kate realizes, both she and Horne are committed to a harmonious use of space that contains, rather than critically deploys, the threats posed by contradiction and difference.

Deutsche's work on public art and public space is apropos here. Deutsche criticizes the way in which discourses about public art, like discourses of urban "redevelopment," repress contradiction, even though, paradoxically, city officials, arts administrators, and neoconservative critics alike invoke contradiction and contestation as one of public art's strengths. Commentators champion the "new public art" of the 1980s and 1990s because it is "for 'the people' ... encourage[s] 'participation' ... promises a democratic spirit of equality" and promotes "accessibility" ("Art and Public Space," 34). Yet, as Deutsche makes clear, such invocations of "democracy," the "public," and even "contested space" depend on "repressing—on establishing as external to the 'public'—the differences and conflicts as well as the outright injustices of urban life" ("Art and Public Space," 38–39). As an example, Deutsche cites a conflict over Jackson Park, in which the "Friends of Jackson Park" (people housed in the vicinity) decided to put a lock on the park's gate at night in order to discourage homeless people from sleeping there. City officials and commentators, pleased that the "public" was "contesting" the meaning of urban space, praised the Friends of Jackson Park for being "determined to keep a park a park" (qtd. in "Art and Public Space," 38). Yet, as Deutsche points out, such "contestation" establishes the homeless as always external to the public and naturalizes the relations of power that *produce* "public space." The demand to "keep a park a park" disallows the participation of the homeless in determining exactly what the space of Jackson Park will mean and assumes instead that the meaning of that particular urban space is secured in advance. Homeless people's presence in Jackson Park foregrounds the contradictions of an urban "redevelopment" that displaces those whose labor is no longer needed; a lock on Jackson Park, in the name of "the public," displaces (yet again) that contradiction.

"Public art" functions in similar ways to "public space," according to Deutsche: public art mutes contradictions even as proponents trumpet "democracy" and universal "accessibility" as its central components. Deutsche writes, "The new public art . . . moves 'beyond decoration' into the field of spatial design in order to affirm, rather than question, its space, to conceal its constitutive social relations" ("Uneven Development," 117). As *People in Trouble* continues, Kate begins to realize that her corporate sponsors expect just such an affirmation of social relations as they are— and indeed, that with her appeals to "universality," she is complicitous in that affirmation. Although Kate's agent implicitly assures her that she sculpts on behalf of "the people" by suggesting that "the work [will] be seen by people on the streets going to work . . . [and will] not be shut up in some exclusive, out-of-the-way gallery" (99), Kate becomes increasingly suspicious of the supposed public and democratic nature of her project. Horne's buildings are newly privatized spaces and his redevelopment of New York City is displacing more and more people from their homes, and Kate begins to comprehend that Horne's support of "public art" outside his buildings smooths over those contradictions.

Ironically, Kate's agent, perhaps "determined to keep a street a street," peoples the city with men and women on their way to work. In her migrations between her apartment and Molly's, however, Kate begins to notice the massive numbers of people *living* on the streets. Once again, her exposure to new queer identities has begun to disrupt the ideas she carries to her artwork. Kate muses to herself, "You see so much more when you walk down the street alone. That's why people work so hard to avoid walking alone too often. What people see when they're alone can drive them mad" (67). To Kate's agent, the city runs like a well-oiled machine, and Kate's work can be part of the technology: people see Kate's sculpture and continue on to work. Stepping out of the herdlike procession, Kate finally notices the contradictions endemic to urban space.

Like her shifting sexual identity, Kate's shifting political identity and her connection to a community of activists take her out of the blind stampede. Near the end of *People in Trouble*, Kate believes she has finally finished her sculpture; then she suddenly learns of the death of Scott, one of the founders of Justice and a friend of hers and Molly's. Scott's funeral is scheduled for the same day as the sculpture's dedication and unveiling. Earlier in the novel, Kate—working to complete her commission yet at the same time troubled by her new sexual and political experiences—had confessed to Scott, "Sometimes a person has to stop talking about art for a moment and take a look around" (166). When she learns of Scott's death, this is precisely what happens:

> She walked outside and *noticed everything*. The buses had been painted a new color. There was a new song on the radio. All the kids were singing it. She passed two parks filled with street people drinking or sleeping or smoking Coke or cigarettes or crying or talking to themselves and to others or dying. She sat with them for a while, once in each park, and smelled their urine and sweat. Every garbage can on Second Avenue had been picked through. She saw the headline on a newsstand: AIDS VICTIMS RIOT.
>
> Three elderly women asked her for money. She gave them everything she had. Then she went to the bank machine and got out more. Four times young men tried to sell her drugs. In each case she bought what they offered without inspection and dropped three bags of marijuana and one crack vial on the sidewalk. There was trash everywhere. The streets were broken and filled with holes. There was a hooker on Twelfth Street who was clutching her vagina and crying. (216–17, emphasis mine)

Suddenly, Kate can no longer harmonize away the contradictions urban existence places before her; she cannot comprehend "people in trouble" (the poor women, the drug dealers, the crying hooker, Scott) through appeals to a vague humanism. Schulman herself insists, "Society is so stratified that people can occupy the same physical space and never see each other, and also have completely different experiences of that space" (qtd. in Munt, "Somewhere," 43). As *People in Trouble* concludes, Kate finally realizes her complicity in the production of space that represses contradictions and stratifications.

Queer Identities in a Crisis

Kate's emerging queer consciousness thus changes her aesthetic. When Kate returns to her apartment, her interaction with Peter confirms that her identity as "artist" has been transformed as decidedly as her sexual and political identities. She listens silently to Peter's lament:

> "I understand you feel a need to be politically active but I think that is something we can do together. Homosexuals don't have a monopoly on morality, you know. We have always agreed that our artwork is our political work. We have always agreed that challenging form is more revolutionary than any political organization ever can be. But if you feel a need to be part of a group, we can do that together. . . . We can be exactly like we were before."
>
> She placed her fingers flat against his chest. It was a wall. It moved. There was hair underneath his shirt. She wanted to dig her fingernails in and tear him apart.
>
> He spoke again. What did he say this time? (217–18)

Kate no longer hears Peter and the ideas he espouses. She cannot base her aesthetic on Peter's ideals; Peter's ideals are, in fact, a wall or barrier blocking her development as an artist. This wall or barrier, however, can be moved, if not completely torn apart. Peter's nostalgic desire for things "exactly like they were before" comes across as incredibly naive, since it endows Kate's previous sexual, political, and artistic identities with an essential wholeness and dismisses Kate's new queer identities as nonessential supplements. "But," as Jacques Derrida insists, "the supplement supplements. It adds only to replace" (145). Kate and Peter *never* were "exactly like they were before," and Kate at this point recognizes that Peter's request is actually a heteronormative demand that she "fix" her identity and disavow the queer relations that are constantly reshaping it.

She and Peter cannot be exactly like they were before, and Kate cannot see space exactly as she did before. Kate's conception of Peter's ideas as a wall that can be moved, however, demonstrates Kate's acceptance that her aesthetic, like her sexual and political identities, need not be understood as static. A final scene—the dedication of Kate's sculpture—starkly represents how far Kate has come. Ronald Horne will preside over the dedication, which takes place on the day of Scott's funeral. Although the narrator records silence as the scene opens, no one can mute the discord of this coincidence: "Kate looked closely at the crowd. There were some people she knew from Justice meetings. . . . There were no words. They did not touch. There were no embraces, only anger and a shared determination that passed between them.... [Scott's coffin] was placed in the hearse without eulogy or speeches" (219–20).

"There were no words" because Schulman has by now firmly established the process this group goes through to form a collective and disruptive queer identity; as anger and shared determination come together, "go ... go ... go" again pulsates beneath this scene without needing to be spoken. And indeed, once in the streets, the group does begin to move, even stopping traffic: "[Kate] climbed over cars, disregarded them. When there are that many people the traffic can't move. When that many people walk together the traffic has to stop" (220). The group walks directly to the space outside the building where Horne is beginning the speech that will dedicate Kate's artwork.

Although homeless people occupy almost all urban locations in a "redeveloped" city such as New York, "authorities" generally round the homeless up and displace them for "public" events such as political rallies, holidays, and dedications. When Horne sees Kate and her queer group approaching, he similarly tries to displace them and the contradictions they embody: "He was searching for just the right throwaway comment to invalidate all the people in front of him and at the same time make great copy for the front page of the next day's *New York Post*. But nothing very clever seemed to come to mind" (221). After the group surges forward, upsetting vehicles and cameras, Kate climbs atop an overturned CNN van and looks at the artwork spread out in front of her. The language that describes the confusion that follows, as Kate puts the "finishing touches" on her piece, suggests that she has moved far from her commitment to a universalizing, high-modernist aesthetic:

> Kate pushed harder than she had ever pushed and clawed her way to the front of the stage, catching and tearing her flesh on the splintered police sawhorses that lay mangled everywhere. Then she climbed under it, crawling on the dirt and garbage over wires, rags, cans of paint and turpentine. She watched her own hands turn black and her arms cake with dirt and blood surrounded by the moving spikes of pants legs bobbing around her. Dragging the cans and power lines to the base of the collage's wooden frames, she looked back at the chaos behind her. Each gesture was too large and so unusual that the action passed before her like a high-speed silent film. Only there was no silence. (221–22)

Kate's artwork goes up in flames, engulfing Ronald Horne, who will indeed make the news but in a way he never anticipated: "Real-estate

Queer Identities in a Crisis

mogul Ronald Horne met a fiery death today when a freak accident occurred during a riot by AIDS victims. An art installation designed for the inauguration of a new health club caught fire and enveloped the billionaire developer in a flaming collage" (224). Kate's corporate sponsors may require harmonious uses of space and containment of chaos and contradiction, but Justice displays a different aesthetic altogether, one that critiques what it was "designed for." A "club" where the few pay for "health" simultaneously denies health and well-being to the many relegated to perpetual nonmember status. Critically and collectively *deploying* chaos and contradiction, Kate and her cohorts insist that such contradictions be made public. Urban space is contested space, and Justice's "flaming" aesthetic works in the end to flaunt that dictum.

Perestroika Redux

Just as the beginning of Schulman's novel could be subtitled, à la Kushner, "Millennium Approaches," so too could the conclusion be subtitled "Perestroika": the mingling, messiness, collective contestation, and hope that characterize the theory staged in *Angels in America* transform Kate in *People in Trouble,* who in turn works with Justice to incorporate those ideas into her sculpture. Ironically, it is not at all clear in the novel whether Schulman endorses Kate's newfound aesthetic. The final chapter focuses on Molly and only obliquely and dismissively mentions Kate: "Kate developed a high profile as a result of Horne's death and could be read about in an essay by Gary Indiana in the *Village Voice* and one by Barbara Kruger in *ArtForum*. In fact, Kate began working extensively in burning installations and quickly got commissions from a number of Northern European countries to come start fires there" (225). There is a fair amount of cynicism in this removal of Kate from the scene, especially since Molly remains behind, with Justice, in New York City. Moreover, the geographic distance might stand as both figure for and confirmation of what various biphobic figures maintain throughout *People in Trouble:* Kate is always already distanced from the gay community, not really committed to "our" struggle.[22]

It is possible, however, to look critically at Schulman's perhaps unintentional slippage from "flaming" to "burning." If we understand a "flaming" aesthetic as alive, brilliant, or—as Kushner might note—*faaaaabulous!* then a "burning" aesthetic, given Schulman's cynicism, might suggest the opposite: faded brilliance, world-weariness, resignation. Yet, although

Kate's cooptation by "the establishment" may be inevitable, this need not mean that she loses her critical edge and forgets the lessons she has learned throughout *People in Trouble* about complicitous critique; indeed, one might reasonably expect at this point that Kate will continue to contest from the "inside," in queer ways, the meanings exacted by "the establishment." The citation of Kruger and Indiana is, in this sense, particularly relevant: Hutcheon often uses Kruger's photographs, with their simultaneous use and abuse of high modernism, as examples of a critical postmodernism that parodies discourses about high art, the media, gender, and sexuality, and Indiana's very *name* suggests complicity and critique, since it is at once the quintessential Midwestern town, immortalized in song and technicolor by a cherubic Ronnie Howard, *and* the signature of a "New Queer Writer" who writes about children, sexuality, and violence.[23] More important, though, the slippage from "flaming" to "burning" belies the ways in which "complicitous critique" describes ACT UP's and Schulman's (and Kushner's) *own* aesthetic strategies.

Douglas Crimp and Adam Rolston, for instance, draw attention to the strategies used by cultural workers in ACT UP:

> If their sophisticated postmodern style has gained art world attention and much-needed funding for Gran Fury [a graphic arts group within ACT UP], the collective has accepted it only hesitantly, often biting the hand that feeds. Their first poster commission from an art institution was discharged with a message about art world complacency: WITH 42,000 DEAD, ART IS NOT ENOUGH. (19)

ACT UP, in short, reconfigures its complicity, using "art world attention" to spotlight "art world complacency." Similarly, Schulman's own "flaming" aesthetic should be seen as both complicitous and critical, especially since she links her work to Kate's by titling both her novel and Kate's sculpture *People in Trouble*. In the last sentence of the novel, Molly and her friends angrily head out to another demonstration, because—as the narrator explains—"there was nothing more to say" (228). Like Kate with her sculpture and ACT UP with their graphics, Schulman bites the hand that feeds (or reads) here, implicitly suggesting, as she lays down her smoking pen, that these words—or, more specifically, the act of writing or reading them—will never be enough. As with the conclusion to *Angels in America*, so too with (both) *People in Trouble*(s): "The Great Work *Begins*" (*P*, 148, emphasis mine).

In the opening scene of *Perestroika,* Kushner introduces a minor character who is played by the actor playing Hannah, Joe's Mormon mother who is transformed by queerness over the course of the play. Aleksii Antedilluvianovich Prelapsarianov, "the World's Oldest Living Bolshevik," speaks in "the Hall of Deputies, the Kremlin," in January 1986 (*P,* 13). Stage directions explain that this character is *"unimaginably old and totally blind"* (*P,* 13). He stands at the front of the stage and demands:

> What System of Thought have these Reformers to present to this mad swirling planetary disorganization, to the Inevident Welter of fact, event, phenomenon, calamity? Do they have, as we did, a beautiful Theory, as bold, as Grand, as comprehensive a construct. . . . You who live in this Sour Little Age cannot imagine the grandeur of the prospect we gazed upon: like standing atop the highest peak in the mighty Caucasus, and viewing in one all-knowing glance the mountainous, granite order of creation. You cannot imagine it. I weep for you. (*P,* 13–14)

According to the World's Oldest Living Bolshevik, the "next Beautiful Theory" must be shaped and absorbed *before* the people head to "the barricades": "If the snake sheds his skin before a new skin is ready, naked he will be in the world, prey to the forces of chaos" (*P,* 14).

Directly behind this speech, however, Kushner restages the ending to *Millennium Approaches:* the angel has just crashed through Prior's ceiling and is hovering above his bed. Such a juxtaposition throws the World's Oldest Living Bolshevik's words into crisis: the chaos has already burst in upon Prior; he has had no opportunity to shape, in advance, an autonomous theory and identity. In short, the straight theory that the World's Oldest Living Bolshevik espouses no longer suffices in this queer world. What is needed instead—what was playing in the streets and what *Angels in America* and *People in Trouble* affirm—is queer perestroika: identities-and theories-in-process, not "viewing in one all-knowing glance the mountainous, granite order of creation" but rather collectively and continuously multiplying and reshaping locations for the production of identity, theory, activism, and art; not standing, in solitude, on "the highest peak in the Caucasus" but acting up, in solidarity, across differences in coalition with others.

Epilogue

Post-Queer?

By concluding with Sarah Schulman, ACT UP, and queers in the street, I have come full circle, since my first chapter concluded with Audre Lorde and the resistant identities she observed being shaped and reshaped in the streets a decade earlier: "My lasting image of that spring . . . was of women whom I knew . . . and women whose names were unknown to me, leading a march through the streets of Boston behind a broad banner stitched with a line from Barbara Deming: 'WE CANNOT LIVE WITHOUT OUR LIVES' " (Lorde, *Need*, 3). The connection is perhaps more than coincidental, since Schulman studied under Lorde at Hunter College in the early 1980s. Schulman writes, "She told us, 'That you can't fight City Hall is a rumor being circulated by City Hall' " (*My American History*, xvii). As far as Lorde was concerned, power was not concentrated on high; women working together as friends and lovers could both rewrite the rumors being circulated about their powerlessness and effect a new world.

The Lorde-Schulman connection is appropriate, given my intention in this project of reading the Queer Renaissance in and through, rather than above, the larger queer social context of the period. The classroom here, notably, facilitates such a reading: it provides neither a pure origin nor an ultimate end for the identities I have explored in this study. Instead, the classroom, for both Lorde and Schulman, is a location contiguous to other locations; both women are simultaneously coming from and going to someplace else. Schulman does not simply learn how to be queer when she gets to Hunter College and reads about it in a book, but neither do her books (or Lorde's, or those read in Lorde's classroom) simply "reflect" queer identities shaped elsewhere. The renaissance of queer creative work and the renaissance of queer identities and political analyses have been mutually constitutive. Each represents and fuels the other.

In the past few years, however, some gay writers have appeared who want queers to stop this flurry of reproductive activity. In this epilogue, I consider briefly whether the emergence of writers such as Bruce Bawer and Andrew Sullivan marks the beginning of a "post-queer" moment. Bawer, Sullivan, and others have gained a great deal of attention by calling for such a moment: their emphasis is on individuality and an abstract individual freedom rather than on relational, fluid identities; they stress not a critique of but an accommodation and assimilation to contemporary society and its institutions. If the Queer Renaissance constructs collective identities intent on disrupting dominant hierarchical understandings of sex, gender, sexuality, race, and class, does the emergence of neoconservative gay writers committed to the status quo or gay scientists who want to ground homosexuality in biology mark a waning of the Queer Renaissance?

Bawer, for one, has virtually sounded the death knell for "queerness": "Today, reasonable gay voices are beginning to be heard in the media. [My writing] is both a cause of this phenomenon and a symptom of it. Also symptomatic are the decline of ACT UP, the dissolution of Queer Nation, and the growing influence of the Log Cabin Republicans" ("No Truce," 74). I conclude, however, that the Queer Renaissance is ongoing despite, and indeed because of, the prominence given to such writers. When such writers can be taken as "representative," it is clear that, in many ways, the queer work I have been examining, and that has been developing for more than fifteen years, has only just begun and is now needed more than ever.

Bawer has forcefully denounced the flamboyance of queers of all kinds: drag queens, leather folk, sex radicals. These groups, according to Bawer, stand between gay men (Bawer has very little to say about lesbians) and acceptance by heterosexuals: "If the heterosexual majority ever comes to accept homosexuality, it will do so because it has seen homosexuals in suits and ties, not nipple clamps and bike pants; it will do so because it has seen homosexuals showing respect for civilization, not attempting to subvert it" (*A Place*, 51). Gay Pride Day, especially, worries Bawer:

> It seemed to me . . . that the sort of pride on display in the Gay Pride Day march was, in many cases, not so much pride in the sense of "self-respect" or "dignity" than pride in the sense of "arrogance," "conceit," "hubris." Real pride, after all, is a hard-won individual attribute. It doesn't come from being gay, or from belonging to *any* group. It can come, however, from dealing with the fact of your homosexuality in a responsible and mature manner,

from not using it as a club to beat other people with or as an excuse to behave irresponsibly or unseriously. (*A Place*, 159)

As an antidote to this "irresponsibility," Bawer offers his book *A Place at the Table: The Gay Individual in American Society*: "I felt that if the image of homosexuals that the march projected was ever to be set right, those of us who were displeased with it in its present form couldn't keep away entirely. We had to do *something*" (157). *A Place at the Table*, then, purports to fix the image, to set it right, by distancing "mainstream gays" (35) from the antics of those pesky queers.

Of course, Bawer's irritation with those who supposedly use their sexuality "as a club to beat other people with" completely mystifies the fact that it is precisely those people who really *have* been beaten with clubs, in ever-increasing numbers, over the past few decades. Moreover, Bawer's disdain for groups and his deification of the individual are ahistorical: the space in which someone like Bawer can confidently be a "gay individual in American society" was forged over time by the very flamboyant groups he would disavow. The fact that Bawer's arguments are easy to counter, however, has not kept the straight media from showering *A Place at the Table* with hyperbolic praise. On the front cover of Bawer's volume, the *New York Times*'s Christopher Lehmann-Haupt declares *A Place at the Table* "an intelligent and eye-opening book" that "smashes the common stereotypes of gay people to smithereens." On the back cover, the *Wall Street Journal*'s Jonathan Rauch writes, "Of all the sinkholes in American politics, the debate over homosexuality is the rankest. . . . With the bracingly rational passion of a writer who can think and feel at the same time, [Bawer] charts a path out of the swamp." And on the inside, John Fink of the *Chicago Tribune* insists, "If there is one book about homosexuality and gay rights that everyone should read, it is probably this one." Bawer worries in *A Place at the Table* that queers (swamp rats?) represent gay life to straight America. Fink's suggestion that Bawer's book is the one gay book everyone should read, however, implies that our threatening representation might be contained. Bawer's book alone, apparently, can speak for us all.

Meanwhile, even as neoconservative writers like Bawer win acclaim by lambasting the "rowdier" elements of queer culture, biologists are searching for the gene that would tidy up the mess that is human sexuality, securing once and for all a biological origin for sexual orientation. Simon

Epilogue: Post-Queer?

LeVay is the neurobiologist most associated with this movement. In *The Sexual Brain*, LeVay writes:

> It is not unrealistic to expect a gene or genes influencing sexual orientation to be identified within the next few years, since there are at least three laboratories in the United States alone that are working on the topic. If such genes are found, it will be possible to ask where, when, and how these genes exert their effects, and hence to gain a more basic understanding of the biological mechanisms that make us straight or gay. (127)

Whereas the queer identities in this study have sought to unsettle and denaturalize the mechanisms of power that produce our current understandings of identity, the gay gene LeVay and his colleagues long for would fix and naturalize sexual identity.

These various developments indeed suggest that we are potentially moving or have moved to a post-queer moment. At the very least, these developments highlight the ongoing tension between liberal reformers and radical liberationists that I focused on, following John D'Emilio, in my introduction. Just as the later Mattachine Society and the Daughters of Bilitis advocated a professional, suit-and-tie approach to homosexual rights that discounted the structural critique of American society advanced by the early Mattachine Society, and just as the Gay Activists Alliance's single-minded focus on gay rights trumped the Gay Liberation Front's commitment to coalition with other movements for liberation, so too could the rise of gay neoconservatism and a renewed faith in "experts" be seen as a "retreat to respectability" (D'Emilio, *Sexual Politics*, 75) that signals the end of the Queer Renaissance.

But, as I have already suggested, it does not have to be that way. We queers need not be contained, and one "representative" need not (and indeed, cannot) speak for us all. This is, in the final analysis, a *queer* renaissance, and there is no reason to expect that it will follow a predictable (straight?) trajectory that simply reproduces the mistakes of the past. Furthermore, these developments might be read as constituting another beginning as much as an end. Queer analysis, after all, *commences* by questioning the boundaries established by others: as Gloria Anzaldúa writes, "The street reader looks at an experience as something that's alive and moving or about to move"; "Queer readers want to interact, to repeat back or reflect or mirror, but also do more than just reflect back or mirror—to add to the dialogue" ("To(o) Queer," 259, 256). Anzaldúa's reflecting back or mirroring is not a pure reflection but rather a refraction, bringing into view those issues that are hidden or effaced by the border guards. In the contemporary context, then, a queer reading might begin by asking: Whom does the fixing of boundaries around a gay gene or of representatives for lesbians and gay men serve? Why are these boundaries and representatives being established at this particular time? How are these boundaries intersected by others, and what is to be gained from interrogating or crossing them?

As far as biology is concerned, the answer to the first question, to many, would seem self-evident: clearly (they would say), *gays and lesbians* are served by the search for the gay gene, and by the positioning of an "expert" like LeVay as our representative. One of Bawer's main theses, for instance, is that (well-behaved) homosexuality should be accepted because it is most definitely *not* a choice; he therefore loudly applauds "a scientific study purportedly demonstrating a correlation between homosexuality and a certain pattern of genetic markers add[ing] to the growing body of evidence that sexual orientation is hereditary" (*A Place,* 56). LeVay has been loudly applauded in other arenas as well, even being hailed as a hero at the Los Angeles Gay Pride Parade. And in a recent informal poll, 61 percent of readers of the lesbian and gay newsmagazine *The Advocate* said that it would help the movement if homosexuality were found to be biologically determined (February 6, 1996, 8).

A queer analysis, however, always attentive to connections across differences, might complicate the question: Why are sexual identities being fixed in the brain at this particular time? Or, more specifically (and perhaps more provocatively), does it matter that *The Sexual Brain* emerged one year before the fanfare surrounding *The Bell Curve,* Richard J. Herrnstein and Charles Murray's "study" that purportedly grounds poverty and other social inequities in biology? Siobhan Somerville implicitly makes this link when, after probing the connections between the "scientific racism" of the late nineteenth century and the contemporaneous emergence of the medicalized homosexual body, she suggests that a queer inquiry into these historical connections might also consider how "these analogies [have] been used to organize bodies in other historical moments" and how "the current effort to rebiologize sexual orientation and to invoke the vocabulary of immutable difference reflect[s] or influence[s] existing cultural anxieties and desires about racialized bodies" (265–66). Such a query might qualify the self-evidence of the assumption that lesbians and gay men are served by the pursuit of a gay gene.

Epilogue: Post-Queer?
———————

There are several ways in which the effort to rebiologize sexual orientation reflects existing cultural anxieties about race. Most important, the two reflect each other in the ways in which they focus our vision. In an attempt to identify the anxieties centralized in *The Bell Curve*, Steven Fraser writes:

> At a time when most indices record expanding inequalities in American life—not only in income and wealth distribution, but in public and private schooling, in matters of health care, even in our varying capacities to rear the newborn—*The Bell Curve* naturalizes those phenomena, turns them into inescapable symptoms of a biological class fate. At the same time, by associating the "cognitive underclass" [Herrnstein and Murray's term for those "genetically predisposed" to lower IQs] with every grisly or disturbing form of social behavior, from crime to unwed teenage motherhood, the authors direct our gaze away from those institutional centers of power that in an earlier era might have had to shoulder the blame for our most grievous inequalities and social pathologies. (4–5)

A similar refocusing of our gaze is at work in *The Sexual Brain*, I would argue, despite LeVay's best intentions: the book directs our gaze away from the institutions that secure and maintain heterosexual dominance—indeed, away from the institution of heterosexuality itself—to a naturalized homosexuality. As Jonathan Katz writes in *The Invention of Heterosexuality* (a book that is, I think, the antithesis—or the Anzaldúan refraction—of *The Sexual Brain*), "Rarely do we focus for long on the riddle of heterosexuality—our gaze turns quickly to 'the problem of homosexuality' " (15). By focusing our gaze once again on "the problem of homosexuality" (indeed, focusing our gaze *microscopically* on that "problem"), the search for a gay gene only accelerates the turn away from a critique of heterosexuality. And just as *The Bell Curve* lets economic institutions off the hook, allowing those in power to regret (perhaps), but not change, the "expanding inequalities in American life," so, too, *The Sexual Brain* lets the institution(s) of heterosexuality off the hook. If a gay gene is secured, there is no reason to assume that homophobia will suddenly end. Indeed, in a culture already primed to see difference as a regrettable biological fact, there is nothing to keep heterosexuals from seeing homosexuality similarly as a natural but regrettable biological destiny, all the while doing nothing to change the institutions that secure heterosexual dominance. And whether or not they understand themselves as having a gay gene, in a

Epilogue: Post-Queer?

world where homosexuality is the "aberration" and heterosexuality the "norm," young gay men and lesbians will still kill themselves.

This is especially true given the ways that the "gay gene" has already been appropriated by the radical right. In a document that was used in the campaign for Colorado's Amendment 2, the measure that prohibited local communities from establishing ordinances that would protect lesbian and gay civil rights and that was later struck down by the U.S. Supreme Court, Tony Marco writes, "Many 'natural' or possibly 'innate' behaviors of both animals and human beings remain unprotected or strictly controlled by society. The striking behavior of poisonous snakes is perfectly natural. Do we argue that 'because snakebites are natural' people ought to welcome and take no steps to protect themselves from venomous vipers?" The right wing likes to disavow the connection between its rhetoric and violence, but this analogy, I think, makes the connection unavoidable: most people cornered by a venomous viper would strike to kill.

As I stressed in my introduction, however, the "institutional centers of power" did "shoulder the blame" in an earlier era: the early Mattachine Society launched a Marxist critique of the organization of American society, particularly the organization of the American family; the Gay Liberation Front made connections between homosexual oppression and a host of other oppressions that are secured in a capitalist and patriarchal society. It is these earlier moments and impulses that are implicitly and explicitly cited and reshaped in the contemporary Queer Renaissance. And at a time when studies such as *The Bell Curve* and *The Sexual Brain* would fix difference in biology before or instead of attending to ongoing structural inequalities, such a queer renaissance is needed more than ever. As Lisa Duggan points out in her afterword to Katz's book, with a nod to anthropologist Carole S. Vance:

> We see headlines announcing the existence of a "gay brain," but no such reporting on the multiplying historical studies that show sexual identity to be cross-culturally and historically variable. We wait to open a copy of *USA Today* to read "Heterosexuality Not 'Natural,' Not 'Normal,' Study Finds." Chances are, we'll be waiting a long time. (194)

To Duggan, that is why studies like Katz's, which contest heteronormative assumptions, are so vital (Duggan, 196). As Katz himself writes, "*Heterosexual* and *homosexual* refer to a historically specific system of domination—of socially unequal sexes and eroticisms. . . . Biological determinism is misconceived intellectually, as well as politically loathsome. For it places the problem in our bodies, not in our society" (189). In contrast, Katz's study, along with the studies and identities multiplying in the Queer Renaissance, locates the problem in society, not in our queer bodies and eroticisms.

If, despite these cautions, *The Bell Curve* and *The Sexual Brain* still seem to be at opposite ends of the spectrum, we should be aware of at least one commentator for whom they are not. David Duke has recently stated:

> I think there is a genetic predisposition to it [homosexuality]. . . . I've read the genetic studies, and I think there is definitely a predisposition to it. But you know what is so funny about all of that? *The New York Times* says stuff like, We can't blame gays for their behavior because they are born that way. That's the argument. Well, don't they realize that the same law of genetics, the same differences in the physical aspects of the brain, could account for differences in personality and races and so forth? I mean, it follows naturally. (qtd. in Boulard, 32)

I mean, it follows naturally. Duke's "straight talk" here could be seen as the antithesis of the statement I identified in the last chapter as a byword for my project: "This is not in the Text, We *deviate*." At the same time, Duke's statement makes clear that deviation from what supposedly "follows naturally" is crucial: queer identities are needed that refuse to acquiesce to a gay biologism or gay neoconservatism, especially when (or precisely because) those movements are used to underwrite the marking and policing of "others." In the process of realizing that "deviation," moreover, such queer identities can and should continue to challenge an array of other conclusions, from all points on the political spectrum, that likewise "follow naturally" from heteronormative "common sense": David Duke's conclusion, for instance, that an "indelible, unwashable AIDS tattoo" would protect people from "AIDS carriers" (qtd. in Boulard, 32), or Bruce Bawer's conclusion that but for the "irresponsible antics" of queers (*A Place*, 222), upstanding lesbians and gay men would be accepted into American society. Queer analyses demonstrate that the "irresponsible antics" of queers are responsible not only for forging a few spaces more conducive to "upstanding" gay and lesbian desire but also for exposing how exclusion of lesbians and gay men (and many, many others) is built into the very structure of American society, and for imagining a world

Epilogue: Post-Queer?

shaped otherwise. The latter queer work is ongoing and has only just begun.

Queer activists and theorists will undoubtedly continue to look critically at neoconservative rhetoric seeking to move "beyond queer"; after all, as a Queer Nation sticker that was ubiquitous a few years ago announces, "Queers Bash Back." Of course, it is possible to argue that the search for the gay gene and recent gay neoconservative writing are not really queer bashing; that they are, instead, merely strategic moves; and that despite their flaws, they nonetheless help to advance the gay and lesbian movement. They are bridges. In response, I would turn again to Moraga and Anzaldúa's *This Bridge Called My Back:* "A bridge gets walked over," Moraga writes in her preface to that collection, "over and over and over again" (xv). Moraga's insight suggests that we ask ourselves: If the books that have been so championed by the mainstream press recently are bridges, on whose backs are those bridges built? Bawer's "gay individual in American society" requires the queer other for his self-definition. Ironically, the same might be said about many queer theorists and activists. The latter, however, try not to disavow the relationship. As Anzaldúa asserts, "We have come to realize that we are not alone in our struggles nor separate nor autonomous but that we—white black straight queer female male—are connected and interdependent" ("La Prieta," iv).

In my analysis in this project of various queer identities (Zami, queer trickster, mestiza queer, AIDS activist/artist), I have stressed that the work of imagining and shaping a queer world occurs both inside and outside the texts I have examined, and that "inside" and "outside" are mutually constitutive. Ironically, Bawer recognizes this, since the chapter in *A Place at the Table* that criticizes parades and protests is the same chapter that condemns the queer literature of the past fifteen years. "Poetry is not a luxury," goes the famous phrase by Audre Lorde (*Sister Outsider,* 36). This study insists that neither is poetry (or fiction or drama) an addendum, added onto or rising above queer activism or theory. Instead, the texts of the Queer Renaissance are intersections, or crossroads, where diverse queer communities both read and write, observe and shape, their own experiences and identities.

Epilogue: Post-Queer?

Notes

Notes to the Introduction

1. For an excellent overview of "the gay and lesbian publishing boom," see William J. Mann. Mann cites a *Publishers Weekly* estimate that about 3 percent of the fifty-eight thousand titles published in 1993, or just under two thousand titles, were lesbian and gay, though he also notes, "Exact figures are hard to come by, if only because of the fluid nature of what constitutes a 'gay book' " (25).

Lambda Book Report's 1991 article "Decade Dance" considered how "gay and lesbian literature took off in the 1980s" and included a profile of those whom *LBR* saw as the fifty "most influential people in the industry" during that decade (10). Such a profile, especially of those "in the *industry*," would have been virtually unthinkable fifteen years earlier. Gay novelist Richard Hall's article "Gay Fiction Comes Home," which appeared on the front page of the *New York Times Book Review* in 1988, was seen by some as an indication that mainstream journalism was finally acknowledging the incredible productivity of openly gay writers (Nelson, "Towards a Transgressive Aesthetic," 16). The first Lambda Literary Awards ("Lammies") were presented in 1989. See Labonte, 60–61, for a discussion of how, by 1994, these awards were taken very seriously by mainstream publishers.

My use of "rare" to describe openly lesbian and gay work in the 1970s is relative to the boom in the 1980s and 1990s; many openly gay and lesbian works were, of course, written or performed in the 1970s. Newly formed feminist presses such as Daughters, Inc., were particularly important for lesbian writers, many of whom got their start in such presses during the 1970s (Rita Mae Brown is the most famous example). Still, as Bonnie Zimmerman makes clear, the 1980s represent a significant advance: "Between 1973 and 1981, an average of only five lesbian novels was published each year; between 1984 and 1987, that number had jumped to twenty-three, and recent figures indicate that the pace is quickening" (207). For men, the shift is perhaps even more apparent: of the nearly five hundred primary works mentioned in the various entries in Emmanuel Nelson's *Contemporary Gay American Novelists: A Bio-Bibliographical Critical Sourcebook*, well over half were published in the 1980s and 1990s. About one-fifth were published in the 1970s, with another one-fifth published in all the decades prior to the 1970s. Even this calculation, however, may be a bit deceiving, since many gay writers who published prior to 1980 published more openly gay work after 1980.

2. Sedgwick's comments on renaissances make clear that scholars are beginning to see same-sex desires, affections, and activities as central to many literary periods; hence the "cultural phenomenon" I examine here is the explosion of *openly* lesbian and gay writing. I do not mean to champion fixed identities through this focus

(quite the opposite, in fact), only to note that something unprecedented has indeed occurred. Although "lesbian" desires, for instance, are certainly discernible in a novel such as Nella Larsen's *Passing* (1929) and in the Harlem Renaissance in general, there is still a significant difference between Larsen's novel and openly lesbian work such as Audre Lorde's *Zami: A New Spelling of My Name* (1982).

3. See, for example, Crimp, "Right On, Girlfriend!"; Duggan, "Making It Perfectly Queer"; Edelman, 112–17; Halperin, 62–67. *Out/Look*, the now defunct national lesbian and gay quarterly, published a special issue on the "Birth of a Queer Nation" in 1991. I discuss more thoroughly how my own use of "queer" fits into this collective project later in this introduction.

4. In 1992, Dennis Cooper published *Discontents: New Queer Writers*, an anthology of angry, graphic, and often violent short stories, essays, comic strips, and interviews. *Discontents* brought together many different queer writers, some of whom I mention briefly at the end of this introduction. Sarah Schulman is the only writer considered in *The Queer Renaissance* whose work is consistently linked to this movement. For another discussion of the New Queer Writers, see Latzky.

5. On the relationship of urban renewal to dislocation and polarization of rich and poor, see Williams and Smith. Williams and Smith also mention, briefly, Detroit's Renaissance Center (204). See also my discussion of Schulman's novel *People in Trouble* in chapter 4.

6. It is perhaps not surprising that I first formulated these thoughts in a run-down Admiral Benbow Inn in downtown Memphis, a city similarly beset by "urban renewal." I have no doubt that the majority of Memphis's poor and African American residents are still waiting for the construction of the monstrous Great American Pyramid on the banks of the Mississippi River to improve their lives.

7. Although Crimp's article is concerned primarily with the visual arts, Michael Denneny's comment makes it clear that similar rhetoric has been used in discussions of the literature of AIDS. Denneny's ideas on the subject haven't gotten any better of late:

> Great writers have always been reactionary. . . . It was true of 19th-century Russian literature and 18th-century English literature and almost assuredly will be true today. Political people are appalled by reality as it is and want to change it. Great artists are people who find intense beauty in the way life is and want to memorialize it. (Qtd. in DeLynn, 55)

For another literary example of appeals to the "transcendent," consider David Leavitt's comments about Susan Sontag's short story "The Way We Live Now." Leavitt writes, "Sontag . . . had written a story that transcended horror and greed, and which was therefore redemptive, if not of AIDS itself, then at least of the processes by which people cope with it" (28). For an alternative perspective on Sontag, see D. A. Miller, who criticizes what he sees as patronizing "urbanity" in Sontag's *AIDS and Its Metaphors:* "Sontag is right when she says that *AIDS and Its Metaphors* is 'not another book about AIDS'; rather it is a book (to be set next to Allan Bloom's or E.D. Hirsch's) that defends this culture, whose value . . . the epidemic provides a usefully extreme opportunity for once again recommending" (218).

Notes to the Introduction

8. I consider the interrelation of art and activism more fully in chapter 4. On these issues, see Doug Sadownick, who asserts, "ACT UP's grassroots war against AIDS is escalating, and the ammunition is art" (26). Sadownick demonstrates that Crimp's ideas about activists and artists are shared by other members of ACT UP:

> Video artist and ACT UP member Phil Zwickler finds it "revolting" and "telling" that art presenters would "still try and shove 'art for art's sake' shit down our throats." Performance artist Tim Miller finds the art world still cloven between those who vie for transcendence and those who want to fix the world. "The challenge of this time," he says, "is for artists to also be citizens, social activists, journalists; the time when you just get to sit in your studio and make art product is over. This is no different from the Latin American model of the citizen artist, or a playwright soon to be president of Czechoslovakia or the student artists in Tienanmen Square." (29)

Miller's comments already begin to indicate that the concept of a global renaissance, like the concept of the artistic generally, might be resignified, as something other than an escape from secular history.

9. Quotations from *Sexual Politics, Sexual Communities* are cited parenthetically as *SP*. Quotations from *Making Trouble* are cited parenthetically as *MT*. Other analyses of the 1950s and 1970s that I have found useful in compiling and contextualizing this section include Adam; Duberman, *Cures* and *Stonewall*; Kennedy and Davis; Kissack; Nestle. George Chauncey's *Gay New York: Gender, Urban Culture, and the Making of the Gay Male World, 1890–1940* takes on what Chauncey labels "the myth of invisibility" (3): the belief that prior to World War II, gay men and lesbians were so isolated from one another that community formation was virtually impossible. Chauncey debunks this myth by providing extensive evidence for a vibrant and highly visible gay male culture in New York City in the first third of the twentieth century. *Gay New York* suggests that the historical moments I have chosen to survey are not necessarily the only moments when lesbians and gay men shaped identities across differences and critiqued heteronormativity and thus are not the only two historical moments to be recalled in the Queer Renaissance. Future work in gay and lesbian history will undoubtedly uncover even more locations when and where lesbians and gay men forged fluid and disruptive identities.

10. On this topic, see Luis Valdez's play *Zoot Suit*, which details the Zoot Suit Riots of the 1940s, when a group of Chicanos were sent to prison without substantial evidence for the murder of a Sleepy Lagoon man. Valdez's play was part of his Teatro Campesino (Farmer's Theater) and part of the Chicano Renaissance.

11. Compare, as well, Joan Nestle's memories: "We needed the Lesbian air of the Sea Colony to breathe the life we could not anywhere else, those of us who wanted to see women dance, make love, wear shirts and pants. Here, and in other bars like this one, we found each other and the space to be a sexually powerful butch-femme community" (37).

12. I discuss this shift, along with the GLF/GAA strategy of "coming out," in chapter 1.

13. For an excellent collection of essays on the sex wars of the early 1980s, see

Duggan and Hunter. Analyses by writers of color and others sensitive to the divisions within both Anglo-American feminism and lesbian and gay politics include Beam; Bulkin, Smith, and Pratt; Hemphill, *Brother to Brother*; Hull, Scott, and Smith; Lorde, *Sister Outsider* and "What Is at Stake"; Martin; Moraga and Anzaldúa.

14. On the Lesbian Avengers, see Schulman, *My American History*, 277–324; Dewan. Schulman implies that the activist spirit in this group reinvigorated ACT UP (*My American History*, 311).

15. For overviews of the Harlem Renaissance that fill out some of the tensions I discuss in these paragraphs, see Lewis; Singh, 1–39. Gates's "The Trope of a New Negro and the Reconstruction of the Image of the Black" traces the vicissitudes of the term *New Negro* from the nineteenth century through the Harlem Renaissance.

16. On the Native American Renaissance, see Lincoln; on the Hawaiian Renaissance, see Sumida.

17. At times Moraga's critique of America and of nationalism leads her to posit another, Chicano nationalism. In chapter 3, I am more critical of Moraga and of this alternative.

18. Senator Jesse Helms (R–N.C.) and Representative Robert Dornan (R–Calif.) are two of the most vocally homophobic members of Congress; Pete Williams was a spokesperson for the Pentagon in the Bush administration and was outed by Signorile and others in protest over the military's policy of discharging lesbians and gay men. Vigorous opposition to the nomination of Clarence Thomas to the Supreme Court in 1991 arose mainly because of charges brought by a former employee, Anita Hill, although both his record on civil rights and his judicial qualifications in general also were and are highly questionable. Senate hearings on the Thomas-Hill controversy were held in the fall of 1991. Barbara Mikulski was, at the time, one of only two women in the Senate; she was the only one of the two to support Hill (and civil rights generally) by opposing Thomas's nomination. Barney Frank (D–Mass.), Gerry Studds (D–Mass.), and Steve Gunderson (R–Wis.) were the first openly gay members of Congress. Dr. Joycelyn Elders served as surgeon general in the Clinton administration until she was dismissed in 1994 because of her comments on masturbation.

Elders's comments about the length of her telephone conversation with Bill Clinton were made on the *Larry King Live* television show. There are numerous other examples of Elders's willingness to take on various queer identities, and there is no doubt that such a willingness hastened her dismissal. When asked by the newspaper *USA Weekend* why she agreed to grant a "controversial" interview to *The Advocate*, Elders asserted, "Why shouldn't I talk to *The Advocate?* I would do it again." And when critics of her opinions on the necessity of condom use began to call her the "condom queen," she told the *New York Times Magazine*, "If I could be the condom queen and get every young person who is engaged in sex to use a condom in the United States, I would wear a crown on my head with a condom on it! I would!" These facts about Elders were drawn from the "Agenda" section in the following issues of *The Advocate*: March 8, 1994; July 12, 1994; March 7 and 12, 1995. Elders was criticized in particular by some religious leaders for talking to the gay and lesbian press; she insisted that she would do so again, and after her dismissal, she even contributed book reviews to *The Advocate*. See the article by Elders, "Three-Ring Circus."

My comments in this section have obviously focused on the dearth of "queers in Washington." Although I still disagree with Signorile's use of the concept, I would agree with his assertion that there are, indeed, "queers in Hollywood." Signorile and I, however, would not necessarily have the same people in mind, since I would include in that category, for instance, television comedian Roseanne.

19. Rich Tafel is head of the gay Republican group known as the Log Cabin Republicans. Bruce Bawer is the author of *A Place at the Table: The Gay Individual in American Society*. I engage more directly with Bawer in my epilogue.

20. I also develop this argument in chapter 3. See Phelan, 151–54, for another discussion of these conflicts. It is interesting that Phelan is wary of how *queer* might "deny the colonization of lesbians and people of color that occurs within 'gay' politics" (154), even though all the queer theorists she cites in her discussion are women (Arlene Stein, Gayle Rubin, Robyn Ochs, and Lisa Duggan).

Although Wiegman criticizes "the deployment of *queer* so far," she provides no example of such a deployment. Wiegman thinks that Teresa de Lauretis coined the term *queer theory*, which is perhaps part of the problem, since de Lauretis is so anxious in her introduction to the special issue of *differences* on queer theory to distance the concept from actual queer activists (de Lauretis, "Queer Theory," xvii n. 2). Since I was participating in a graduate seminar called "Queer Theory" at the time de Lauretis's volume appeared, I am skeptical about positioning her as the individual author of the concept. In other locations, Wiegman's thoughts on queer theory are more complicated. In a recent review of books by Judith Butler and Eve Sedgwick, for instance, she concludes approvingly that "identity is always out of place" in the queer theory of these two writers (Wiegman, review, 895). *Who Can Speak? Authority and Critical Identity*, a collection of essays edited by Judith Roof and Wiegman, additionally contains several engagements with queer theory.

21. I am reminded here of the assertions of an audience member at the final plenary session of "InQueery/InTheory/InDeed," the Sixth Annual Lesbian and Gay Studies Conference held at the University of Iowa in November 1994. Audience members' comments generally revolved around predictable issues of exclusion and marginalization at the conference. One woman, however, chose to register her criticism in a unique—and to my mind, highly productive—way: after reciting a list of authors, publication dates, and titles ("Cherríe Moraga and Gloria Anzaldúa, 1981, *This Bridge Called My Back* . . . Audre Lorde, 1982, *Zami: A New Spelling of My Name* . . . Gloria Anzaldúa, 1987, *Borderlands/La Frontera: The New Mestiza*"), the conference participant asserted, "*That* is queer theory." In other words, far from being mere "additions," these women writers of color are always already on the inside, *authorizing* queer theory—not in the (patronizing) sense of merely looking on and giving approval to someone else's project but rather in the sense of writing (and living) the history of queer theory themselves.

Notes to the Introduction

Notes to Chapter 1

1. John D'Emilio explains that homophile activists adopted the slogan "Gay is Good" in 1968 (*Making Trouble*, 239). Barry Adam notes that Franklin Kameny of the Mattachine Society of Washington, D.C., had used the phrase as early as 1964: "In [the] face of the MSNY [Mattachine Society of New York] president's traditional homophile contention that 'we must lose the label of homosexual organizations,' Kameny asserted simply that 'gay is good!' " (71). Kameny was consciously referencing African American rhetoric, such as the slogan "Black is Beautiful." For a discussion of the influence on the early gay movement of the rhetoric of African American and Latino groups such as the Black Panthers and the Young Lords, see D'Emilio, *Making Trouble*, 240–41. On Stonewall generally, see Duberman, *Stonewall*.

2. See the essays included in Jay and Young. On the GLF, see D'Emilio, *Sexual Politics*, 233–35, and *Making Trouble*, 239–46; Adam, 73–89; Kissack. Adam specifically recounts the GLF and GAA (Gay Activists Alliance) zaps that helped pave the way for the APA shift (81–82). On the Radicalesbians, see Echols, 215–17, 232; Kissack, 121–23. The construction of the woman-identified woman enabled heterosexual feminists to identify more fully with their lesbian sisters, but it was, in many ways, a conservative move. Alice Echols argues that it was "designed to assuage heterosexual feminists' fears about lesbianism" (215); consequently, it ended up desexualizing lesbianism. Still, despite its evasion of "the knotty problem of sexuality," the construction at least temporarily "redefined lesbianism as the quintessential act of political solidarity with other women" (Echols, 217).

3. I have already mentioned the re-presentation of Civil Rights rhetoric in Edmund White's fictional account of Stonewall. The name Gay Liberation Front itself was meant to give tribute to the liberation struggles in Vietnam and Algeria (Duberman, *Stonewall*, 217).

4. For a good overview of feminist standpoint epistemology, as well as an "archeology of standpoint theory" (76), see Sandra Harding. Harding explains that feminist standpoint theory emerges from an engagement with Marxism (53–54). On this point, see Haraway, 186–87. By translating standpoint theory to a queer context, I am trying to further coalition building among theorists; like Harding, I recognize that "even though standpoint arguments are most fully articulated as such in feminist writings, they appear in the scientific projects of all the new social movements" (54). Echols's overview of radical feminism demonstrates that the boundaries between the different groups engaging in this self-reflexive constructionism were often blurred.

5. On this shift, see also D'Emilio, "Foreword," xxiv–xxviii, and *Making Trouble*, 239–51.

6. I am grateful to Steve Amarnick for helping me sort out some of the issues I am working with here. I am not dismissing the psychological importance of coming out, nor am I denying that Oprah Winfrey's sensitivity to coming out is empowering to thousands of gay and lesbian individuals. Rather, I am suggesting that the "coming out equals self-respect" model alone can be equally disempowering for

the gay and lesbian *movement,* and for the many other lesbian and gay people who too infrequently see themselves represented in any other way.

7. For a counterexample, see John Preston. The very fact that Preston can say, "I always shake my head in disbelief when I read critics who think the coming out novel is just a stage we're going through" (39), suggests that many critics have expressed their reservations about the genre. Indeed, Preston's article is in the same issue of *Lambda Book Report* that includes Sarah Schulman's derisive comments about the coming-out story (see Fries). In his introduction to the most recent edition of *A Boy's Own Story,* White himself notes the reservations that have been expressed about the genre: "Now [1994] there's an excess of coming-out novels, and critics talk of creating a ban against any further ones" ("On the Line," xv).

8. Neither White nor Lorde has necessarily identified with the concept of "queer" as it is deployed in this chapter and throughout this study, although White has begun to use the term *queer* more frequently, generally as a synonym for gay men and lesbians. See White, "The Personal Is Political: Queer Fiction and Criticism," in *The Burning Library,* 367–77. The work of Lorde (and other women of color) in the early 1980s, however, helped usher in the queer theory and activism of the later 1980s by facilitating the emergence of the disruptive identities that are at the center of the Queer Renaissance—identities that are not fixed in advance but are rather constantly reshaped in interaction with other identities. See chapter 3 for a fuller consideration of these issues in relation to Gloria Anzaldúa and the 1981 publication of *This Bridge Called My Back;* see my introduction, for a consideration of these issues in relation to my own use of the term *queer.* Some of Lorde's readers, of course, do identify with the term *queer* and deploy it in various ways, as my discussion of *Afrekete: An Anthology of Black Lesbian Writing* later in this chapter highlights.

For another reading of *Zami* through and as feminist positionality theory, see Carlston, 226, 231–32, 236. On positionality theory in relation to Lorde's 1986 collection of poetry *Our Dead Behind Us,* see Hull, 155, 159.

9. My thoughts on the ways in which *A Boy's Own Story* disrupts heterosexist understandings of linear sexual development are indebted to Kenneth Kidd.

10. White himself has at other times disavowed the possibility that *A Boy's Own Story* might be somehow representative; he writes, "The novel is not a political tract, nor is it meant to be representative or typical" ("On the Line," xii). My larger point here, however, is that the invisibility of whiteness allows for *A Boy's Own Story* to be cast as representative regardless of White's (clearly contradictory) intentions. The packaging of the novel underscores this: in spite of White's disavowal, a blurb on the back cover from the *New York Times*'s Christopher Lehmann-Haupt announces, "It is any boy's story. . . . For all I know, it may be any girl's story as well." The Plume paperback has gone through at least three cover designs since 1982, each utilizing a photograph of a different young (white) boy.

11. I am grateful to Michael Thurston for pointing out this connection to me.

12. Barbara Smith has made a similar point (Bulkin, Smith, and Pratt, 75–76).

13. This interpretation attempts to resist what Sagri Dhairyam points out about critical responses to Lorde's poetry: "The relational, shifting points of the politics

of identity enacted by and through Lorde's poems are stilled by their recuperation into canons of feminine or lesbian identity" (243). Nonetheless, I have framed this interpretation in a chapter about "coming out," and this, coupled with my own gay male location, might still the "shifting points of the politics of identity" yet again, recuperating Lorde, this time, into a rapidly expanding canon of "queer theory." This tension within "queerness," which I discuss at greater length in chapter 3, is unavoidable, but I hope that a negotiation of the tension will fuel, rather than forestall, the work of queer theory.

14. Lorde's work has influenced the shaping and reshaping of so many readers, writers, and communities that it would be impossible to compile a comprehensive list of the locations where such reinvention has occurred. *Celebrate the Life and Legacy of Audre Lorde*, a booklet distributed for Lorde's memorial service in New York City on January 18, 1993, particularly attests to the scope of her vision and influence. *Celebrate the Life and Legacy* includes tributes from, among many others, Palestinian feminists, groups fighting for Hawaiian independence, the Organization of Women Writers of Africa, and Men of All Colors Together. I am grateful to Steve Amarnick for sending me a copy of this document.

15. In 1992 a revised edition of *Chosen Poems—Old and New* was published as *Undersong*. In that collection, Lorde reiterated her commitment to revision: "The process of revision is, I believe, crucial to the integrity and lasting power of a poem. The problem in reworking any poem is always when to let go of it, refusing to give in to the desire to have that particular poem *do it all*, say it all, become the mythical, unattainable Universal Poem" (xiii).

16. For white gay male creative work that is more self-reflexive about whiteness or about positionality, respectively, see Allan Gurganus's 1990 collection of stories *White People* and Tom Joslin and Peter Friedman's 1993 film *Silverlake Life: The View from Here*. Gurganus's stories explore both gay and nongay white life in North Carolina, and Joslin and Friedman's film is a collective effort (often depending on who had the strength to work the camera) at documenting Joslin's and his lover Mark Massi's deaths from AIDS. The position from which the camera "sees" is repeatedly foregrounded and complicated. For a discussion of embodied and communal identity in the work of another white gay male author, Robert Glück, see Jackson. See also Crimp, "Right On, Girlfriend!" and my discussion of Tony Kushner and "queer perestroika" in chapter 4, for considerations of the sort of collective identity I discuss throughout this chapter.

17. Jewelle Gomez notes, significantly, that "commercial companies . . . would publish Audre's poems but could not bring themselves to publish the more explicit ideas of her essays" (7). On White's sometimes rocky experiences with publishers, see Bonetti, 101–2.

18. I am grateful to Stacy Alaimo for calling my attention to this series. The Book-of-the-Month Club instituted a similar series with fewer authors but—initially—the same problems: included are Baldwin *(Giovanni's Room)*, White (*A Boy's Own Story* and *The Beautiful Room Is Empty* ["available here in one exclusive volume"]), and Rita Mae Brown *(Rubyfruit Jungle,* published in 1973). After Lorde's death in 1992, however, an "exclusive three-in-one volume" of *Zami, Sister Outsider,* and *Undersong* was the first new addition to the Book-of-the-

Month Club series. This addition highlights the difficulty of making overly hasty generalizations about either White's or Lorde's canonicity. Also, I should note that, despite mainstream attempts to cast White as "America's most influential gay writer," such attempts have hardly garnered him nationwide fame. White has found such fame instead in European countries: in France, White is considered by many to be the most important American writer since Henry James, and in England, as he himself explains, *A Boy's Own Story* "made me so well known that English fans are always astonished to learn that most Americans don't know who I am" ("On the Line," xix).

19. Since, at the time of this award, Lorde was in Berlin undergoing treatment for the cancer she had been battling for more than a decade (and which eventually took her life), Jewelle Gomez, another black lesbian writer, delivered Lorde's speech. The "I" of Lorde's speech is thus destabilized in a way similar to that of the "I" in "Need," discussed above.

20. White's "greatest hit" list is as follows: among non-American writers, "Marcel Proust, Virginia Woolf, Colette, Jean Genet, Thomas Mann, Christopher Isherwood, Ronald Firbank," and among Americans, "Elizabeth Bishop, James Merrill, and John Ashbery" ("Twenty Years On," 5). Overall, I might add, White's 1989 acceptance speech is about two and a half times longer than Lorde's 1990 speech.

21. Such bittersweet isolation is conveyed by the very title of White's novel: "*The Beautiful Room Is Empty* . . . takes its title from one of Kafka's letters alluding to the unfortunate inability of two people (or perhaps two psyches) to inhabit a single space" (Radel, 184). White's beautiful and empty room contrasts significantly with Lorde's "house of difference," where cohabitation, though never easy, is both possible and necessary for survival.

Notes to Chapter 2

1. Vito Russo lists lesbian and gay characters, the films in which they appear, and the causes of their deaths in his "Necrology" in *The Celluloid Closet: Homosexuality in the Movies* (347–49). In the 1930s the Hays Office, headed by former postmaster general Will Hays, was responsible for the creation of the Motion Picture Production Code. The motion picture industry used this code to regulate itself (Russo, 31). Under the Hays code, virtually all portrayals of homosexuality were negative, and many ended in death, so that audiences would see that "vice" was appropriately "punished." My thanks to Ramona Curry for discussing the Hays code with me.

2. "Widely available" is an understatement; migration-to-the-big-city novels could compete against coming-out stories for the title of "Most Common Lesbian/ Gay Genre." Pre-Stonewall works that turn upon migrations to the city include Ann Bannon's Beebo Brinker series (for example, *Beebo Brinker* [1962]; the back cover declares, "She landed in New York, fresh off the farm") and John Rechy's *City of Night* (1963). Post-Stonewall explorations of the trope include Armistead Maupin's Tales of the City series (for example, *Tales of the City* [1978]; the front cover of the first paperback edition depicts a female figure with luggage, dwarfed

and awed by the immensity of the Golden Gate Bridge), Andrew Holleran's *Dancer from the Dance* (1978), and Edmund White's *The Beautiful Room Is Empty* (1988). Ethan Mordden's *I've a Feeling We're Not in Kansas Anymore* (1985) explicitly thematizes the disjunction between the city and the "provinces."

Of course, as Gates himself notes, the migration from South to North (and the corresponding shift from rural to urban) is also a trope in the African American literary tradition (*Signifying Monkey*, xxv). In a way, suggesting that Randall Kenan replicate this trope precludes him from signifying on it (see note 11, below).

In the Queer Renaissance, the dominance of the migration-to-the-big-city theme has been implicitly challenged by various Southern writers, including Kenan. For a few of the many texts in which Southern writers consider how queer subjectivity is shaped in the backwoods, marshes, and trailer parks of the South, see Allan Gurganus's *White People* (1990), Blanche McCrary Boyd's *The Revolution of Little Girls* (1991), and Dorothy Allison's *Bastard out of Carolina* (1992). See also Kenan and Allison's conversation about Southern queer literature, "Spies Like Us: Talking between the Lines."

3. The second chapter of *The Signifying Monkey*, "The Signifying Monkey and the Language of Signifyin(g): Rhetorical Difference and the Orders of Meaning" (44–88), provides a thorough explanation of the black concepts of "Signification" and "Signifyin(g)." "The bracketed *g*," Gates writes, "enables me to connote the fact that this word is, more often than not, spoken by black people without the final *g* as 'signifyin' "' (46).

4. This presumption, of course, may be a bit hasty. Gates himself, earlier in the interview I have been citing, notes that "a lot of gay black men in Harlem . . . are tired of being used for batting practice" (in Rowell, 454).

5. "Vogueing," developed by black and Latino gay men in New York City, is a form of dance in which dancers imitate and implicitly critique "high-fashion" styles and poses, such as those depicted in *Vogue* magazine. "Snapping" is a gesture of pride and defiance used to "read," punctuate, or invalidate another's discourse (Becquer, 8–12).

6. Michel Foucault's famous formulation is relevant here:

> There is not, on the one side, a discourse of power, and opposite it, another discourse that runs counter to it. Discourses are tactical elements or blocks operating in the field of force relations; there can exist different and even contradictory discourses within the same strategy; they can, on the contrary, circulate without changing their form from one strategy to another, opposing strategy. (101–2)

7. Despite this disclaimer, I think an earlier article of mine on *A Visitation of Spirits* did disarm Becquer's analysis (see McRuer, "A Visitation of Difference"); I hope that my indebtedness to Becquer's argument is clearer here (see note 22, below).

8. The theme of "coming home" runs throughout Hemphill's work. This quotation comes from his essay "Does Your Mama Know about Me?" Later in *Ceremonies*, in "Loyalty," Hemphill makes a similar point: "We will not go away with our

issues of sexuality. We are coming home" (64). See also Joseph Beam, "Brother to Brother: Words from the Heart":

> When I speak of home, I mean not only the familial constellation from which I grew, but the entire Black community: the Black press, the Black church, Black academicians, the Black literati, and the Black left. Where is my reflection? I am most often rendered invisible, perceived as a threat to the family, or am tolerated if I am silent and inconspicuous. I cannot go home as who I am and that hurts me deeply. (*In the Life*, 231)

Hemphill's work, with its insistence that "*I am* coming home," explicitly responds to Beam's lament here.

9. For another brief overview of *A Visitation of Spirits*, see my bio-bibliographical article "Randall Kenan," 234–35.

10. Reverend Barden reappears in *Let the Dead Bury Their Dead*, Kenan's collection of short stories. In "Ragnarök! The Day the Gods Die," Barden's internal thoughts are juxtaposed with his pontifications from the pulpit. "Ragnarök!" is, on the surface, the record of Barden's eulogy to the late Sister Louise Tate of the First Baptist Church. This eulogy is interrupted, however, by Barden's parenthetical meditations on his decades-long affair with the woman. Barden's hypocrisy in this story helps to de-authorize the bigotry he preaches in *A Visitation of Spirits*.

11. Interestingly, and *pace* Gates, both of Kenan's significations here move an "urban" story to the rural location of Tims Creek. *A Christmas Carol*, of course, is set in nineteenth-century London. *Go Tell It on the Mountain* is set primarily in New York. Several of Baldwin's characters come to New York *from* the South, suggesting that moving the story from New York *to* the South (which exactly reverses the situation) is part of Kenan's signification on Baldwin.

12. Similar passages occur elsewhere in *Go Tell It on the Mountain*; for example, "[John] wanted to stop and turn to Elisha, and tell him . . . something for which he found no words" (219). Emmanuel Nelson discusses such passages in his examination of homoeroticism in *Go Tell It on the Mountain* ("James Baldwin," 9–11).

13. I have provided only a skeletal outline of the ways in which *A Visitation of Spirits* signifies on *Go Tell It on the Mountain*, since to do more would be beyond the scope of this chapter. But it is not just in the story of Horace that Kenan signifies on Baldwin. Several sections of *A Visitation of Spirits* focus on older members of the community (Zeke and Ruth) who explore their pasts through internal monologue or through "dialogue" with God. As I mention briefly later, I read these sections as signifying on the second part of Baldwin's novel, "The Prayers of the Saints" (63–189).

For an analysis of other black gay significations on the church, see Nero, 238–43. As I suggested, Baldwin as well is quite critical of the church. For a more explicit and autobiographical critique, see Baldwin's *The Fire Next Time*:

> Being in the pulpit was like being in the theatre; I was behind the scenes and knew how the illusion was worked. . . . I knew, though I did not wish to know it, that I had no respect for the people with whom I worked. I could not have said it then, but I also knew that if I continued I would soon have

no respect for myself. . . . I really mean that there was no love in the church. It was a mask for hatred and self-hatred and despair. (55–58)

See Edelman, 68–71, for an analysis of the ways in which Baldwin resignifies the concept of salvation in his last novel, *Just above My Head*. I return to Baldwin in the next section of this chapter, where—through a consideration of Jimmy Greene—I am more explicit about how the church might be "saved." The "other sort of church" *A Visitation of Spirits* envisions through Jimmy might be understood as a local manifestation of the "other myths of queer positionality" I advocate in chapter 1.

14. A few pages before this scene, Kenan playfully underscores that his story should be seen not in a direct line of descent from but rather as a signification on Dickens. Horace is ostensibly discussing, with one of his lovers, the historical inaccuracies of the theatrical production of the history of the Cross family, but his comment ironically speaks to (and invalidates) the parallels between *A Visitation of Spirits* and *A Christmas Carol*: "[This play] is more than a little inaccurate, to tell the truth. I didn't have a great-great-great-grandfather named Ebenezer" (224).

15. Eve Sedgwick discusses the Department of Health and Human Services report in her article "Queer and Now":

I think everyone who does gay and lesbian studies is haunted by the suicides of adolescents. To us, the hard statistics come easy: that queer teenagers are two to three times likelier to attempt suicide, and to accomplish it, than others; that up to 30 percent of teen suicides are likely to be gay or lesbian; that a third of lesbian and gay teenagers say they have attempted suicide; that minority queer adolescents are at even more extreme risk. (*Tendencies*, 1)

16. If we take into account the annual number of deaths from lung cancer that can be linked to cigarette use, then the tobacco idyll itself, even without the suicide that immediately precedes it, is dependent on numerous sacrifices for the "good of the community." My thanks to Elizabeth Davies for suggesting this to me.

17. The other epigraph to *A Visitation of Spirits* is from William Gibson's *Neuromancer*: "To call up a demon you must learn its name. Men dreamed that, once, but now it is real in another way" (epigraph page; Gibson, 243).

The Dickens epigraph is a commentary on how Kenan's signification on *A Christmas Carol* should be read. One way (among many) to read the Gibson epigraph is as a commentary on *A Visitation of Spirits*'s other major signification, on Baldwin. Since Kenan's novel "outs" *Go Tell It on the Mountain*, it rejects the tradition of coding homosexuality as the "unnameable" or "unspeakable" and instead "learns its names."

18. Actually, although I focus on Foucault, I do not mean to suggest that the other writers Jimmy is reading are insignificant. Foucault most clearly introduces my argument about the ways in which sexual meanings have become unstable for Jimmy; later in this section, I discuss the transformations of Jimmy's public life (as minister), and in that context it might be as appropriate to consider why Jimmy is reading Erasmus or Augustine (*Confessions?*). Still, I focus on Foucault at this

point because Jimmy's reasons for reading Foucault are a bit more ambiguous than his reasons for reading some of the others. After all, although John Hope Franklin (or C. L. Franklin), Benjamin Quarles, and Frantz Fanon are obviously important to Jimmy, he precedes their names with a touchstone that explains why: "black history."

19. The translation is Ed Cohen's.

20. Perhaps I should say that my Foucauldian fantasies are not intended to "name" in the *standard* English sense of that word. On the trope of naming in the black literary tradition, see Gates, *Signifying Monkey,* 55, 69, 82, 87.

21. On the tension between minoritizing and universalizing views of homo/heterosexual definition, see Sedgwick, *Epistemology of the Closet,* 82–86.

22. Mercer writes:

The challenge of sameness entails the recognition that we share the same planet, even if we live in different worlds. We inhabit a discursive universe with a finite number of symbolic resources which can nevertheless be appropriated and articulated into a potentially infinite number of representations. Identities and differences are constructed out of a common stock of signs, and it is through the combination and substitution of these shared elements that antagonism becomes representable as such. ("1968," 427)

In general, this section on Jimmy and the "challenge of sameness" that Horace poses is the part of my argument that differs most sharply from my earlier article on *A Visitation of Spirits.* In "A Visitation of Difference: Randall Kenan and Black Queer Theory," my critique of identity politics tended to elide the theoretical potential of subversive sameness.

23. With this view, Kenan positions himself as part of a strong tradition that rejects the oppressive elements of the African American church but embraces its more progressive, visionary elements. Baldwin is part of this tradition as well. Cornel West would perhaps identify Baldwin's and Kenan's views as related to what he calls "prophetic moral reasoning." According to West, prophetic moral reasoning

encourages a coalition strategy that solicits genuine solidarity with those deeply committed to antiracist struggle. . . . A prophetic framework replaces black cultural conservatism with black cultural democracy. Instead of authoritarian sensibilities that subordinate women or degrade gays and lesbians, black cultural democracy promotes the equality of black women and men and the humanity of black gays and lesbians. In short, black cultural democracy rejects the pervasive patriarchy and homophobia in black [and white] American life. (397–98)

24. In *A Visitation of Spirits,* although Rabbi helps Jimmy rewrite the "traditional" Christianity of Tims Creek, North Carolina, it is possible to read this ostensible rewriting as closer to the original spirit of Christianity. Many of Christ's disciples, of course, called him "Rabbi." I'm grateful to Amy Farmer for reminding me of this.

25. Indeed, Gates's own tributes to Houston Baker often suggest as much; see,

for example, his aside to Baker in "Canon-Formation, Literary History, and the Afro-American Tradition," 15.

26. In 1994, Chelsea House Publishers launched a series of biographies intended for young lesbians and gay men, *Lives of Notable Gay Men and Lesbians*, under the general editorship of Martin Duberman. Kenan's biography of James Baldwin was the first installment in this series. See Kenan, *James Baldwin*. See also V. Hunt's recent interview with Kenan, in which Kenan cites Baldwin's influence in his decision to become a writer and identifies Baldwin as "the one other person [he] can really be paired with" (Hunt 412, 415).

27. The complete title of the story is "Let the Dead Bury Their Dead; Being the Annotated Oral History of the Former Maroon Society called Snatchit and then Tearshirt and later the Town of Tims Creek, North Carolina [circa 1854–1985]" (271). "Let the Dead Bury Their Dead" was originally conceived as part of *A Visitation of Spirits* (Hunt, 417).

28. I am suggesting that the emergence of Menes/Pharaoh marks a "resurrection," of sorts, for Jimmy, but Jimmy's death might be read ironically in another sense: Jimmy dies on March 12, 1998. March 12 is Kenan's birthday.

Notes to Chapter 3

1. The best study of male "homosociality" in literature is Eve Kosofsky Sedgwick's *Between Men: English Literature and Male Homosocial Desire*. In *Between Men*, Sedgwick examines "erotic triangles" in which the bond between two (male) rivals for a (female) beloved's affection is often as strong, or stronger, than the bond between either rival and the beloved (21). This erotic economy facilitates the exchange of women but simultaneously requires a structural homophobia that sharply proscribes the men's relationships with each other, thereby ensuring their participation in the patriarchal system.

Although Sedgwick argues that, at the end of the nineteenth century, this homosocial system began to give way "to a discussion of male homosexuality and homophobia as we know them" (202), a "male bonding" or homosociality that nonetheless requires a structural homophobia obviously continued to exist in various forms into and throughout the twentieth century. Robin Wood, for example, argues that the 1970s "buddy film" requires "an explicitly homosexual character" who "has the function of a disclaimer—our boys are not like *that*" (228–29). Kerouac's novels, which also make use of such queer disclaimers, are antecedents for such films. Of course, the homosocial system of the buddy film and of Kerouac's texts becomes somewhat difficult to sustain when, as in Kerouac's *The Subterraneans*, the protagonist ends up sleeping with the queer disclaimer (72–74); drugs and alcohol, however, are always conveniently on hand to explain (away) the lapse. Although this structural homophobia makes Kerouac a fascinating object of analysis for contemporary queer inquiry, I think it also prohibits consideration of him as the "classical gay writer" Sarah Schulman considers him to be (*My American History*, 167); hence my description of him as an "unlikely candidate" for inclusion in my study.

2. The United States, Canada, and Mexico signed the North American Free

Trade Agreement (NAFTA) in 1993. Many regulations on goods and services crossing the border were lifted; the agreement was intended to provide all three countries with increased access to the others' markets. Project Censored includes "NAFTA's Broken Promises" among its top ten censored stories of 1995. Less than two years after passage of the agreement, many American corporations have cut jobs in the United States—more than 150,000 in 1994 alone—and moved their plants to Mexico, where they have exploited both workers and the environment in blatant violation of labor rights and environmental regulations in that country.

3. Teresa de Lauretis's insight here comes from her analysis of Barbara Smith's landmark "Toward a Black Feminist Criticism." Turning to Gloria T. Hull, Patricia Bell Scott, and Barbara Smith's 1982 anthology *All the Women Are White, All the Blacks Are Men, but Some of Us Are Brave,* de Lauretis adds, "The term 'blacks' does not include (comprehend) black women any more than the term 'man' (white men) includes or comprehends white women. The black feminist concept of a simultaneity of oppressions means that the layers are not parallel but imbricated into one another; the systems of oppression are interlocking and mutually determining" (de Lauretis, "Eccentric Subjects," 134). In general, Andrew Ross's analysis in *No Respect: Intellectuals and Popular Culture* cannot accommodate such observations: Ross has his "race" chapter (read: black men) and his "gender" chapter (read: white women), but never do the two meet.

4. In Kerouac's work, the particular coming together of *attraction to* and *revulsion for* women of color is perhaps presented most starkly in *The Subterraneans,* in the relationship between Leo Percepied and Mardou Fox, a young African American woman. Although his affair with Mardou is passionate, Leo repeatedly abandons her, often for explicitly racist reasons: "I wake from the scream of beermares and see beside me the Negro woman with parted lips sleeping and little bits of white pillow stuffing her black hair, feel almost revulsion, realize what a beast I am for feeling anything near it" (24). Despite the protagonist's apparent awareness of it, the attraction-revulsion pattern repeats throughout *The Subterraneans.*

5. For an incisive overview of the *corrido* tradition, see R. Saldívar, 26–42. See also J. Saldívar, 49–84 (esp. 51–56).

6. Harper goes on to connect the elision of specificity that results from the mass-cultural marketability of marginality to the similar elision of specificity that can occur in academic analyses of social marginality (195). For another consideration of the marketability of a "fashionable" queerness, see Clark.

7. Of course, inevitable disappointment has been a component of many, many theoretical movements. Slavoj Žižek argues that identity becomes a rallying point in political movements when subjects phantasmatically invest identity with an expectation of wholeness. Such wholeness will always be exposed as fictive; hence inevitable disappointment occurs when the identificatory sign fails to live up to its original promise (cited in Butler, *Bodies That Matter,* 209). As an alternative to this politicization of identification, Judith Butler offers the politicization of *disidentification:* "What are the possibilities of politicizing *disidentification,* this experience of *misrecognition,* this uneasy sense of standing under a sign to which one does and does not belong? . . . It may be that the affirmation of that slippage, that failure of

identification is itself the point of departure for a more democratizing affirmation of internal difference" (*Bodies That Matter*, 219). My reading of Anzaldúa and this chapter in general are very much indebted to Butler's ideas; and as my conclusion should make clear, my reading of Butler is, in turn, indebted to Anzaldúa. As Butler herself notes, she is not the first to suggest such a politicization of disidentification:

> To understand "women" as a permanent site of contest, or as a feminist site of agonistic struggle, is to presume that there can be no closure on the category and that, for politically significant reasons, there ought never to be. . . . The numerous refusals on the part of "women" to accept the descriptions offered in the name of "women" not only attest to the specific violences that a partial concept enforces, but to the constitutive impossibility of an impartial or comprehensive concept or category. (221)

See Riley, whom Butler herself cites, for another feminist argument suggesting a contestatory relation to the sign *woman;* see also Snitow, 9.

8. Norma Alarcón writes:

> The most remarkable tendency in the work reviewed in this essay [Alarcón's "The Theoretical Subject(s) of *This Bridge Called My Back* and Anglo-American Feminism"] is the implicit or explicit acknowledgment that, on the one hand, women of color are excluded from feminist theorizing on the subject of consciousness and, on the other, that though excluded from theory, their books are read in the classroom and/or duly (foot)noted. (39)

Although not specifically "feminist" or "queer," Henry Giroux's work provides some of the more glaring examples of this relegation to the margins: although he wrote a book called *Border Crossings*, he virtually ignored Chicana/o scholarship. Anzaldúa shows up on one page, in an epigraph for Giroux's own thoughts on "The Politics of Voice and Difference" (168).

9. Through her representation of this process, Anzaldúa cites one of the legacies of the Chicano Renaissance. Luis Valdez's Brechtian *actos*, or short one-act plays, were designed to incite audience members to action (such as joining the union or striking) through careful consideration of their social locations. *Los Vendidos* (The sell-outs), in particular, encouraged audiences to resist an assimilationist Mexican American identity and to assume instead a critical Chicano identity. See Valdez and El Teatro Campesino. Anzaldúa improves on her predecessors in that the identity she posits is more fluid and multiple than the male-centered identity of the Chicano Renaissance (Yarbro-Bejarano, 12). For more on the Chicano Renaissance, see my introduction.

10. My interpretation in this section, with its emphasis on specificity over and against appropriation, intersects with Shane Phelan's; see Phelan, 57–75. Phelan argues that Anzaldúa's mestiza consciousness "has been an avenue for white women to develop a new understanding of alliance" that precludes simply adopting another's perspective as one's own (73).

11. In *Lesbian Utopics*, Jagose criticizes those who "figure 'lesbian' as utopic and outside dominant conceptual frameworks" (5). Jagose situates Anzaldúa's borderlands as a site for such lesbian utopic thinking. At the other end of the spectrum,

Cherríe Moraga argues, "Ironically, the most profound message of *La Frontera* I believe has very little to do with lesbians. . . . Lesbian desire is not a compelling force in the book" ("Algo secretamente amado," 154–55). Too lesbian, not lesbian enough—Anzaldúa is caught between colliding critics as well as cultures (and I am not innocent of participation in the conflict; see note 15, below).

12. According to Raiskin, the very term *mulatto* reflects this conflation, since it is a racial categorization that draws its name from the sterile product (the mule) of an "unnatural" sexual coupling (157). For more on the historical linkage of the mulatto and the homosexual, see Somerville, 256–60.

13. Similar points, of course, could be made about the work of other women of color, such as Audre Lorde (see chapter 1). I have already discussed briefly Moraga and Anzaldúa; see, in addition, Sandoval; B. Smith, "Toward a Black Feminist Criticism"; Hull, Scott, and Smith.

14. Chela Sandoval sees this sort of mobility as central to "U.S. Third World Feminism" generally (10–17, esp. 14–15). For another analysis explicitly juxtaposing this sort of mobility to what I label an "unlimited access" mobility, which maintains relations of domination-subordination by allowing white, male, and heterosexual identities to go unmarked, see Dhaliwal, 87, 93–96. The mobility Anzaldúa performs has affinities with the affirmation of "mixing and migration" that Tony Kushner stages in *Angels in America*. See my discussion of *Angels in America* and Sarah Schulman's *People in Trouble* in chapter 4.

15. I am implicated in Anzaldúa's comments here, since I am a white and male writer whose identity as such often can and does go unmarked and unremarked. In this chapter, and in this project generally, I am attempting to take comments such as Anzaldúa's seriously; to counter the tendency to include lesbians of color as footnotes that validate a writer's ability to be "inclusive" while nonetheless maintaining a white center and colored margin (see, for example, my comments on Giroux in note 8, above), I am attempting to position the work of lesbian and gay writers of color as at the very center of the Queer Renaissance. However, despite my arguments against "hipness" in this chapter, my declared intentions and my commitment to the politics of alliance do not fully displace me from the potentially patronizing position of (white) hostess at a hip and inclusive queer party. I leave this as a necessary tension in my work; attempting to smooth away this tension would, I think, be an example of the very "escapes from identity" against which I have argued in this chapter.

16. Nor is Anzaldúa's lament that white gay men and lesbians "police the queer person of color with theory" a simple denunciation of "theory." Elsewhere, Anzaldúa writes, "Because . . . what passes for theory these days is forbidden territory for us, it is *vital* that we occupy theorizing space, that we not allow whitemen and women solely to occupy it. By bringing in our own approaches and methodologies, we transform that theorizing space" (*Making Face*, xxv). This quote suggests not only that theory is used to police the queer person of color but also that the queer person of color with theory is policed. Anzaldúa resists, *with theory*, that policing.

17. For examples crediting *This Bridge Called My Back* with revolutionizing feminism, see de Lauretis, *Technologies*, 10; Sandoval, 5; Quintana, 112–15, 139–

40. Lisa Duggan also writes, "The elaboration of . . . a ['queer'] locale within feminist theory could work a radical magic similar to that of the category 'women of color.' As many feminists have argued, the category 'women of color' as proposed in such ground-breaking anthologies as *This Bridge Called My Back*, is a significant conceptual and political innovation" ("Making It Perfectly Queer," 25). I agree with Duggan here, while giving an added twist to her argument: "women of color" is not simply *like* "queer"; it was theorized *as* "queer" well before queer theory became hip (particularly, as I have suggested, in Anzaldúa's "La Prieta"). But this extension of Duggan's argument is actually indebted to Duggan herself, who in 1991 taught the first "Queer Theory" course at the University of Illinois at Urbana-Champaign, and whose syllabus placed *This Bridge Called My Back* in just such an "originary" position within queer theory.

Making Face, Making Soul extends the disruptive and queer tradition of *This Bridge Called My Back* from the first page of Anzaldúa's introduction, where she explores "*gestos subversivos*, political subversive gestures, the piercing look that questions or challenges, the look that says, 'Don't walk all over me,' the one that says, 'Get out of my face' " (xv). Connection and coalition are central issues in *Making Face, Making Soul*, but as with *This Bridge Called My Back*, and as this quote illustrates, these connections are never simply celebratory.

Notes to Chapter 4

1. Quotations from *Angels in America: Millennium Approaches* are cited parenthetically as *MA*. Quotations from *Angels in America: Perestroika* are cited parenthetically as *P*.

2. Biblical scholars generally agree that the earliest strand in Genesis, Exodus, and Numbers was written by a single author, J, who lived around the tenth century B.C.E. Harold Bloom argues that J was a woman and that later authors seriously revised her work, tempering her irony and taming her impish Yahweh. More normative versions of Judaism and Christianity, which Bloom thinks would be unrecognizable to J, stemmed from these revisions. Kushner acknowledges his debt to Bloom's reading of J's Jacob story in his "Playwright's Notes" for *Perestroika* (*P*, 7).

3. The first national tour of *Angels in America*, directed by Michael Mayer, originated in Chicago at the Royal George Theatre, with a cast made up of both Chicago and New York actors. In the spirit of my second chapter's commitment to redefining centers and margins, I focus mostly on this national production—rather than the "original" Broadway production—when I comment on the performance of *Angels in America*. Mayer describes the production as "different conceptually from the New York version," which was "too complicated technically to be tourable." My theses about the performance of identity in *Angels in America* actually work best in conjunction with the national production, which Mayer describes, alternatively, as "actor-driven" (qtd. in Rossen, 32).

4. Undoubtedly, the contradictory nature of this scene was appreciated more fully in the Tel Aviv production. My thanks to Dan Sharon of the Asher Library at Chicago's Spertus Institute of Jewish Studies, for providing me with translations of these Hebrew passages.

5. Kushner has Walter Benjamin's contradictory "angel of history" in mind here. Benjamin analyzes a Paul Klee painting, "Angelus Novus," that "shows an angel looking as though he is about to move away from something he is fixedly contemplating" (257). Benjamin reads this angel, whose wings are open, as being blown backward into the future, toward which he refuses to look. The wind is so strong that the angel can no longer close his wings (257–58). Both Kushner's and Klee/Benjamin's angels, then, simultaneously represent stasis and extreme movement.

6. I am thinking in this section not only of Eve Sedgwick's formulation of her own deconstructive project (*Epistemology*, 9–10) but also—through my insistence that Prior moves to a new location—of her recognition that "a deconstructive understanding of these binarisms," although necessary, is not "sufficient to disable them" (10). With this in mind, it is important to point out that while each of my chapters might be said to perform a deconstructive analysis, each additionally attempts to supplement such an analysis with an examination of new queer identities that work to refuse the terms of the binary relations from which they emerge and which they cite. As the preceding chapter suggests, however, following Gloria Anzaldúa and Judith Butler, this is an ongoing project, in that each new performance of "queerness" can and will generate other exclusions that must be critically negotiated.

7. A local production of *Angels in America* at the Station Theater in Urbana, Illinois, augmented the queerness of the angel by casting Shelley Holt in the role. In a small community such as Urbana-Champaign, many audience members would undoubtedly remember (and bring to their watching of *Angels in America*) Holt's performance of Benita in Brad Fraser's *Unidentified Human Remains and the True Nature of Love*. Benita is the queer psychic who seems to know everything about everyone in Edmonton, where Fraser's play is set.

8. Rob Baker credits Robert Chesley's 1984 *Night Sweat* as the first AIDS play to present onstage gay sex scenes and positions *Angels in America* as the next major play to do so (184). In general, most of the major plays about AIDS have presented a more subdued sexuality or have—as with Larry Kramer's *The Normal Heart*—actually preached against gay male "promiscuity." Kramer's semi-autobiographical character Ned Weeks opines, "Why is it we can only talk about our sexuality, and so relentlessly? You know, Mickey, all we've created is generations of guys who can't deal with each other as anything but erections" (Kramer, 58). For pointed critiques of *The Normal Heart*, see Crimp, "How to Have Promiscuity," 246–53; Román, 209–11.

9. The audience for Kushner's attack on "the myth of the Individual" reaches beyond the readership of *Perestroika*: Kushner originally published this piece in the *New York Times*, and he republished it in his recent collection of essays. See Kushner, *Thinking*, 33–40.

10. Although I have not focused much on the Roy Cohn plot in *Angels in America*, it is nonetheless an important element of the play. As Kushner explains, "Part of the impulse to write *Angels in America* came from the way this man who I hated got an obituary in the *Nation* by Robert Sherrill that was completely homophobic. The question of forgiveness may be the hardest political question

people face. . . . But forgiveness, if it means anything, has to be incredibly hard to come by" (qtd. in Tucker, 33). My point here is that Kushner thematizes "forgiveness" and affirmation of the character's humanity in the play but does not uncritically absorb these themes into the vision of political solidarity in the end.

Scott Tucker has some potentially valid reservations about Kushner's inclusion of Cohn in the play. Tucker insists that, "as an emblematic figure of reaction in the 1980s," Cohn

> cannot really bear the burden Kushner places upon him. . . . William F. Buckley, for example, is an equally grotesque and dramatic figure who once proposed tattooing all HIV-positive people for easy identification—and his political power far exceeded Roy Cohn's during that decade. Introducing a *living* public menace in the play would have made "the question of forgiveness" Kushner raises a great deal more challenging and pointed. . . . [Cohn's] *presence* in the play is not the problem, but it underscores the complete *absence* of the main players in power during those years. (33–34)

"Complete absence," however, is a misnomer. Reagan, in particular, is a constant and looming presence in these characters' lives—a menacing presence that would have been *diluted*, I think, had Kushner actually embodied Reagan as a character. Kushner is very much aware of "the main players in power" during these years, and it is these players against which some (and only some) of his characters are united in the end.

11. Kushner explains in his "Playwright's Notes" that the cases cited in this scene are actual cases with some names and circumstances changed (*P*, 8). Louis confronts Joe with only a few specific cases, but it is clear that Joe has written many more. The first involved plaintiffs on Staten Island who were suing a New Jersey toothpaste company because the smoke from the company's factory had led to the hospitalization of at least three children. The judge ruled that the plaintiffs had no case because the Air and Water Protection Act, which they were citing, did not apply to people, only to air and water. The second involved a gay soldier who filed an appeal when the army kicked him out and cheated him of his pension. Although the soldier got his pension again, the judge's decision stated that it was only because the army in this case had foreknowledge of the soldier's homosexuality, and that homosexuals are still not guaranteed to equal protection under the law (*P*, 109–10).

12. Moreover, conservative critics *did* feel excluded: "The crowd-pleasing swipes at conservatives, Republicans, and Mormons, an occasional irritant in Part I, have multiplied this time to fill the dramatic vacuum" (Olson, 72); "The playwright is not given to moderation in expression. He says Ronald Reagan will go down in history as a 'tremendously evil' man, who ran a 'closet-fascist government' " (Grenier, 54).

13. Kushner, in turn, reiterates his commitment to solidarity over and over again in his interviews and writings. See, particularly, his response to neoconservative writers Andrew Sullivan and Bruce Bawer:

> What of the things gay children have to fear, in common with all children? What of the planetary despoilment that kills us? Or the financial necessity

that drives some of us into unsafe, insecure, stupid, demeaning and ill-paying jobs? Or the unemployment that impoverishes some of us? Or the racism some of us face? Or the rape some of us fear? What about AIDS? Is it enough to say, Not our problem? Of course gay and lesbian politics is a progressive politics: It depends on progress for the accomplishment of any of its goals. Is there any progressive politics that recognizes no connectedness, no border-crossings, no solidarity or possibility for mutual aid? ("A Socialism of the Skin," 13)

14. Kushner himself has implied that "ongoing dialogue" for him includes dialogue with lesbian and gay novelists such as Schulman:

[Interviewer]: Larry Kramer wrote in *The Advocate* last year that the gay novel is a dead form; the only interesting work happening in gay literature is in the theater. What is your reaction to that?
Tony Kushner: Oh, Larry! I don't know what he's talking about, because he's gone off to write a novel as far as I know.
I just read Michael Cunningham's new novel *[Flesh and Blood]*, which is just astonishing. And Chris Bram has a new novel *[Father of Frankenstein]*, which is amazing. I think Sarah Schulman writes amazing novels. Certainly there's Dorothy Allison—I think *Bastard out of Carolina* is one of the best things I've ever read. So I don't agree at all. (Lowenthal, 11)

Kushner provides an extended blurb on the back cover of Schulman's most recent novel, *Rat Bohemia*, and quotes approvingly from *Rat Bohemia* in the preface to his collection of essays (*Thinking*, ix).

15. On Donald Trump and the Trump Tower, see Crimp and Rolston, 122.

16. During the summer of 1988, medical waste (catheter bags, sutures, hypodermic needles, and vials of blood—some of which tested positive for HIV) washed ashore on beaches from Long Island to Staten Island.

17. On the Tompkins Square Park Riots, see N. Smith, 59.

18. For a more extended consideration of the issues in this paragraph, see my discussion in chapter 2 of Randall Kenan's character Jimmy Greene from *A Visitation of Spirits*.

19. The dance floor is an appropriate location for this announcement, since it has been, historically, an important site for the (re)fashioning of queer identities. See, for example, my overview in chapter 2 of Marcos Becquer's reading of *Tongues Untied* and *Paris Is Burning*, as well as Becquer and José Gatti's more extensive analysis of vogueing.

20. Edward King, in *Safety in Numbers: Safer Sex and Gay Men*, criticizes ACT UP and coalition work, suggesting that they have contributed to the contemporary "degaying" of AIDS (191–92). King's analysis focuses primarily on Britain, where the degaying of AIDS has proven disastrous for gay men: the British government has shifted funding away from organizations that address the specific needs of gay men, even though the vast majority of people living with AIDS in Britain are gay men.

King's study in general is important and convincing, but in his zeal to critique the degaying of AIDS, I think he conflates universalizing ("AIDS is everyone's problem") and coalition. Perhaps this conflation is necessary, given the particular problems in Britain that King addresses. Throughout my analysis, however, I hope it has been clear that "coalition" entails coming together to face, not efface, the specific needs of various groups. In the United States, moreover, many people living with AIDS are already located in multiple communities: gay and bisexual men of color, particularly, have been disproportionately impacted by the epidemic. Audre Lorde's comments from chapter 1 are again apropos here: "It was a while before we came to realize that our place was the very house of difference rather than the security of any one particular difference" (Zami, 226).

21. See especially Bordowitz, "Picture a Coalition," which provides an overview of the Testing the Limits Collective, a group of video activists who documented many of ACT UP's early actions. See also Bordowitz, "The AIDS Crisis Is Ridiculous"; Saalfield; Saalfield and Navarro, 367–65.

22. Schulman's own position on this issue is unclear, but she maintains that People in Trouble's "principal idea . . . was how personal homophobia becomes societal neglect" (in Loewenstein, 220; see also Schulman, My American History, xviii). Since it is unclear whether she is referring here to Molly's or Kate's "personal homophobia," Schulman's statement is fairly ambiguous. Either way, however, it is problematic and biphobic: Does Molly's personal homophobia lead her to neglect her activism and "the community" by "wasting time" with a "straight" woman? Or does Kate's personal homophobia prevent her from making a "real" commitment to the gay and lesbian world?

Whenever I have taught this novel, Kate's character initially has elicited the standard biphobic litany from students: she "can't make up her mind," is "indecisive and mean," treats both Molly and Peter "unfairly," and so forth. Invariably, however, discussion gravitates toward Kate, who—given the profound shifts she experiences throughout the novel—is a more seductive character than either Molly or Peter. Schulman's attempts to contain Kate (by providing readers with a theme through which to read her: "personal homophobia becomes societal neglect") are never, I think, entirely successful.

23. I am thinking here of Gary Indiana's disturbing contribution to the anthology Discontents: New Queer Writers: "He goes to a party where a five year old child gets passed around for everyone to fuck, and then it's chopped up with steak knives and consumed" (167). Schulman is also a contributor to this anthology, so if her citation of Indiana in People in Trouble is parodic, she herself is nonetheless allied with him in at least one queer venue.

Works Cited

Abelove, Henry, Michèle Aina Barale, and David M. Halperin, eds. *The Lesbian and Gay Studies Reader.* New York: Routledge, 1993.

Adam, Barry. *The Rise of a Gay and Lesbian Movement.* Boston: Twayne, 1987.

Alarcón, Norma. "The Theoretical Subject(s) of *This Bridge Called My Back* and Anglo-American Feminism." In Calderón and Saldívar, 28–39.

Alcoff, Linda. "Cultural Feminism versus Post-Structuralism: The Identity Crisis in Feminist Theory." *Signs: Journal of Women in Culture and Society* 13 (1988): 405–36.

Alexander, Elizabeth. " 'Coming Out Blackened and Whole': Fragmentation and Reintegration in Audre Lorde's *Zami* and *The Cancer Journals.*" *American Literary History* 6 (1994): 695–715.

Allison, Dorothy. *Bastard out of Carolina.* New York: Plume/Penguin Books, 1992.

Altman, Dennis. "AIDS and the Reconceptualization of Homosexuality." In *A Leap in the Dark: AIDS, Art and Contemporary Cultures,* edited by Allan Klusaček and Ken Morrison, 32–43. Montreal: Véhicule Press, 1993.

Anzaldúa, Gloria. *Borderlands/La Frontera: The New Mestiza.* San Francisco: Aunt Lute Books, 1987.

———. "Bridge, Drawbridge, Sandbar or Island: *Lesbians-of-Color Hacienda Alianzas.*" In *Bridges of Power: Women's Multicultural Alliances,* edited by Lisa Albrecht and Rose M. Brewer, 216–31. Philadelphia: New Society, 1990.

———. *Friends from the Other Side/Amigos del otro lado.* Illustrated by Consuelo Méndez. San Francisco: Children's Book Press/Libros para niños, 1993.

———. "La Prieta." In Moraga and Anzaldúa, 198–209.

———. "To(o) Queer the Writer—Loca, escritora y chicana." In Warland, 249–63.

———, ed. *Making Face, Making Soul/Haciendo Caras: Creative and Critical Perspectives by Feminists of Color.* San Francisco: Aunt Lute Books, 1990.

Avena, Thomas. "Interview with Edmund White." In *Life Sentences: Writers, Artists, and AIDS,* edited by Thomas Avena, 213–46. San Francisco: Mercury House, 1994.

Bad Object-Choices, ed. *How Do I Look?: Queer Film and Video.* Seattle: Bay Press, 1991.

Baker, Rob. *The Art of AIDS.* New York: Continuum, 1994.

Bakhtin, Mikhail M. *The Dialogic Imagination.* Translated by Caryl Emerson and Michael Holquist. Edited by Michael Holquist. Austin: University of Texas Press, 1981.

Baldwin, James. *The Fire Next Time.* New York: Dell, 1963.

———. *Go Tell It on the Mountain.* 1953. Reprint, New York: Dell, 1981.

Bannon, Ann. *Beebo Brinker.* 1962. Reprint, Tallahassee: Naiad Press, 1986.

Bawer, Bruce. "No Truce for Bruce." *10 Percent* (November–December 1994): 62–65+.

———. *A Place at the Table: The Gay Individual in American Society.* New York: Touchstone/Simon, 1993.

———, ed. *Beyond Queer: Challenging Gay Left Orthodoxy.* New York: Free Press, 1996.

Beam, Joseph, ed. *In the Life: A Black Gay Anthology.* Boston: Alyson, 1986.

Becquer, Marcos. "Snap!thology and Other Discursive Practices in *Tongues Untied.*" *Wide Angle* 13, 2 (1991): 6–17.

Becquer, Marcos, and José Gatti. "Elements of Vogue." *Third Text* (December 1991–January 1992): 65–81.

Behrens, Bill. "Come Out, Wherever You Are, and Friends Won't Turn Away." *Daily Illini,* 10 October 1990, 19.

Benjamin, Walter. *Illuminations.* Translated by Harry Zohn. New York: Schocken Books, 1968.

Bergman, David. "Edmund White." In Nelson, *Contemporary Gay American Novelists,* 386–94.

———. *Gaiety Transfigured: Gay Self-Representation in American Literature.* Madison: University of Wisconsin Press, 1991.

Berlant, Lauren, and Michael Warner. "Guest Column. What Does Queer Theory Teach Us about *X?*" *PMLA* 110 (1995): 343–49.

Bérubé, Michael. *Marginal Forces/Cultural Centers: Tolson, Pynchon, and the Politics of the Canon.* Ithaca, N.Y.: Cornell University Press, 1992.

"Birth of a Queer Nation." *Out/Look* 11 (1991): 12–23.

Bloom, Harold. Commentary on *The Book of J,* translated by David Rosenberg, 173–322. New York: Vintage/Random House, 1990.

Bonetti, Kay. "An Interview with Edmund White." *Missouri Review* 13 (1990): 89–110.

Bordowitz, Gregg. "The AIDS Crisis Is Ridiculous." In Gever, Greyson, and Parmar, 209–24.

———. "Picture a Coalition." In Crimp, *AIDS,* 183–96.

Boulard, Garry. "The Man behind the Mask." *The Advocate* (2 May 1995): 29–35.

Boyd, Blanche McCrary. *The Revolution of Little Girls.* New York: Vintage/Random House, 1991.

Brownworth, Victoria. "On Publishing: Indecent Advances." *Lambda Book Report* (January–February 1995): 49.

Bulkin, Elly, Barbara Smith, and Minnie Bruce Pratt. *Yours in Struggle: Three Feminist Perspectives on Anti-Semitism and Racism.* New York: Long Haul Press, 1984.

Butler, Judith. *Bodies That Matter: On the Discursive Limits of "Sex".* New York: Routledge, 1993.

———. *Gender Trouble: Feminism and the Subversion of Identity.* New York: Routledge, 1990.

———. "Imitation and Gender Insubordination." In Fuss, *Inside/Out,* 13–31.

Calderón, Héctor, and José David Saldívar, eds. *Criticism in the Borderlands: Stud-

ies in Chicano Literature, Culture, and Ideology. Durham, N.C.: Duke University Press, 1991.

Carlston, Erin G. "*Zami* and the Politics of Plural Identity." In *Sexual Practice/ Textual Theory: Lesbian Cultural Criticism,* edited by Susan J. Wolfe and Julia Penelope, 226–36. Cambridge: Blackwell, 1993.

Celebrate the Life and Legacy of Audre Lorde. Memorial service booklet. Cathedral Church of St. John the Divine, New York, 18 January 1993.

Chauncey, George. *Gay New York: Gender, Urban Culture, and the Making of the Gay Male World, 1890–1940.* New York: Basic Books, 1994.

Chesley, Robert. *Hard Plays/Stiff Parts: The Homoerotic Plays of Robert Chesley.* San Francisco: Alamo Square Press, 1990.

Clark, Danae. "Commodity Lesbianism." In Abelove, Barale, and Halperin, 186–201.

Clum, John M. *Acting Gay: Male Homosexuality in Modern Drama.* Rev. ed. New York: Columbia University Press, 1994.

Cohen, Ed. "Constructing Gender." In *The Columbia History of the American Novel,* edited by Emory Elliott, 542–57. New York: Columbia University Press, 1991.

———. "Foucauldian Necrologies: 'Gay' 'Politics'? Politically Gay?" *Textual Practice* 2 (1988): 87–101.

———. "Who Are 'We'? Gay 'Identity' as Political (E)motion (A Theoretical Rumination)." In Fuss, *Inside/Out,* 71–92.

Cooper, Dennis, ed. *Discontents: New Queer Writers.* New York: Amethyst Press, 1992.

Cornwell, Anita. " 'I Am Black, Woman, and Poet': An Interview with Audre Lorde." In *Black Lesbian in White America,* 35–50. Tallahassee: Naiad Press, 1983.

Crimp, Douglas. "How to Have Promiscuity in an Epidemic." In Crimp, *AIDS,* 237–71.

———. Introduction. In Crimp, *AIDS,* 3–16.

———. "Mourning and Militancy." In Ferguson et al., 233–45.

———. "Right On, Girlfriend!" *Social Text* 33 (1992): 2–18.

———, ed. *AIDS: Cultural Analysis/Cultural Activism.* Cambridge, Mass.: MIT Press, 1987.

Crimp, Douglas, with Adam Rolston. *AIDS DemoGraphics.* Seattle: Bay Press, 1990.

Dayan, Joan. " 'A Receptacle for that Race of Men': Blood, Boundaries, and Mutations of Theory." *American Literature* 67 (1995): 801–13.

"Decade Dance: The 80s." *Lambda Book Report* (March–April 1991): 10–13.

de Lauretis, Teresa. "Eccentric Subjects: Feminist Theory and Historical Consciousness." *Feminist Studies* 16 (1990): 115–50.

———. "Film and the Visible." In Bad Object-Choices, 223–76.

———. *Technologies of Gender: Essays on Theory, Film, and Fiction.* Bloomington: Indiana University Press, 1987.

———. "Queer Theory: Lesbian and Gay Sexualities. *An Introduction.*" *differences: A Journal of Feminist Cultural Studies* 3, 2 (1991): iii–xviii.

Works Cited

239

DeLillo, Don. *White Noise*. New York: Viking, 1985.

DeLynn, Jane. "Crown Jewel." *The Advocate* (21 February 1995): 52–55.

D'Emilio, John. Foreword. In Jay and Young, xi–xxix.

————. *Making Trouble: Essays on Gay History, Politics, and the University*. New York: Routledge, 1992.

————. *Sexual Politics, Sexual Communities: The Making of a Homosexual Minority in the United States, 1940–1970*. Chicago: University of Chicago Press, 1983.

D'Emilio, John, and Estelle B. Freedman. *Intimate Matters: A History of Sexuality in America*. New York: Harper & Row, 1988.

Derrida, Jacques. *Of Grammatology*. Translated by Gayatri Chakravorty Spivak. Baltimore: Johns Hopkins University Press, 1974.

Deutsche, Rosalyn. "Art and Public Space: Questions of Democracy." *Social Text* 33 (1992): 34–53.

————. "Uneven Development: Public Art in New York City." In Ferguson et al., 107–30.

Dewan, Shaila. "15 Minutes of Flame." *10 Percent* (November–December 1994): 48–51+.

Dhairyam, Sagri. " 'Artifacts for Survival': Remapping the Contours of Poetry with Audre Lorde." *Feminist Studies* 18 (1992): 229–56.

Dhaliwal, Amarpal. "Response to Stanley Aronowitz's 'The Situation of the Left in the United States.' " *Socialist Review* 23, 3 (1994): 81–98.

Doan, Laura, ed. *The Lesbian Postmodern*. New York: Columbia University Press, 1994.

Duberman, Martin. *Cures: A Gay Man's Odyssey*. New York: Dutton, 1991.

————. *Stonewall*. New York: Dutton, 1993.

Duggan, Lisa. Afterword. In Katz, 193–96.

————. "Making It Perfectly Queer." *Socialist Review* 22, 1 (1992): 11–31.

————. "The Trials of Alice Mitchell: Sensationalism, Sexology, and the Lesbian Subject in Turn-of-the-Century America." *Signs: Journal of Women in Culture and Society* 18 (1993): 791–814.

Duggan, Lisa, and Nan D. Hunter. *Sex Wars: Sexual Dissent and Political Culture*. New York: Routledge, 1995.

Dyer, Richard. "White." *Screen* 29, 4 (1988): 44–64.

Echols, Alice. *Daring to Be Bad: Radical Feminism in America, 1967–1975*. Minneapolis: University of Minnesota Press, 1989.

Edelman, Lee. *Homographesis: Essays in Gay Literary and Cultural Theory*. New York: Routledge, 1994.

Elders, Joycelyn. "Three-Ring Circus." *The Advocate* (31 October 1995): 58–60.

Eliot, T.S. *The Complete Poems and Plays 1909–1950*. San Diego: Harcourt Brace Jovanovich, 1971.

Ellison, Ralph. *Invisible Man*. 1952. Reprint, New York: Vintage/Random House, 1972.

Ferguson, Russell, Martha Gever, Trinh T. Minh-ha, and Cornel West, eds. *Out There: Marginalization and Contemporary Cultures*. New York: New Museum of Contemporary Art and MIT Press, 1990.

Works Cited

Foucault, Michel. *The History of Sexuality*. Volume 1. Translated by Robert Hurley. New York: Random House, 1978.

Fraser, Brad. *Unidentified Human Remains and the True Nature of Love*. Winnipeg: Blizzard, 1990.

Fraser, Steven, ed. *The Bell Curve Wars: Race, Intelligence, and the Future of America*. New York: Basic Books, 1995.

Freedman, Diane P. *An Alchemy of Genres: Cross-Genre Writing by American Feminist Poet-Critics*. Charlottesville: University Press of Virginia, 1992.

Freixas, Claudio. Introduction to *Afro-Cuban Poetry de Oshún a Yemayá*, 12–28. Miami: Ediciones Universal, 1978.

Friend, Tad. "Avenging Angel." *Vogue* (November 1992): 158 + .

Fries, Kenny. "Fighting False Symbols: Sarah Schulman Searches for a Satisfying Lesbian Identity." *Lambda Book Report* (January–February 1993): 7–9.

Fuss, Diana. *Essentially Speaking: Feminism, Nature and Difference*. New York: Routledge, 1989.

———, ed. *Inside/Out: Lesbian Theories, Gay Theories*. New York: Routledge, 1991.

Gates, David, with Maggie Malone. "An 'Explosion' of Gay Writing." *Newsweek* (10 May 1993): 58.

Gates, Henry Louis, Jr. "Canon-Formation, Literary History, and the Afro-American Tradition: From the Seen to the Told." In *Afro-American Literary Study in the 1990s*, edited by Houston A. Baker, Jr., and Patricia Redmond, 14–50. Chicago: University of Chicago Press, 1989.

———. *The Signifying Monkey: A Theory of African-American Literary Criticism*. New York: Oxford University Press, 1988.

———. "The Trope of a New Negro and the Reconstruction of the Image of the Black." *Representations* 24 (1988): 129–55.

Gever, Martha, John Greyson, and Pratibha Parmar, eds. *Queer Looks: Perspectives on Lesbian and Gay Film and Video*. New York: Routledge, 1993.

Gibson, William. *Neuromancer*. New York: Ace Books, 1984.

Giroux, Henry. *Border Crossings: Cultural Workers and the Politics of Education*. New York: Routledge, 1992.

Gomez, Jewelle. "Black Lesbian Feminist Warrior Poet Mother." *Lambda Book Report* (March–April 1993): 6–7.

Gonzales, Rodolfo. *I Am Joaquín/Yo Soy Joaquín*. 1967. Reprint, New York: Bantam Books, 1972.

Greenblatt, Stephen, and Giles Gunn, eds. *Redrawing the Boundaries: The Transformation of English and American Literary Studies*. New York: MLA, 1992.

Grenier, Richard. "The Homosexual Millennium: Is It Here? Is It Approaching?" *National Review* (7 June 1993): 52–56.

Gurganus, Allan. *White People: Stories and Novellas*. New York: Ballantine Books, 1990.

Gutiérrez, Ramón A. "Community, Patriarchy and Individualism: The Politics of Chicano History and the Dream of Equality." *American Quarterly* 46 (1993): 44–72.

Works Cited

Hall, Richard. "Gay Fiction Comes Home." *New York Times Book Review,* 19 June 1988, 3+.

Halperin, David. *Saint Foucault: Towards a Gay Hagiography.* New York: Oxford University Press, 1995.

Hamilton-Little, Dominic. "Award-Winning *Angels in America* Comes to Chicago." *OutLines* (September 1994): 18.

Haraway, Donna J. *Simians, Cyborgs, and Women: The Reinvention of Nature.* New York: Routledge, 1991.

Harding, Sandra. "Rethinking Standpoint Epistemology: What Is 'Strong Objectivity'?" In *Feminist Epistemologies,* edited by Linda Alcoff and Elizabeth Potter, 49–82. New York: Routledge, 1993.

Harper, Phillip Brian. *Framing the Margins: The Social Logic of Postmodern Culture.* New York: Oxford University Press, 1994.

Hemphill, Essex. *Ceremonies.* New York: Plume/Penguin Books, 1992.

———, ed. *Brother to Brother: New Writings by Black Gay Men.* Boston: Alyson, 1991.

Holleran, Andrew. *Dancer from the Dance.* New York: Plume/Penguin Books, 1978.

Hull, Gloria T. "Living on the Line: Audre Lorde and *Our Dead Behind Us.*" In *Changing Our Own Words: Essays on Criticism, Theory, and Writing by Black Women,* edited by Cheryl A. Wall, 150–72. New Brunswick, N.J.: Rutgers University Press, 1989.

Hull, Gloria T., Patricia Bell Scott, and Barbara Smith, eds. *All the Women Are White, All the Blacks Are Men, but Some of Us Are Brave: Black Women's Studies.* New York: Feminist Press, 1982.

Hunt, V. "A Conversation with Randall Kenan." *African American Review* 29 (1995): 411–20.

Hutcheon, Linda. *The Politics of Postmodernism.* London: Routledge, 1989.

Indiana, Gary. "Reproduction." In Cooper, 167–70.

Jackson, Earl, Jr. "Scandalous Subjects: Robert Glück's Embodied Narratives." *differences: A Journal of Feminist Cultural Studies* 3, 2 (1991): 112–34.

Jagose, Annamarie. *Lesbian Utopics.* New York: Routledge, 1994.

Jay, Karla, and Allen Young, eds. *Out of the Closets: Voices of Gay Liberation.* 1972. Reprint, New York: New York University Press, 1992.

Jones, Joyce. "Affirmative-Action Watch: More Racial Injustice in the Justice Department." *Black Enterprise* (April 1994): 18.

Joslin, Tom, and Peter Friedman, directors. *Silverlake Life: The View from Here.* 96 minutes. Zeitgeist, 1993. VHS.

Kaplan, Carla. "The Erotics of Talk: 'That Oldest Human Longing' in *Their Eyes Were Watching God.*" *American Literature* 67 (1995): 115–42.

Katz, Jonathan. *The Invention of Heterosexuality.* New York: Dutton, 1995.

Keating, AnnLouise. "Making 'our shattered faces whole': The Black Goddess and Audre Lorde's Revision of Patriarchal Myth." *Frontiers: A Journal of Women's Studies* 13 (1992): 20–33.

Kenan, Randall. *James Baldwin.* New York: Chelsea House, 1994.

———. *Let the Dead Bury Their Dead and Other Stories.* San Diego: Harcourt Brace Jovanovich, 1992.

————. *A Visitation of Spirits*. New York: Anchor/Doubleday, 1989.

Kenan, Randall, and Dorothy Allison. "Spies Like Us: Talking between the Lines." *Voice Literary Supplement* (September 1993): 26–27.

Kennedy, Elizabeth Lapovsky, and Madeline D. Davis. *Boots of Leather, Slippers of Gold: The History of a Lesbian Community*. New York: Penguin Books, 1993.

Kerouac, Jack. *On the Road*. 1957. Reprint, New York: Viking, 1976.

————. *The Subterraneans*. New York: Grove Press, 1958.

King, Edward. *Safety in Numbers: Safer Sex and Gay Men*. New York: Routledge, 1993.

King, Katie. "Audre Lorde's Lacquered Layerings: The Lesbian Bar as a Site of Literary Production." *Cultural Studies* 2 (1988): 321–42.

Kissack, Terence. "Freaking Fag Revolutionaries: New York's Gay Liberation Front, 1969–1971." *Radical History Review* 62 (1995): 104–34.

Kramer, Larry. *The Normal Heart*. New York: Plume/Penguin Books, 1985.

Kroll, Jack. "A Broadway Godsend." *Newsweek* (10 May 1993): 56–58.

Kushner, Tony. *Angels in America: A Gay Fantasia on National Themes*. Part One: *Millennium Approaches*. New York: Theatre Communications, 1993.

————. *Angels in America: A Gay Fantasia on National Themes*. Part Two: *Perestroika*. New York: Theatre Communications, 1994.

————. "Foreword: Notes Toward a Theater of the Fabulous." In *Staging Gay Lives: An Anthology of Contemporary Gay Theater*, edited by John M. Clum, vii–ix. Boulder, Colo.: Westview Press, 1996.

————. "A Socialism of the Skin." *The Nation* (4 July 1994): 9–14. Reprinted in Kushner, *Thinking*, 19–32.

————. *Thinking about the Longstanding Problems of Virtue and Happiness (Essays, a Play, Two Poems and a Prayer)*. New York: Theatre Communications, 1995.

Labonte, Richard. "Title Bout." *The Advocate* (28 June 1994): 60–61.

Latzky, Eric. "Queer Perspectives: Snapshots from the New Garde." *Lambda Book Report* (July–August 1991): 14–15.

Leavitt, David. "The Way I Live Now." *New York Times Magazine* (9 July 1989): 28 +.

LeVay, Simon. *The Sexual Brain*. Cambridge, Mass.: MIT Press, 1993.

Lewis, David Levering. *When Harlem Was in Vogue*. New York: Knopf, 1981.

Liebman, Marvin. *Coming Out Conservative: An Autobiography*. San Francisco: Chronicle, 1992.

Lincoln, Kenneth. *Native American Renaissance*. Berkeley: University of California Press, 1983.

Loewenstein, Andrea Freud. "Troubled Times." Interview with Sarah Schulman. In Warland, 217–26.

Lorde, Audre. *The Black Unicorn*. New York: Norton, 1978.

————. *Chosen Poems—Old and New*. New York: Norton, 1982.

————. "Dear Joe." *Callaloo* 14 (1991): 47–48.

————. *Need: A Chorale of Black Woman Voices*. Latham, N.Y.: Kitchen Table: Women of Color Press, 1990.

Works Cited

———. *Sister Outsider*. Crossing Press Feminist Series. Freedom, Calif.: Crossing Press, 1984.

———. *Undersong: Chosen Poems Old and New*. Rev. ed. New York: Norton, 1992.

———. "What Is at Stake in Lesbian and Gay Publishing Today." *Callaloo* 14 (1991): 65–66.

———. *Zami: A New Spelling of My Name*. Crossing Press Feminist Series. Trumansburg, N.Y.: Crossing Press, 1982.

Lowenthal, Michael. "On Art, *Angels,* and 'Mostmodern Fascism.' " Interview with Tony Kushner. *Harvard Gay and Lesbian Review* 2, 2 (1995): 10–12.

Mann, William J. "The Gay and Lesbian Publishing Boom." *Harvard Gay and Lesbian Review* 2, 2 (1995): 24–27.

Marco, Tony. "Special Class Protections for Self-Alleged Gays: A Question of 'Orientation' and Consequences." Available online @ http://www.iclnet.org/clm/marco/marco10.html; INTERNET.

Marcus, Leah S. "Renaissance/Early Modern Studies." In Greenblatt and Gunn, 41–63.

Martin, Biddy. "Lesbian Identity and Autobiographical Difference[s]." In *Life/Lines: Theorizing Women's Autobiography,* edited by Bella Brodzki and Celeste Schenck, 77–103. Ithaca, N.Y.: Cornell University Press, 1988.

Maupin, Armistead. *Tales of the City*. New York: Harper & Row, 1978.

McKinley, Catherine E. Introduction to *Afrekete: An Anthology of Black Lesbian Writing,* edited by Catherine E. McKinley and L. Joyce Delaney, xi–xvii. New York: Anchor/Doubleday, 1995.

McRuer, Robert. "Randall Kenan." In Nelson, *Contemporary Gay American Novelists,* 232–36.

———. "A Visitation of Difference: Randall Kenan and Black Queer Theory." In *Critical Essays: Gay and Lesbian Writers of Color,* edited by Emmanuel Nelson, 221–32. New York: Haworth Press, 1993.

Mercer, Kobena. " '1968': Periodizing Postmodern Politics and Identity." In *Cultural Studies,* edited by Lawrence Grossberg, Cary Nelson, and Paula Treichler, 424–49. New York: Routledge, 1992.

———. "Skin Head Sex Thing: Racial Difference and the Homoerotic Imaginary." In Bad Object-Choices, 169–222.

Miller, D.A. "Sontag's Urbanity." In Abelove, Barale, and Halperin, 212–20.

Minson, Jeffrey. *Genealogies of Morals: Nietzsche, Foucault, Donzelot and the Eccentricity of Ethics*. London: Macmillan, 1985.

Miracky, James J. "A Vision of Life Past Hope." *America* (5 March 1994): 12–13.

Mirandé, Alfredo, and Evangelina Enríquez. *La Chicana: The Mexican-American Woman*. Chicago: University of Chicago Press, 1979.

Moraga, Cherríe. "Algo secretamente amado." Review of *Borderlands/La Frontera,* by Gloria Anzaldúa. *Third Woman: The Sexuality of Latinas* 4 (1989): 151–56.

———. *The Last Generation*. Boston: South End, 1993.

———. Preface. In Moraga and Anzaldúa, xiii–xix.

Moraga, Cherríe, and Gloria Anzaldúa, eds. *This Bridge Called My Back: Writings* by *Radical Women of Color*. 2d ed. Latham, N.Y.: Kitchen Table: Women of Color Press, 1983.

Mordden, Ethan. *I've a Feeling We're Not in Kansas Anymore*. New York: St. Martin's, 1985.

Morrison, Toni. *Playing in the Dark: Whiteness and the American Literary Imagination*. New York: Vintage/Random House, 1992.

Morton, Donald. "The Politics of Queer Theory in the (Post)Modern Moment." *Genders* 17 (1993): 120–50.

Muñoz, Carlos, Jr. *Youth, Identity, Power: The Chicano Movement*. London: Verso, 1989.

Munt, Sally. " 'Somewhere over the Rainbow . . .': Postmodernism and the Fiction of Sarah Schulman." In Munt, *New Lesbian Criticism*, 33–50.

———, ed. *New Lesbian Criticism: Literary and Cultural Readings*. New York: Columbia University Press, 1992.

Nelson, Emmanuel. "James Baldwin." In Nelson, *Contemporary Gay American Novelists*, 6–24.

———. "Towards a Transgressive Aesthetic: Gay Readings of Black Writing." *James White Review: A Gay Men's Literary Quarterly* 11, 3 (1994): 15–17.

———, ed. *Contemporary Gay American Novelists: A Bio-Bibliographical Critical Sourcebook*. Westport, Conn.: Greenwood, 1993.

Nero, Charles I. "Toward a Black Gay Aesthetic: Signifying in Contemporary Black Gay Literature." In Hemphill, *Brother to Brother*, 229–52.

Nestle, Joan. *A Restricted Country*. Ithaca, N.Y.: Firebrand Books, 1987.

Ohmann, Richard. "The Shaping of a U.S. Canon: U.S. Fiction, 1960–1975." In *Canons*, edited by Robert von Hallberg, 377–401. Chicago: University of Chicago Press, 1983.

Olson, Walter. "Winged Defeat." *National Review* (24 January 1994): 71–73.

Paredes, Américo. *"With His Pistol in His Hand": A Border Ballad and Its Hero*. Austin: University of Texas Press, 1958.

Pease, Donald E. Introduction to *The American Renaissance Reconsidered*, edited by Walter Benn Michaels and Donald E. Pease, vii–xi. Baltimore: Johns Hopkins University Press, 1985.

Phelan, Shane. *Getting Specific: Postmodern Lesbian Politics*. Minneapolis: University of Minnesota Press, 1994.

Preston, John. "Prognostications." *Lambda Book Report* (January–February 1993): 39.

Project Censored. "NAFTA's Broken Promises." Available online @ http://zippy.sonoma.edu/ProjectCensored/stories1995.html; INTERNET.

Quintana, Alvina E. *Home Girls: Chicana Literary Voices*. Philadelphia: Temple University Press, 1996.

Radel, Nicholas F. "Self as Other: The Politics of Identity in the Works of Edmund White." In *Queer Words, Queer Images: Communication and the Construction of Homosexuality*, edited by Jeffrey Ringer, 175–92. New York: New York University Press, 1994.

Radicalesbians. "The Woman-Identified Woman." In Jay and Young, 172–77.

Works Cited

Raiskin, Judith. "Inverts and Hybrids: Lesbian Rewritings of Sexual and Racial Identities." In Doan, 156–72.

Rechy, John. *City of Night*. New York: Ballantine Books, 1963.

Riley, Denise. *Am I That Name?: Feminism and the Category of "Women" in History*. New York: Macmillan, 1989.

Román, David. "Performing All Our Lives: AIDS, Performance, Community." In *Critical Theory and Performance*, edited by Janelle Reinelt and Joseph Roach, 208–21. Ann Arbor: University of Michigan Press, 1992.

Roof, Judith, and Robyn Wiegman, eds. *Who Can Speak? Authority and Critical Identity*. Urbana: University of Illinois Press, 1995.

Ross, Andrew. *No Respect: Intellectuals and Popular Culture*. New York: Routledge, 1989.

Rossen, Jeff. " 'Angels' in Middle America." *Gay Chicago Magazine* (8 September 1994): 30–32.

Rowell, Charles H. Interview with Henry Louis Gates, Jr. *Callaloo* 14 (1991): 444–63.

Russo, Vito. *The Celluloid Closet: Homosexuality in the Movies*. Rev. ed. New York: Harper & Row, 1987.

Ruta, Suzanne. "On Why Gay Teenagers Are Committing Suicide." *Wigwag* (March 1990): 12–14.

Saalfield, Catherine. "On the Make: Activist Video Collectives." In Gever, Greyson, and Parmar, 21–37.

Saalfield, Catherine, and Ray Navarro. "Shocking Pink Praxis: Race and Gender on the ACT UP Frontlines." In Fuss, *Inside/Out*, 341–69.

Sadownick, Doug. "ACT UP Makes a Spectacle of AIDS." *High Performance* 13, 1 (1990): 26–31.

Saldívar, José David. *The Dialectics of Our America: Genealogy, Cultural Critique, and Literary History*. Durham, N.C.: Duke University Press, 1991.

Saldívar, Ramón. *Chicano Narrative: The Dialectics of Difference*. Madison: University of Wisconsin Press, 1990.

Sandla, Robert. "The Angel Has Landed." *Stagebill* (September 1994): 31–33.

Sandoval, Chela. "U.S. Third World Feminism: The Theory and Method of Oppositional Consciousness in the Postmodern World." *Genders* 10 (1991): 1–24.

Schulman, Leonard. "Imagining Other Lives." *Time* (30 July 1990): 58–60.

Schulman, Sarah. *My American History: Lesbian and Gay Life During the Reagan/Bush Years*. New York: Routledge, 1994.

———. *People in Trouble*. New York: Plume/Penguin Books, 1990.

———. *Rat Bohemia*. New York: Dutton, 1995.

Sedgwick, Eve Kosofsky. *Between Men: English Literature and Male Homosocial Desire*. New York: Columbia University Press, 1985.

———. *Epistemology of the Closet*. Berkeley: University of California Press, 1990.

———. *Tendencies*. Durham, N.C.: Duke University Press, 1993.

Signorile, Michelangelo. *Queer in America: Sex, the Media, and the Closets of Power*. New York: Anchor/Doubleday, 1993.

Singh, Amritjit. *The Novels of the Harlem Renaissance: Twelve Black Writers, 1923–1933*. University Park, Pa.: Penn State University Press, 1976.

Works Cited

Smith, Barbara. "Toward a Black Feminist Criticism." In Hull, Scott, and Smith, 157–75.

———. "The Truth That Never Hurts: Black Lesbians in Fiction in the 1980s." In *Third World Women and the Politics of Feminism*, edited by Chandra Talpade Mohanty, Ann Russo, and Lourdes Torres, 101–29. Bloomington: Indiana University Press, 1991.

Smith, Neil. "Contours of a Spatialized Politics: Homeless Vehicles and the Production of Geographical Scale." *Social Text* 33 (1992): 54–81.

Smith, Sidonie. "The Autobiographical Manifesto: Identities, Temporalities, Politics." In *Autobiography and Questions of Gender*, edited by Shirley Neuman, 186–212. London: Cass, 1991.

Smith, Valerie. "Gender and Afro-Americanist Literary Theory and Criticism." In *Speaking of Gender*, edited by Elaine Showalter, 56–70. New York: Routledge, 1989.

Smyth, Cherry. *Lesbians Talk Queer Notions*. London: Scarlet Press, 1992.

Snitow, Ann. "A Gender Diary." In *Conflicts in Feminism*, edited by Marianne Hirsch and Evelyn Fox Keller, 9–43. New York: Routledge, 1990.

Somerville, Siobhan. "Scientific Racism and the Emergence of the Homosexual Body." *Journal of the History of Sexuality* 5 (1994): 243–66.

Sumida, Stephen. *And the View from the Shore: Literary Traditions of Hawaii*. Seattle: University of Washington Press, 1991.

Treichler, Paula. "How to Have Theory in an Epidemic: The Evolution of AIDS Treatment Activism." In *Technoculture*, edited by Constance Penley and Andrew Ross, 57–106. Minneapolis: University of Minnesota Press, 1991.

Trinh T. Minh-ha. *Woman, Native, Other*. Bloomington: Indiana University Press, 1989.

Tucker, Scott. "Our Queer World: A Storm Blowing from Paradise." *The Humanist* (November–December 1993): 32–35.

Tytell, John. *Naked Angels: Kerouac, Ginsberg, Burroughs*. New York: Grove, 1976.

Valdez, Luis. *Zoot Suit and Other Plays*. Houston: Arte Publico Press, 1992.

Valdez, Luis, and El Teatro Campesino. *Luis Valdez—Early Works: Actos, Bernabé and Pensamiento Serpentino*. Houston: Arte Publico Press, 1990.

Van Leer, David. "Beyond the Margins." *New Republic* (12 October 1992): 50–53.

Warland, Betsy, ed. *Inversions: Writings by Dykes, Queers and Lesbians*. Vancouver: Press Gang, 1991.

Warner, Michael. "Introduction: Fear of a Queer Planet." *Social Text* 9, 4 (1991): 5–17.

West, Cornel. "Black Leadership and the Pitfalls of Racial Reasoning." In *Race-ing Justice, En-gendering Power: Essays on Anita Hill, Clarence Thomas and the Construction of Social Reality*, edited by Toni Morrison, 390–401. New York: Pantheon Books, 1992.

White, Edmund. *The Beautiful Room Is Empty*. New York: Knopf, 1988.

———. *A Boy's Own Story*. New York: Plume/Penguin Books, 1982.

———. *The Burning Library: Essays*. Edited by David Bergman. New York: Knopf, 1994.

———. *Nocturnes for the King of Naples*. New York: St. Martin's, 1978.

Works Cited

————. "On the Line." Introduction to *A Boy's Own Story*, ix–xix. New York: Plume/Penguin Books, 1994.

————. "Twenty Years On . . ." *Lambda Rising Book Report* (June–July 1989): 4–5.

————, ed. *The Faber Book of Gay Short Stories*. London: Faber & Faber, 1991.

Wiegman, Robyn. "Introduction: Mapping the Lesbian Postmodern." In Doan, 1–20.

————. Review of *Bodies That Matter: On the Discursive Limits of "Sex"*, by Judith Butler, and *Tendencies*, by Eve Kosofsky Sedgwick. *American Literature* 67 (1995): 893–95.

Williams, Peter, and Neil Smith. "From 'Renaissance' to Restructuring: The Dynamics of Contemporary Urban Development." In *Gentrification of the City*, edited by Neil Smith and Peter Williams, 204–24. Boston: Allen & Unwin, 1986.

Wilson, Anna. "Audre Lorde and the African-American Tradition: When the Family Is Not Enough." In Munt, *New Lesbian Criticism*, 75–93.

Wilson, Craig. "Gay-Fiction Anthology Opens Doors to Debate." *USA Today*, 14 November 1991, 8D.

Wojnarowicz, David. *Close to the Knives: A Memoir of Disintegration*. New York: Vintage/Random House, 1991.

Wood, Robin. *Hollywood from Vietnam to Reagan*. New York: Columbia University Press, 1986.

Yarbro-Bejarano, Yvonne. "Gloria Anzaldúa's *Borderlands/La Frontera*: Cultural Studies, 'Difference,' and the Non-Unitary Subject." *Cultural Critique* 29 (1994): 5–28.

Young, Allen. "Out of the Closets, into the Streets." In Jay and Young, 6–31.

Zimmerman, Bonnie. *The Safe Sea of Women: Lesbian Fiction, 1969–1989*. Boston: Beacon Press, 1990.

Index

activism: AIDS, 9, 14–16, 30, 156, 171–72, 173–74, 188–95, 199–202; antiwar, 13; feminist, 60–62, 205; housing, 181, 191–93, 197–98; queer, 3, 33, 152–53, 167, 169, 171–72, 173–74, 176, 178–80, 204, 205, 212–13, 219 n. 20, 221 n. 8. *See also* ACT UP; Black Panthers; Chicano movement; civil rights movement; Daughters of Bilitis; Gay Activists Alliance; Gay Liberation Front; Lesbian Avengers; Mattachine Society; Queer Nation; Radicalesbians; Student Nonviolent Coordinating Committee; Young Lords

ACT UP (AIDS Coalition to Unleash Power), 3–4, 9, 15–16, 20, 30, 156, 173, 178, 180, 191–94, 203, 205, 206, 217 n. 8, 218 n. 14, 235–36 n. 20, 236 n. 21

Adam, Barry, 217 n. 9, 220 nn. 1, 2

Advocate, The, 209, 218–19 n. 18

Afrekete, 53, 54–55, 56–57

Afrekete: An Anthology of Black Lesbian Writing (McKinley and Delaney), 56–57, 221 n. 8

African American studies: theories of signification, 30, 69–70, 79–82, 85–90, 93, 95–97, 102, 111–13, 114–15, 224 nn. 2, 3, 225 n. 11, 225–26 n. 13, 226 nn. 14, 17, 227 n. 20. *See also* Gates, Henry Louis, Jr.; Kenan; queer trickster

AIDS: in *Angels in America*, 157–59, 162–63, 164, 170–74, 175, 176, 233–34 n. 10; "degaying" of, 235–36 n. 20; and medical waste, 181, 235 n. 16; in *People in Trouble*, 156, 181, 188–95, 199–202; and political rebirth, 14–16; quilt, 174; and the radical right, 212; and renaissance discourse, 3, 5, 8–9, 216 n. 7, 217 n. 8; in *Silverlake Life*, 222 n. 16

AIDS activist, as identity, 4, 30, 31, 128, 155–56, 159, 171–72, 173–74, 178–80, 188–95, 199–202, 213

Alarcón, Norma, 230 n. 8

Alcoff, Linda, 34–35, 52–53, 55, 56

Alexander, Elizabeth, 62

Allison, Dorothy, 64, 224 n. 2, 235 n. 14

Altman, Dennis, 14

American Psychiatric Association (APA), 14, 32, 220 n. 2

American Renaissance (New England Renaissance), 1, 5–6, 7

Angels in America: Broadway production of, 170, 177, 232 n. 3; Royal George Theatre (Chicago) production of, 162, 164–65, 166–67, 172, 174, 232 n. 3; Station Theater (Urbana, Ill.) production of, 233 n. 7; Tel Aviv production of, 232 n. 4

Anzaldúa, Gloria, ix, 22, 28, 116–18, 168, 210, 230 nn. 7, 8, 9, 10, 230–31 n. 11, 231 nn. 14, 15, 233 n. 6; *Borderlands/La Frontera*, 30, 116, 125, 128–31, 132–47, 148–49, 149–50, 151, 153, 219 n. 21; "Bridge, Drawbridge, Sandbar or Island: Lesbians-of-Color Hacienda Alianzas," 147–48, 152, 153, 154; "*La conciencia de la mestiza*/Towards a New Consciousness," 128, 136, 139–42, 143–46, 148–49, 149; *Friends from the Other Side/Amigos del otro lado*, 131–32; "The Homeland, Aztlán/El otro México," 129–31, 132–39, 145; *Making Face, Making Soul/Haciendo Caras*, 153, 231 n. 16, 232 n. 17; "La Prieta," 141, 143, 146, 213, 232 n. 17; and queerness, 116–17, 128, 142–53, 221 n. 8; "To(o) Queer the Writer—Loca, escritora y chicana," 145–46, 147, 148, 151–53, 208–9. *See also* borders; new mestiza; *This Bridge Called My Back*

Ashbery, John, 223 n. 20

Augustine, 99, 226 n. 18

Baker, Houston, 227–28 n. 25

Baker, Rob, 171, 173, 233 n. 8

Bakhtin, Mikhail, 90

Baldwin, James, 46, 47–50, 111–13, 227 n. 23, 228 n. 26; *The Fire Next Time*, 111–12, 225–26 n. 13; *Giovanni's Room*, 63, 69, 222 n. 18; *Go Tell It on the Mountain*, 79–82, 97, 98, 225 nn. 11, 12, 13, 226 n. 17; *Just Above My Head*, 49, 226 n. 13

Bannon, Ann, 223 n. 2

Bawer, Bruce, 206, 234 n. 13; *Beyond Queer*, 28; *A Place at the Table*, 206–7, 209, 212, 213, 219 n. 19

Beam, Joseph, 62; *In the Life*, 49, 218 n. 13, 225 n. 8

Beatles, the, 186

Becquer, Marcos, 70–73, 75, 76, 85, 224 nn. 5, 7, 235 n. 19

Behrens, Bill, 38

Bellamy, Dodie, 29

Bell Curve, The (Herrnstein and Murray), 209–12

Benjamin, Walter, 169, 192, 233 n. 5

Bergman, David, 43, 49; *Gaiety Transfigured*, 24, 47–48

Berlant, Lauren, 126

Bérubé, Michael, 64, 65

Bill Whitehead Memorial Award, 66

biology, 30–31, 207–13

bisexuality, 128, 156, 180–87, 202, 236 n. 22

Bishop, Elizabeth, 223 n. 20

Black Panthers, 13, 220 n. 1

Bloom, Allan, 216 n. 7

Bloom, Harold, 159, 163, 232 n. 2

Book of J, 159, 175, 232 n. 2

Book-of-the-Month Club, 2, 222–23 n. 18

borders: academic, 30, 117, 118, 124–28; and border guards, 30, 117–18, 119, 128, 130, 131–32, 134, 137, 148, 149–50, 208–9; and Chicana/o theory, 116–17, 122–24, 141, 230 n. 8; and queer theory, 116–17, 123, 124–28; United States-Mexican, 30, 117, 118–22, 129–41, 176. *See also* Anzaldúa; Kerouac

Bordowitz, Gregg, 236 n. 21

Boyd, Blanche McCrary, 224 n. 2

Bram, Christopher, 235 n. 14

Brown, John, 24

Brown, Rita Mae, 215 n. 1, 222 n. 18

Brownworth, Victoria, 64

Bryant, Anita, 15

Buckley, William F., 234 n. 10

Bulkin, Elly, 218 n. 13

Burroughs, William S., 29

Bush, George, 4, 218 n. 18

butch/femme identities, 88, 183–84, 217 n. 11

Butler, Judith, 83, 219 n. 20, 233 n. 6; *Bodies That Matter*, 150–51, 152–53, 229–30 n. 7; *Gender Trouble*, 87–88, 103, 185–86, 189–90

Calderón, Héctor, 123

canons: American, 116; lesbian and gay, 62–66, 222–23 n. 18

Carlston, Erin G., 221 n. 8

Cervantes, Lorna Dee, 22

Chalfant, Kathleen, 170

Chauncey, George, 217 n. 9

Chelsea House Publishers, 228 n. 26

Chesley, Robert, 233 n. 8

Chicano movement (El Movimiento), 17–20, 22, 23, 218 n. 17

Chicano Renaissance, 5, 17–20, 21, 22, 23, 24, 217 n. 10, 230 n. 9

Chicano/a studies, 122–24, 135, 141, 145, 229 n. 5, 230 nn. 8, 9. *See also* borders

Christianity: Fundamentalist, 69, 75, 77–78, 79–82, 105; revisions of, 77–78, 82, 93, 94, 106–12, 225–26 n. 13, 227 nn. 23, 24. *See also* Baldwin; Kenan

civil rights movement, 13, 32, 120, 220 n. 3

Clark, Danae, 229 n. 6

Clinton, Bill, vii, 218 n. 18

Clum, John, 155, 165–66, 170, 172

Cohen, Ed, 39, 64, 72, 227 n. 19

Cohn, Roy, 157, 158, 160, 167, 170, 176, 233–34 n. 10

Colette, 223 n. 20

Colorado, 211

Combahee River Collective, 47

coming out, 29–30, 217 n. 12; and apositionality, 40–46, 66–67; and collective identity, 32–33, 52–57, 59–62, 66–68; critiques of, 33, 35–39, 220–21 n. 6, 221 n. 7; and positionality theory, 33, 35–39, 52–53, 55–57, 60–62, 66–68. *See also* coming-out stories

coming-out stories, 29–30, 33, 36, 37–39, 40–46, 50–51, 52–53, 62, 67–68, 221 n. 7, 223 n. 2. *See also* Lorde; White

confession, 76–78, 97–111, 226 n. 18

Congress, United States, vii, 25–26, 218 n. 18

Cooper, Dennis, 5, 29, 216 n. 4

Cortés, Hernán, 135

Index

Cowan, Patricia, 60
Crimp, Douglas, 8–9, 177–78, 188–89, 191–92, 203, 216 nn. 3, 7, 217 n. 8, 222 n. 16, 233 n. 8, 235 n. 15
Crossing Press Feminist Series, 52, 62
cultural studies, 5–6, 124, 126
Cunningham, Michael, 235 n. 14

Daily Prayer Book/Ha-Siddur Ha-Shalem, 164
Daughters, Inc., 215 n. 1
Daughters of Bilitis (DOB), 12, 208
Davis, Madeline D., 12, 217 n. 9
deconstruction, 70–73, 160, 168–69, 170, 171, 196–97, 200, 233 n. 6
Defense of Marriage Act (DOMA), vii
Delaney, L. Joyce, 56
de Lauretis, Teresa, 120, 178, 219 n. 20, 229 n. 3, 231 n. 17
DeLillo, Don, 43, 44
D'Emilio, John, 10–17, 73, 220 n. 5; *Making Trouble*, 10–16, 36, 217 n. 9, 220 nn. 1, 2, 5; *Sexual Politics, Sexual Communities*, 10–12, 208, 217 n. 9, 220 n. 2
Deming, Barbara, 60, 61, 205
Denneny, Michael, 9, 216 n. 7
Derrida, Jacques, 200
Details, 126
Detroit, 6–7, 216 n. 5
Deutsche, Rosalyn, 192, 195, 197–98
Dewan, Shaila, 218 n. 14
Dhairyam, Sagri, 55, 221–22 n. 13
Dhaliwal, Amarpal, 231 n. 14
Dickens, Charles: *A Christmas Carol*, 74, 79, 84, 88, 95–96, 225 n. 11, 226 nn. 14, 17
Donne, John, 104
Dornan, Robert, 25, 218 n. 18
Duberman, Martin, 228 n. 26; *Cures*, 35–36, 217 n. 9; *Stonewall*, 67, 217 n. 9, 220 nn. 1, 3
DuBois, W. E. B., 21
Duggan, Lisa, 41–42, 77–78, 124–25, 126, 211, 216 n. 3, 217–18 n. 13, 219 n. 20, 232 n. 17
Duke, David, 212
Dyer, Richard, 35, 42, 43

Echols, Alice, 220 nn. 2, 4
Edelman, Lee, 216 n. 3, 226 n. 13
Elders, Joycelyn, 26, 218–19 n. 18

Eliot, T.S., 196
Ellison, Ralph, 40, 102
Enríquez, Evangelina, 135
Erasmus, 99, 226 n. 18
essentialism, 36–37, 40, 41–42, 47, 53, 56, 68, 127, 132

Fanon, Frantz, 99, 227 n. 18
feminism, 17, 215 n. 1, 229–30 n. 7; academic, 63, 65, 151–53; and gay and lesbian politics, 14–15, 152–53; lesbian, 14, 15; and the New Left, 120; and positionality theory, 29, 33–35, 37–39, 52, 55–56, 68, 220 n. 4, 221 n. 8; and race, 23, 35, 123–24, 148, 151–53, 218 n. 13, 229 n. 3, 230 nn. 8, 10, 231 nn. 13, 14, 231–32 n. 17; radical, 13, 16, 32–33, 220 nn. 2, 4
Fink, John, 207
Firbank, Ronald, 223 n. 20
Flight of the Mind, 1
Flowers, Reg, 174
Forbes, Malcolm, 27
Fordyce, Kent, 46
Foster, Jodie, 27
Foucault, Michel, 99–101, 224 n. 6, 226–27 n. 18, 227 n. 20
Frank, Barney, 26, 218 n. 18
Franklin, C. L., 99, 227 n. 18
Franklin, John Hope, 99, 227 n. 18
Fraser, Brad, 233 n. 7
Fraser, Steven, 210
Frazier, Demita, 61
Freedman, Diane, 134
Freedman, Estelle B., 73
Freixas, Claudio, 134
Freud, Sigmund, 99
Friedman, Peter, 222 n. 16
Fung, Richard, 22
Fuss, Diana, 72; *Essentially Speaking*, 37, 47

Gates, David, 2
Gates, Henry Louis, Jr., 69–70, 75, 96, 112–13, 115, 224 n. 4, 225 n. 11; and Houston Baker, 227–28 n. 25; *The Signifying Monkey*, 69–70, 85–89, 93, 95, 102, 112–13, 115, 224 nn. 2, 3, 227 n. 20; "Trope of a New Negro," 21, 218 n. 15
Gatti, José, 235 n. 19
Gay Activists Alliance (GAA), 13–14, 35–36, 208, 217 n. 12, 220 n. 2

Index

Gay Liberation Front (GLF), 3, 10, 12–14, 16, 29, 32–33, 35–37, 208, 211, 217 n. 12, 220 nn. 2, 3
Gay Pride Day, 3–4, 24, 206–7, 209
Genet, Jean, 29, 223 n. 20
Gibson, William, 226 n. 17
Giroux, Henry, 124, 125–26, 230 n. 8, 231 n. 15
Glück, Robert, 35, 222 n. 16
Goldman, Emma, 127
Goldstein, Richard, 9
Gomez, Jewelle, 222 n. 17, 223 n. 19
Gonzales, Rodolfo "Corky": I Am Joaquín/ Yo Soy Joaquín, 18–20, 22
Gorbachev, Mikhail, 172–73
Graham, Bobbie Jean, 60
Greenblatt, Stephen, 124, 125
Grenier, Richard, 234 n. 12
Gronniosaw, Ukawsaw, 102
Gunderson, Steve, 26, 218 n. 18
Gunn, Giles, 124, 125
Gurganus, Allan, 222 n. 16, 224 n. 2

Hall, Richard, 38, 215 n. 1
Halperin, David, 216 n. 3
Haraway, Donna, 34–35, 37, 39, 43, 50, 52, 56, 61, 220 n. 4
Harding, Sandra, 220 n. 4
Harlem Renaissance (New Negro Renaissance), 1, 5, 17, 20–22, 23, 24, 216 n. 2, 218 n. 15
Harper, Phillip Brian, 126, 229 n. 6
Hawaii, vii–viii
Hawaiian Renaissance, 24, 218 n. 16
Hay, Harry, 10–11
Hays, Will, 69, 223 n. 1
Health and Human Services, U.S. Department of, 89, 226 n. 15
Helms, Jesse, 25, 218 n. 18
Hemphill, Essex: Brother to Brother, 47, 218 n. 13; Ceremonies, 73, 224–25 n. 8
Herrnstein, Richard J., 209–12
heterosexuality: black gay critiques of, 71–73; instability of, 87–88, 98–106, 168, 180–87, 195, 200, 226–27 n. 18, 228 n. 1; invention of, 210–12; and mobility, 117, 119, 147–48, 154–55, 231 n. 14; and queer perestroika, 175–77. See also queer trickster
Hill, Anita, 218 n. 18
hipsters, 117–18, 118–22, 124, 126–27, 128,
130, 136, 137, 139, 147, 150, 151–52, 153–54, 196, 231 n. 15, 232 n. 17. See also Kerouac
Hirsch, E.D., 216 n. 7
Holleran, Andrew, 48, 49, 224 n. 2
Holt, Shelley, 233 n. 7
homelessness, 181, 187, 190, 191–93, 197–99, 201
homosociality, 116, 228 n. 1
Howard, Ronnie, 203
Hubbard, Jim, 194
Hull, Gloria T., 218 n. 13, 221 n. 8, 229 n. 3, 231 n. 13
Hunter, Nan, 217–18 n. 13
Hurston, Zora Neale, 112–13
Hutcheon, Linda, 196–97, 203

identity politics, 37, 72, 227 n. 22
Immigration and Naturalization Service, U.S., 131
Indiana, Gary, 202, 203, 236 n. 23
individualism, 36, 56, 160, 167, 170, 174–78, 206–7, 213, 233 n. 9, 234–35 n. 13
InQueery/InTheory/InDeed Conference, 219 n. 21
invisibility, 39–40, 42–46, 66, 66–67, 221 n. 10
Isherwood, Christopher, 223 n. 20

Jackson, Jr., Earl, 35, 222 n. 16
Jagose, Annamarie, 140, 230–31 n. 11
James, Henry, 223 n. 18
Jay, Karla, 220 n. 2
Johnson, Charles, 21
Johnson, James Weldon, 20, 21
Jones, Joyce, 131
Joslin, Tom, 222 n. 16
Julien, Isaac, 22
Jung, Carl, 99
Justice, U.S. Department of, 131

Kafka, Franz, 223 n. 21
Kameny, Franklin, 220 n. 1
Kaplan, Carla, 21
Katz, Jonathan Ned: The Invention of Heterosexuality, 210–12
Keating, AnnLouise, 54
Kenan, Randall, ix, 28, 224 n. 2; and James Baldwin, 79–82, 97, 98, 111–13, 225 nn. 11, 13, 226 n. 17, 227 n. 23, 228 n. 26; and Charles Dickens, 74, 79, 84, 88, 95–96,

225 n. 11, 226 nn. 14, 17; and critique of community, 69–71, 73, 74–75, 82–93; and disruption of heterosexuality, 95, 98–106; *Let the Dead Bury Their Dead,* 94, 113–15, 225 n. 10, 228 nn. 27, 28; and transformation of community, 75, 78–79, 93–97, 99, 106–12, 114–15, 141; *A Visitation of Spirits,* 30, 69–71, 73–113, 114, 115, 143, 225 nn. 9, 10, 225–26 n. 13, 226 nn. 14, 17, 226–27 n. 18, 227 nn. 22, 24, 228 n. 27, 235 n. 18. *See also* queer trickster

Kennedy, Elizabeth Lapovsky, 12, 217 n. 9
Kerouac, Jack, 126; *On the Road,* 116–22, 123, 124, 125, 126, 126–27, 130, 135, 136, 137, 147, 153–54; *The Subterraneans,* 228 n. 1, 229 n. 4
Killian, Kevin, 29
King, Edward, 235–36 n. 20
King, Katie, 52, 56
King, Larry, 218 n. 18
Kissack, Terence, 13, 217 n. 9, 220 n. 2
Kitchen Table: Women of Color Press, 60–62
Klee, Paul, 233 n. 5
Koch, Ed, 179, 191–92
Kramer, Larry, 48, 49, 233 n. 8, 235 n. 14
Kruger, Barbara, 202, 203
Kushner, Tony, ix, 126, 179, 202–3, 233 n. 5, 235 n. 14; *Angels in America,* 30, 155–78, 179, 180, 189, 202, 203, 204, 231 n. 14, 232 nn. 1, 2, 233–34 n. 10, 234 n. 11; critical response to, 155, 171–72, 175–77, 234 nn. 10, 12; "Notes Toward a Theater of the Fabulous," 169, 171; and queer activism, 156, 167–68, 171–72, 173–74, 176, 178–79, 204; and queer perestroika, 30, 155–56, 159, 160, 170–71, 171–73, 175–78, 204, 222 n. 16; and queer sexuality, 159, 160–63, 164–66, 168–72, 177–78, 233 n. 8; "A Socialism of the Skin," 234–35 n. 13; *Thinking about the Longstanding Problems of Virtue and Happiness,* 179, 233 n. 9. *See also* AIDS activist, as identity

Labonte, Richard, 215 n. 1
Lacan, Jacques, 85
Lambda Book Report, 215 n. 1, 221 n. 7
Lambda Literary Awards, 1, 155, 215 n. 1
Larsen, Nella, 216 n. 2
Latzky, Eric, 29, 216 n. 4
Leavitt, David, 29, 216 n. 7

Lehmann-Haupt, Christopher, 207, 221 n. 10
lesbian and gay studies, ix, 210–12, 217 n. 9. *See also* literary studies; queer theory
Lesbian Avengers, 16, 218 n. 14
lesbian chic, 126
LeVay, Simon, 209; *The Sexual Brain,* 207–12
Lewis, David Levering, 218 n. 15
Liebman, Marvin, 37
Lincoln, Kenneth, 218 n. 16
literary studies, 124–25, 215–16 n. 2; American, ix, 2, 44, 47–50, 116; lesbian and gay, ix, 1, 2–3, 47–50, 62–66, 215 n. 1, 235 n. 14. *See also* renaissance discourse
Livingston, Jennie: *Paris Is Burning,* 71, 235 n. 19
Locke, Alain, 21
Log Cabin Republicans, 206, 219 n. 19
Lorde, Audre, ix, 28, 41, 47, 65–66, 205, 221–22 n. 13, 222 n. 17, 223 nn. 19, 20, 21, 230 n. 13; *The Black Unicorn,* 62, 134; "Brother Alvin," 62; *Chosen Poems—Old and New,* 53, 57–60, 146, 222 n. 15; "Dear Joe," 62; memorial service, 222 n. 14; "Need: A Choral of Black Women's Voices," 59–62, 67, 147, 205, 223 n. 19; *Our Dead Behind Us,* 221 n. 8; *Sister Outsider,* 63, 213, 218 n. 13, 222 n. 18; *Undersong,* 222 nn. 14, 18; "What Is at Stake in Lesbian and Gay Publishing Today," 66, 218 n. 13; *Zami: A New Spelling of My Name,* 29–30, 33, 39, 43, 51–57, 58, 59, 60, 62, 67, 68, 70, 75, 141, 175, 216 n. 2, 219 n. 21, 221 n. 8, 222 n. 18, 236 n. 20. *See also* Zami, as identity

Maddy, Yulisa Amadu, 49
Malinche, La, 135–36
Mann, Thomas, 223 n. 20
Mann, William J., 215 n. 1
Marco, Tony, 211
Marcus, Leah S., 7–8
marginality, vii–x, 39–40, 42, 72–73, 78–79, 95, 115, 126, 128, 147, 219 n. 21, 221 n. 10, 229 n. 6, 230 n. 8, 231 n. 15, 232 n. 3; and New Queer Writers, 29; and region, 30, 69, 73, 75, 87, 90, 99, 115; and renaissance discourse, 6–10
marriage, gay and lesbian, vii–viii
Martin, Biddy, 37, 51, 218 n. 13
Martin, Robert K., 48

Index

Marx, Karl, 178
Massi, Mark, 222 n. 16
Mattachine Society, 3, 10–11, 12, 13, 14, 16, 208, 211, 220 n. 1
Maupin, Armistead, 223–24 n. 2
Mayer, Michael, 172, 232 n. 3
McCarthy, Joseph, 157, 177
McKenna, Teresa, 123
McKinley, Catherine E., 56–57
McRuer, Robert, 112, 224 n. 7, 225 n. 9, 227 n. 22
Men Stopping Rape, 61
Mercer, Kobena, 50, 105–6, 227 n. 22
Merrill, James, 223 n. 20
migration, urban: in gay and lesbian literature, 69–70, 89, 115, 223–24 n. 2
Mikulski, Barbara, 25, 218 n. 18
Miller, D. A., 216 n. 7
Miller, Tim, 217 n. 8
Minson, Jeffrey, 37
Mirandé, Alfredo, 135
modernism, 24, 195–97, 201, 203
Modern Language Association (MLA), 63, 124
Moraga, Cherríe, 47, 123–24, 146–47, 213, 230–31 n. 11; *The Last Generation*, 23–24, 145, 218 n. 17. *See also This Bridge Called My Back*
Mordden, Ethan, 224 n. 2
Morrison, Toni, 43, 63, 64; *Playing in the Dark*, 44, 45; *Sula*, 43
Morton, Donald, 127–28
MTV, 126
Muñoz, Carlos, Jr., 19
Murray, Charles, 209–12
Murrieta, Joaquín, 19–20

National Black Men's Health Network, 61
National Coalition of Black Lesbians and Gays (NCBLG), 61
National Coming Out Day, 38
Native American Renaissance, 24, 218 n. 16
Navarro, Ray, 236 n. 21
Nazi Germany, 20
Nelson, Emmanuel, 49–50, 215 n. 1, 225 n. 12
neoconservatism, gay, 30–31, 206–13, 219 n. 19, 234–35 n. 13
Nero, Charles I., 225
Nestle, Joan, 217 nn. 9, 11
New American Library, 51, 62

new historicism, 5–6
new mestiza, 4, 31, 130–36, 139–54, 168, 213, 230 n. 10; and agency, 149–53; and critical mobility, 30, 117, 125, 128, 140–41, 147–48, 150, 154, 231 n. 14
New Negro identity, 20–21, 218 n. 15
New Queer Writers, 5, 25–31, 203, 216 n. 4, 236 n. 3
New Right, 15, 211–12
Newsweek, 2, 65
New York Lesbian and Gay Experimental Film Festival, 194
North American Free Trade Agreement (NAFTA), 117, 228–29 n. 2
North Carolina, 30, 69, 70–71, 73, 75–79, 90–93, 94, 113, 176, 222 n. 16, 228 n. 27. *See also* Kenan
Norton and Company, W. W., 60, 62
Novazcek, Ruth, 28

Oakland Men's Project, 61
Ochs, Robyn, 219 n. 20
Ohmann, Richard, 63–64, 65
Okazawa-Rey, Margo, 61
Olson, Walter, 234 n. 12
Other Countries, 1
Out/Look, 216 n. 3
OutWrite Conference, 179
Oyá, 135

Paredes, Américo, 122–23
Paz, Octavio, 135
Pease, Donald E., 5–6
Penthouse, 49
performativity, 30, 87–88, 103–4, 127–28, 136, 146–47, 150–53, 155–56, 159, 167, 168–69, 173–75, 178–79, 182
Persephone Press, 52, 62
Phelan, Shane, 219 n. 20, 230 n. 10
Pittsburgh, 6
postmodernism, 89, 127, 156, 180, 196–97, 203
poststructuralism, 3, 52–53, 58, 70–73, 200. *See also* deconstruction
Pratt, Minnie Bruce, 218 n. 13
Preston, John, 221 n. 7
Proust, Marcel, 223 n. 20
public art, 179–80, 195, 197–99, 200–202
Pulitzer Prize, 155, 179
Pynchon, Thomas, 63

Index

Quality Paperback Book Club (QPB), 63
Quarles, Benjamin, 99, 227 n. 18
queer, as concept, 16, 22, 24, 25–29, 82, 115,
128, 142–45, 147, 150–53, 167, 176, 186,
216 n. 3, 219 n. 20, 221 n. 8, 232 n. 17
queer identities, ix, 3–4, 16–17, 117, 126,
128, 141, 155–56, 159, 167–68, 173–74,
176, 177–78, 178–80, 183–87, 204, 205–6,
208, 212–13, 218–19 n. 18, 221 n. 8,
224 n. 2., 233 n. 6, 235 n. 19. *See also*
AIDS activist, as identity; new mestiza;
queer trickster; Zami, as identity
Queer Nation, 16, 145, 173, 206, 213, 216 n.
3
Queer Renaissance: and biology, 30–31, 206,
207–13; and Chicano Renaissance, 5, 17–
20, 22, 23–24; as confluence of cultural
production and political analysis, 4, 9–10,
17, 156, 167, 205, 213; and cultural production, viii, 1–3, 155, 213, 215 n. 1; and
Harlem Renaissance, 5, 17, 20–22, 23, 24;
and gay neoconservatism, 30–31, 206–13;
and lesbian and gay marketplace, 65–66;
and radical queer political analysis, viii, 3,
5, 167–68; and region, 73, 115, 176, 223–
24 n. 2; and reinvention of identity, 3–4,
16, 38–39, 51, 53, 62, 123, 141, 149, 156,
167–68, 170, 176, 177–78, 189, 205, 206,
213, 217 n. 9, 221 n. 8; and *This Bridge
Called My Back*, 123–24, 153, 221 n. 8,
231–32 n. 17
"Queers Bash Back," 213
queer theory, 213, 216 n. 3, 219 nn. 20, 21,
220 n. 4, 222 n. 13, 231 n. 16, 232 n. 17;
and borders, 116–17, 124–28; critiques of,
127–28, 150–53; and identity, 3, 16–17,
213, 221 n. 8; and region, 69, 72–73; staging of, 155, 159, 166, 171–72, 175–78,
178–79, 204
queer trickster, 4, 30, 31, 70, 75, 78–79, 86–
88, 93–97, 98, 100, 105, 114–15, 128, 141,
213
Quiñones, Tirsa, 146–47
Quintana, Alvina E., 231–32 n. 17

race: and coming-out stories, 33, 36, 40, 41–
46, 50–51; and essentialism, 40, 41–42, 47;
and gay male literary criticism, 47–50;
and the Justice Department, 131; and lesbian and gay politics, 15, 71–73, 152–53,
218 n. 13; and lesbian and gay antholog-

ies, 28, 46–47, 153; and lesbian and gay
awards, 66, 179; and the New Left, 120;
and positionality theory, 35; and
queerness, 27–29, 151–53, 213, 219 n. 21,
221 n. 8; and scientific racism, 209–12.
See also African American studies, Chi-
cano/a studies, feminism, new mestiza,
whiteness
Radel, Nicholas, 223 n. 21
Radicalesbians, 32–33, 37, 220 n. 2
Raiskin, Judith, 142, 231 n. 12
Rauch, Jonathan, 207
Reagan, Ronald, 9, 157, 175, 191, 234 nn.
10, 12
Rechy, John, 49–50, 223 n. 2
region: and queerness, 30, 69–70, 72–73,
115, 176, 223–24 n. 2; and whiteness, 43–
44, 46. *See also* borders; Hawaii; North
Carolina; urban space
Renaissance, the (Italian and English Renais-
sance), 1, 7–8
Renaissance Center (Detroit), 6–7, 216 n. 5
renaissance discourse, 3, 4–5, 5–10, 17, 149,
217 n. 8
Riggs, Marlon: *Tongues Untied*, 71–72,
235 n. 19
Riley, Denise, 230 n. 7
Robertson, Hannah, 165
Rodwell, Craig, 67
Rolston, Adam, 191–92, 203, 235 n. 15
Román, David, 178–79, 233 n. 8
Roof, Judith, 219 n. 20
Roseanne, 219 n. 18
Ross, Andrew, 120, 229 n. 3
Rubin, Gayle, 219 n. 20
Russo, Vito, 69, 223 n. 1
Ruta, Suzanne, 89

Saalfield, Catherine, 236 n. 21
Sadownick, Doug, 217 n. 8
Saldívar, José David, 123, 229 n. 5
Saldívar, Ramón, 229 n. 5
Sandoval, Chela, 56, 231 nn. 13, 14, 17
Schulman, Sarah, ix, 38, 221 n. 7, 235 n. 14;
and artistic identity, 156, 179–80, 190–91,
195–202, 202–3; and film and video production, 193–94; *My American History*,
14–15, 205, 218 n. 14, 228 n. 1, 236 n. 22;
and New Queer Writers, 216 n. 4, 236 n.
23; *People in Trouble*, 30, 156, 179–202,
202–3, 204, 216 n. 5, 231 n. 14, 236 n. 22;

Schulman (Continued)
   and political identity, 156, 179–80, 187–
   95, 197, 199, 200; Rat Bohemia, 235 n. 14;
   and sexual identity, 156, 179, 180–87, 190,
   199, 200. See also AIDS activist, as identity
Scott, Patricia Bell, 218 n. 13, 229 n. 3,
   231 n. 13
Sedgwick, Eve Kosofsky, 17, 24, 127, 219 n.
   20; Between Men, 228 n. 1; Epistemology
   of the Closet, 1, 81, 89, 98–99, 101, 104,
   215 n. 2, 227 n. 21, 233 n. 6; Tendencies,
   3–4, 22–23, 25, 226 n. 15
Sella, Robert, 162, 166–67
Sex Wars, 15, 217–18 n. 13
Sherrill, Robert, 233 n. 10
Signorile, Michelangelo, 25–28; Queer in
   America, 25–27, 218–19 n. 18
"Silence = Death," 20
Singh, Amritjit, 218 n. 15
Smith, Barbara, 47, 51–52, 61, 218 n. 13,
   221 n. 12, 229 n. 3, 231 n. 13
Smith, Bessie, 21
Smith, Neil, 216 n. 5, 235 n. 17
Smith, Sidonie, 136
Smyth, Cherry, 16, 17
snapping, 71–72, 76, 86, 224 n. 5
Snitow, Ann, 230 n. 7
Somerville, Siobhan, 209, 231 n. 12
Sontag, Susan, 216 n. 7
Stein, Arlene, 219 n. 20
Stonewall Inn Riots, 1, 10, 13, 32, 66–67,
   220 nn. 1, 3
Studds, Gerry, 26, 218 n. 18
Student Nonviolent Coordinating Commit-
   tee (SNCC), 120
suicide: gay and lesbian, 69, 70, 74, 82, 86,
   88–90, 92–93, 95–97, 210–11, 226 nn. 15,
   16
Sullivan, Andrew, 206, 234 n. 13
Sumida, Stephen, 218 n. 16
Supreme Court, U.S., 26, 211, 218 n. 18
Swift, Carolyn, 162, 164–65, 166–67

Tafel, Rich, 28, 219 n. 19
Taylor, Elizabeth, 8
Teatro Campesino, 19, 217 n. 10, 230 n. 9
Texas Rangers, 122–23
This Bridge Called My Back (Moraga and
   Anzaldúa), 123–24, 135, 141, 143, 146,

153, 213, 218 n. 13, 219 n. 21, 221 n. 8,
   230 n. 8, 231 n. 13, 231–32 n. 17
Thomas, Clarence, 26, 218 n. 18
Time, 63, 65
Tompkins Square Park Riots, 181, 188,
   235 n. 17
Tony Awards, 155, 179
Toomer, Jean, 21
transsexuality, 185–86
Treichler, Paula, 194
Trinh T. Minh-ha, 55–56
Trump, Donald, 179, 191–92, 235 n. 15
Tucker, Scott, 175–77, 234 n. 10
Tytell, John, 121

urban space, 6–7, 197–99, 201–2, 216 nn. 5,
   6
USA Today, 46, 52

Valdés, Gina, 144
Valdez, Luis, 19, 217 n. 10, 230 n. 9
Vance, Carole S., 211
Van Leer, David, 38
Violet Quill Club, 1
Virgin of Guadalupe, 133, 134
vogueing, 71–72, 76, 85, 86, 224 n. 5, 235 n.
   19

Walker, Alice, 112–13
Warner, Michael, 16–17, 115, 126
Washington, Mary Helen, 112
Wattenburg, Bill, 117
Webb, Walter Prescott, 122–23
West, Cornel, 227 n. 23
White, Edmund, ix, 53, 55, 62–67, 222 n. 17;
   and gay male literary criticism, 47–51;
   The Beautiful Room Is Empty, 32, 34, 38,
   39, 63, 66–67, 220 n. 3, 222 n. 18, 223 n.
   21, 224 n. 2; A Boy's Own Story, 2, 22,
   29–30, 33, 39–46, 47, 50–51, 52, 62, 63,
   67–68, 221 nn. 7, 9, 10, 222–23 n. 18; The
   Burning Library, 41, 221 n. 8; The Faber
   Book of Gay Short Stories, 38, 46–47, 50–
   51; The Farewell Symphony, 39; Nocturnes for the King of Naples, 48, 65;
   "Twenty Years On," 65–66, 223 n. 20
whiteness, 28, 29–30, 35, 36, 37, 40–51, 119–
   22, 131–32, 151–53, 221 n. 10, 222 n. 16,
   230 n. 10, 231 nn. 14, 15, 16

Index

256

Wiegman, Robyn, 28, 219 n. 20
Williams, Pete, 25, 218 n. 18
Williams, Peter, 216 n. 5
Wilson, Anna, 65
Winfrey, Oprah, 38, 220 n. 6
Wojnarowicz, David, 26–28, 29; *Close to the Knives*, 26–27; *Fuck You Faggot Fucker*, 27
Wood, Robin, 228 n. 1
Woolf, Virginia, 223 n. 20

Yarbro-Bejarano, Yvonne, 230 n. 9
Yemayá, 133–34, 136
Young, Allen, 33, 220 n. 2
Young Lords, 220 n. 1

Zami, as identity, 4, 29–30, 31, 55–57, 62, 128, 141, 153, 175, 213
Zimmerman, Bonnie, 215 n. 1
Žižek, Slavoj, 229 n. 7
Zwickler, Phil, 217 n. 8

Index